Volume 3

by Minari Endou

HAMBURG // LONDON // LOS ANGELES // TOKYO

Maria Holic Volume 3
Created by Minari Endou

Translation - Yuko Fukami
English Adaptation - Clint Bickham
Retouch and Lettering - Star Print Brokers
Production Artist - Rui Kyo
Graphic Designer - Chelsea Windlinger

Editor - Cindy Suzuki
Print Production Manager - Lucas Rivera
Managing Editor - Vy Nguyen
Senior Designer - Louis Csontos
Art Director - Al-Insan Lashley
Director of Sales and Manufacturing - Allyson De Simone
Associate Publisher - Marco F. Pavia
President and C.O.O. - John Parker
C.E.O. and Chief Creative Officer - Stu Levy

A TOKYOPOP® Manga

TOKYOPOP and are trademarks or registered trademarks of TOKYOPOP Inc.

TOKYOPOP Inc.
5900 Wilshire Blvd. Suite 2000
Los Angeles, CA 90036

E-mail: info@TOKYOPOP.com
Come visit us online at www.TOKYOPOP.com

© 2008 Minari Endou. First published in Japan in 2008 by MEDIA FACTORY, Inc., Tokyo, Japan. English publication rights arranged through MEDIA FACTORY, Inc. English text copyright © 2010 TOKYOPOP Inc.

All rights reserved. No portion of this book may be reproduced or transmitted in any form or by any means without written permission from the copyright holders. This manga is a work of fiction. Any resemblance to actual events or locales or persons, living or dead, is entirely coincidental.

ISBN: 978-1-4278-1673-3

First TOKYOPOP printing: March 2010

10 9 8 7 6 5 4 3 2 1

Printed in the USA

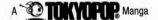

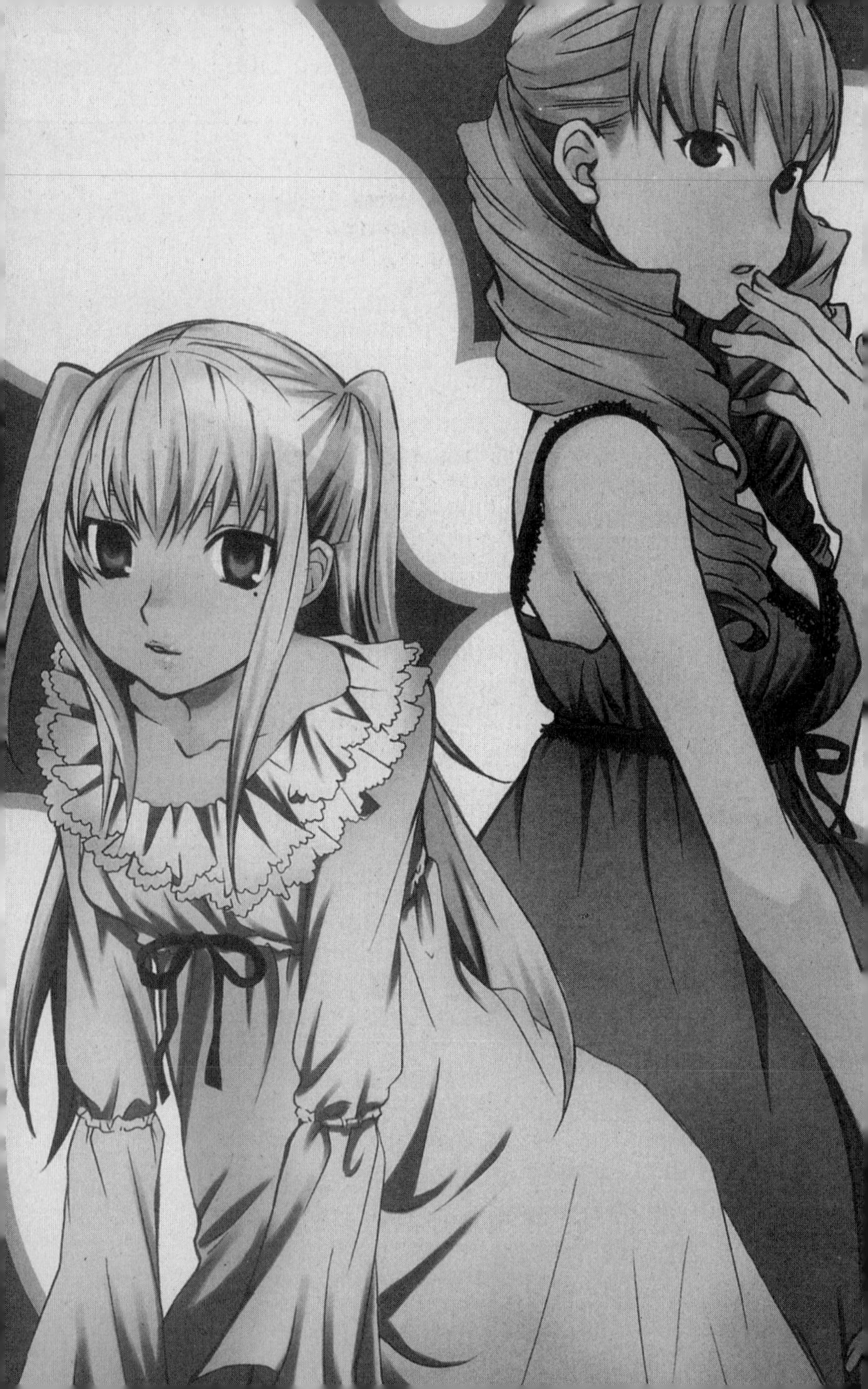

MARIA HOLIC 3

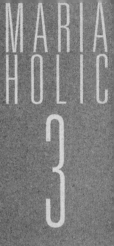

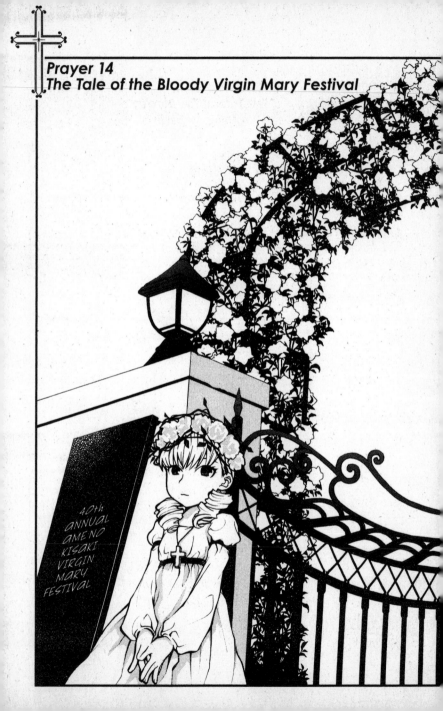

Prayer 14
The Tale of the Bloody Virgin Mary Festival

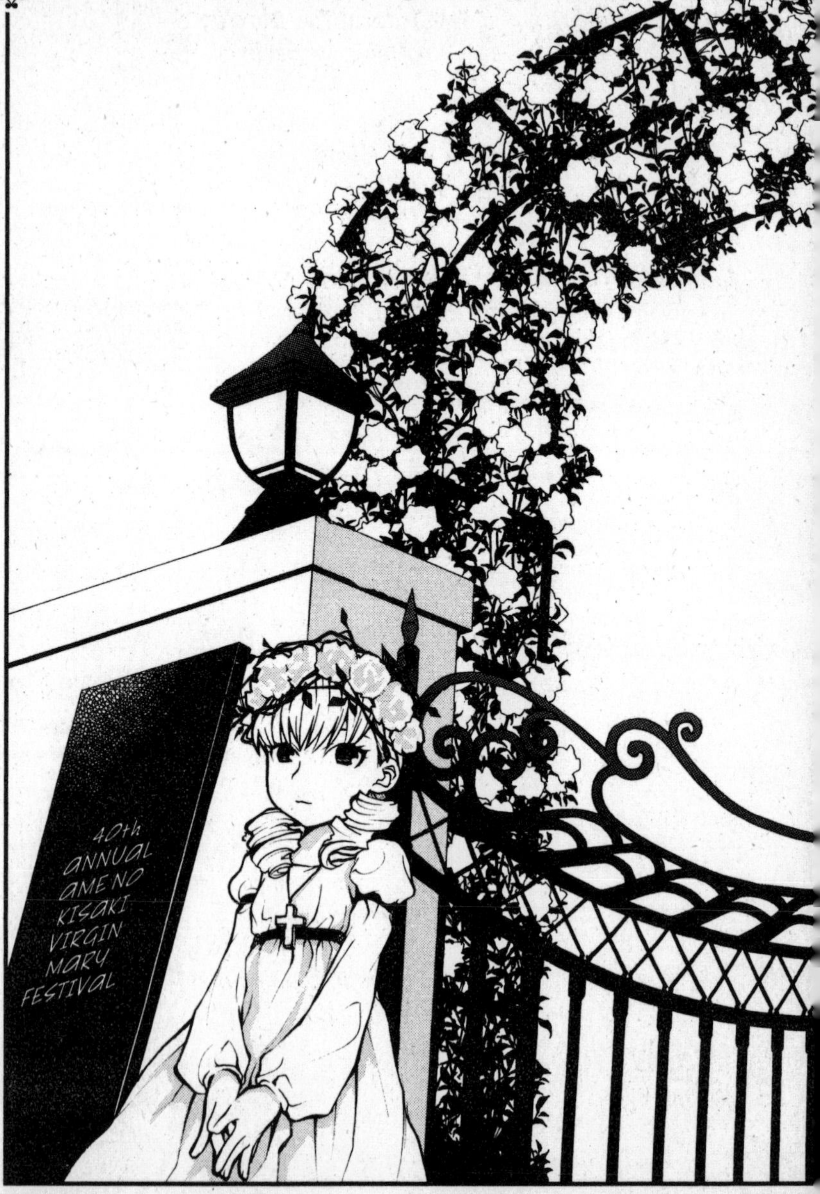
40th
ANNUAL
AME NO
KISAKI
VIRGIN
MARY
FESTIVAL

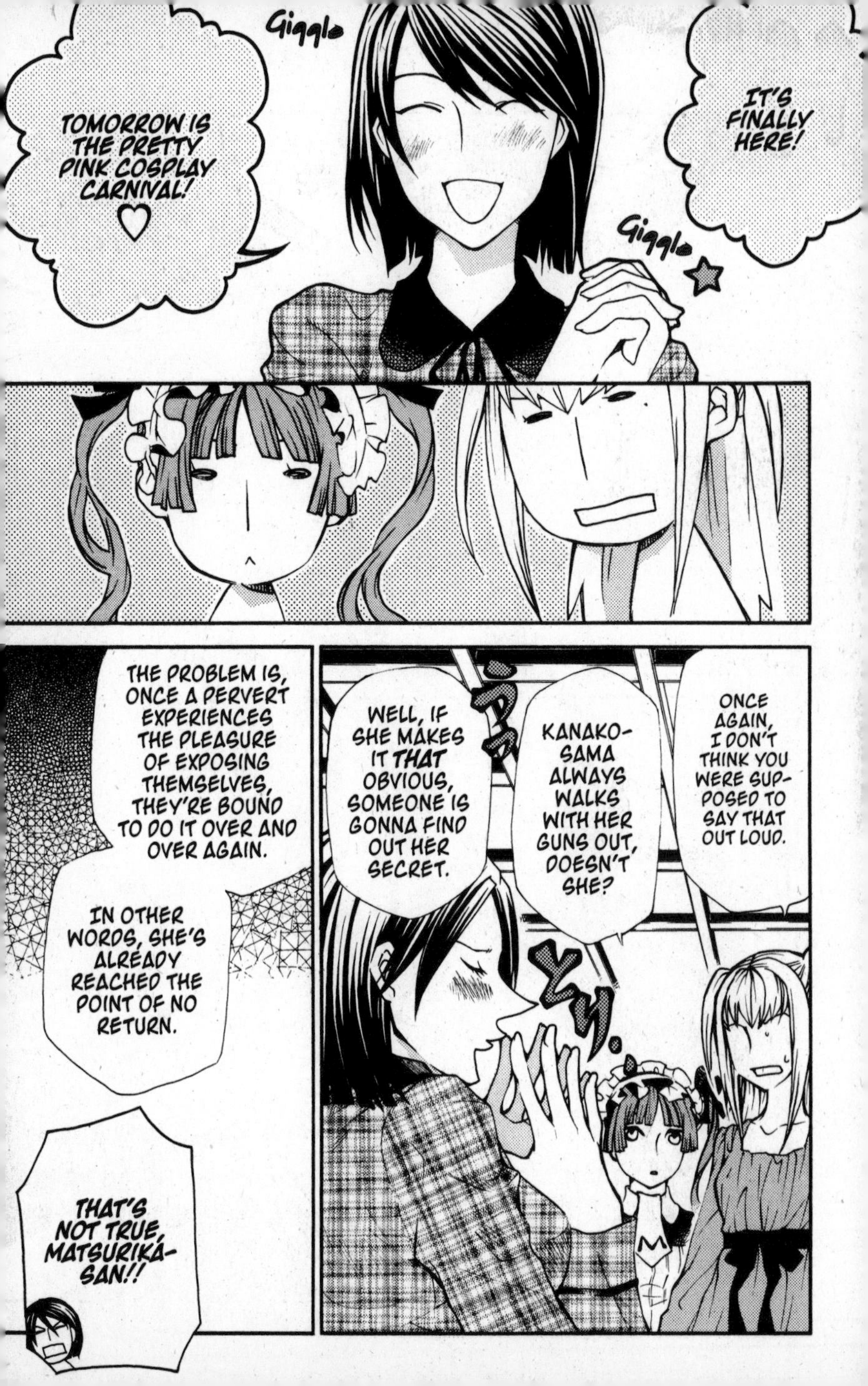
Giggle
IT'S FINALLY HERE!
Giggle
TOMORROW IS THE PRETTY PINK COSPLAY CARNIVAL! ♡
ONCE AGAIN, I DON'T THINK YOU WERE SUP-POSED TO SAY THAT OUT LOUD.
KANAKO-SAMA ALWAYS WALKS WITH HER GUNS OUT, DOESN'T SHE?
WELL, IF SHE MAKES IT THAT OBVIOUS, SOMEONE IS GONNA FIND OUT HER SECRET.
THE PROBLEM IS, ONCE A PERVERT EXPERIENCES THE PLEASURE OF EXPOSING THEMSELVES, THEY'RE BOUND TO DO IT OVER AND OVER AGAIN.
IN OTHER WORDS, SHE'S ALREADY REACHED THE POINT OF NO RETURN.
THAT'S NOT TRUE, MATSURIKA-SAN!!

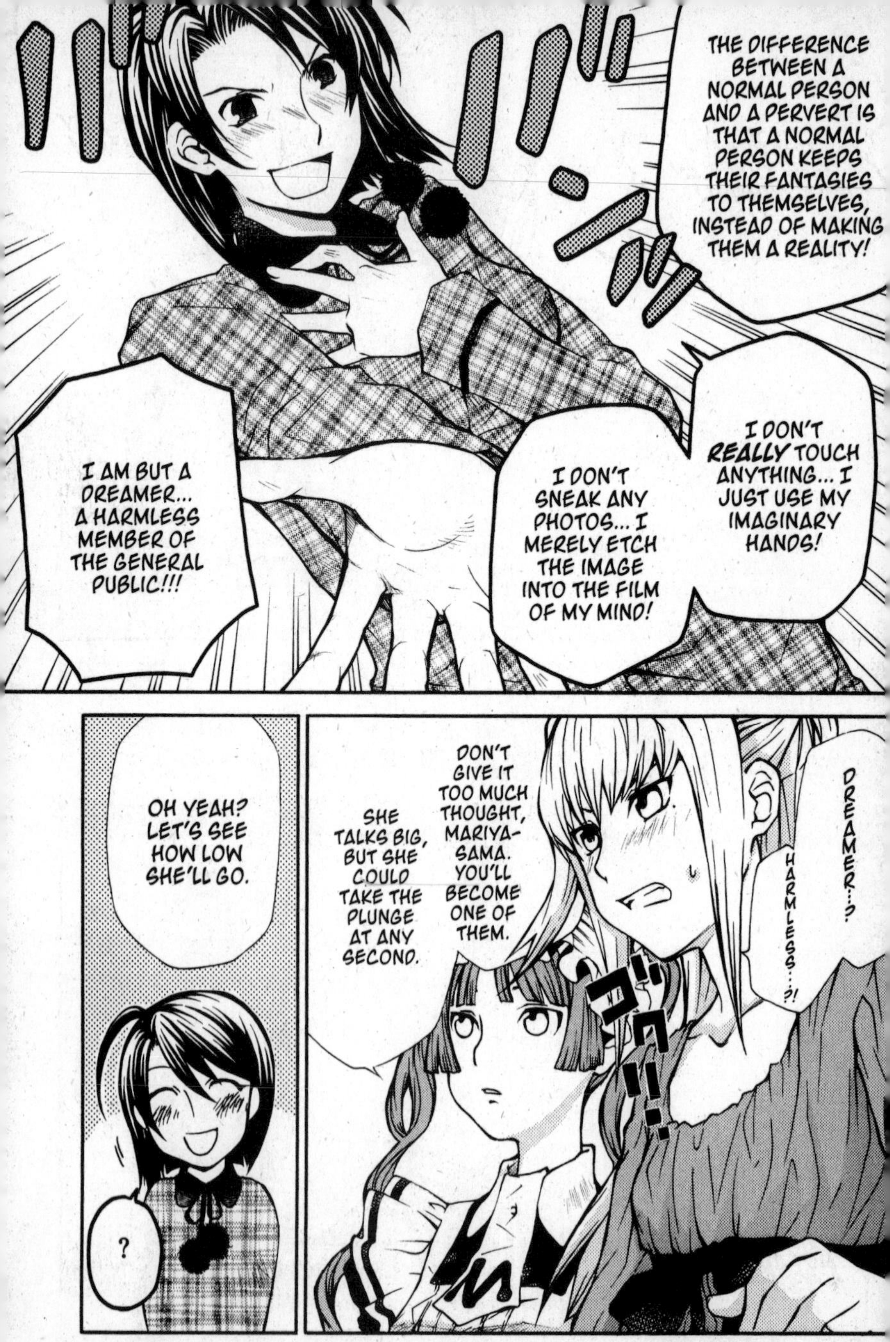
THE DIFFERENCE BETWEEN A NORMAL PERSON AND A PERVERT IS THAT A NORMAL PERSON KEEPS THEIR FANTASIES TO THEMSELVES, INSTEAD OF MAKING THEM A REALITY!
I DON'T *REALLY* TOUCH ANYTHING... I JUST USE MY IMAGINARY HANDS!
I DON'T SNEAK ANY PHOTOS... I MERELY ETCH THE IMAGE INTO THE FILM OF MY MIND!
I AM BUT A DREAMER... A HARMLESS MEMBER OF THE GENERAL PUBLIC!!!
DREAMER...?
HARMLESS...?!
DON'T GIVE IT TOO MUCH THOUGHT, MARIYA-SAMA. YOU'LL BECOME ONE OF THEM.
SHE TALKS BIG, BUT SHE COULD TAKE THE PLUNGE AT ANY SECOND.
OH YEAH? LET'S SEE HOW LOW SHE'LL GO.
?

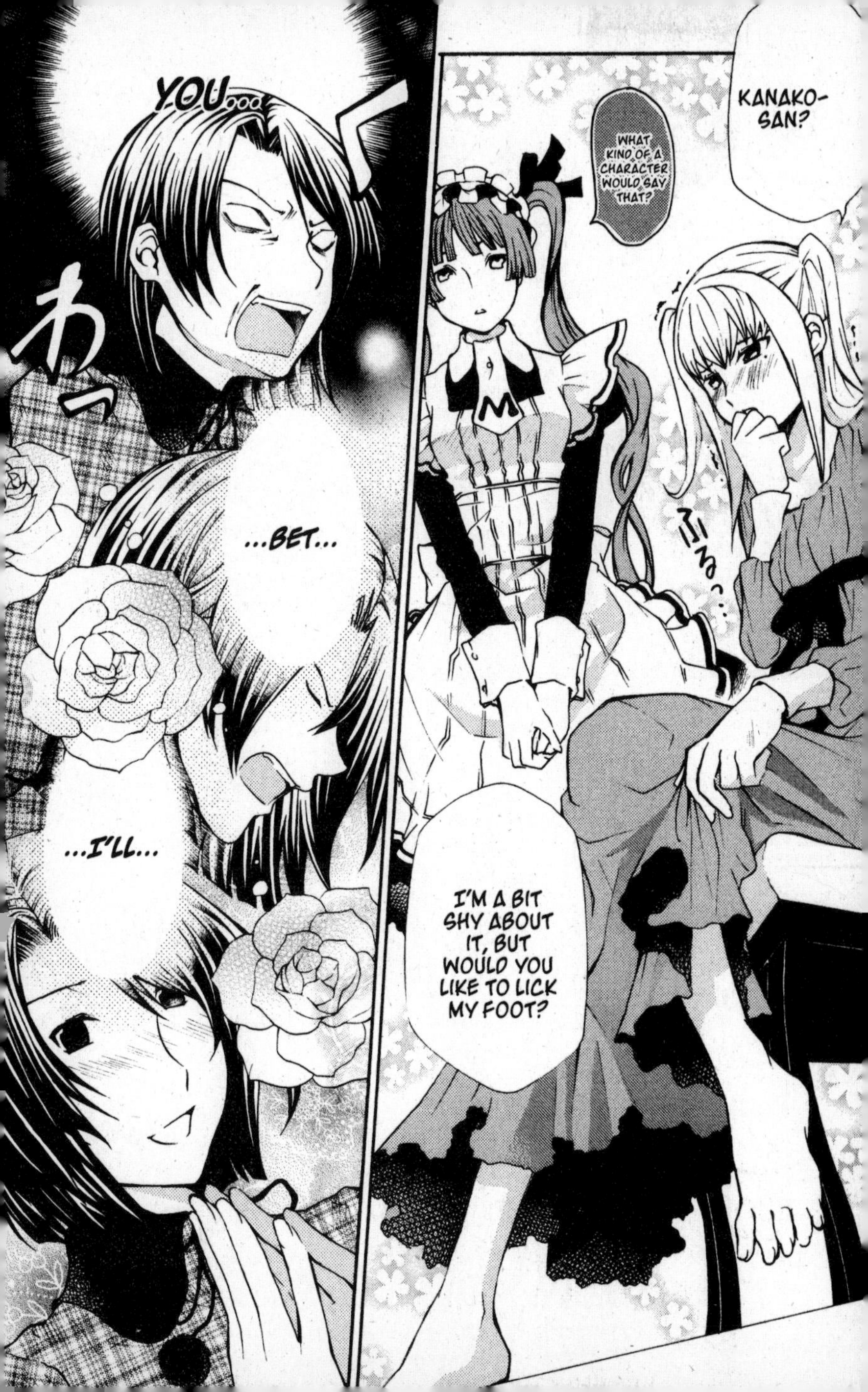
KANAKO-SAN?
WHAT KIND OF A CHARACTER WOULD SAY THAT?
I'M A BIT SHY ABOUT IT, BUT WOULD YOU LIKE TO LICK MY FOOT?
YOU...
わっ
...BET...
...I'LL...

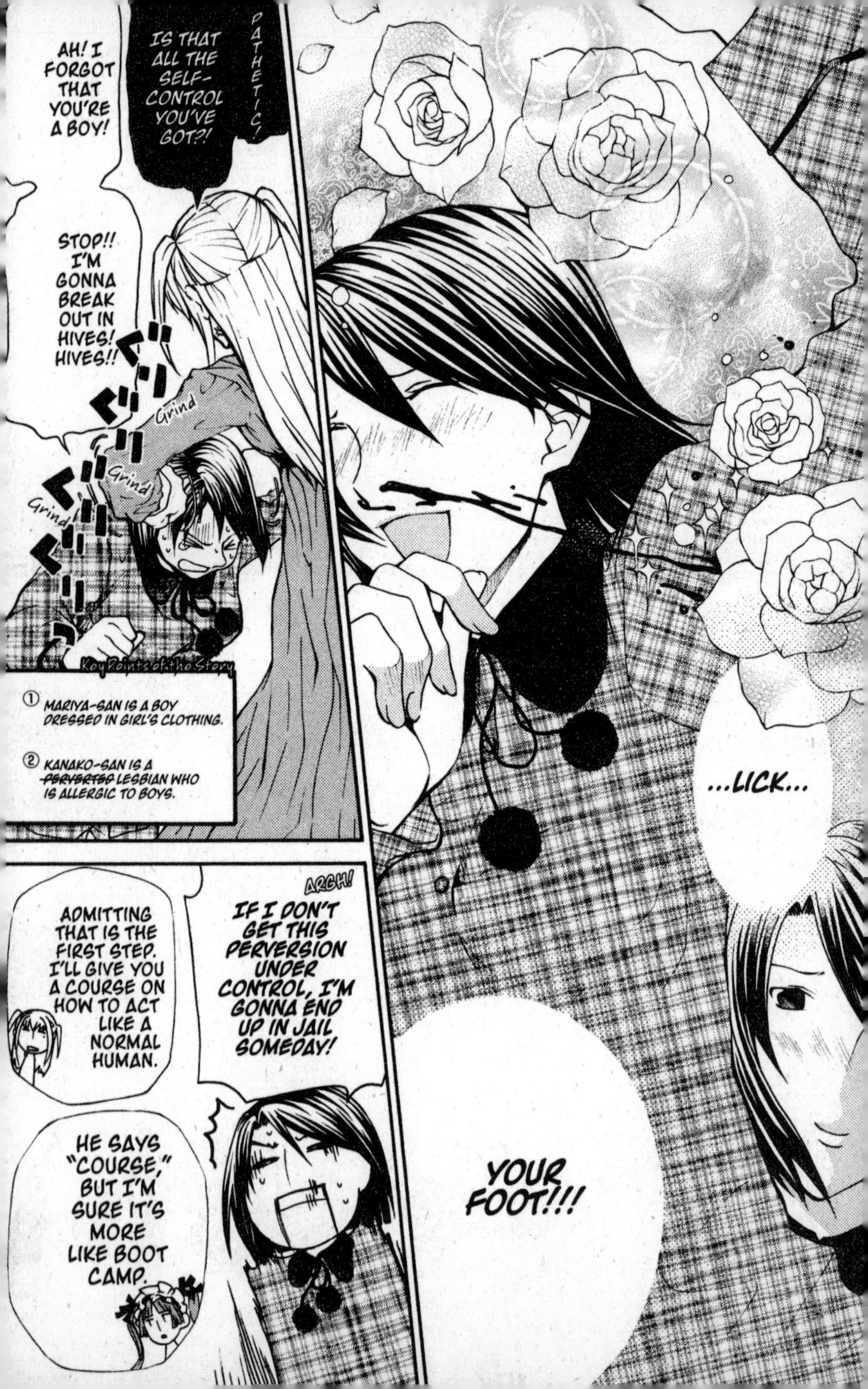
...LICK...
YOUR FOOT!!!
PATHETIC!
IS THAT ALL THE SELF-CONTROL YOU'VE GOT?!
AH! I FORGOT THAT YOU'RE A BOY!
STOP!! I'M GONNA BREAK OUT IN HIVES! HIVES!!
Grind
Grind
Grind
Key Points of the Story
① MARIYA-SAN IS A BOY DRESSED IN GIRL'S CLOTHING.
② KANAKO-SAN IS A ~~PERVERTED~~ LESBIAN WHO IS ALLERGIC TO BOYS.
ARGH!
IF I DON'T GET THIS PERVERSION UNDER CONTROL, I'M GONNA END UP IN JAIL SOMEDAY!
ADMITTING THAT IS THE FIRST STEP. I'LL GIVE YOU A COURSE ON HOW TO ACT LIKE A NORMAL HUMAN.
HE SAYS "COURSE," BUT I'M SURE IT'S MORE LIKE BOOT CAMP.

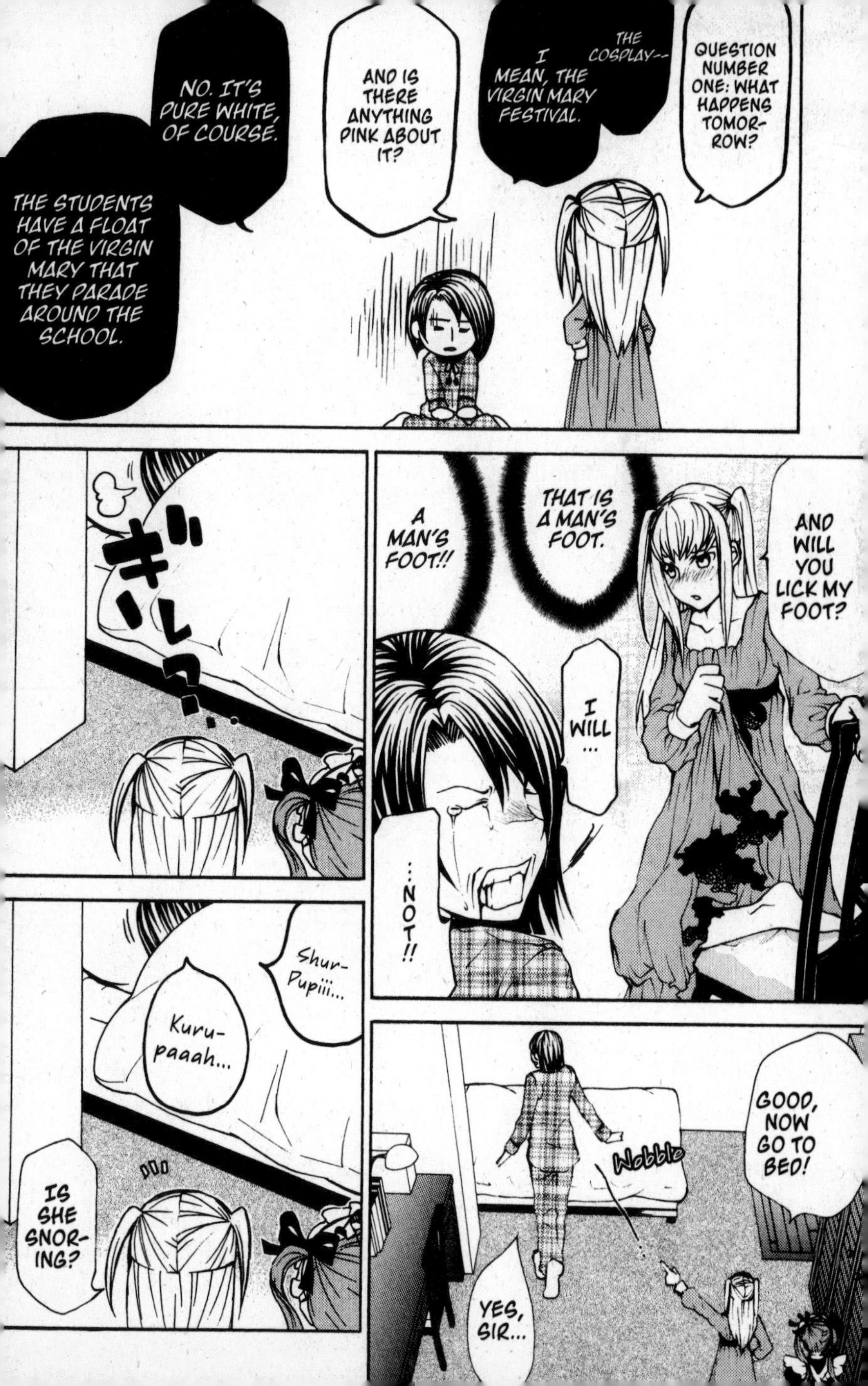
QUESTION NUMBER ONE: WHAT HAPPENS TOMORROW?
THE COSPLAY--
I MEAN, THE VIRGIN MARY FESTIVAL.
AND IS THERE ANYTHING PINK ABOUT IT?
NO. IT'S PURE WHITE, OF COURSE.
THE STUDENTS HAVE A FLOAT OF THE VIRGIN MARY THAT THEY PARADE AROUND THE SCHOOL.
AND WILL YOU LICK MY FOOT?
THAT IS A MAN'S FOOT.
A MAN'S FOOT!!
I WILL...
...NOT!!
GOOD, NOW GO TO BED!
Wobble
YES, SIR...
Shur-Pupiii...
Kuru-paaah...
IS SHE SNORING?

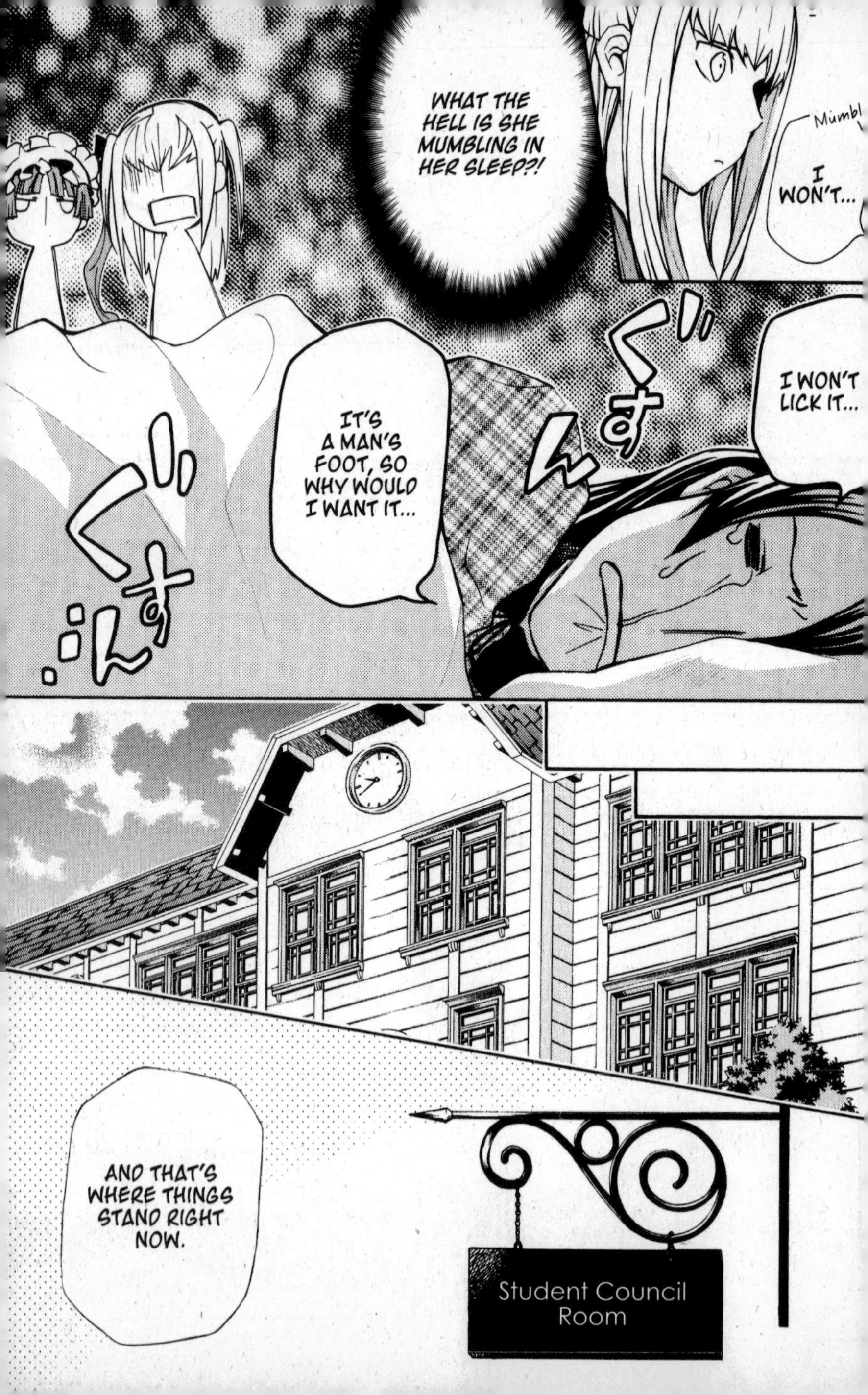
Mumbl
I WON'T...
WHAT THE HELL IS SHE MUMBLING IN HER SLEEP?!
I WON'T LICK IT...
ぐすん
IT'S A MAN'S FOOT, SO WHY WOULD I WANT IT...
ぐすん
AND THAT'S WHERE THINGS STAND RIGHT NOW.
Student Council Room

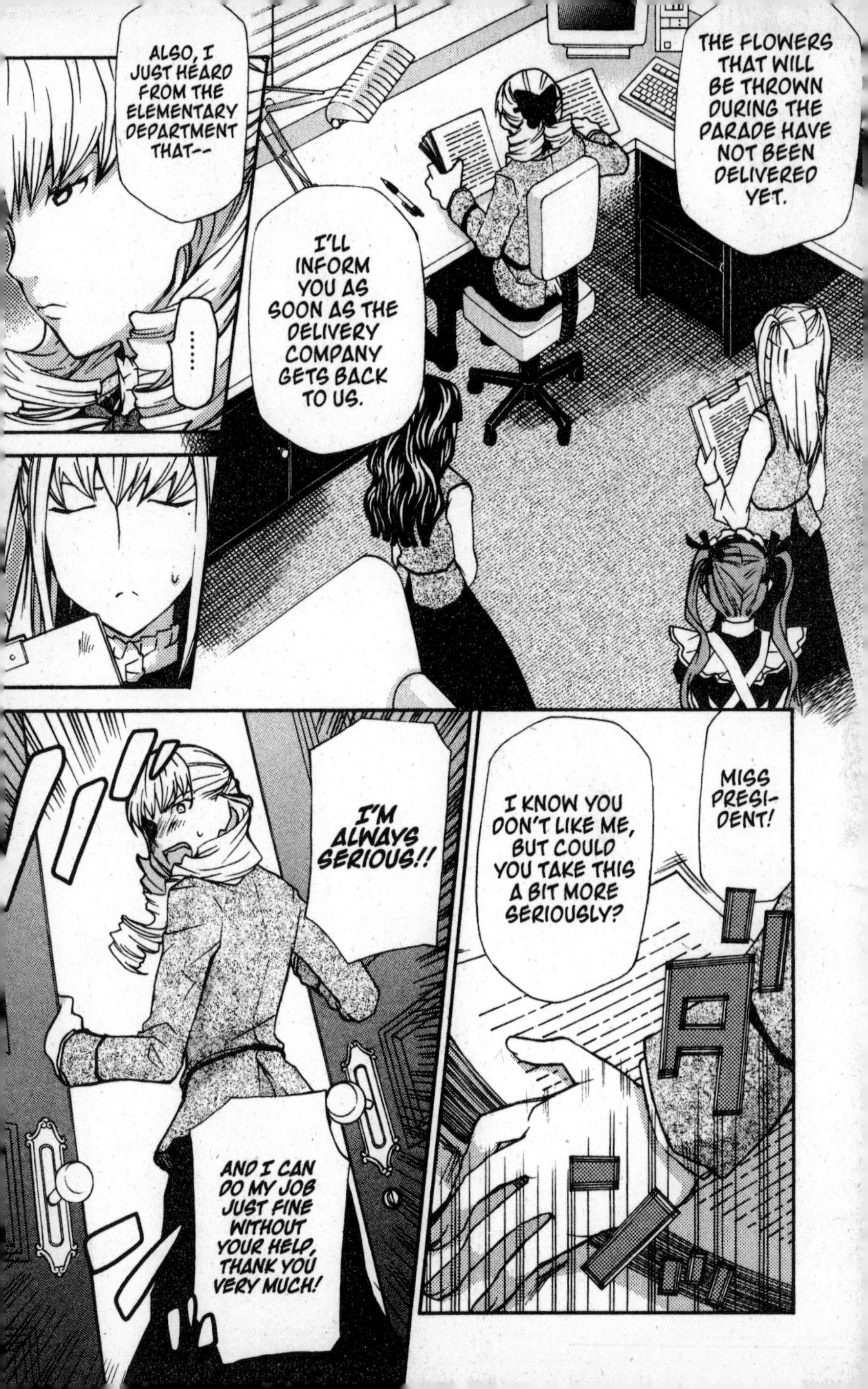
THE FLOWERS THAT WILL BE THROWN DURING THE PARADE HAVE NOT BEEN DELIVERED YET.
I'LL INFORM YOU AS SOON AS THE DELIVERY COMPANY GETS BACK TO US.
ALSO, I JUST HEARD FROM THE ELEMENTARY DEPARTMENT THAT--
......
MISS PRESI-DENT!
I KNOW YOU DON'T LIKE ME, BUT COULD YOU TAKE THIS A BIT MORE SERIOUSLY?
I'M ALWAYS SERIOUS!!
AND I CAN DO MY JOB JUST FINE WITHOUT YOUR HELP, THANK YOU VERY MUCH!

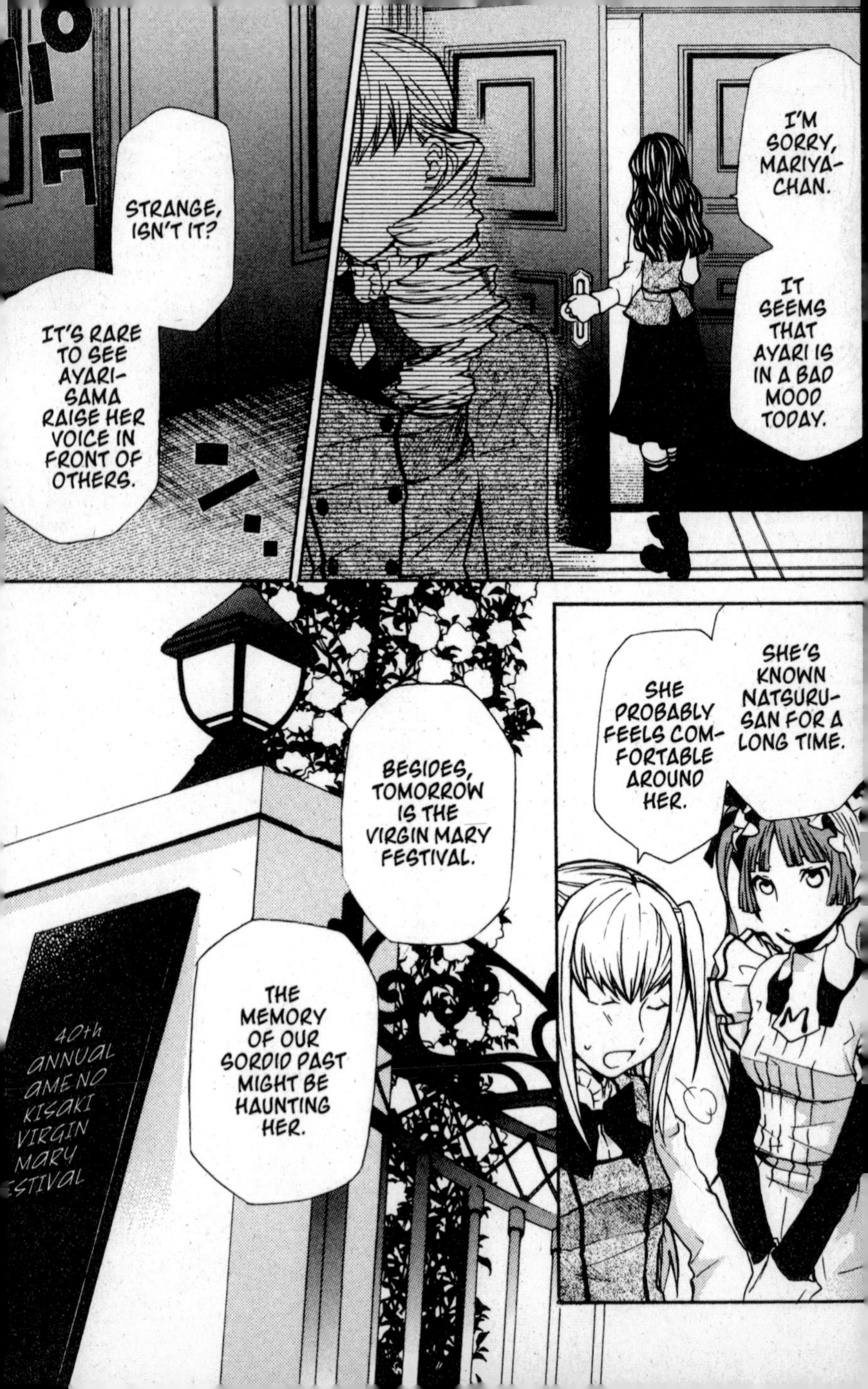
I'M SORRY, MARIYA-CHAN.
IT SEEMS THAT AYARI IS IN A BAD MOOD TODAY.
STRANGE, ISN'T IT?
IT'S RARE TO SEE AYARI-SAMA RAISE HER VOICE IN FRONT OF OTHERS.
SHE'S KNOWN NATSURU-SAN FOR A LONG TIME.
SHE PROBABLY FEELS COM-FORTABLE AROUND HER.
BESIDES, TOMORROW IS THE VIRGIN MARY FESTIVAL.
THE MEMORY OF OUR SORDID PAST MIGHT BE HAUNTING HER.
40th ANNUAL AME NO KISAKI VIRGIN MARY ESTIVAL

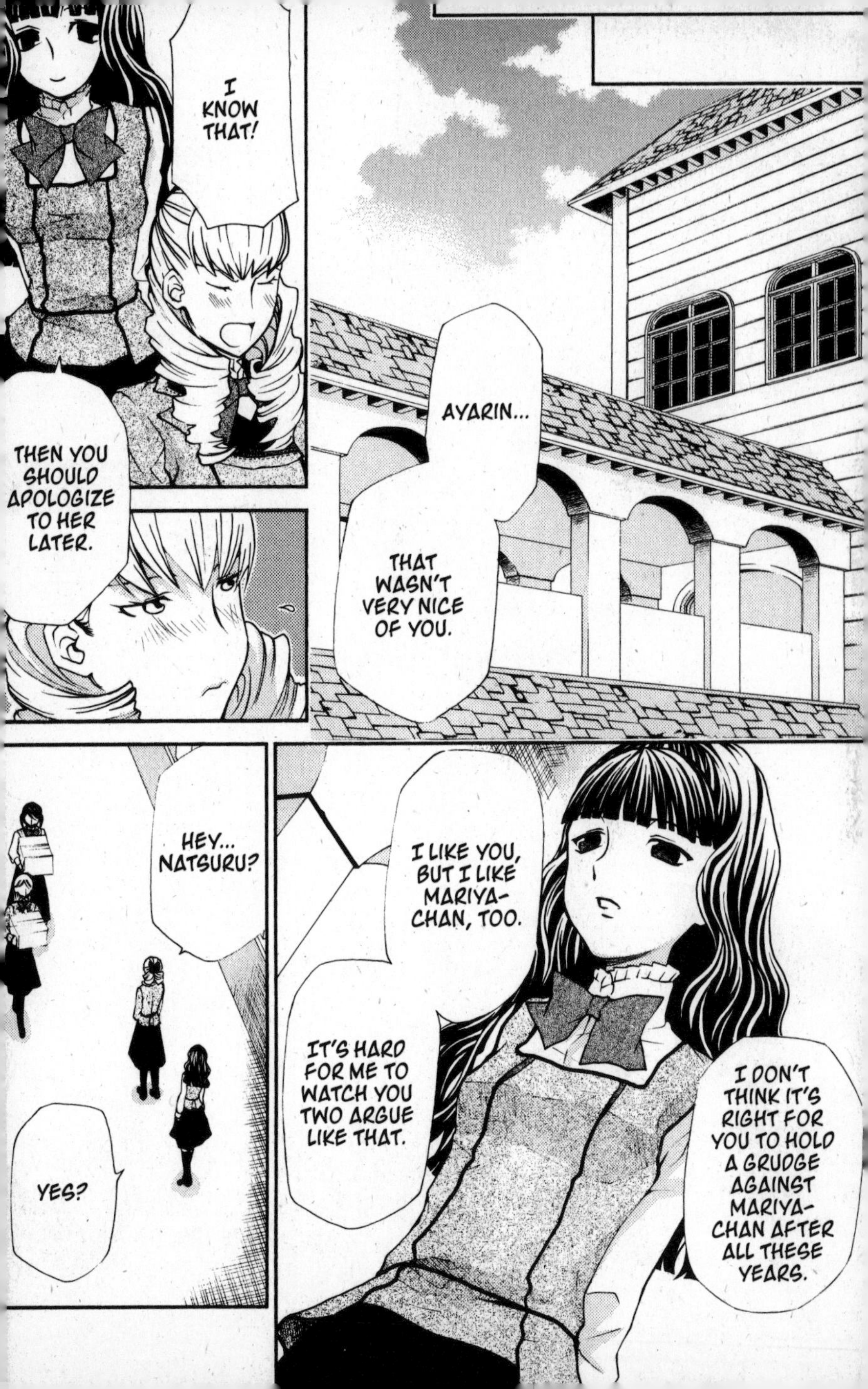
AYARIN...
THAT WASN'T VERY NICE OF YOU.
I KNOW THAT!
THEN YOU SHOULD APOLOGIZE TO HER LATER.
I LIKE YOU, BUT I LIKE MARIYA-CHAN, TOO.
IT'S HARD FOR ME TO WATCH YOU TWO ARGUE LIKE THAT.
I DON'T THINK IT'S RIGHT FOR YOU TO HOLD A GRUDGE AGAINST MARIYA-CHAN AFTER ALL THESE YEARS.
HEY... NATSURU?
YES?

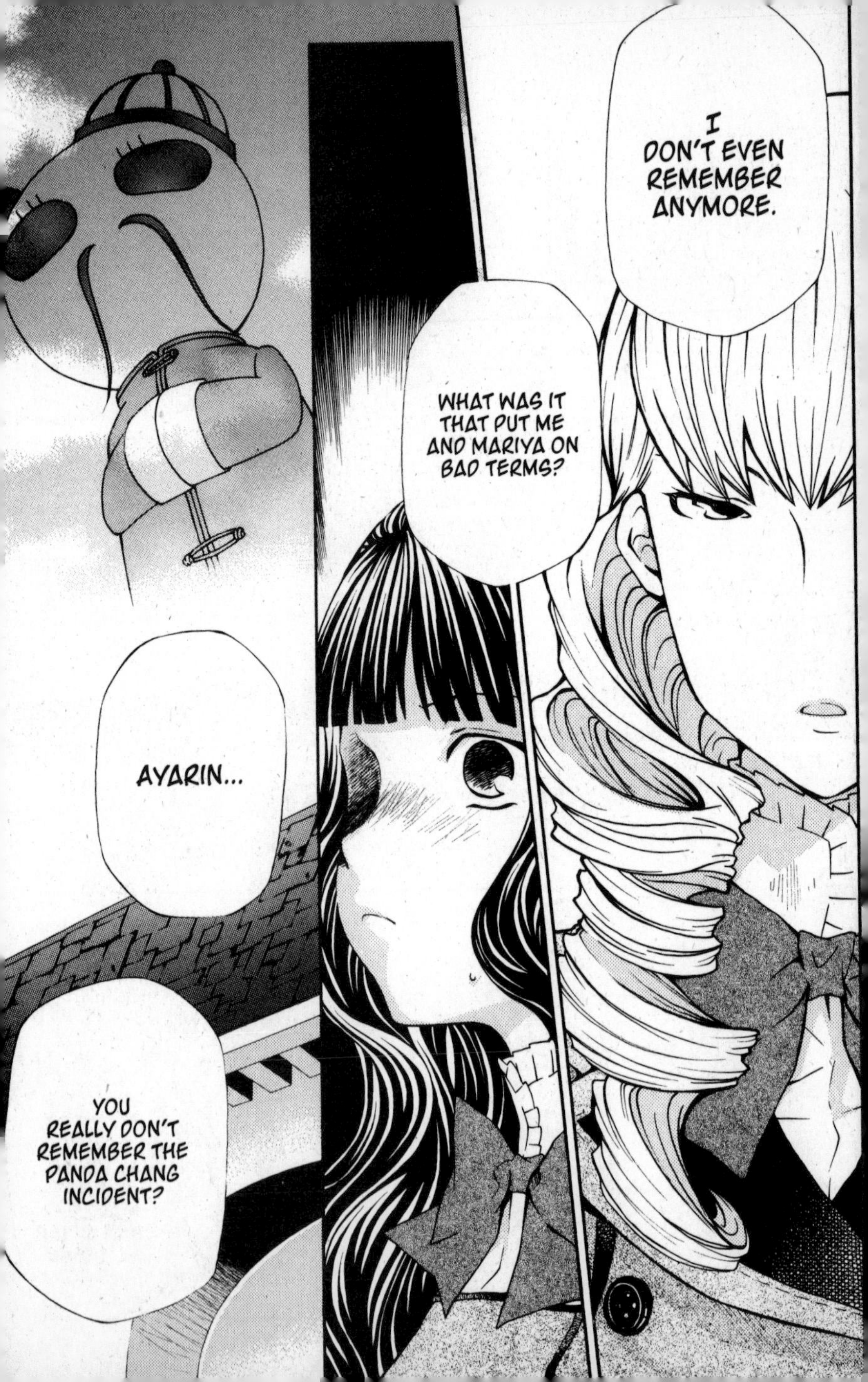
I DON'T EVEN REMEMBER ANYMORE.
WHAT WAS IT THAT PUT ME AND MARIYA ON BAD TERMS?
AYARIN...
YOU REALLY DON'T REMEMBER THE PANDA CHANG INCIDENT?

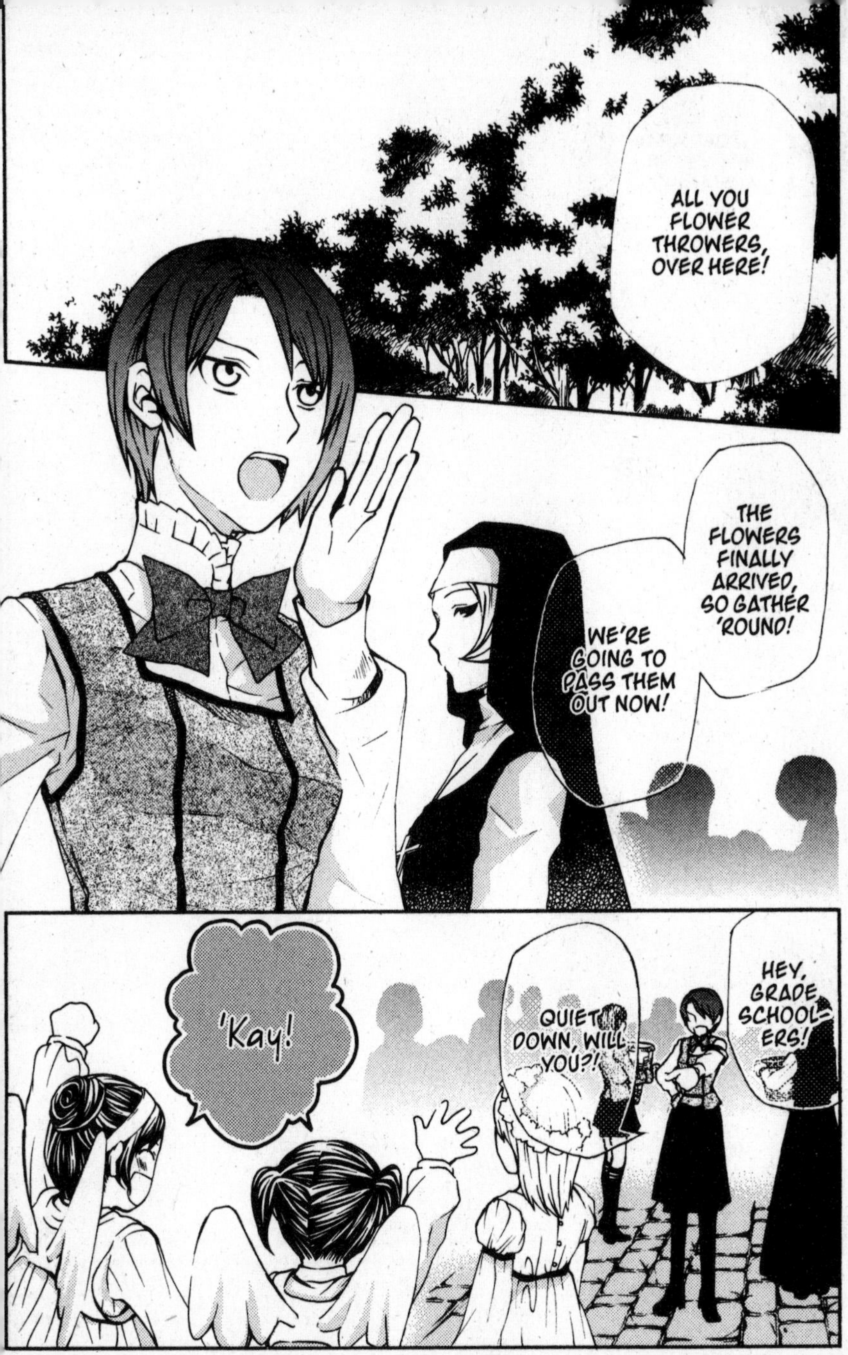
ALL YOU FLOWER THROWERS, OVER HERE!
THE FLOWERS FINALLY ARRIVED, SO GATHER 'ROUND!
WE'RE GOING TO PASS THEM OUT NOW!
HEY, GRADE SCHOOL-ERS!
QUIET DOWN, WILL YOU?!
'Kay!

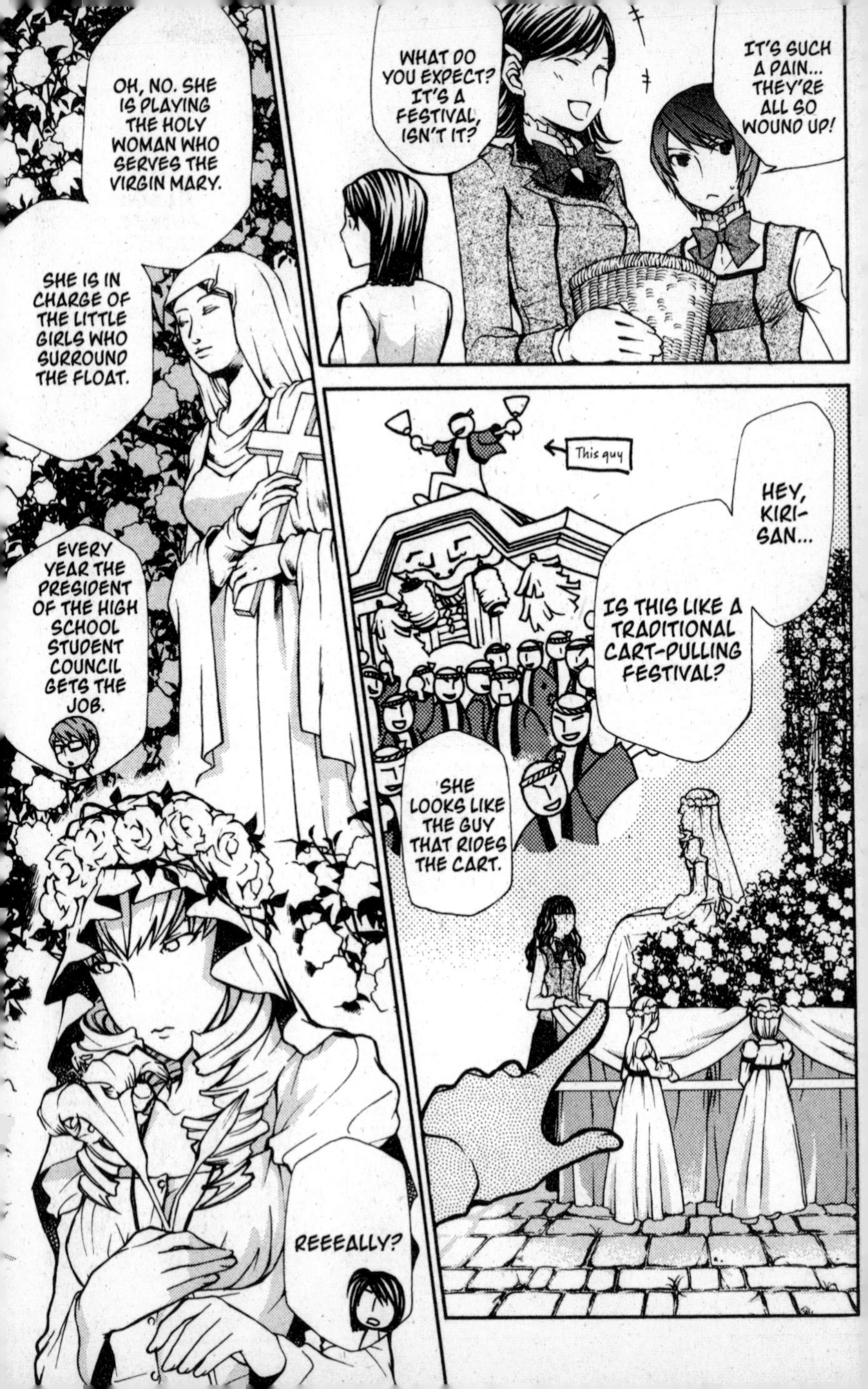
IT'S SUCH A PAIN... THEY'RE ALL SO WOUND UP!
WHAT DO YOU EXPECT? IT'S A FESTIVAL, ISN'T IT?
HEY, KIRI-SAN...
IS THIS LIKE A TRADITIONAL CART-PULLING FESTIVAL?
This guy
SHE LOOKS LIKE THE GUY THAT RIDES THE CART.
OH, NO. SHE IS PLAYING THE HOLY WOMAN WHO SERVES THE VIRGIN MARY.
SHE IS IN CHARGE OF THE LITTLE GIRLS WHO SURROUND THE FLOAT.
EVERY YEAR THE PRESIDENT OF THE HIGH SCHOOL STUDENT COUNCIL GETS THE JOB.
REEEALLY?

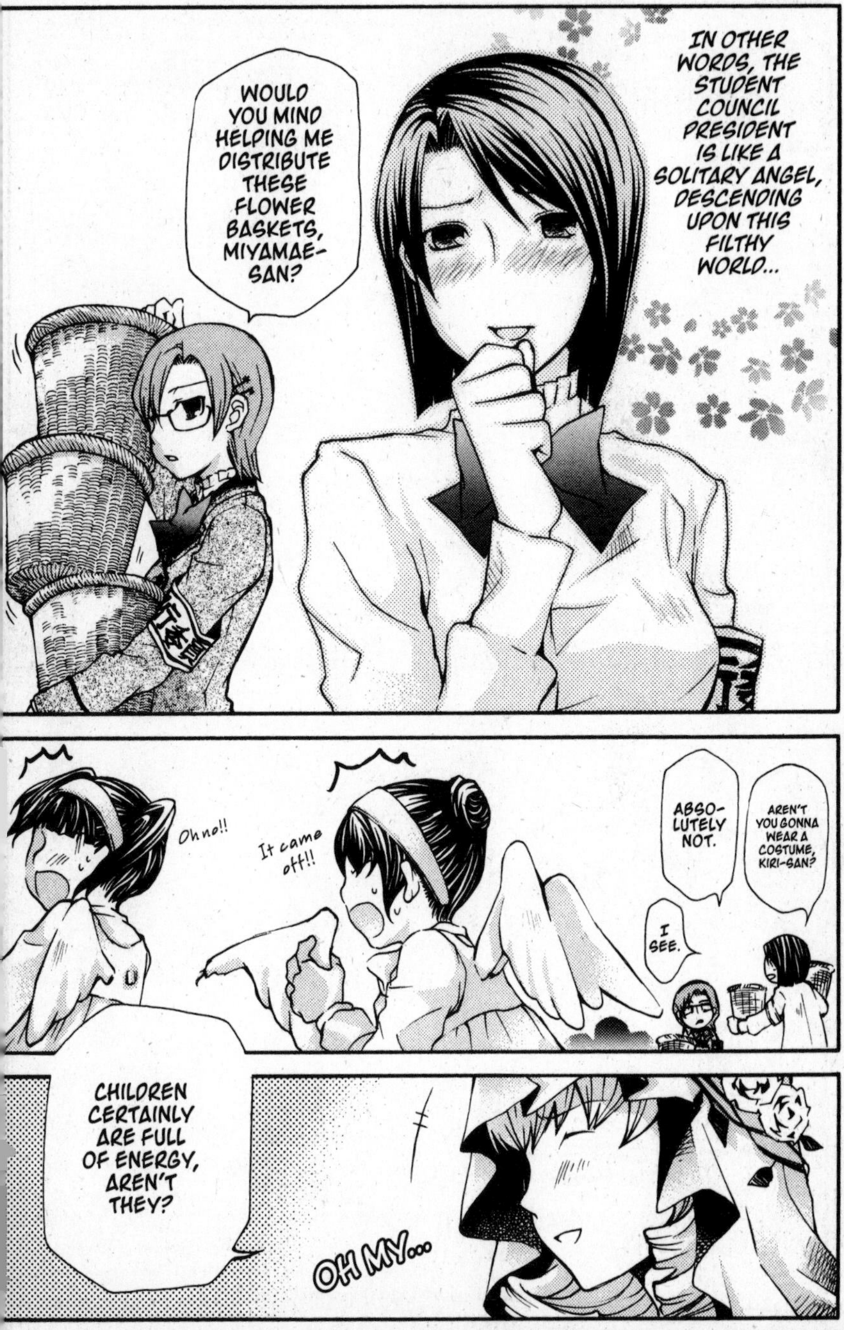
IN OTHER WORDS, THE STUDENT COUNCIL PRESIDENT IS LIKE A SOLITARY ANGEL, DESCENDING UPON THIS FILTHY WORLD...
WOULD YOU MIND HELPING ME DISTRIBUTE THESE FLOWER BASKETS, MIYAMAE-SAN?
AREN'T YOU GONNA WEAR A COSTUME, KIRI-SAN?
ABSO-LUTELY NOT.
I SEE.
It came off!!
Oh no!!
OH MY...
CHILDREN CERTAINLY ARE FULL OF ENERGY, AREN'T THEY?

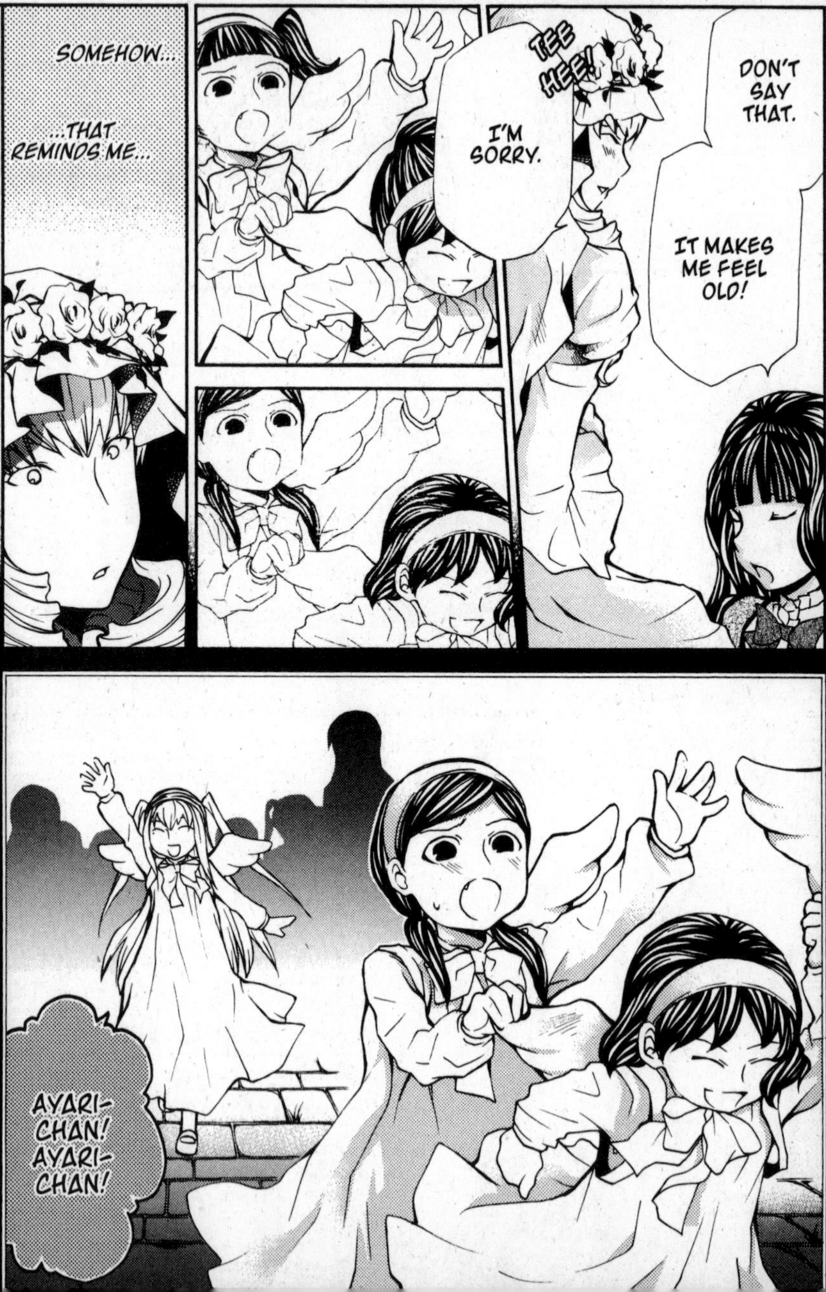
DON'T SAY THAT.
IT MAKES ME FEEL OLD!
TEE HEE!
I'M SORRY.
SOMEHOW...
...THAT REMINDS ME...
AYARI-CHAN! AYARI-CHAN!

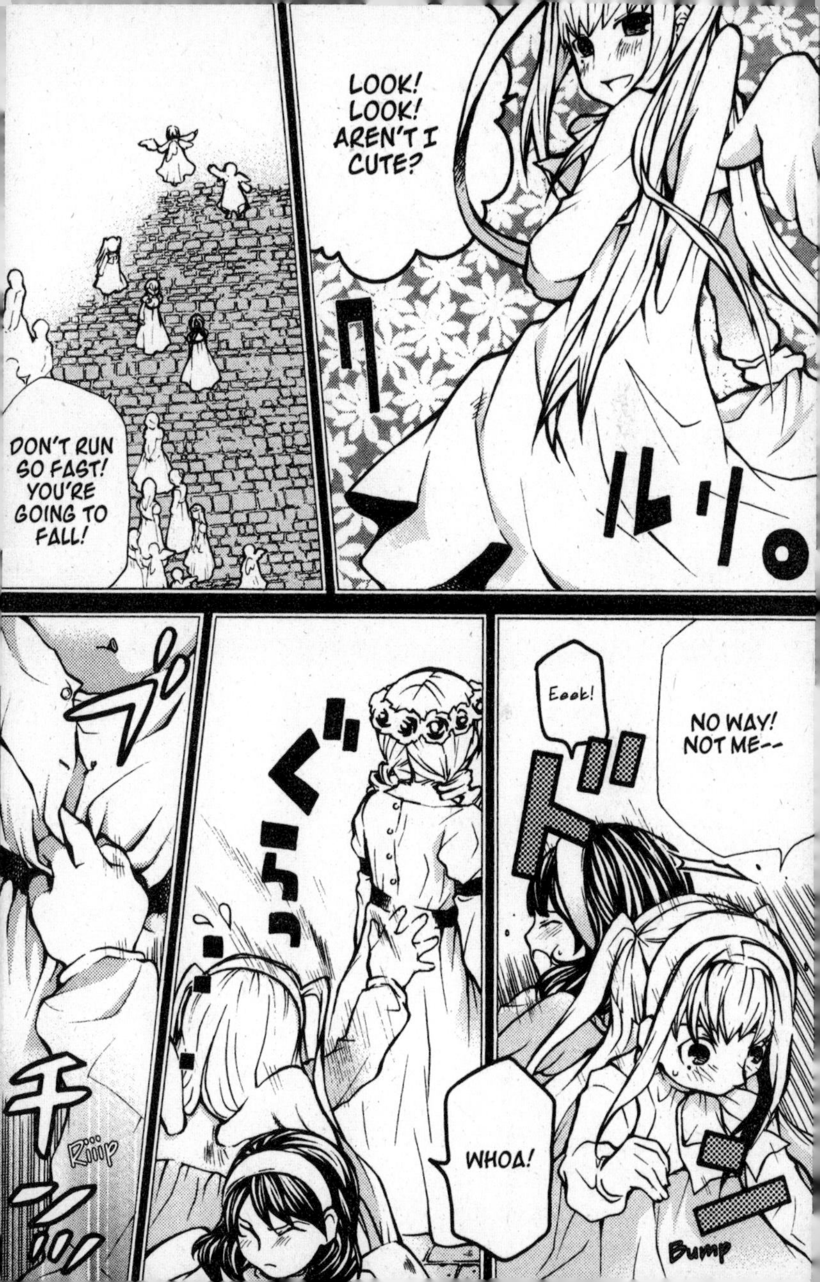
LOOK! LOOK! AREN'T I CUTE?
DON'T RUN SO FAST! YOU'RE GOING TO FALL!
NO WAY! NOT ME--
Eeek!
WHOA!
Bump
Riiip

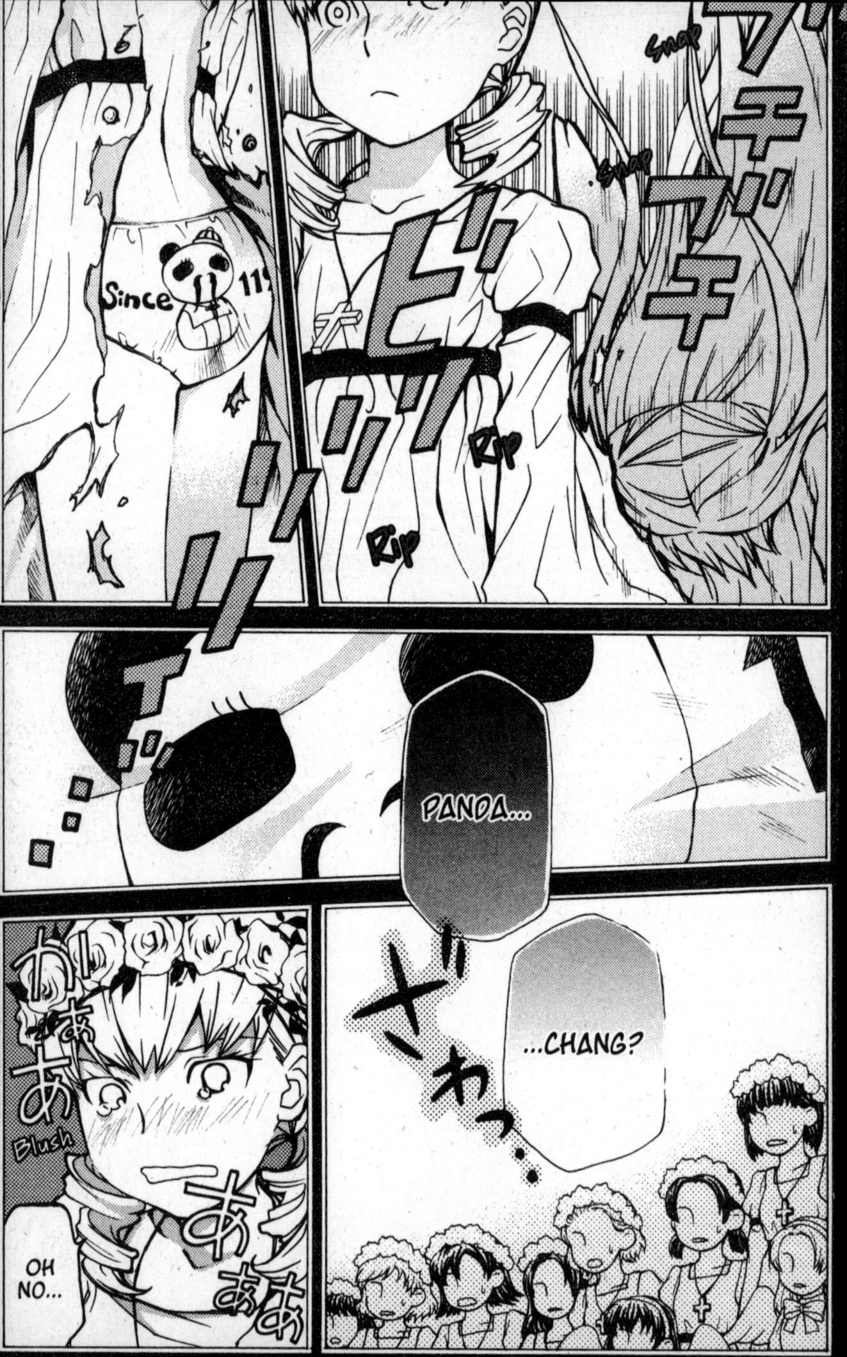

Snap
Snap
Rip
Rip
Since
PANDA...
...CHANG?
ざわっ…
Blush
OH NO...

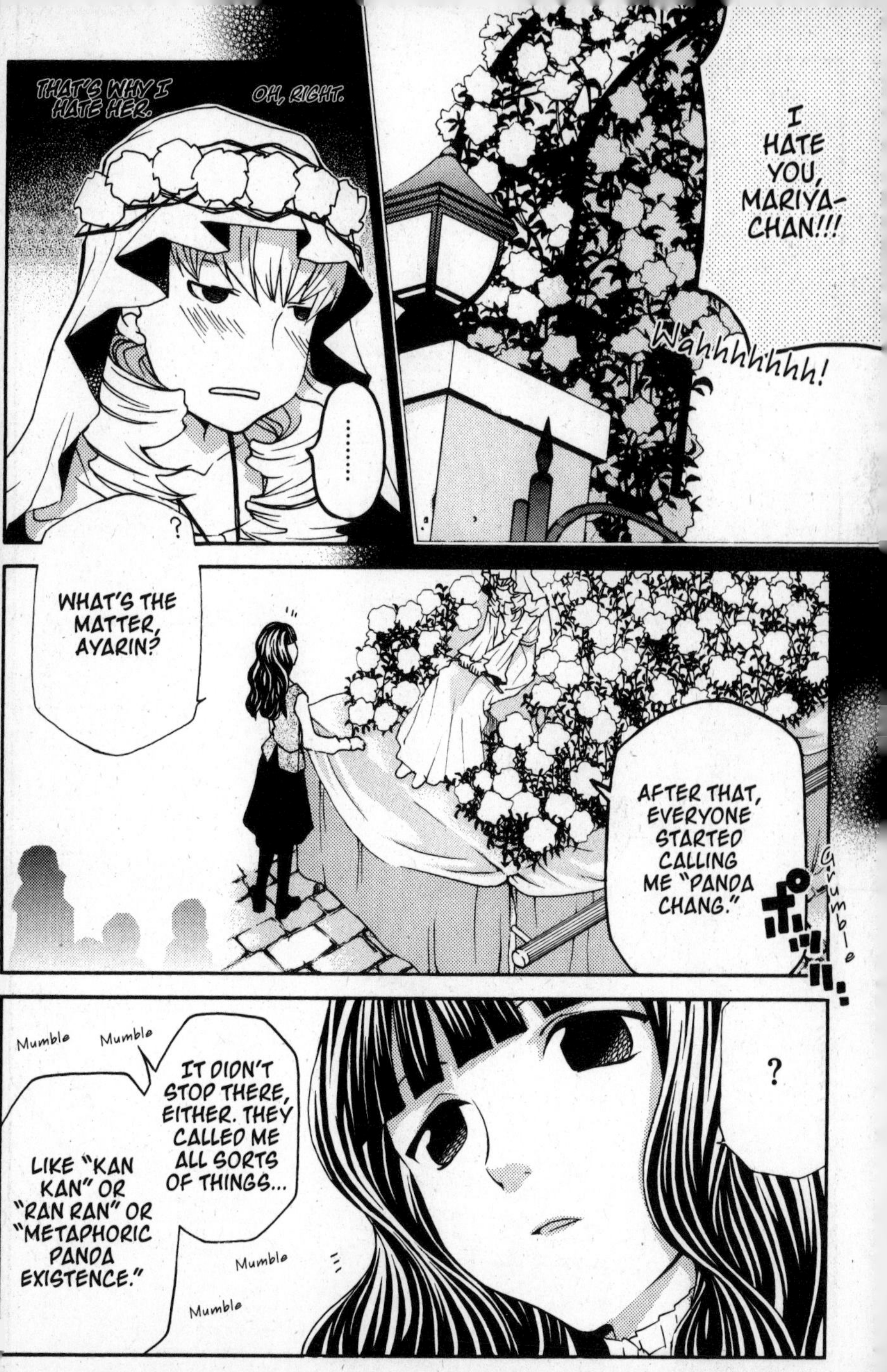
I HATE YOU, MARIYA-CHAN!!!
Wahhhhhhhh!
OH, RIGHT.
THAT'S WHY I HATE HER.
......
?
AFTER THAT, EVERYONE STARTED CALLING ME "PANDA CHANG."
Grumble
WHAT'S THE MATTER, AYARIN?
?
IT DIDN'T STOP THERE, EITHER. THEY CALLED ME ALL SORTS OF THINGS...
Mumble
Mumble
LIKE "KAN KAN" OR "RAN RAN" OR "METAPHORIC PANDA EXISTENCE."
Mumble
Mumble

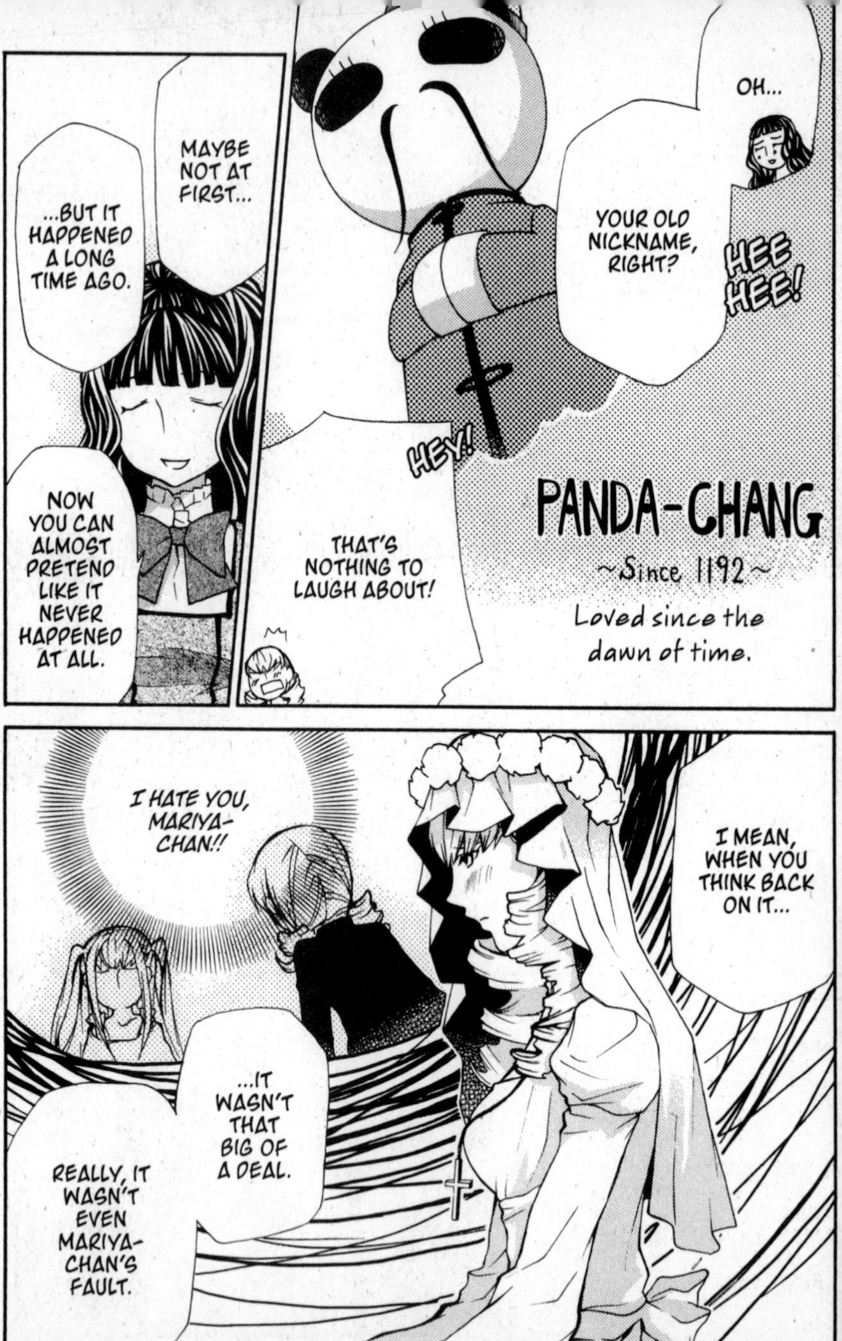
OH...
YOUR OLD NICKNAME, RIGHT?
HEE HEE!
PANDA-CHANG
~Since 1192~
Loved since the dawn of time.
HEY!
THAT'S NOTHING TO LAUGH ABOUT!
MAYBE NOT AT FIRST...
...BUT IT HAPPENED A LONG TIME AGO.
NOW YOU CAN ALMOST PRETEND LIKE IT NEVER HAPPENED AT ALL.
I MEAN, WHEN YOU THINK BACK ON IT...
I HATE YOU, MARIYA-CHAN!!
...IT WASN'T THAT BIG OF A DEAL.
REALLY, IT WASN'T EVEN MARIYA-CHAN'S FAULT.

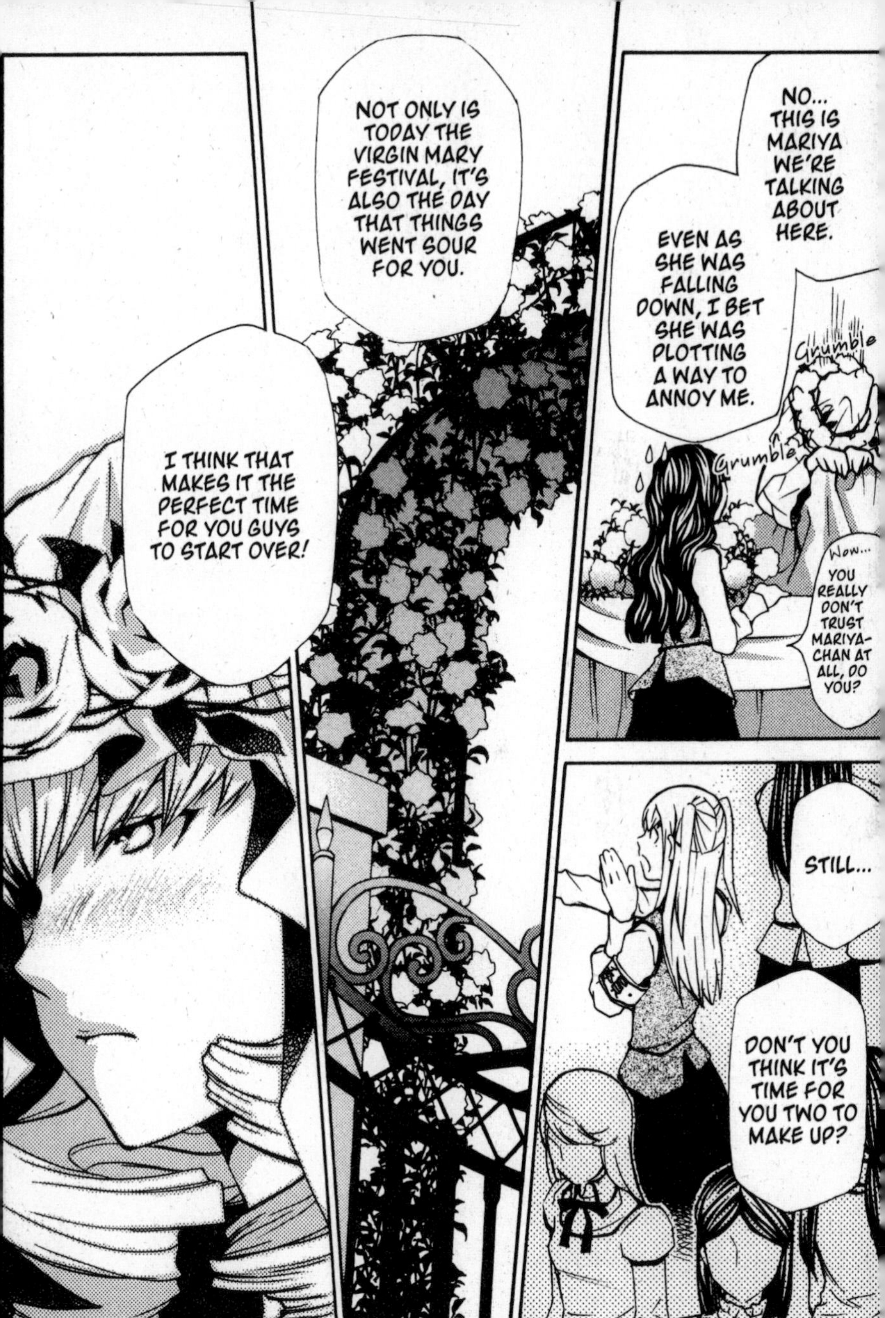
NO... THIS IS MARIYA WE'RE TALKING ABOUT HERE.
EVEN AS SHE WAS FALLING DOWN, I BET SHE WAS PLOTTING A WAY TO ANNOY ME.
Grumble
Grumble
Wow... YOU REALLY DON'T TRUST MARIYA-CHAN AT ALL, DO YOU?
STILL...
DON'T YOU THINK IT'S TIME FOR YOU TWO TO MAKE UP?
NOT ONLY IS TODAY THE VIRGIN MARY FESTIVAL, IT'S ALSO THE DAY THAT THINGS WENT SOUR FOR YOU.
I THINK THAT MAKES IT THE PERFECT TIME FOR YOU GUYS TO START OVER!

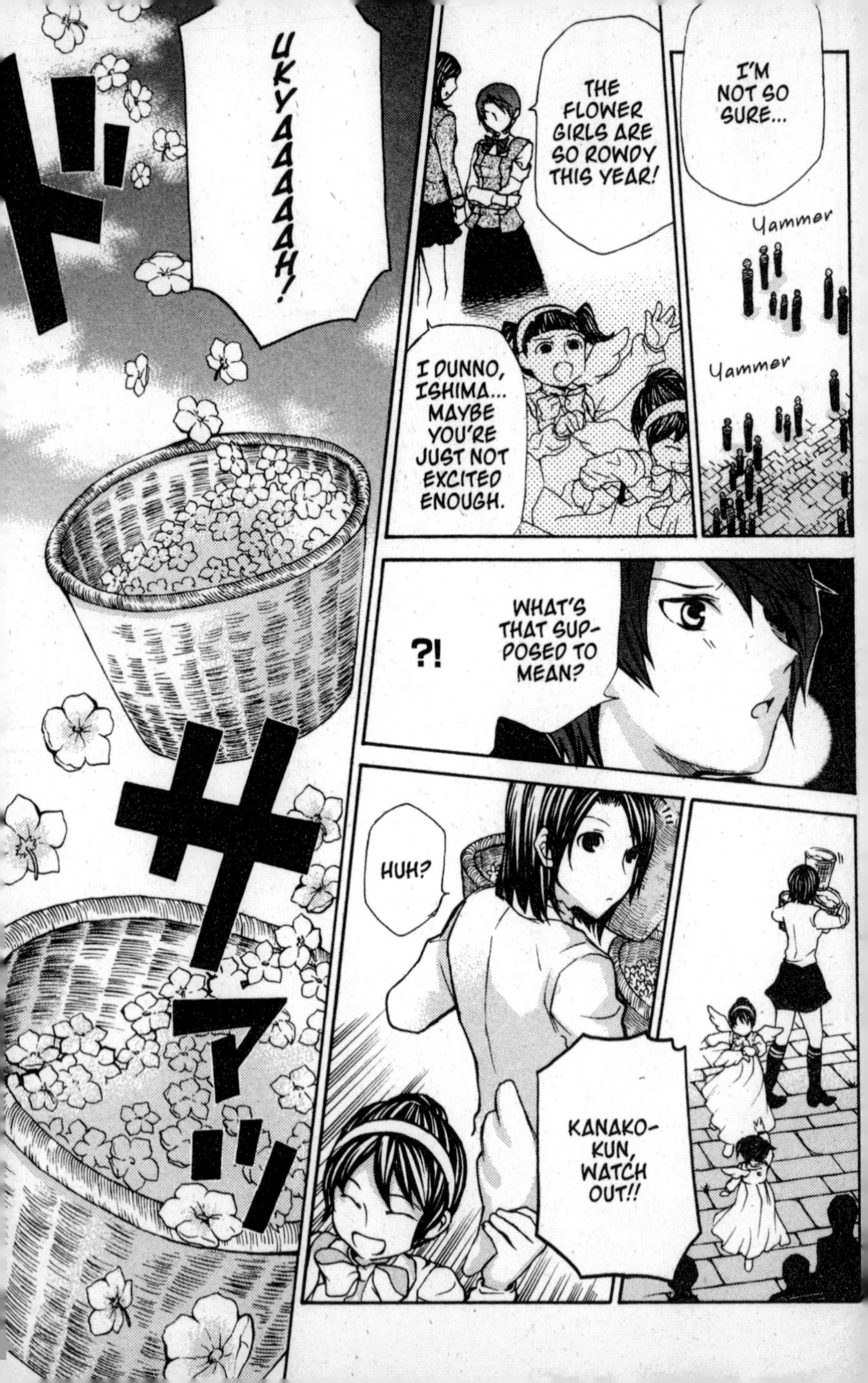
I'M NOT SO SURE...
Yammer
Yammer
THE FLOWER GIRLS ARE SO ROWDY THIS YEAR!
I DUNNO, ISHIMA... MAYBE YOU'RE JUST NOT EXCITED ENOUGH.
WHAT'S THAT SUP-POSED TO MEAN?
?!
KANAKO-KUN, WATCH OUT!!
HUH?
UKYAAAAAAAH!
ド
ザァッ

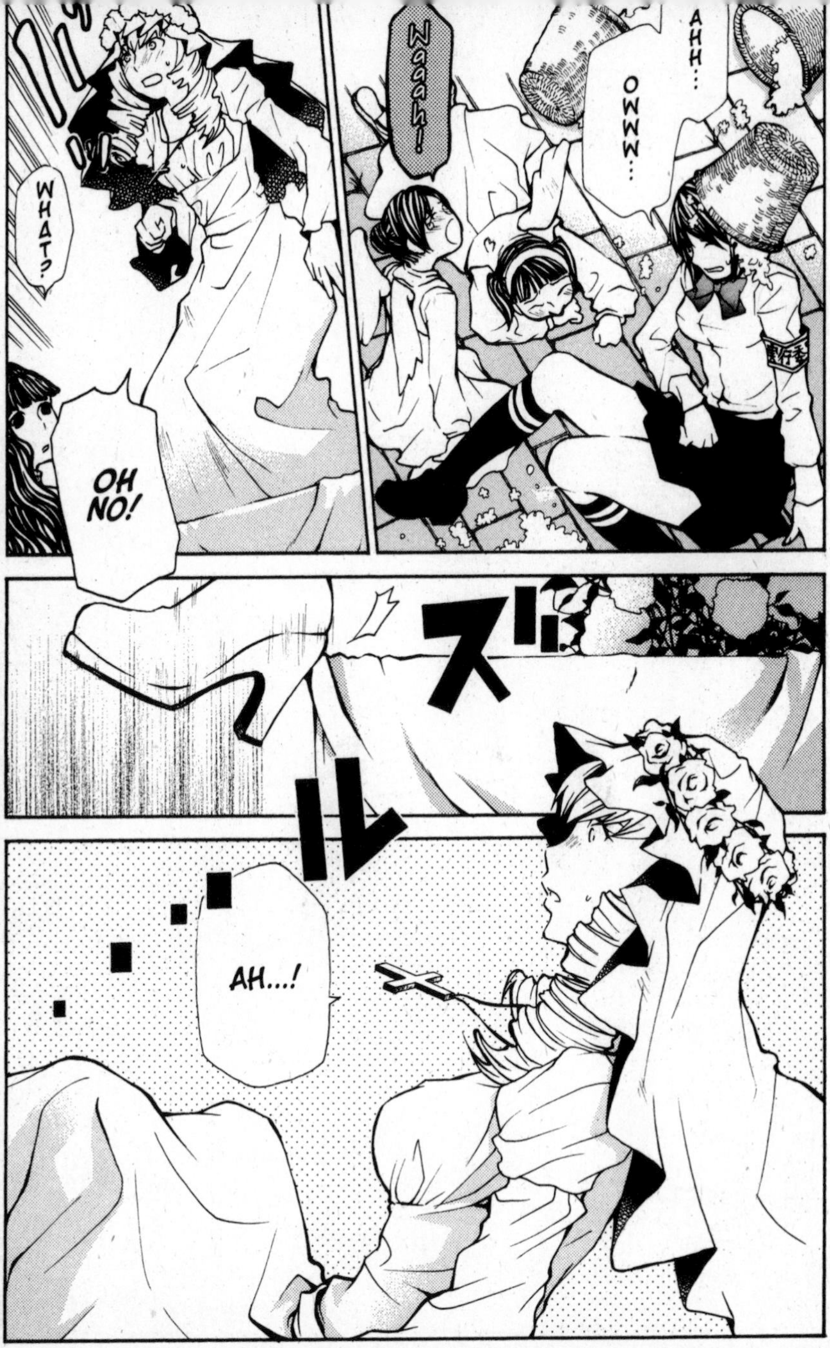
AHH... OWWW...
Waaah!
WHAT?
OH NO!
ズル
AH...!

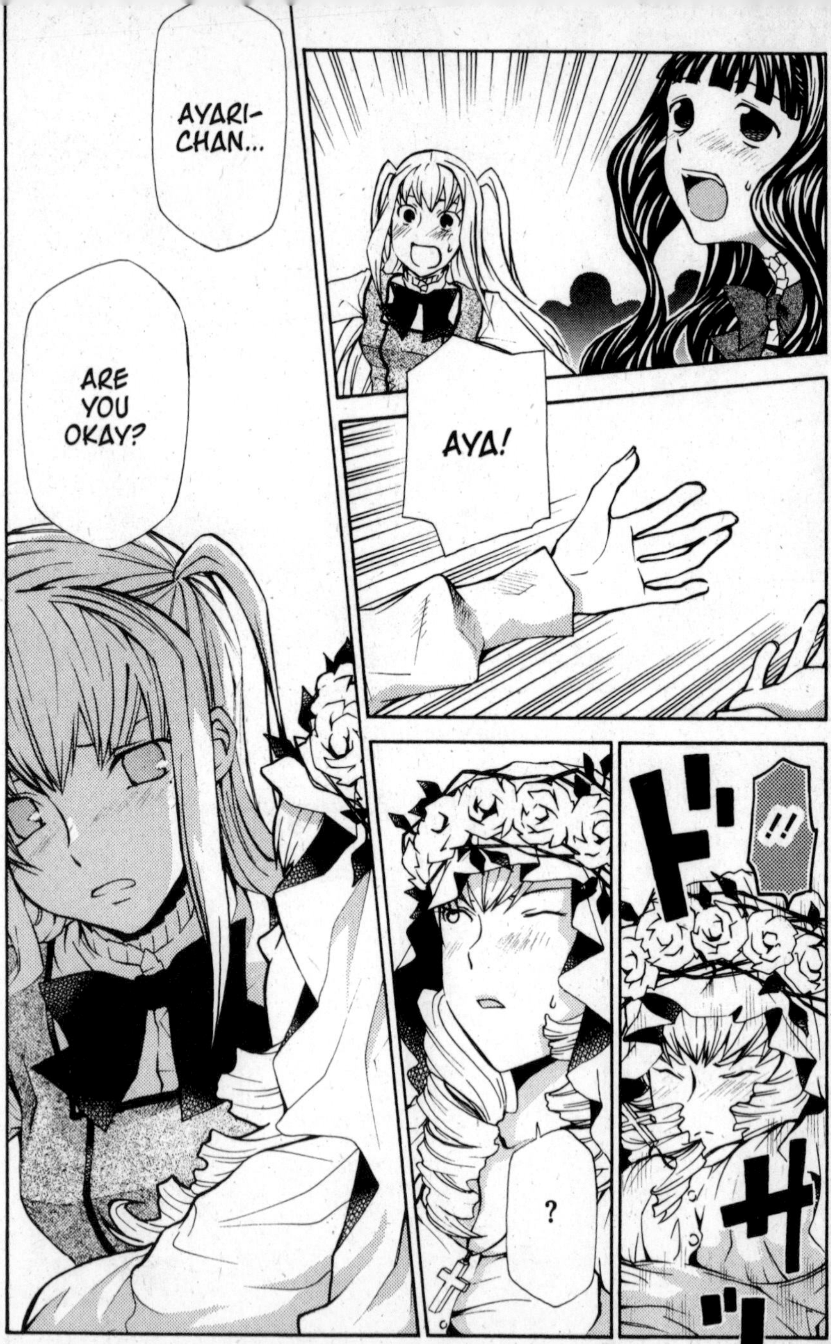
AYA!
!!
ドッ
サッ
?
AYARI-CHAN...
ARE YOU OKAY?

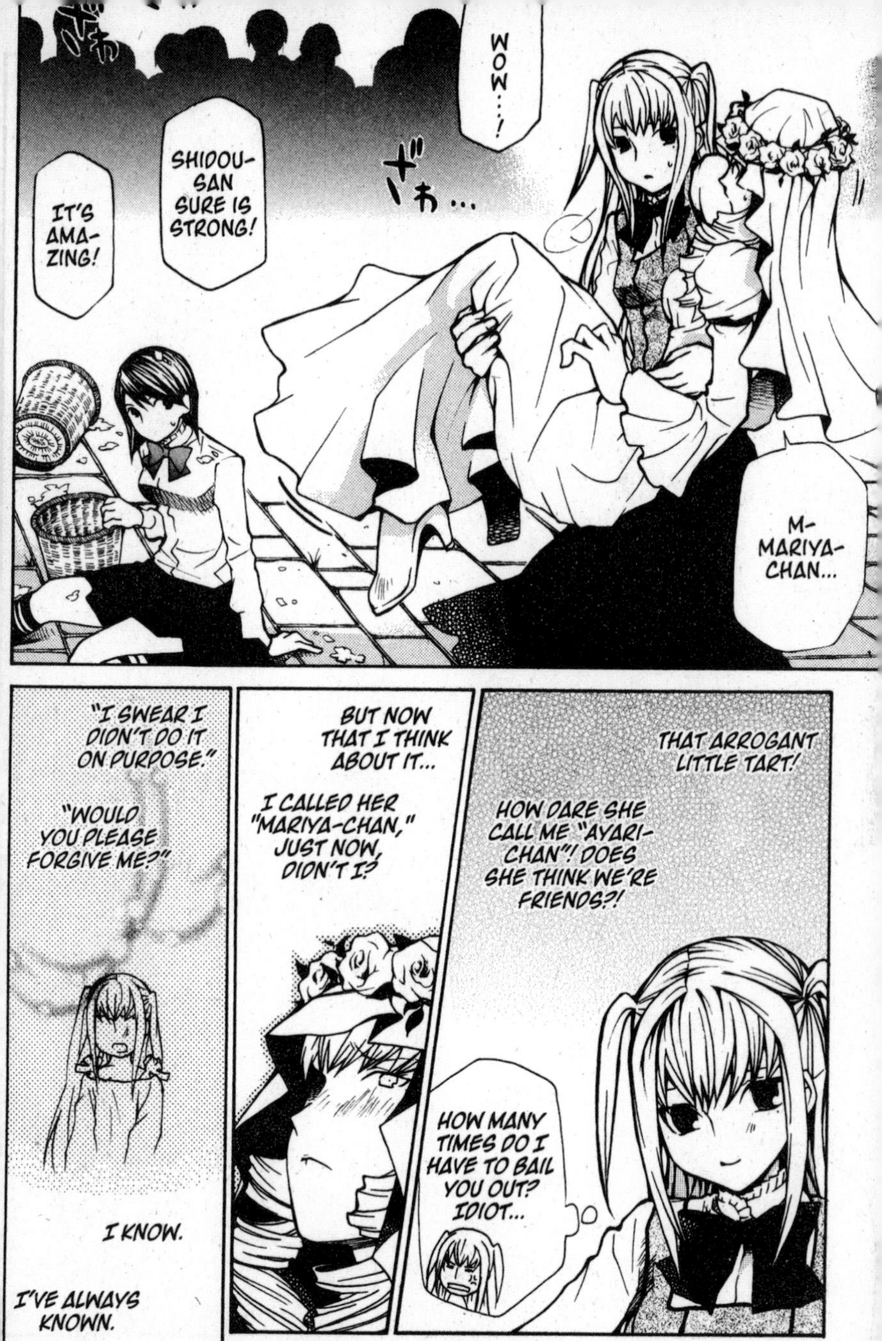
WOW...!
ざわ...
SHIDOU-SAN SURE IS STRONG!
IT'S AMA-ZING!
ざわ
M-MARIYA-CHAN...
THAT ARROGANT LITTLE TART!
HOW DARE SHE CALL ME "AYARI-CHAN"! DOES SHE THINK WE'RE FRIENDS?!
HOW MANY TIMES DO I HAVE TO BAIL YOU OUT? IDIOT...
BUT NOW THAT I THINK ABOUT IT...
I CALLED HER "MARIYA-CHAN," JUST NOW, DIDN'T I?
"I SWEAR I DIDN'T DO IT ON PURPOSE."
"WOULD YOU PLEASE FORGIVE ME?"
I KNOW.
I'VE ALWAYS KNOWN.

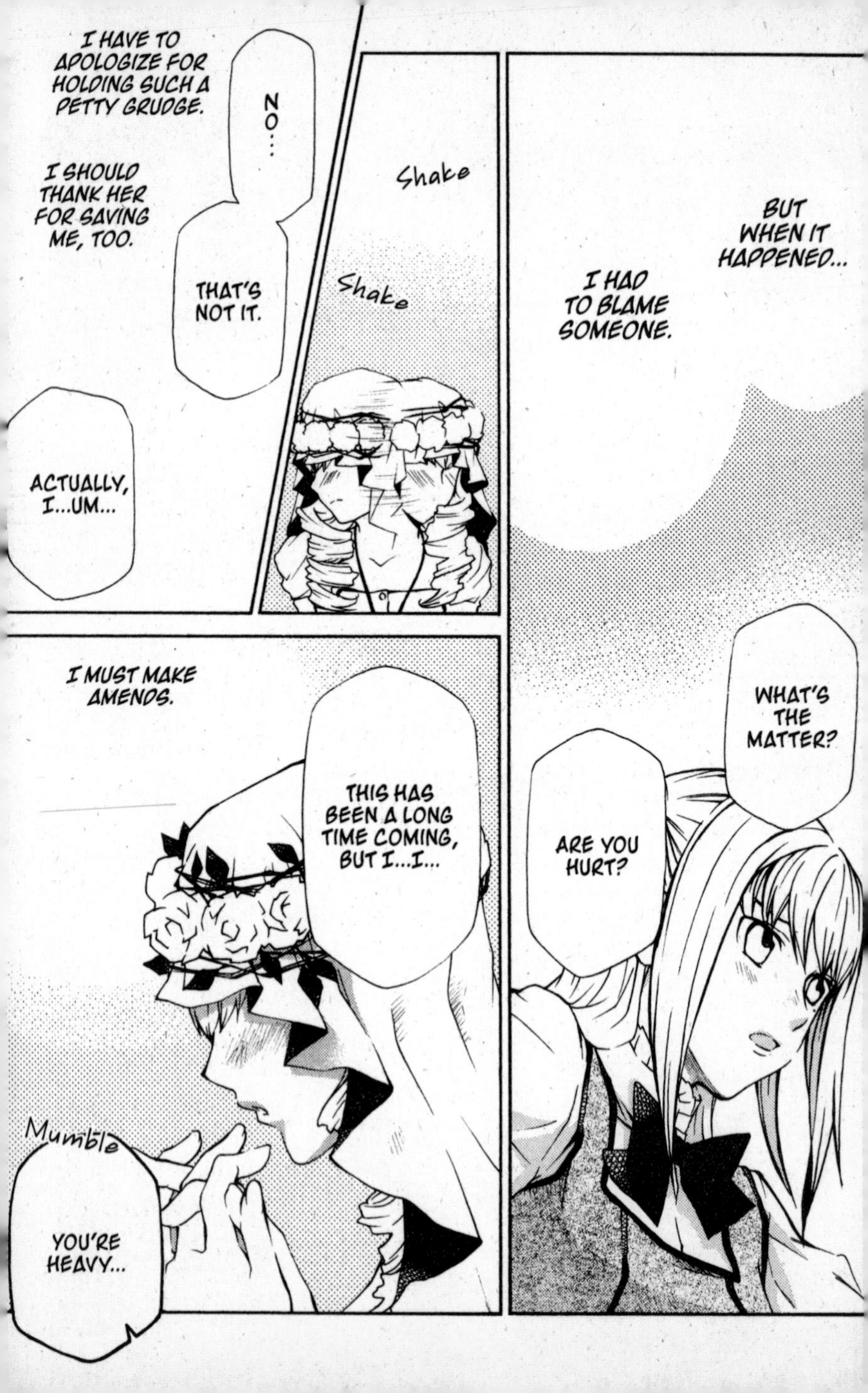
BUT WHEN IT HAPPENED...
I HAD TO BLAME SOMEONE.
WHAT'S THE MATTER?
ARE YOU HURT?
Shake
Shake
I HAVE TO APOLOGIZE FOR HOLDING SUCH A PETTY GRUDGE.
I SHOULD THANK HER FOR SAVING ME, TOO.
NO...
THAT'S NOT IT.
ACTUALLY, I...UM...
I MUST MAKE AMENDS.
THIS HAS BEEN A LONG TIME COMING, BUT I...I...
Mumble
YOU'RE HEAVY...

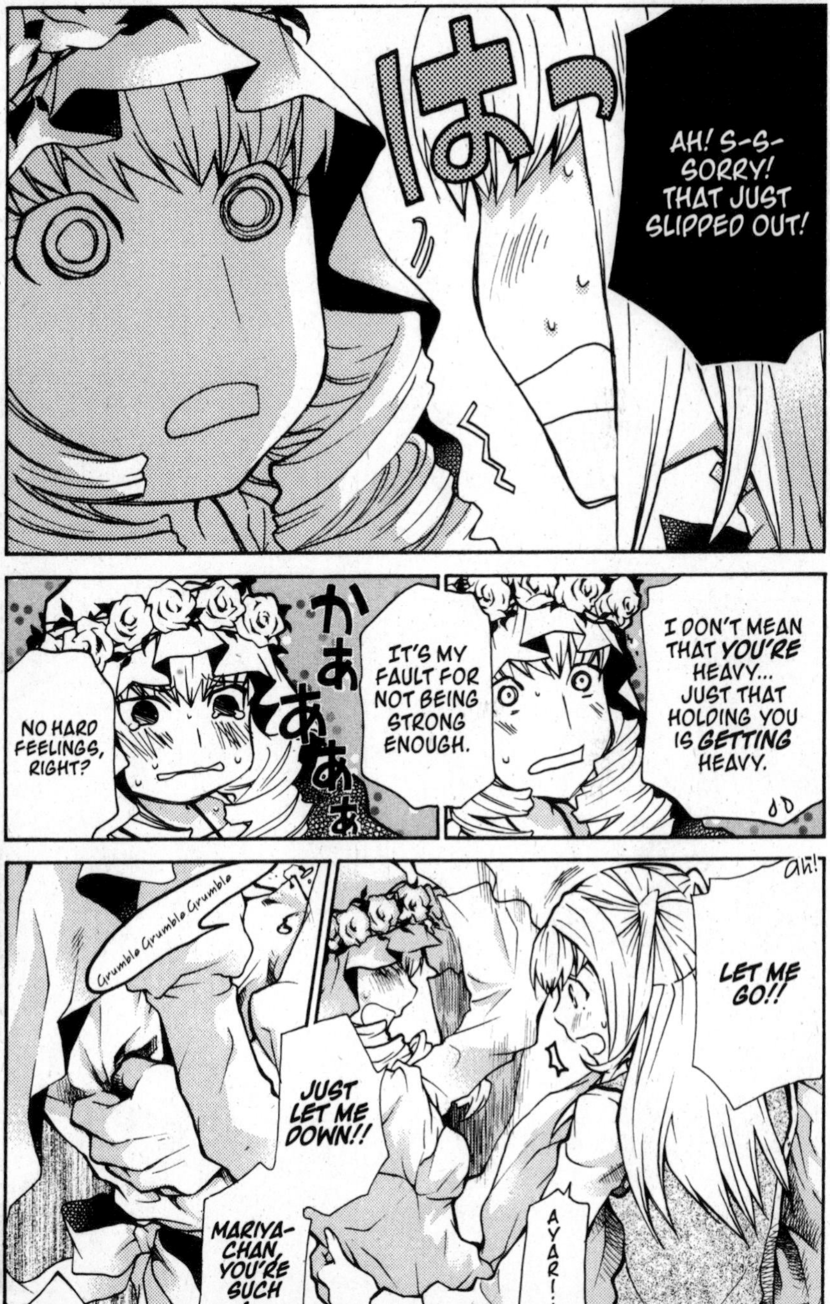
はっ
AH! S-S-SORRY! THAT JUST SLIPPED OUT!
I DON'T MEAN THAT *YOU'RE* HEAVY... JUST THAT HOLDING YOU IS *GETTING* HEAVY.
IT'S MY FAULT FOR NOT BEING STRONG ENOUGH.
かぁあぁぁ
NO HARD FEELINGS, RIGHT?
ah!
LET ME GO!!
JUST LET ME DOWN!!
AYARI...?!
MARIYA-CHAN, YOU'RE SUCH A...
Grumble Grumble Grumble

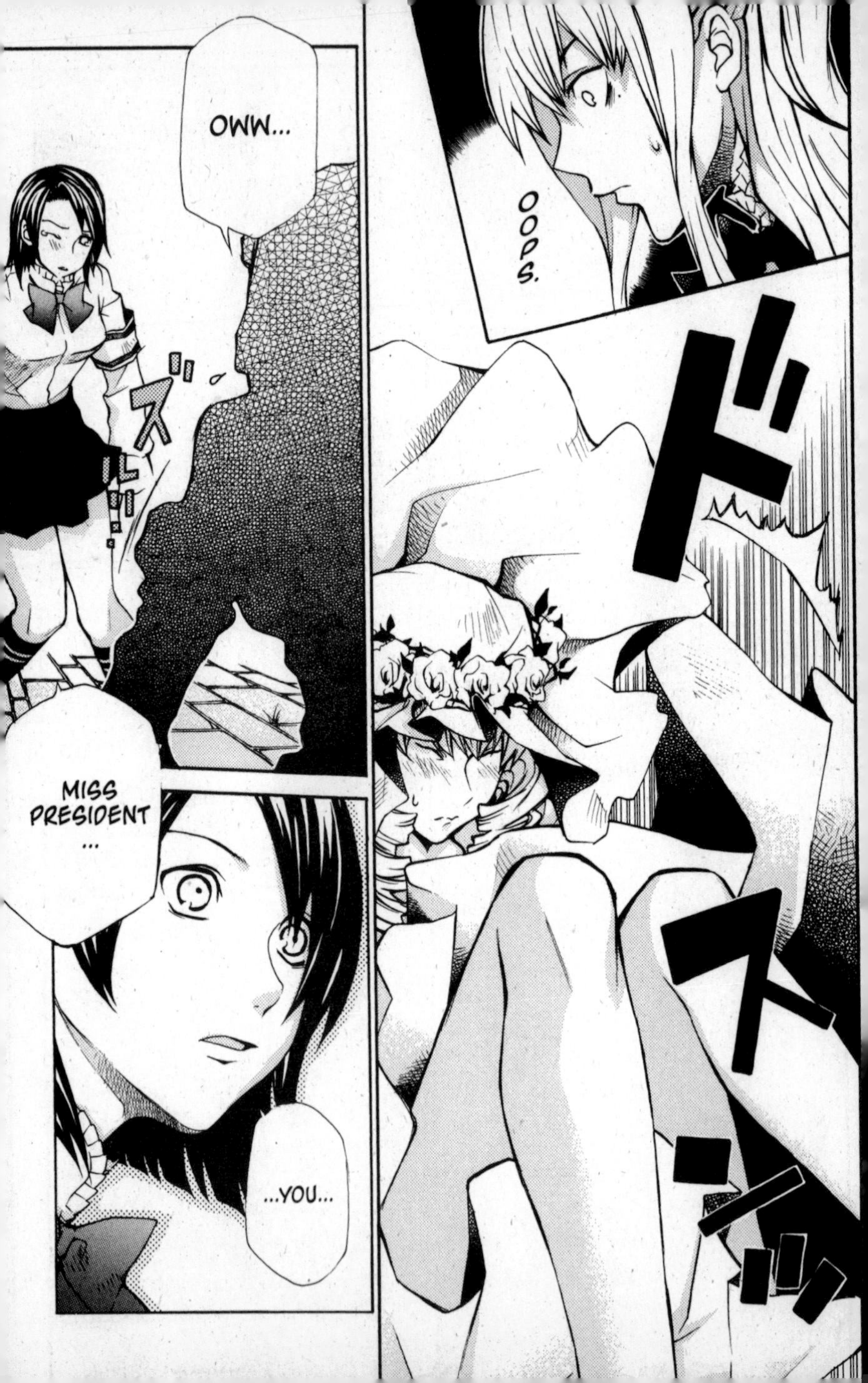
OOPS.
ドスッ
OWW...
ズルッ
MISS PRESIDENT ...
...YOU...

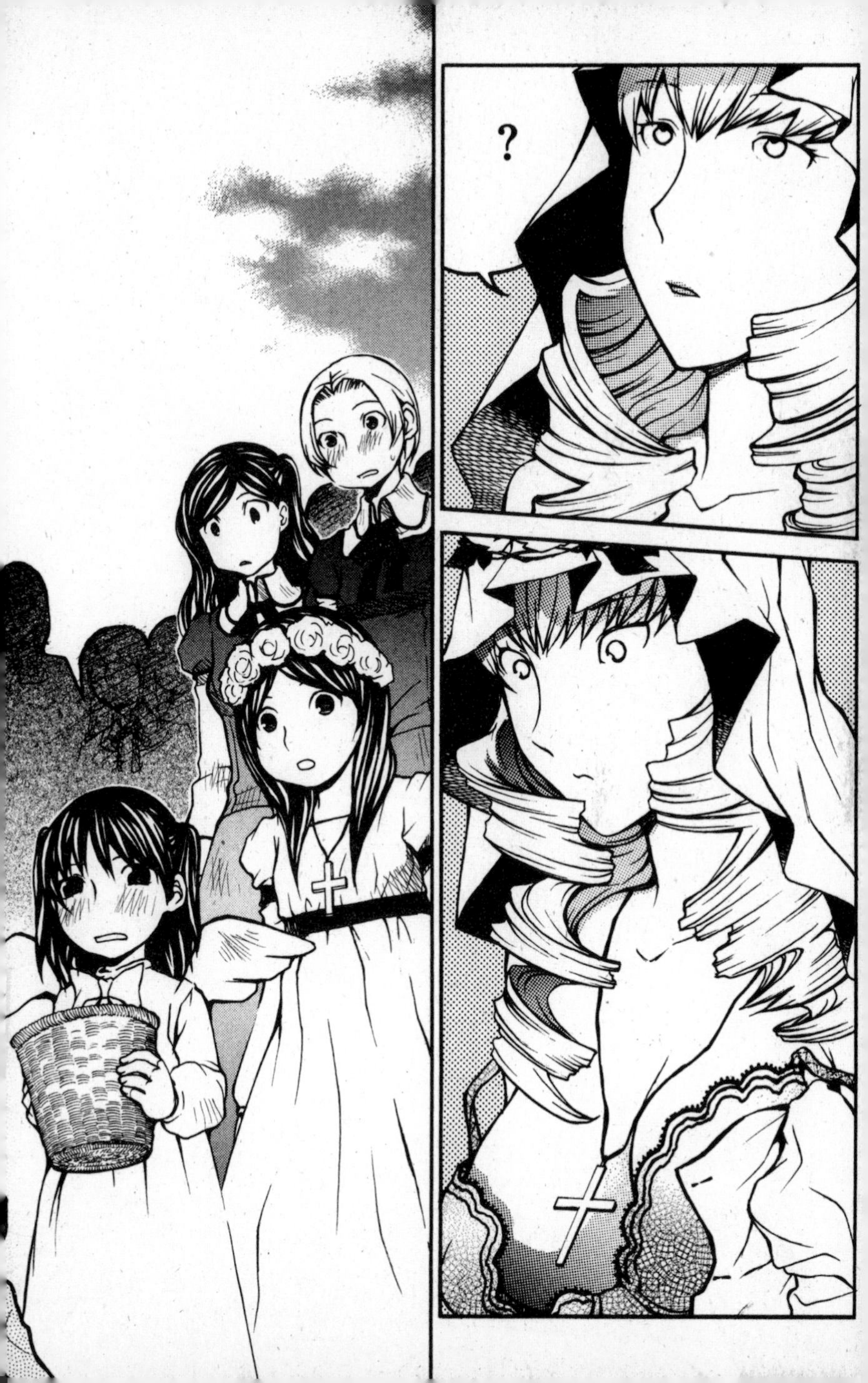
?

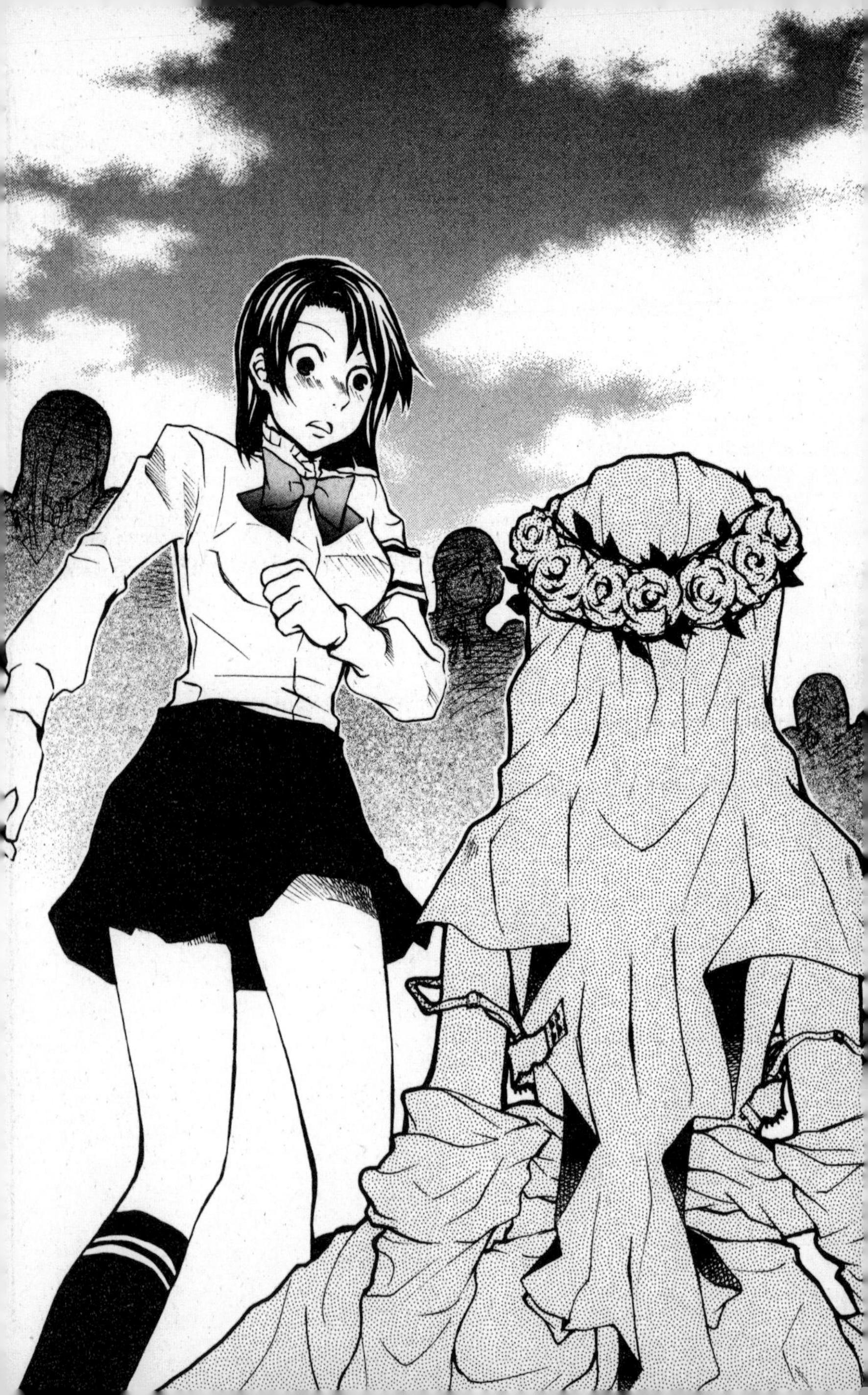

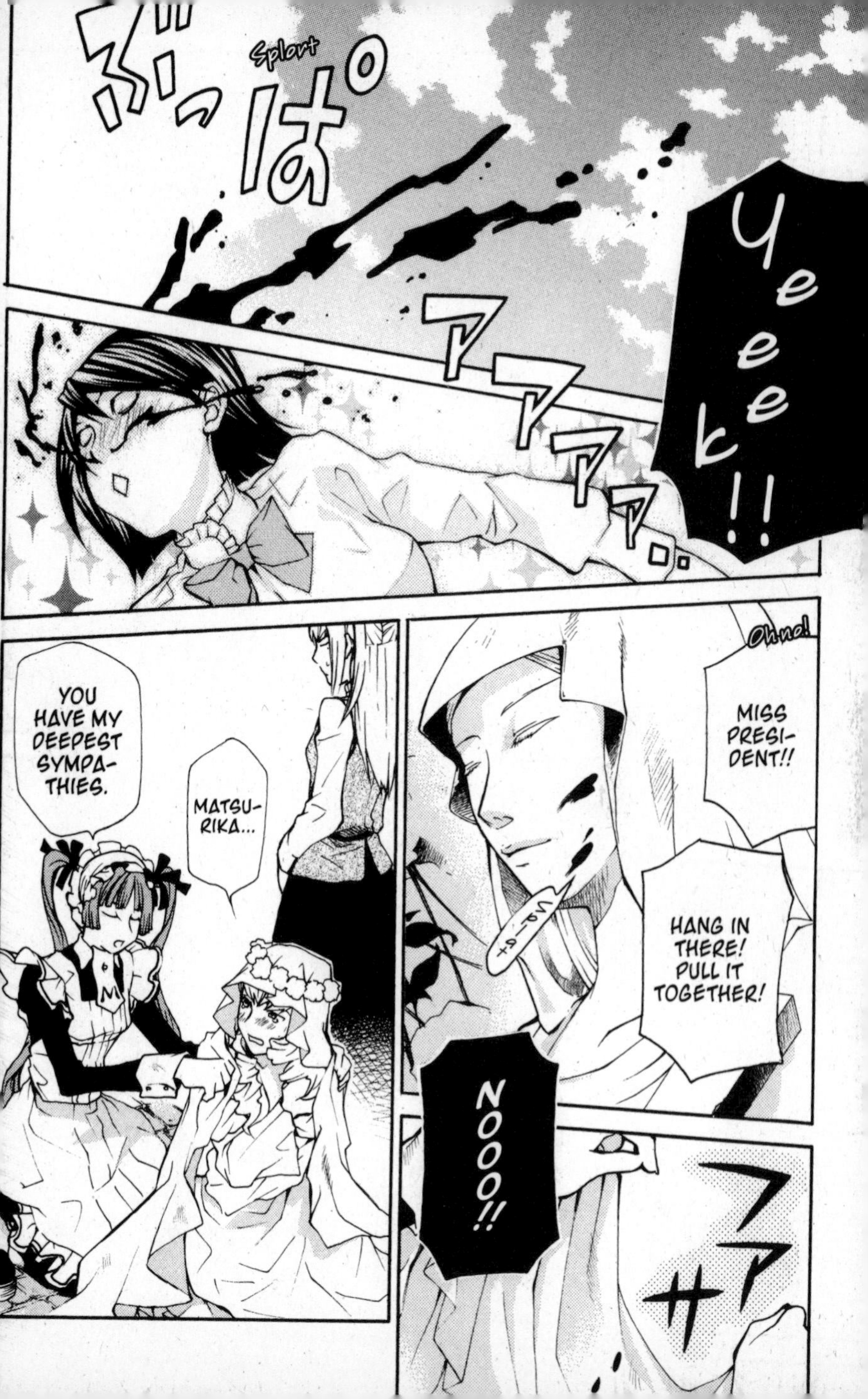

ぶっぱ
Splort
Yeeeek!!
アアアア。。
Oh no!
MISS PRESIDENT!!
HANG IN THERE! PULL IT TOGETHER!
MATSURIKA...
YOU HAVE MY DEEPEST SYMPATHIES.
NOOOO!!
ファサ

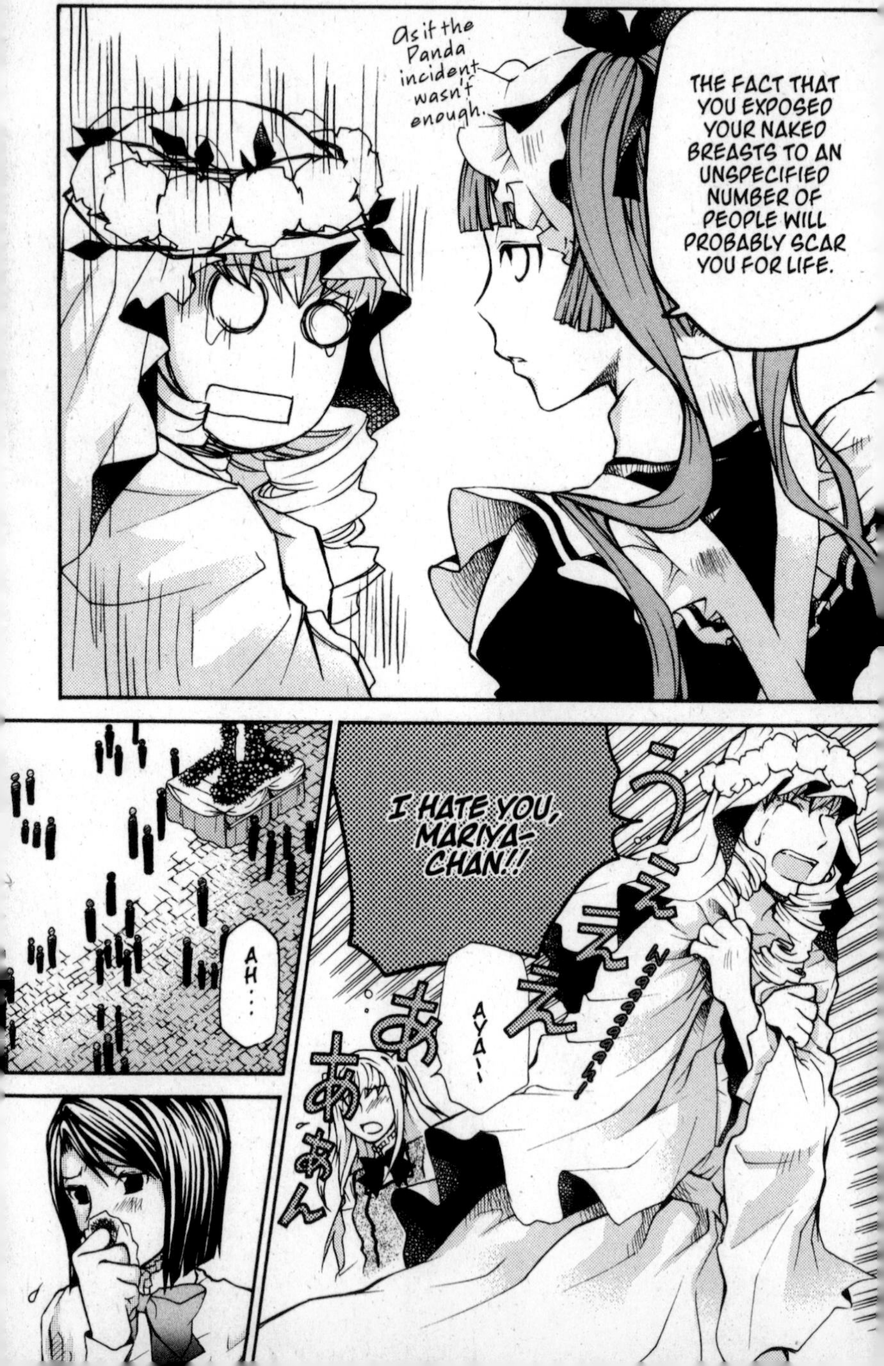
THE FACT THAT YOU EXPOSED YOUR NAKED BREASTS TO AN UNSPECIFIED NUMBER OF PEOPLE WILL PROBABLY SCAR YOU FOR LIFE.
As if the Panda incident wasn't enough.
うえぇぇ
Waaaaaaaaaaaaah!
I HATE YOU, MARIYA-CHAN!!
AYA--
ああぁん
AH...

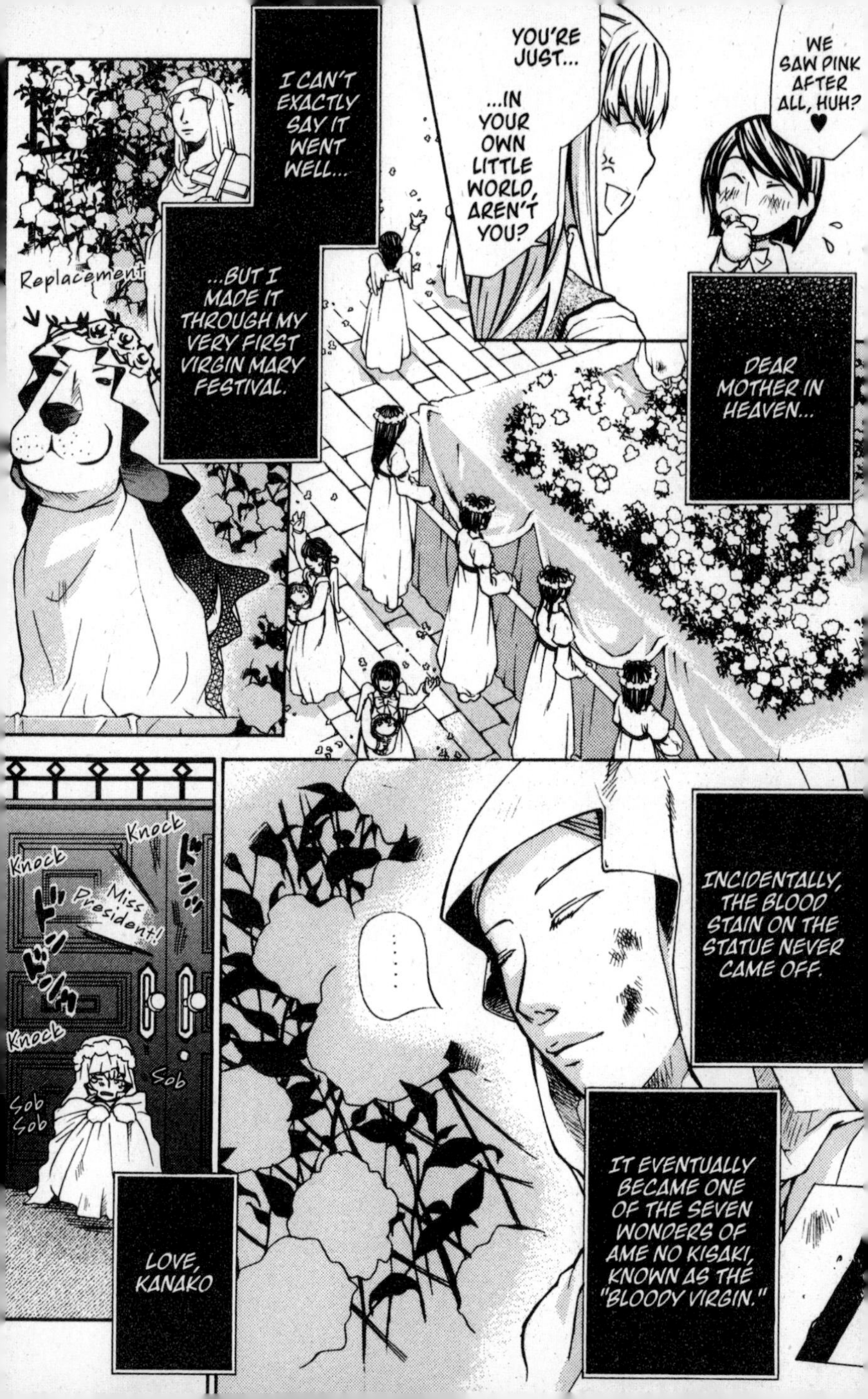
We saw pink after all, huh? ♥
You're just...
...in your own little world, aren't you?
Dear Mother in Heaven...
I can't exactly say it went well...
...but I made it through my very first Virgin Mary Festival.
Replacement
Incidentally, the blood stain on the statue never came off.
......
It eventually became one of the seven wonders of Ame no Kisaki, known as the "Bloody Virgin."
Knock
Knock
Miss President!
Knock
Sob
Sob Sob
Love, Kanako

TONY AND MYTY

DISCOVER WORLD HERITAGE SITES

TONY, THE DREAMY PRANKSTER, AND MYTY, THE CYNIC, WILL TAKE YOU ON A FAST AND FUN TOUR OF WORLD HERITAGE SITES. ☆
STARTS ON THE NEXT BONUS PAGE!

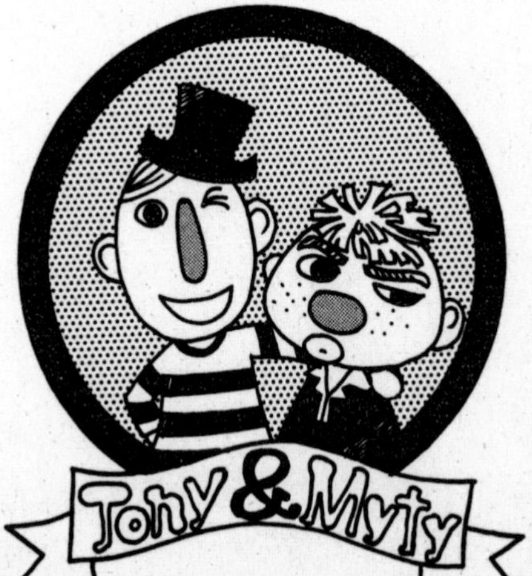
Tony & Myty

Maria✝Holic

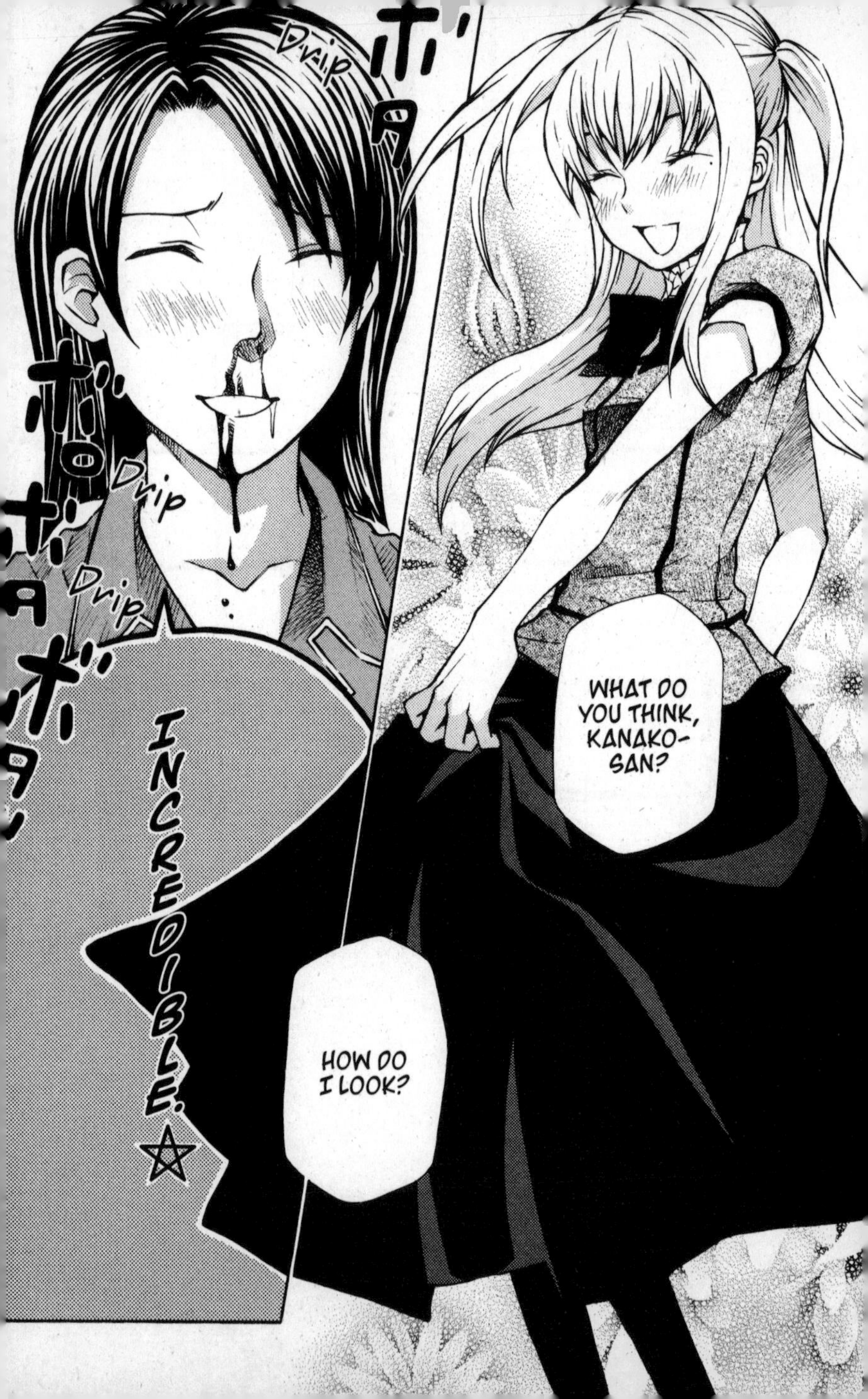
WHAT DO YOU THINK, KANAKO-SAN?
HOW DO I LOOK?
Drip
Drip
Drip
INCREDIBLE.☆

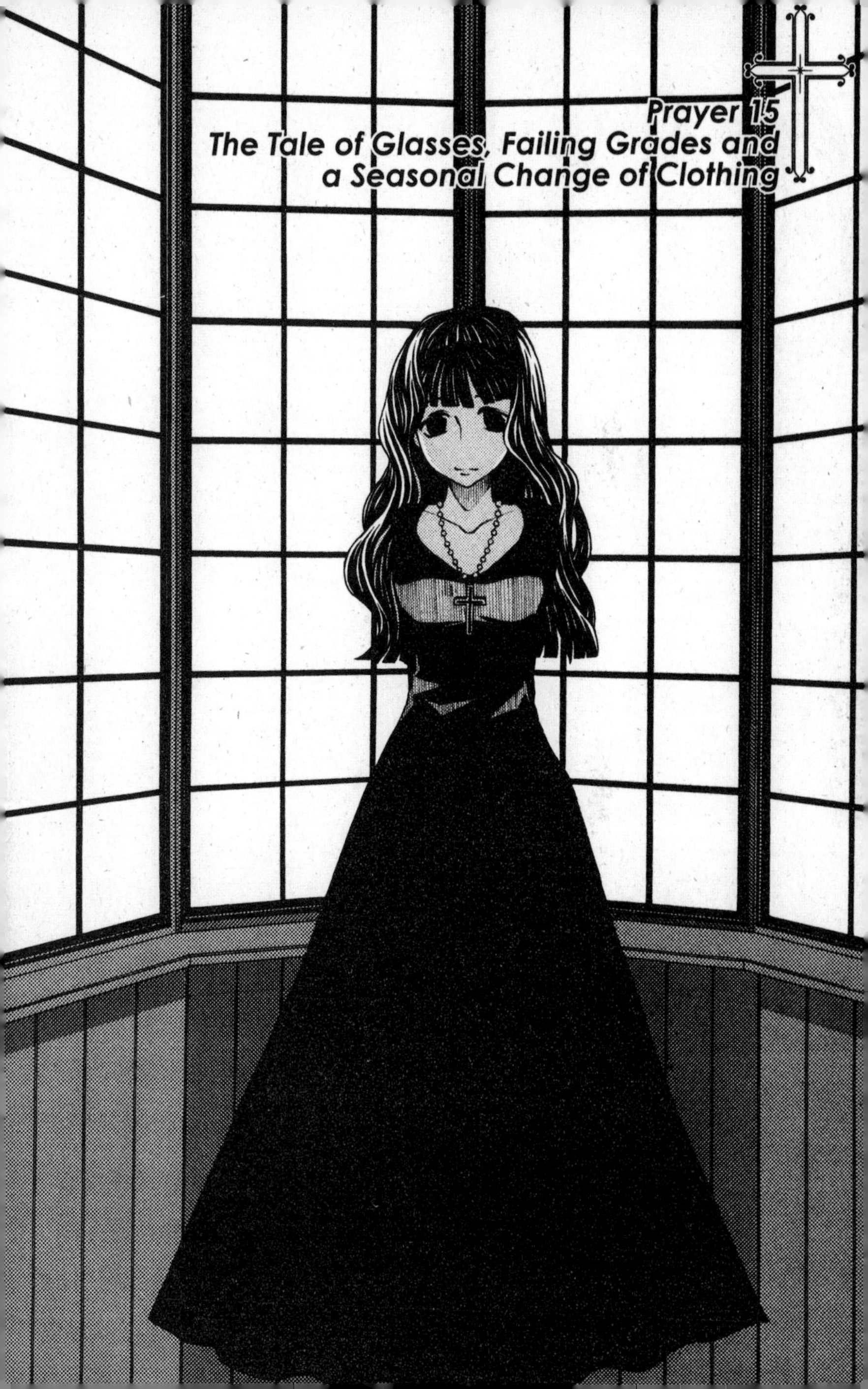
Prayer 15
The Tale of Glasses, Failing Grades and a Seasonal Change of Clothing

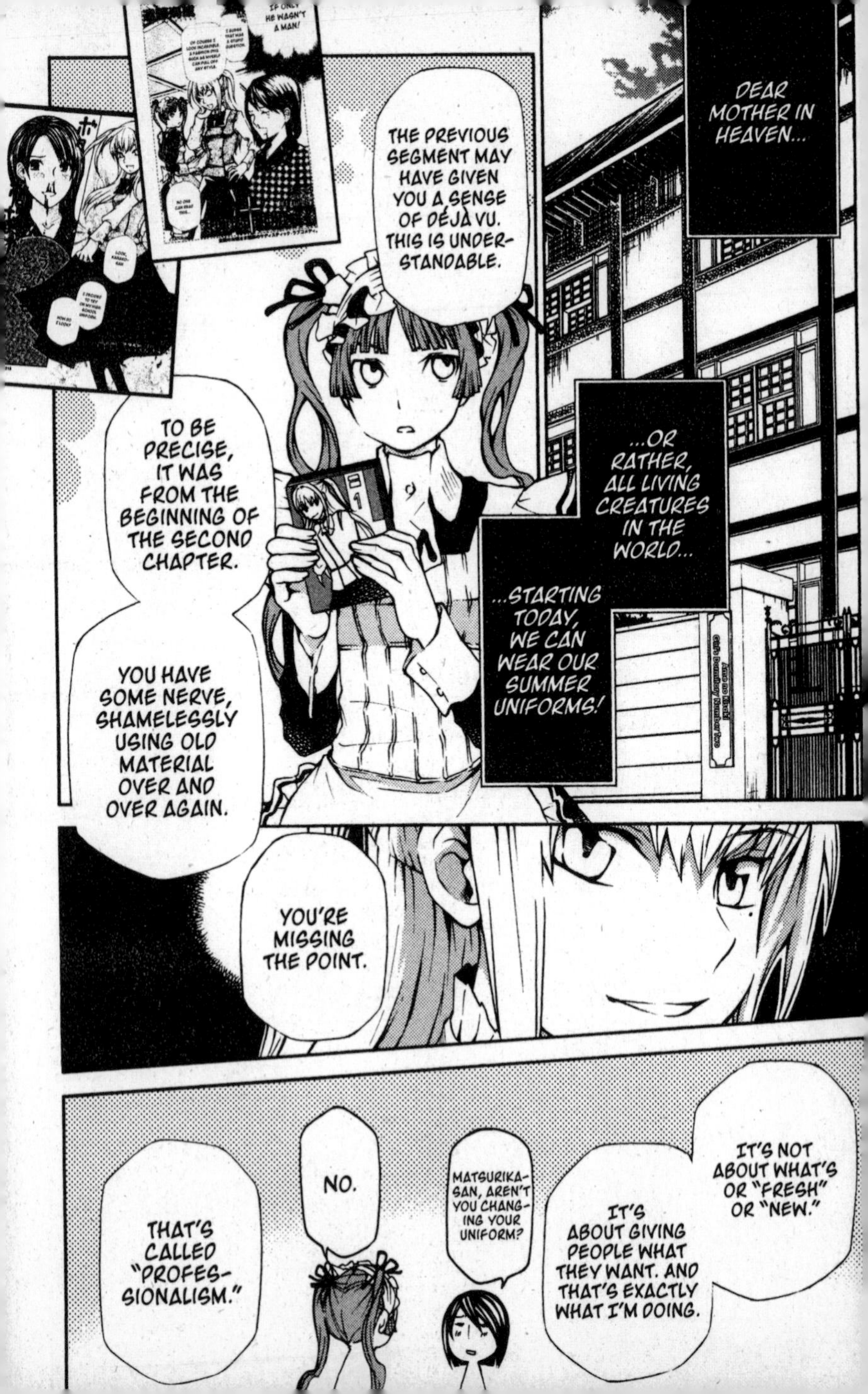
DEAR MOTHER IN HEAVEN...
...OR RATHER, ALL LIVING CREATURES IN THE WORLD...
...STARTING TODAY, WE CAN WEAR OUR SUMMER UNIFORMS!
Ame no Kisaki Girl's Dormitory Number Two
THE PREVIOUS SEGMENT MAY HAVE GIVEN YOU A SENSE OF DÉJÀ VU. THIS IS UNDER-STANDABLE.
TO BE PRECISE, IT WAS FROM THE BEGINNING OF THE SECOND CHAPTER.
IF ONLY HE WASN'T A MAN!
I GUESS THAT WAS A STUPID QUESTION.
NO ONE CAN BEAT THIS...
LOOK, KANAKO-SAN
I DECIDED TO TRY ON MY HIGH SCHOOL UNIFORM.
HOW DO I LOOK?
YOU HAVE SOME NERVE, SHAMELESSLY USING OLD MATERIAL OVER AND OVER AGAIN.
YOU'RE MISSING THE POINT.
IT'S NOT ABOUT WHAT'S OR "FRESH" OR "NEW."
IT'S ABOUT GIVING PEOPLE WHAT THEY WANT. AND THAT'S EXACTLY WHAT I'M DOING.
MATSURIKA-SAN, AREN'T YOU CHANG-ING YOUR UNIFORM?
NO.
THAT'S CALLED "PROFES-SIONALISM."

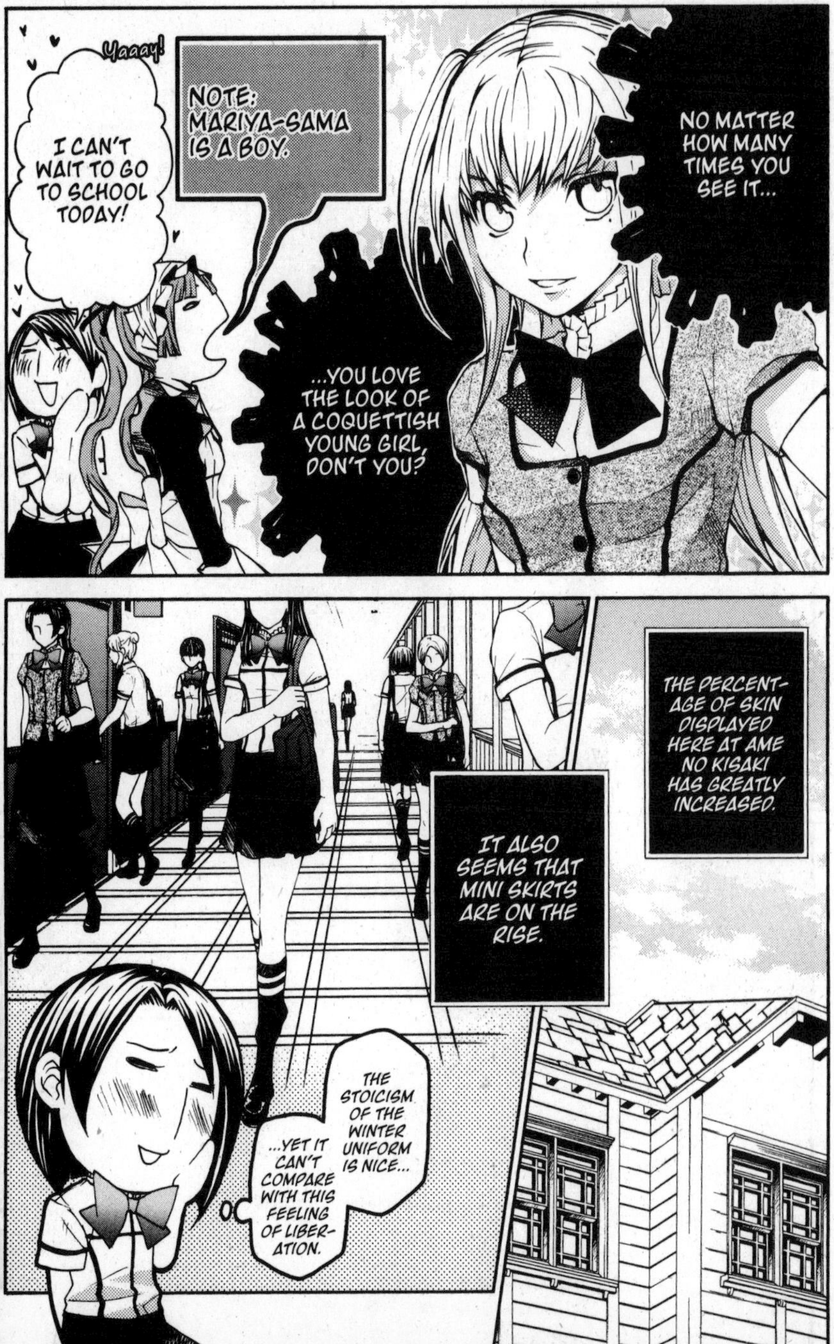
NO MATTER HOW MANY TIMES YOU SEE IT...
...YOU LOVE THE LOOK OF A COQUETTISH YOUNG GIRL, DON'T YOU?
NOTE: MARIYA-SAMA IS A BOY.
Yaaay!
I CAN'T WAIT TO GO TO SCHOOL TODAY!
THE PERCENTAGE OF SKIN DISPLAYED HERE AT AME NO KISAKI HAS GREATLY INCREASED.
IT ALSO SEEMS THAT MINI SKIRTS ARE ON THE RISE.
THE STOICISM OF THE WINTER UNIFORM IS NICE...
...YET IT CAN'T COMPARE WITH THIS FEELING OF LIBERATION.

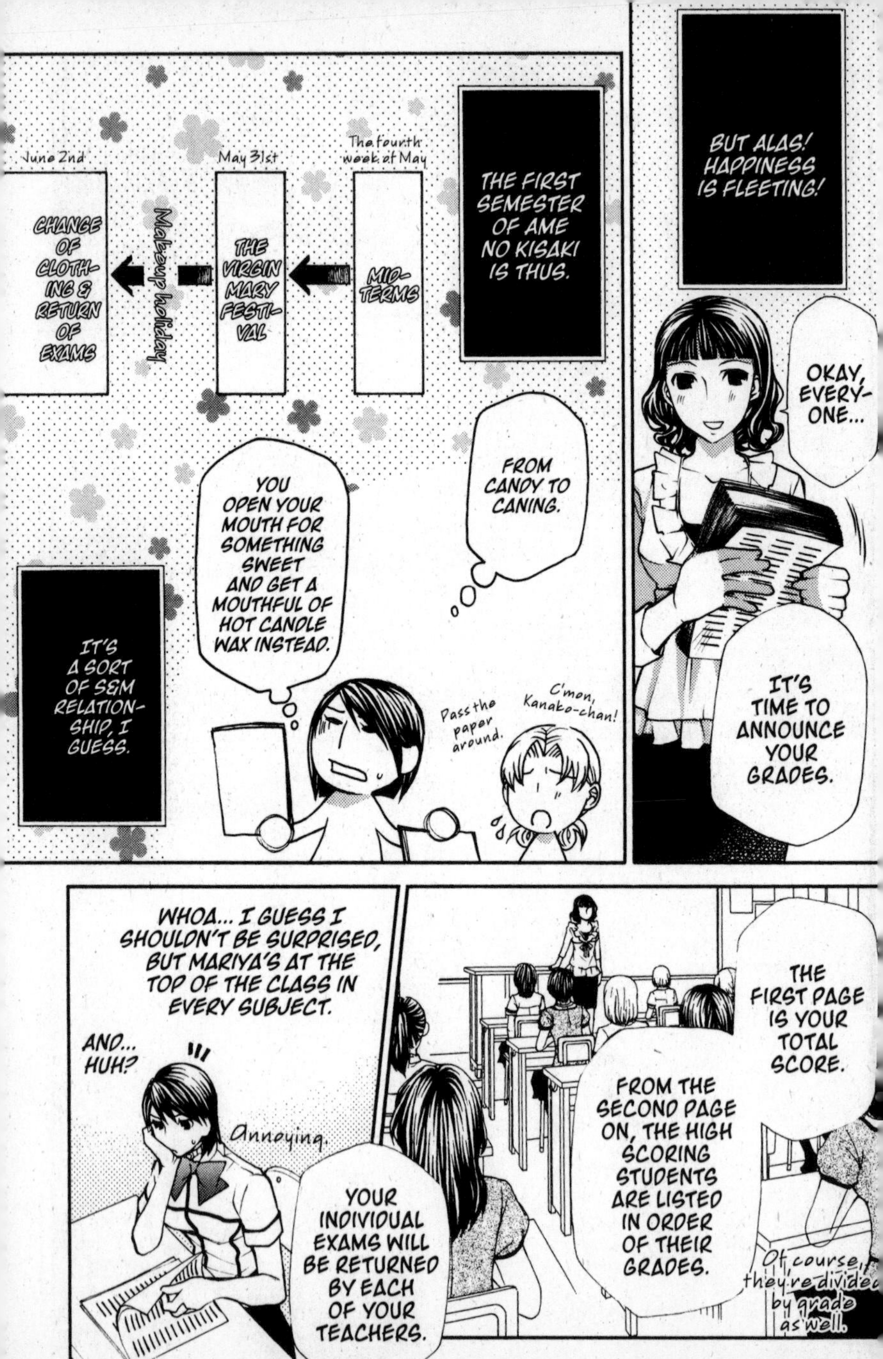
BUT ALAS! HAPPINESS IS FLEETING!
OKAY, EVERYONE...
IT'S TIME TO ANNOUNCE YOUR GRADES.
THE FIRST SEMESTER OF AME NO KISAKI IS THUS.
The fourth week of May
MID-TERMS
May 31st
THE VIRGIN MARY FESTIVAL
Makeup holiday
June 2nd
CHANGE OF CLOTHING & RETURN OF EXAMS
FROM CANDY TO CANING.
C'mon, Kanako-chan!
Pass the paper around.
YOU OPEN YOUR MOUTH FOR SOMETHING SWEET AND GET A MOUTHFUL OF HOT CANDLE WAX INSTEAD.
IT'S A SORT OF S&M RELATIONSHIP, I GUESS.
THE FIRST PAGE IS YOUR TOTAL SCORE.
FROM THE SECOND PAGE ON, THE HIGH SCORING STUDENTS ARE LISTED IN ORDER OF THEIR GRADES.
Of course, they're divided by grade as well.
YOUR INDIVIDUAL EXAMS WILL BE RETURNED BY EACH OF YOUR TEACHERS.
WHOA... I GUESS I SHOULDN'T BE SURPRISED, BUT MARIYA'S AT THE TOP OF THE CLASS IN EVERY SUBJECT.
AND... HUH?
Annoying.

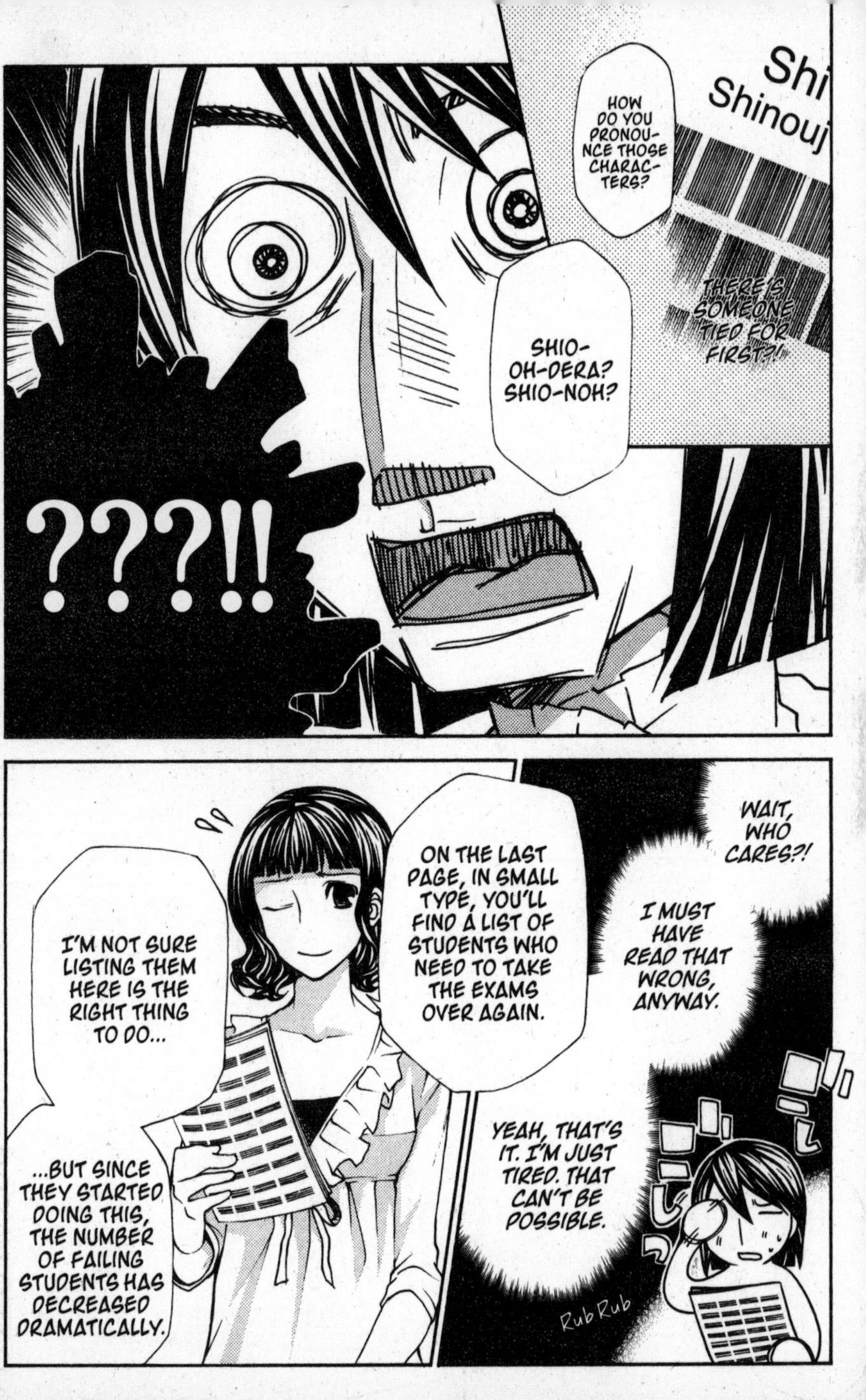
Shi
Shinouj
HOW DO YOU PRONOUNCE THOSE CHARACTERS?
THERE'S SOMEONE TIED FOR FIRST?!
SHIO-OH-DERA? SHIO-NOH?
???!!
WAIT, WHO CARES?!
I MUST HAVE READ THAT WRONG, ANYWAY.
YEAH, THAT'S IT. I'M JUST TIRED. THAT CAN'T BE POSSIBLE.
Rub Rub
ON THE LAST PAGE, IN SMALL TYPE, YOU'LL FIND A LIST OF STUDENTS WHO NEED TO TAKE THE EXAMS OVER AGAIN.
I'M NOT SURE LISTING THEM HERE IS THE RIGHT THING TO DO...
...BUT SINCE THEY STARTED DOING THIS, THE NUMBER OF FAILING STUDENTS HAS DECREASED DRAMATICALLY.

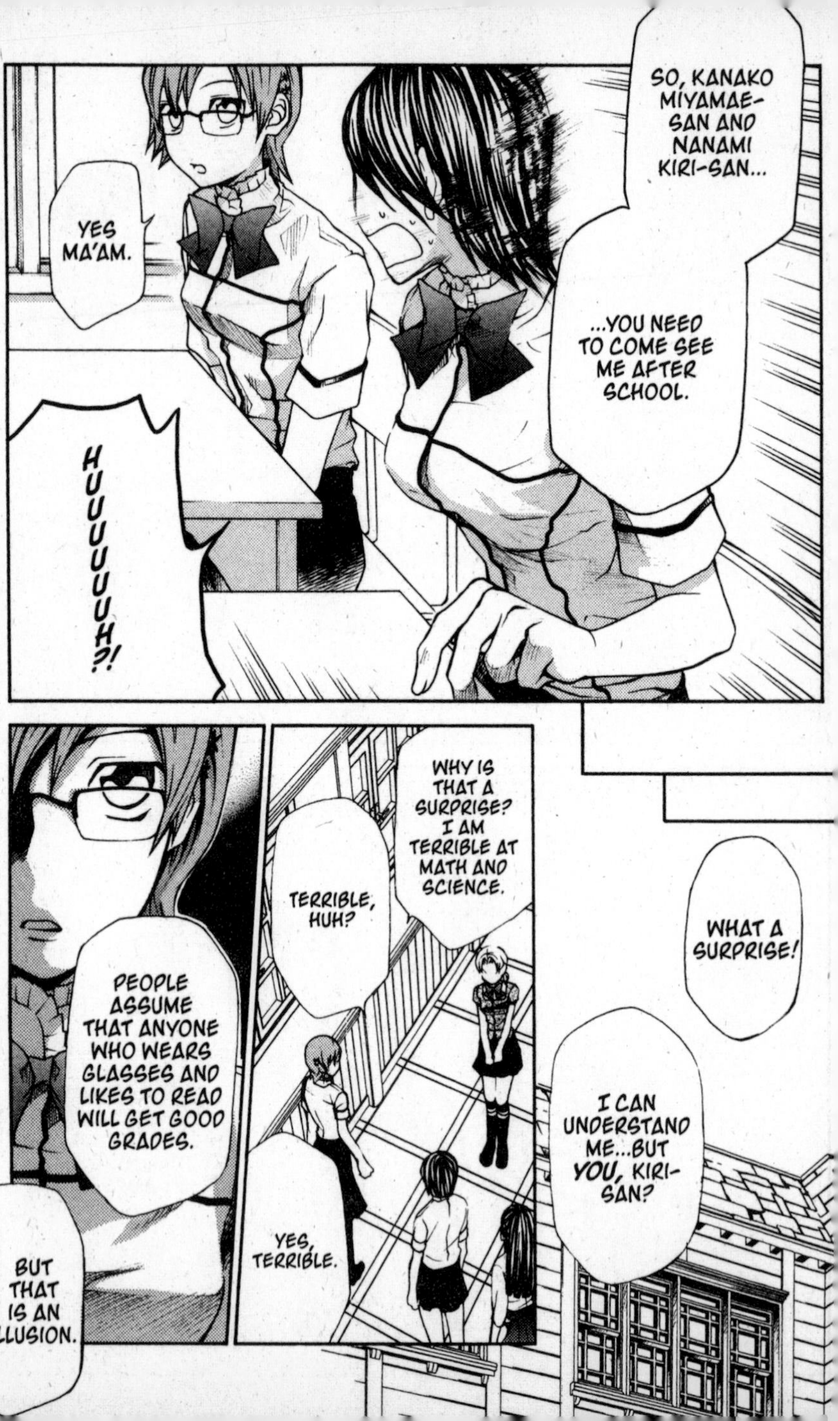
SO, KANAKO MIYAMAE-SAN AND NANAMI KIRI-SAN...
...YOU NEED TO COME SEE ME AFTER SCHOOL.
YES MA'AM.
HUUUUUUUH?!
WHAT A SURPRISE!
I CAN UNDERSTAND ME...BUT *YOU*, KIRI-SAN?
WHY IS THAT A SURPRISE? I AM TERRIBLE AT MATH AND SCIENCE.
TERRIBLE, HUH?
YES, TERRIBLE.
PEOPLE ASSUME THAT ANYONE WHO WEARS GLASSES AND LIKES TO READ WILL GET GOOD GRADES.
BUT THAT IS AN ILLUSION.

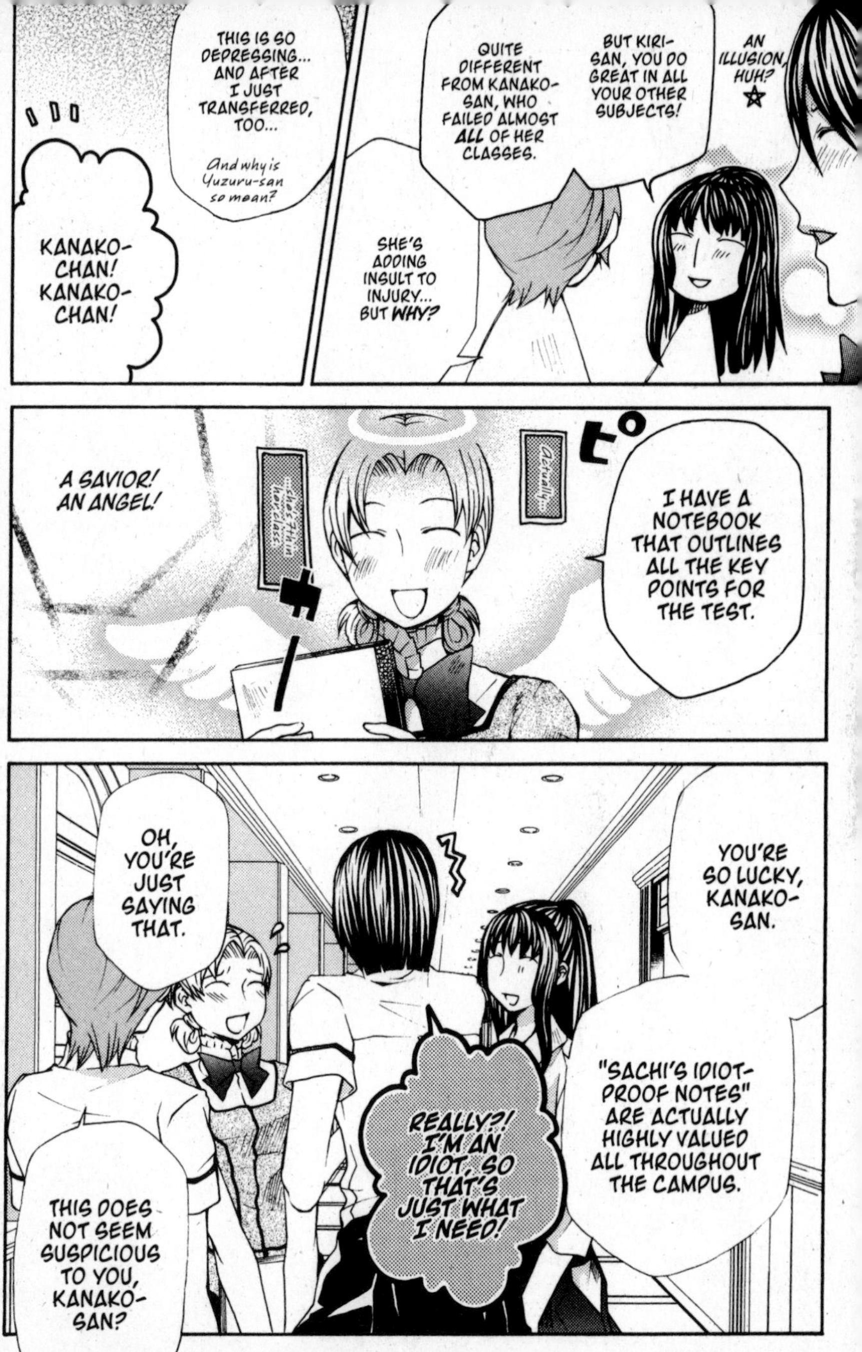
AN ILLUSION, HUH? ☆
BUT KIRI-SAN, YOU DO GREAT IN ALL YOUR OTHER SUBJECTS!
QUITE DIFFERENT FROM KANAKO-SAN, WHO FAILED ALMOST **ALL** OF HER CLASSES.
SHE'S ADDING INSULT TO INJURY... BUT **WHY?**
THIS IS SO DEPRESSING... AND AFTER I JUST TRANSFERRED, TOO...
And why is Yuzuru-san so mean?
KANAKO-CHAN! KANAKO-CHAN!
I HAVE A NOTEBOOK THAT OUTLINES ALL THE KEY POINTS FOR THE TEST.
Actually...
...she's 7th in her class.
A SAVIOR! AN ANGEL!
YOU'RE SO LUCKY, KANAKO-SAN.
"SACHI'S IDIOT-PROOF NOTES" ARE ACTUALLY HIGHLY VALUED ALL THROUGHOUT THE CAMPUS.
OH, YOU'RE JUST SAYING THAT.
REALLY?! I'M AN IDIOT, SO THAT'S JUST WHAT I NEED!
THIS DOES NOT SEEM SUSPICIOUS TO YOU, KANAKO-SAN?

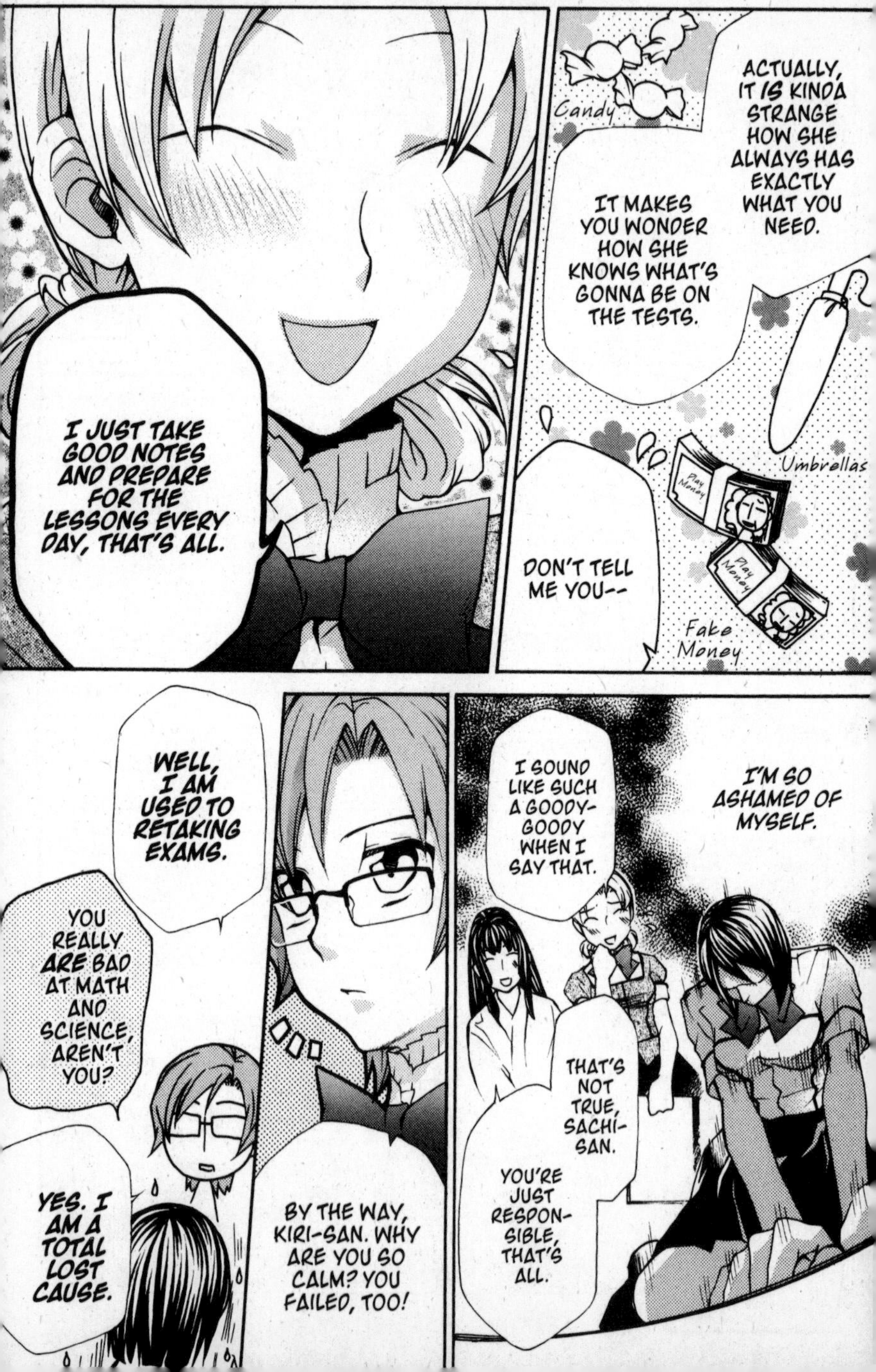
ACTUALLY, IT *IS* KINDA STRANGE HOW SHE ALWAYS HAS EXACTLY WHAT YOU NEED.
Candy
IT MAKES YOU WONDER HOW SHE KNOWS WHAT'S GONNA BE ON THE TESTS.
Umbrellas
Play Money
DON'T TELL ME YOU--
Fake Money
I JUST TAKE GOOD NOTES AND PREPARE FOR THE LESSONS EVERY DAY, THAT'S ALL.
I'M SO ASHAMED OF MYSELF.
I SOUND LIKE SUCH A GOODY-GOODY WHEN I SAY THAT.
THAT'S NOT TRUE, SACHI-SAN.
YOU'RE JUST RESPONSIBLE, THAT'S ALL.
BY THE WAY, KIRI-SAN. WHY ARE YOU SO CALM? YOU FAILED, TOO!
WELL, I AM USED TO RETAKING EXAMS.
YOU REALLY *ARE* BAD AT MATH AND SCIENCE, AREN'T YOU?
YES. I AM A TOTAL LOST CAUSE.

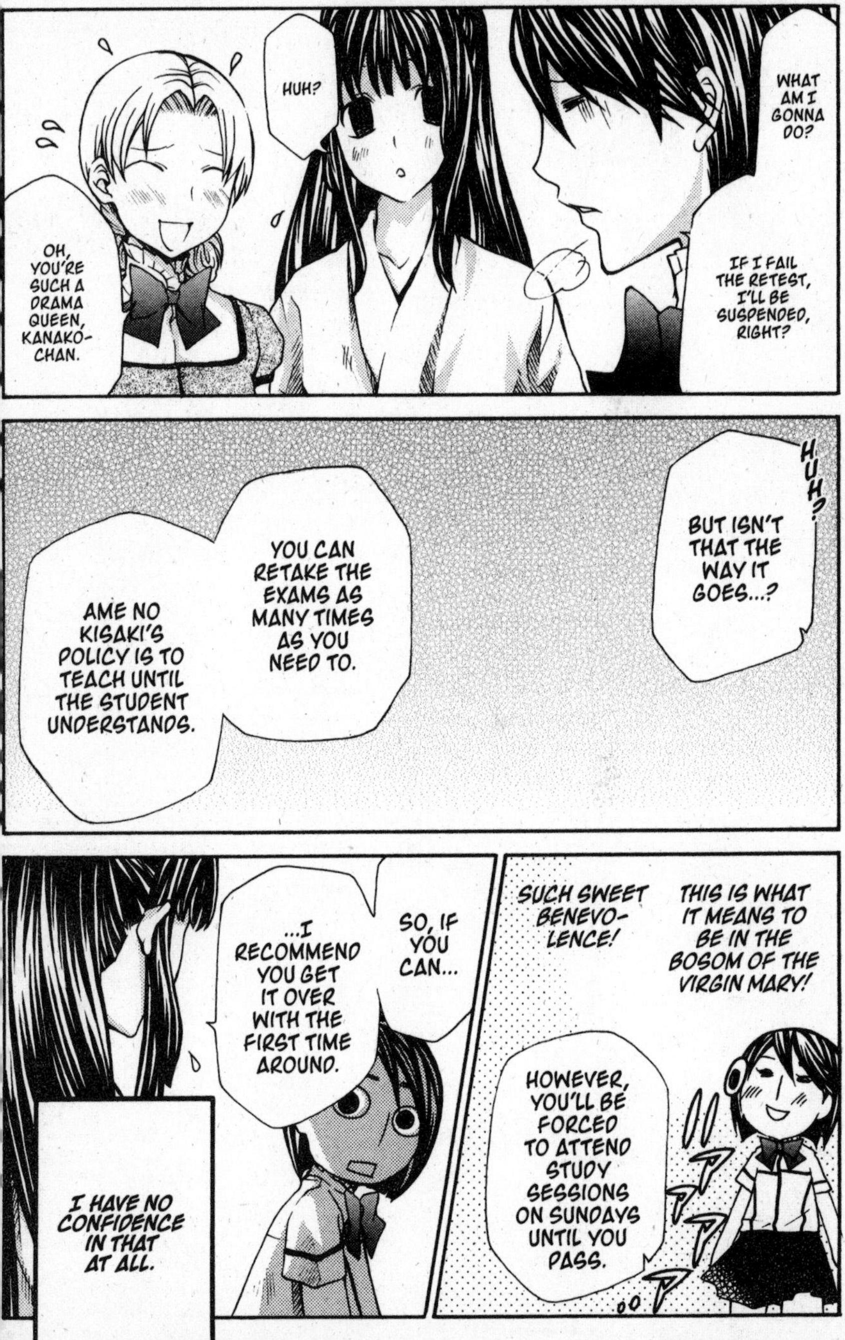
WHAT AM I GONNA DO?
IF I FAIL THE RETEST, I'LL BE SUSPENDED, RIGHT?
HUH?
OH, YOU'RE SUCH A DRAMA QUEEN, KANAKO-CHAN.
HUH?
BUT ISN'T THAT THE WAY IT GOES...?
YOU CAN RETAKE THE EXAMS AS MANY TIMES AS YOU NEED TO.
AME NO KISAKI'S POLICY IS TO TEACH UNTIL THE STUDENT UNDERSTANDS.
THIS IS WHAT IT MEANS TO BE IN THE BOSOM OF THE VIRGIN MARY!
SUCH SWEET BENEVO-LENCE!
HOWEVER, YOU'LL BE FORCED TO ATTEND STUDY SESSIONS ON SUNDAYS UNTIL YOU PASS.
SO, IF YOU CAN...
...I RECOMMEND YOU GET IT OVER WITH THE FIRST TIME AROUND.
I HAVE NO CONFIDENCE IN THAT AT ALL.

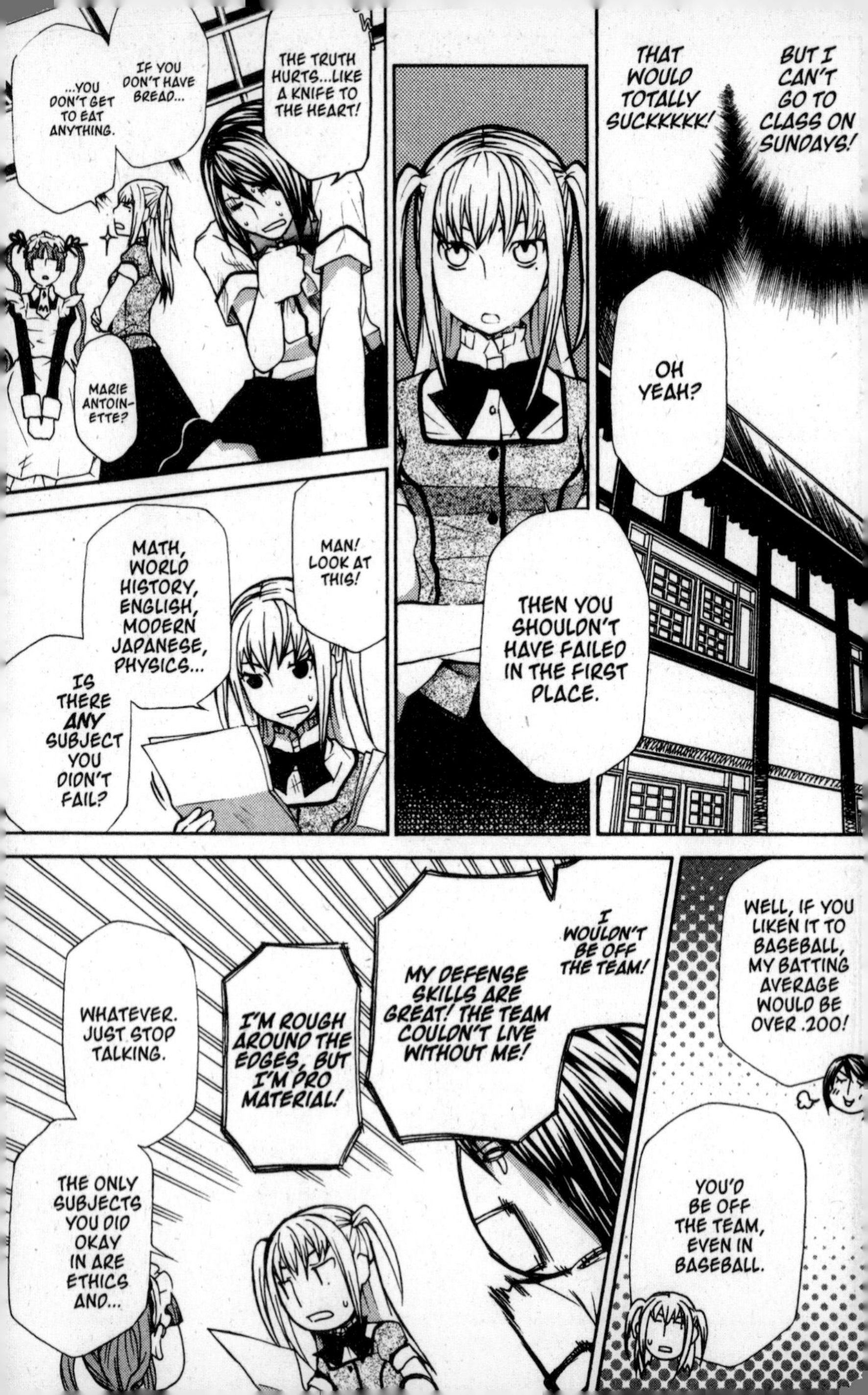

BUT I CAN'T GO TO CLASS ON SUNDAYS!
THAT WOULD TOTALLY SUCKKKKK!
OH YEAH?
THEN YOU SHOULDN'T HAVE FAILED IN THE FIRST PLACE.
THE TRUTH HURTS...LIKE A KNIFE TO THE HEART!
IF YOU DON'T HAVE BREAD...
...YOU DON'T GET TO EAT ANYTHING.
MARIE ANTOIN-ETTE?
MAN! LOOK AT THIS!
MATH, WORLD HISTORY, ENGLISH, MODERN JAPANESE, PHYSICS...
IS THERE ANY SUBJECT YOU DIDN'T FAIL?
WELL, IF YOU LIKEN IT TO BASEBALL, MY BATTING AVERAGE WOULD BE OVER .200!
YOU'D BE OFF THE TEAM, EVEN IN BASEBALL.
I WOULDN'T BE OFF THE TEAM!
MY DEFENSE SKILLS ARE GREAT! THE TEAM COULDN'T LIVE WITHOUT ME!
I'M ROUGH AROUND THE EDGES, BUT I'M PRO MATERIAL!
WHATEVER. JUST STOP TALKING.
THE ONLY SUBJECTS YOU DID OKAY IN ARE ETHICS AND...

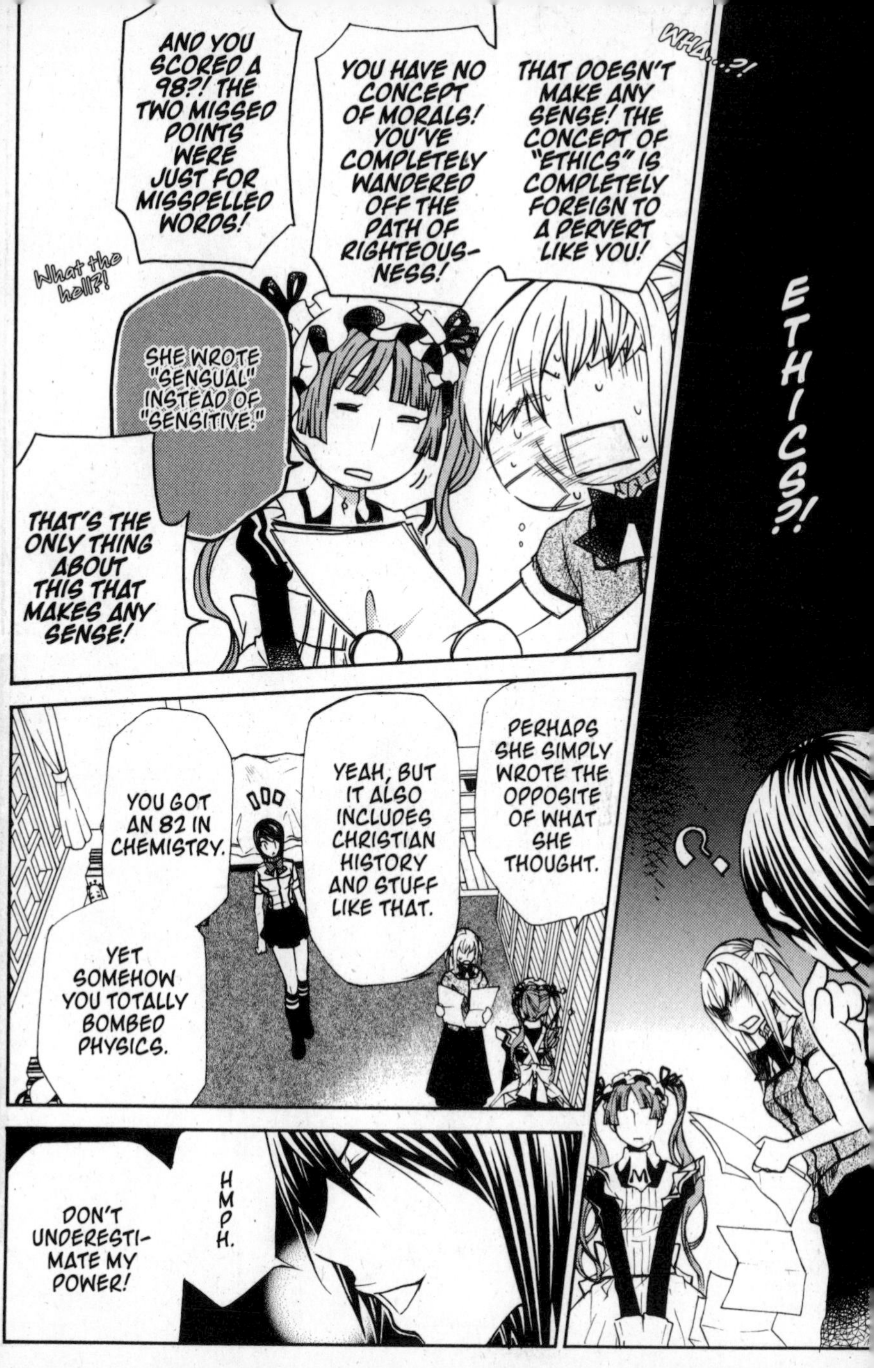
WHA...?!
ETHICS?!
THAT DOESN'T MAKE ANY SENSE! THE CONCEPT OF "ETHICS" IS COMPLETELY FOREIGN TO A PERVERT LIKE YOU!
YOU HAVE NO CONCEPT OF MORALS! YOU'VE COMPLETELY WANDERED OFF THE PATH OF RIGHTEOUS-NESS!
AND YOU SCORED A 98?! THE TWO MISSED POINTS WERE JUST FOR MISSPELLED WORDS!
What the hell?!
SHE WROTE "SENSUAL" INSTEAD OF "SENSITIVE."
THAT'S THE ONLY THING ABOUT THIS THAT MAKES ANY SENSE!
PERHAPS SHE SIMPLY WROTE THE OPPOSITE OF WHAT SHE THOUGHT.
YEAH, BUT IT ALSO INCLUDES CHRISTIAN HISTORY AND STUFF LIKE THAT.
YOU GOT AN 82 IN CHEMISTRY.
YET SOMEHOW YOU TOTALLY BOMBED PHYSICS.
HMPH.
DON'T UNDERESTI-MATE MY POWER!

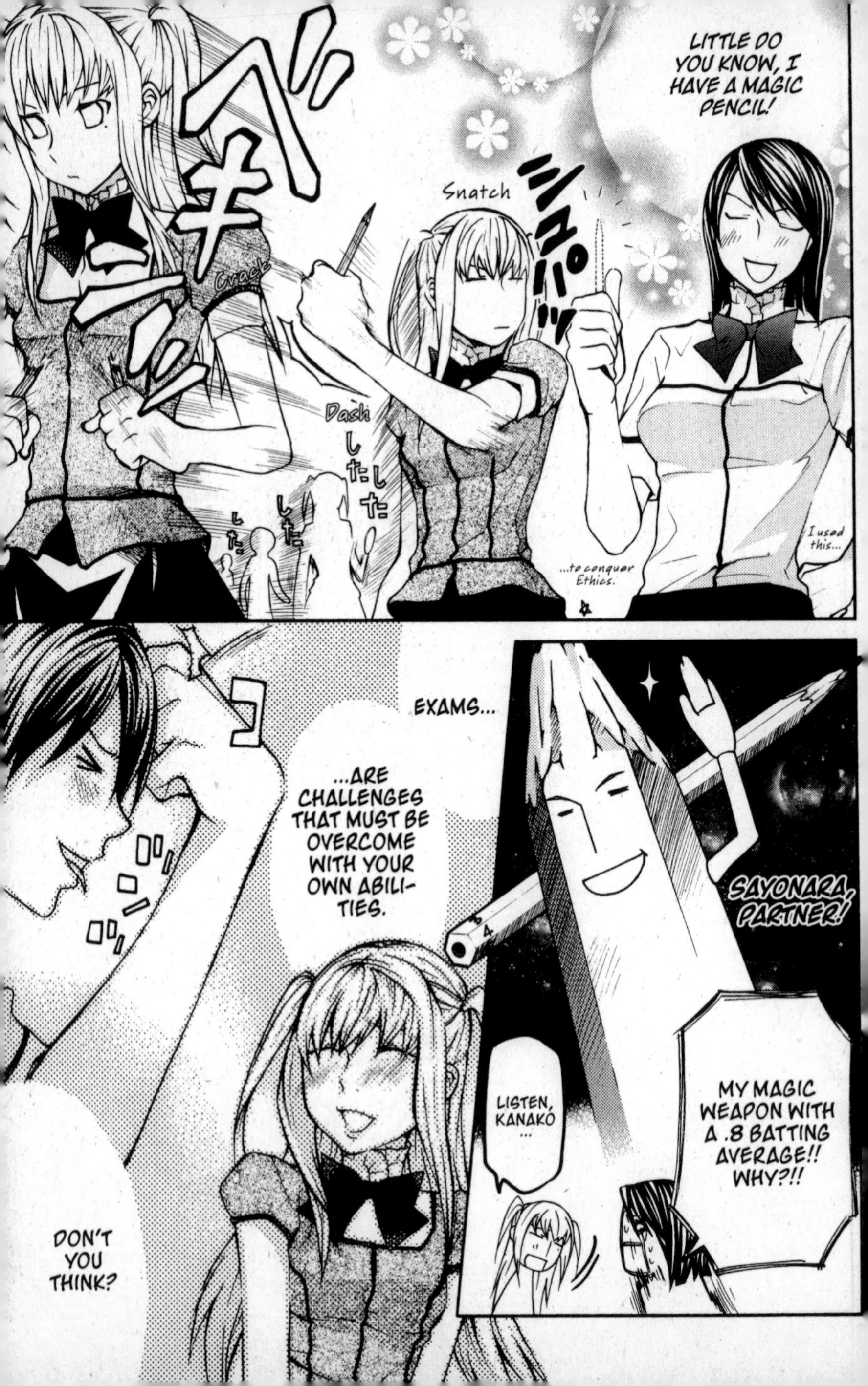
LITTLE DO YOU KNOW, I HAVE A MAGIC PENCIL!
I used this...
...to conquer Ethics.
Snatch
Crack
Dash
したしたしたした
SAYONARA, PARTNER!
MY MAGIC WEAPON WITH A .8 BATTING AVERAGE!! WHY?!!
LISTEN, KANAKO...
EXAMS...
...ARE CHALLENGES THAT MUST BE OVERCOME WITH YOUR OWN ABILITIES.
DON'T YOU THINK?

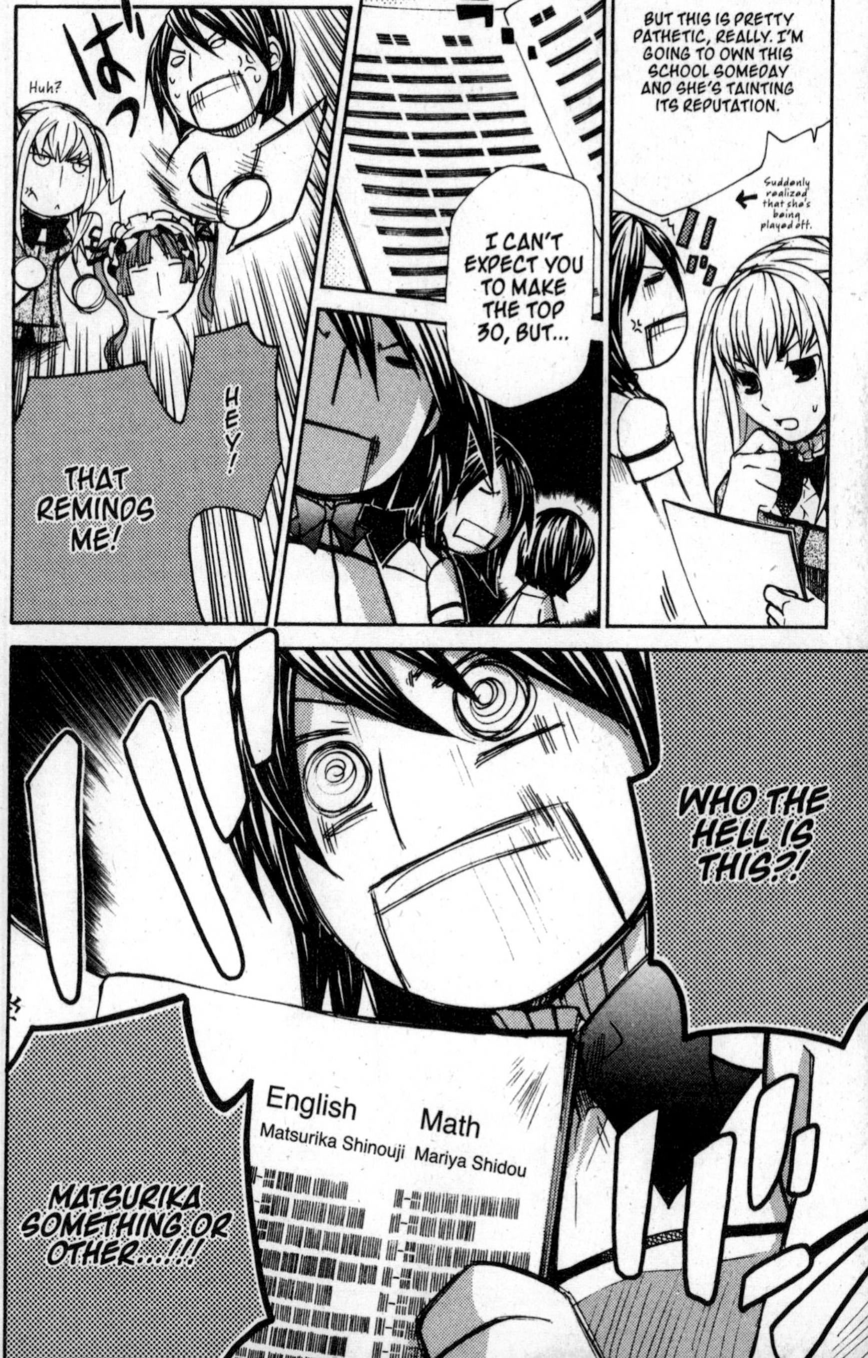
BUT THIS IS PRETTY PATHETIC, REALLY. I'M GOING TO OWN THIS SCHOOL SOMEDAY AND SHE'S TAINTING ITS REPUTATION.
Suddenly realized that she's being played off.
I CAN'T EXPECT YOU TO MAKE THE TOP 30, BUT...
はっ
Huh?
HEY!
THAT REMINDS ME!
WHO THE HELL IS THIS?!
English
Math
Matsurika Shinouji
Mariya Shidou
MATSURIKA SOMETHING OR OTHER...!!!

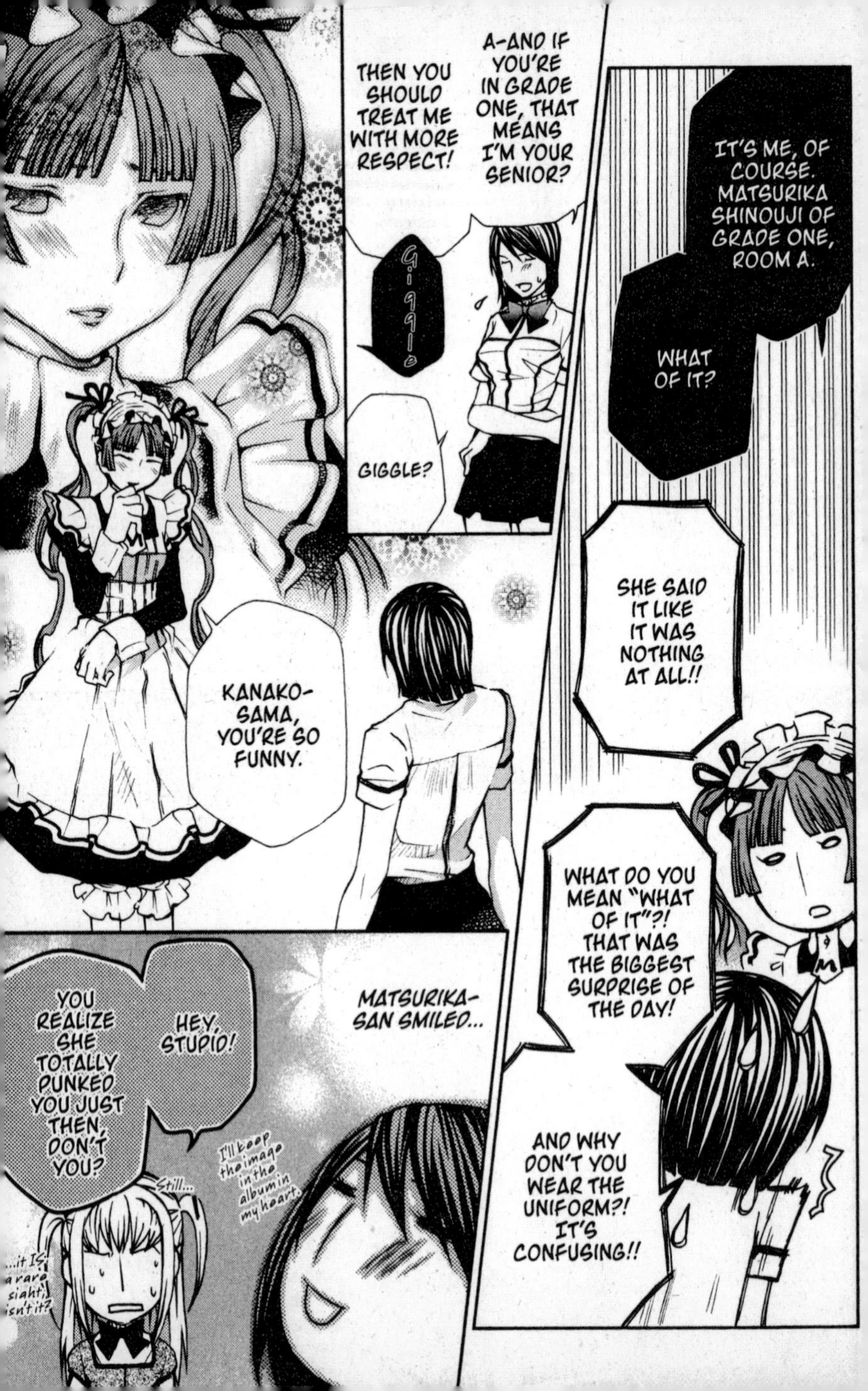
IT'S ME, OF COURSE. MATSURIKA SHINOUJI OF GRADE ONE, ROOM A.
WHAT OF IT?
A-AND IF YOU'RE IN GRADE ONE, THAT MEANS I'M YOUR SENIOR?
THEN YOU SHOULD TREAT ME WITH MORE RESPECT!
Giggle
GIGGLE?
KANAKO-SAMA, YOU'RE SO FUNNY.
SHE SAID IT LIKE IT WAS NOTHING AT ALL!!
WHAT DO YOU MEAN "WHAT OF IT"?! THAT WAS THE BIGGEST SURPRISE OF THE DAY!
AND WHY DON'T YOU WEAR THE UNIFORM?! IT'S CONFUSING!!
MATSURIKA-SAN SMILED...
HEY, STUPID!
YOU REALIZE SHE TOTALLY PUNKED YOU JUST THEN, DON'T YOU?
I'll keep the image in the album in my heart.
Still...
...it IS a rare sight, isn't it?

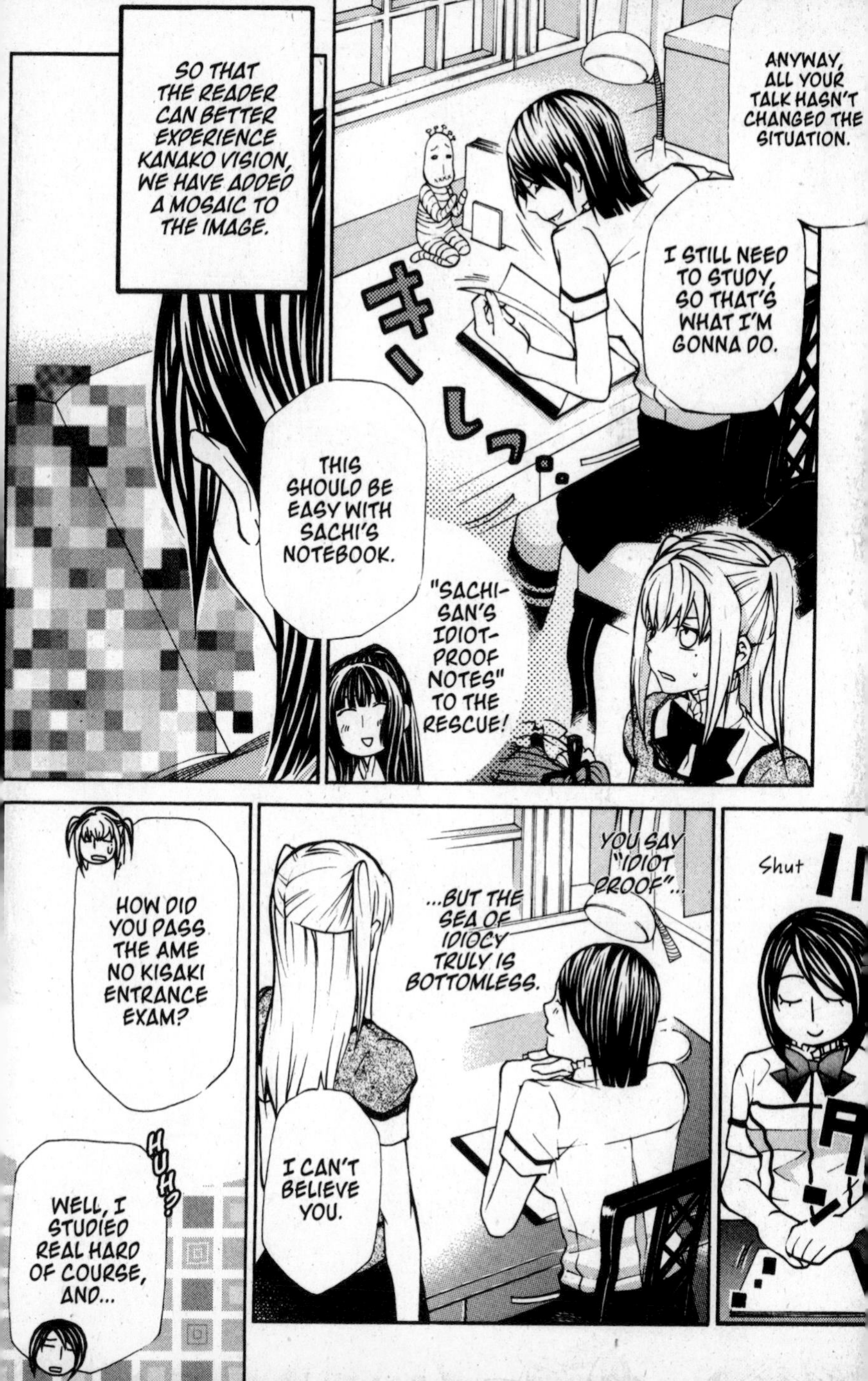
ANYWAY, ALL YOUR TALK HASN'T CHANGED THE SITUATION.
I STILL NEED TO STUDY, SO THAT'S WHAT I'M GONNA DO.
きーしっ
THIS SHOULD BE EASY WITH SACHI'S NOTEBOOK.
"SACHI-SAN'S IDIOT-PROOF NOTES" TO THE RESCUE!
SO THAT THE READER CAN BETTER EXPERIENCE KANAKO VISION, WE HAVE ADDED A MOSAIC TO THE IMAGE.
Shut
YOU SAY "IDIOT PROOF"...
...BUT THE SEA OF IDIOCY TRULY IS BOTTOMLESS.
I CAN'T BELIEVE YOU.
HOW DID YOU PASS THE AME NO KISAKI ENTRANCE EXAM?
HUH?
WELL, I STUDIED REAL HARD OF COURSE, AND...

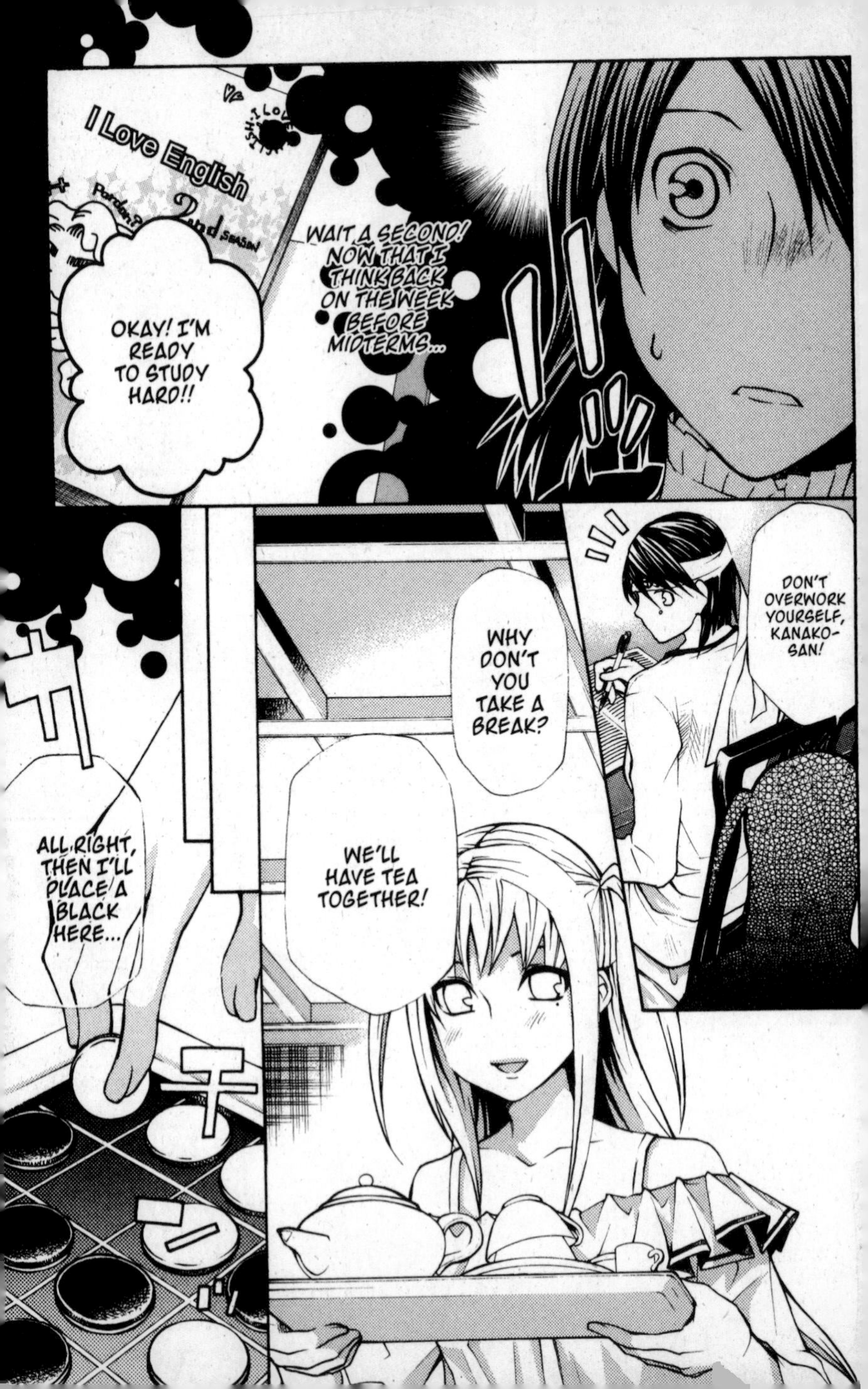
I Love English
2nd SEASON
Pardon?
WAIT A SECOND! NOW THAT I THINK BACK ON THE WEEK BEFORE MIDTERMS...
OKAY! I'M READY TO STUDY HARD!!
DON'T OVERWORK YOURSELF, KANAKO-SAN!
WHY DON'T YOU TAKE A BREAK?
WE'LL HAVE TEA TOGETHER!
ALL RIGHT, THEN I'LL PLACE A BLACK HERE...

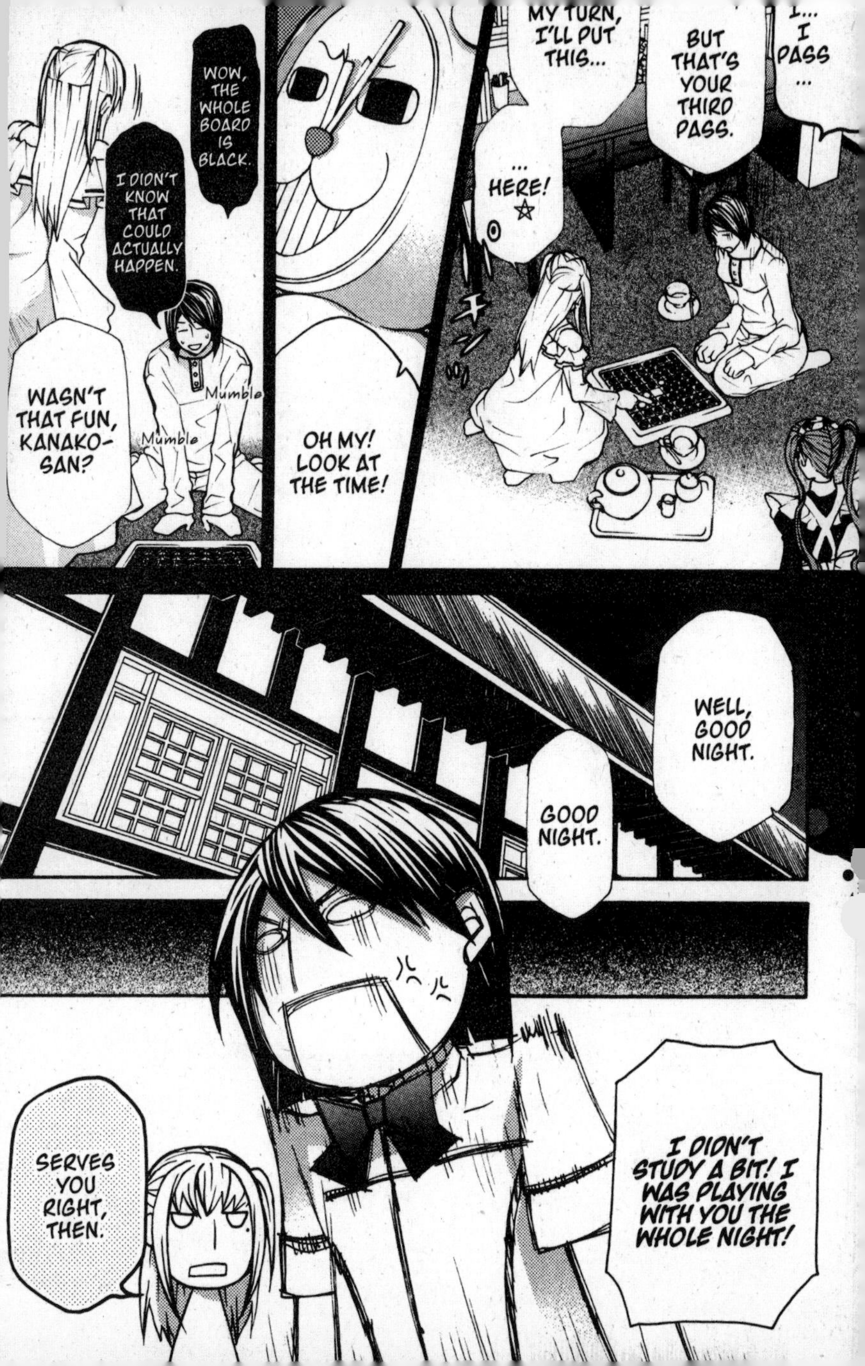
I... I PASS...
BUT THAT'S YOUR THIRD PASS.
MY TURN, I'LL PUT THIS...
...HERE! ☆
OH MY! LOOK AT THE TIME!
WOW, THE WHOLE BOARD IS BLACK.
I DIDN'T KNOW THAT COULD ACTUALLY HAPPEN.
Mumble
Mumble
WASN'T THAT FUN, KANAKO-SAN?
WELL, GOOD NIGHT.
GOOD NIGHT.
I DIDN'T STUDY A BIT! I WAS PLAYING WITH YOU THE WHOLE NIGHT!
SERVES YOU RIGHT, THEN.

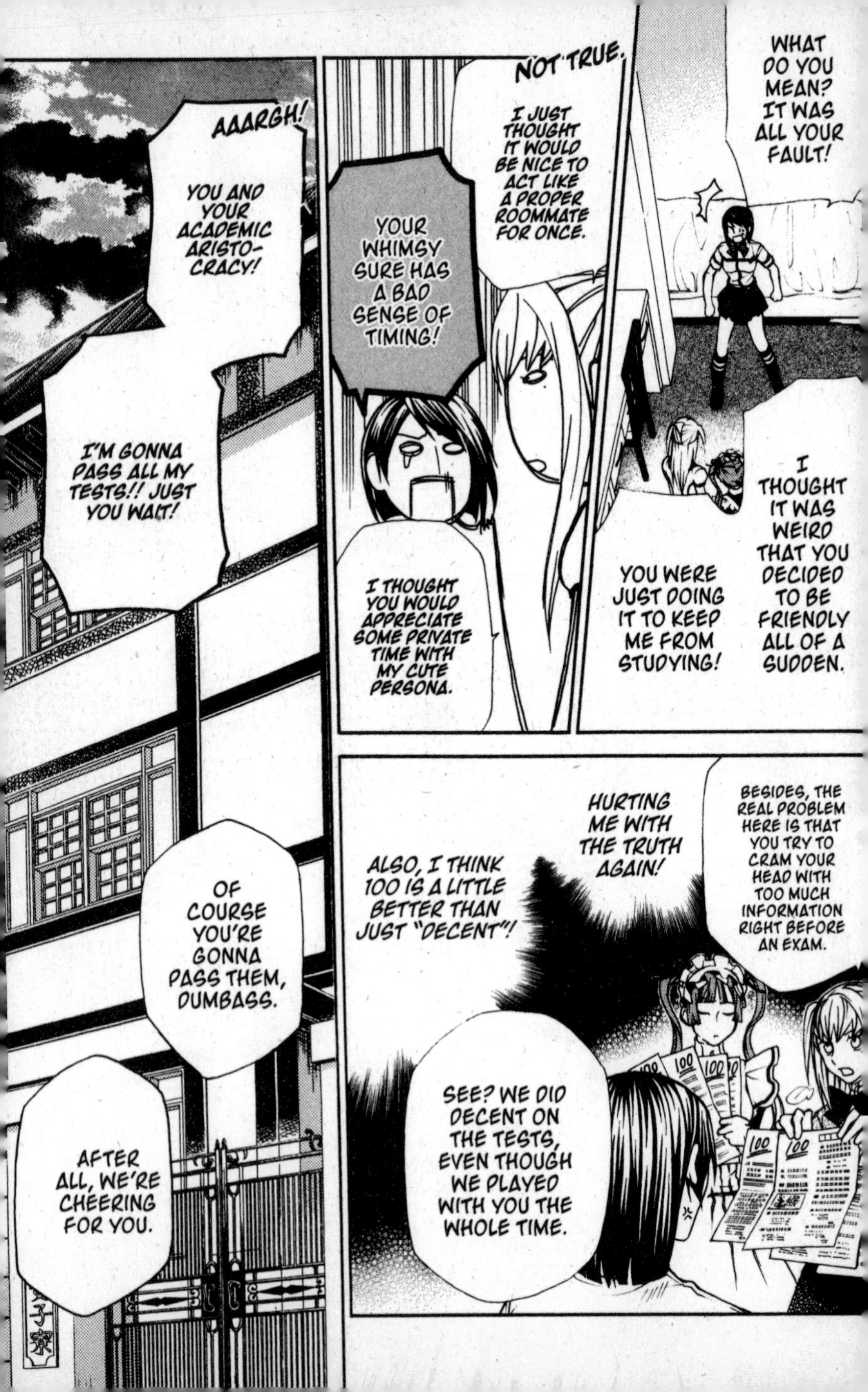
WHAT DO YOU MEAN? IT WAS ALL YOUR FAULT!
I THOUGHT IT WAS WEIRD THAT YOU DECIDED TO BE FRIENDLY ALL OF A SUDDEN.
YOU WERE JUST DOING IT TO KEEP ME FROM STUDYING!
NOT TRUE.
I JUST THOUGHT IT WOULD BE NICE TO ACT LIKE A PROPER ROOMMATE FOR ONCE.
YOUR WHIMSY SURE HAS A BAD SENSE OF TIMING!
I THOUGHT YOU WOULD APPRECIATE SOME PRIVATE TIME WITH MY CUTE PERSONA.
BESIDES, THE REAL PROBLEM HERE IS THAT YOU TRY TO CRAM YOUR HEAD WITH TOO MUCH INFORMATION RIGHT BEFORE AN EXAM.
HURTING ME WITH THE TRUTH AGAIN!
ALSO, I THINK 100 IS A LITTLE BETTER THAN JUST "DECENT"!
SEE? WE DID DECENT ON THE TESTS, EVEN THOUGH WE PLAYED WITH YOU THE WHOLE TIME.
AAARGH!
YOU AND YOUR ACADEMIC ARISTOCRACY!
I'M GONNA PASS ALL MY TESTS!! JUST YOU WAIT!
OF COURSE YOU'RE GONNA PASS THEM, DUMBASS.
AFTER ALL, WE'RE CHEERING FOR YOU.

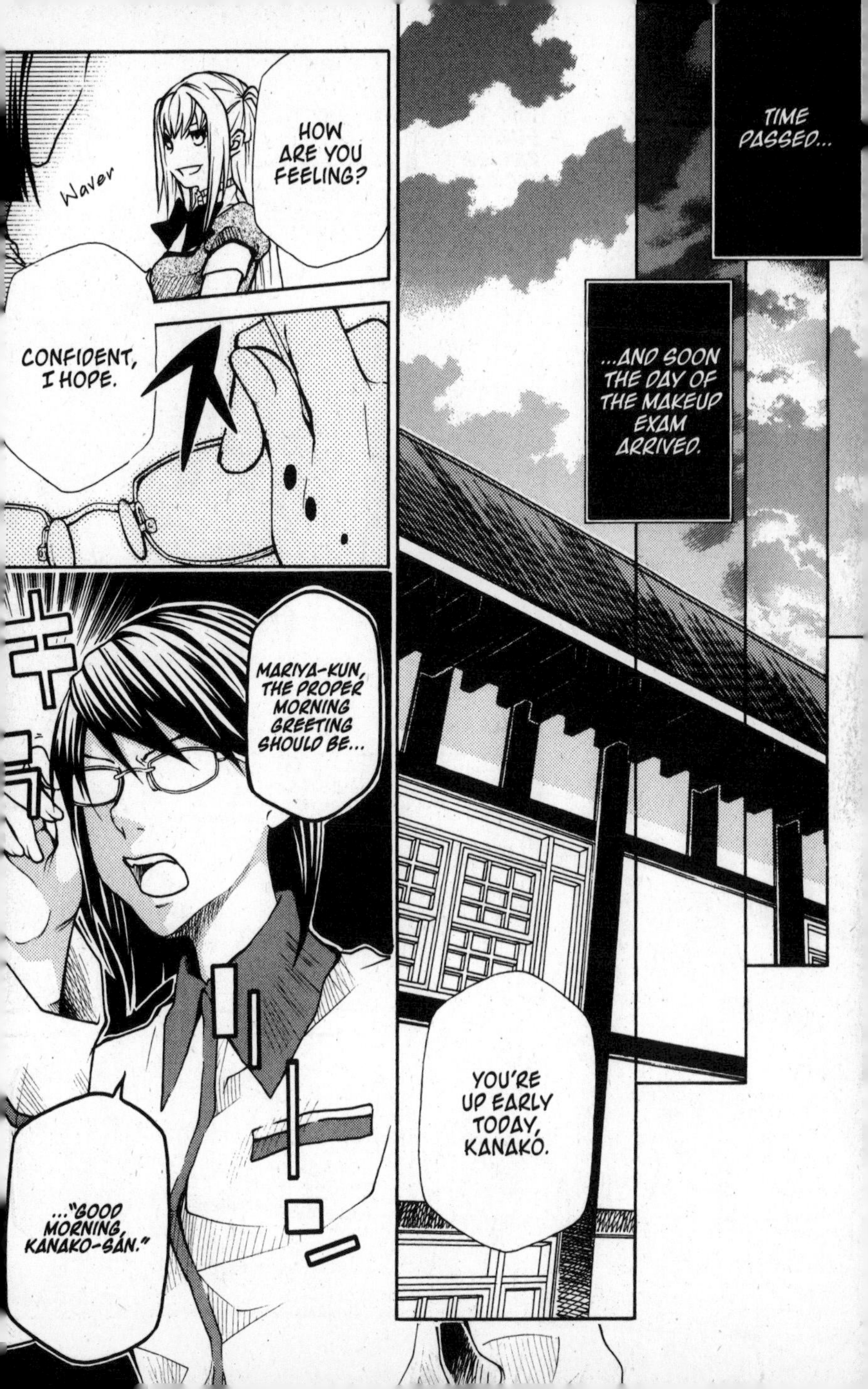
TIME PASSED...
...AND SOON THE DAY OF THE MAKEUP EXAM ARRIVED.
YOU'RE UP EARLY TODAY, KANAKO.
HOW ARE YOU FEELING?
Waver
CONFIDENT, I HOPE.
MARIYA-KUN, THE PROPER MORNING GREETING SHOULD BE...
..."GOOD MORNING, KANAKO-SAN."

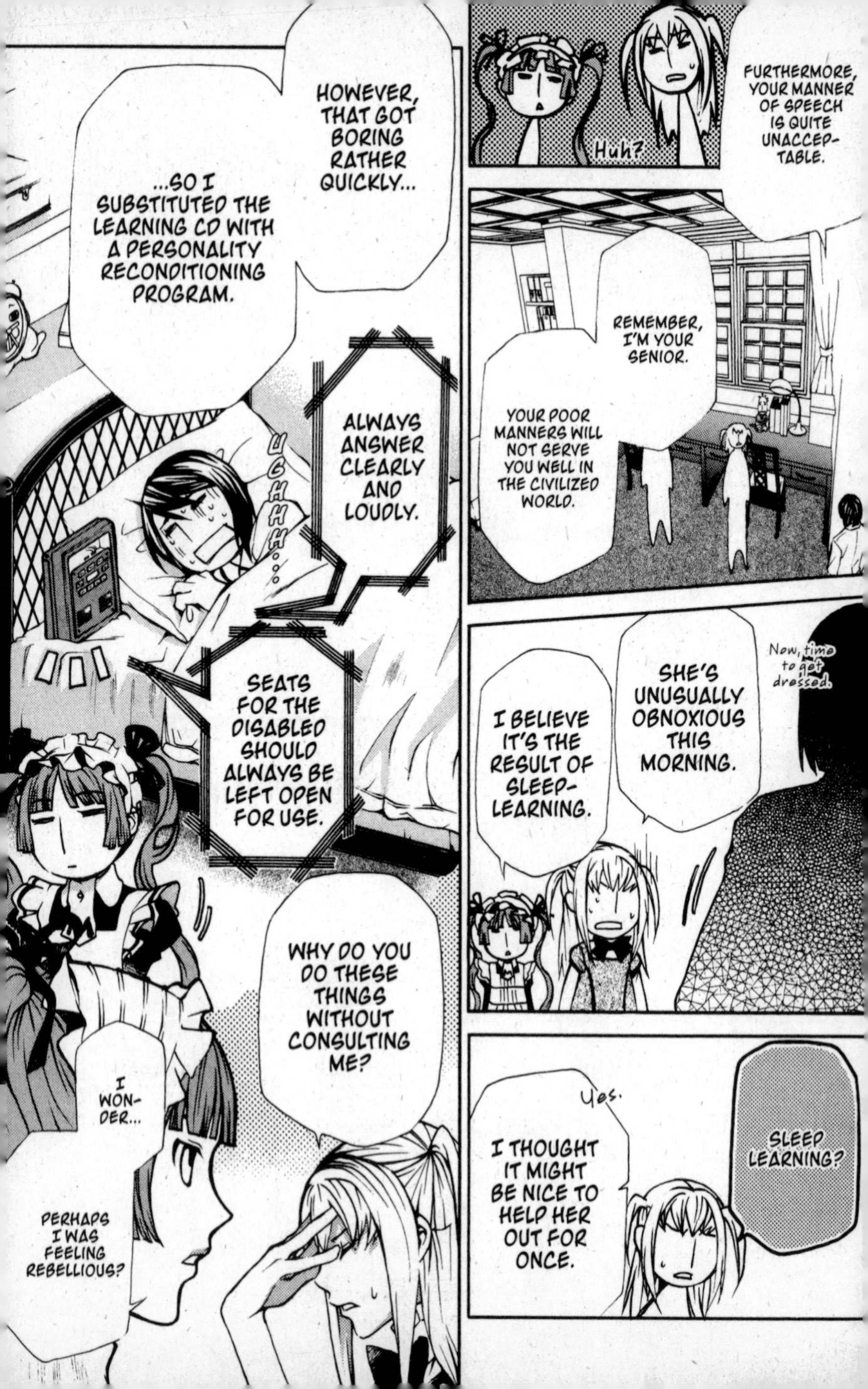
FURTHERMORE, YOUR MANNER OF SPEECH IS QUITE UNACCEPTABLE.
Huh?
REMEMBER, I'M YOUR SENIOR.
YOUR POOR MANNERS WILL NOT SERVE YOU WELL IN THE CIVILIZED WORLD.
Now, time to get dressed.
SHE'S UNUSUALLY OBNOXIOUS THIS MORNING.
I BELIEVE IT'S THE RESULT OF SLEEP-LEARNING.
SLEEP LEARNING?
Yes.
I THOUGHT IT MIGHT BE NICE TO HELP HER OUT FOR ONCE.
HOWEVER, THAT GOT BORING RATHER QUICKLY...
...SO I SUBSTITUTED THE LEARNING CD WITH A PERSONALITY RECONDITIONING PROGRAM.
UGHHH...
ALWAYS ANSWER CLEARLY AND LOUDLY.
SEATS FOR THE DISABLED SHOULD ALWAYS BE LEFT OPEN FOR USE.
WHY DO YOU DO THESE THINGS WITHOUT CONSULTING ME?
I WONDER...
PERHAPS I WAS FEELING REBELLIOUS?

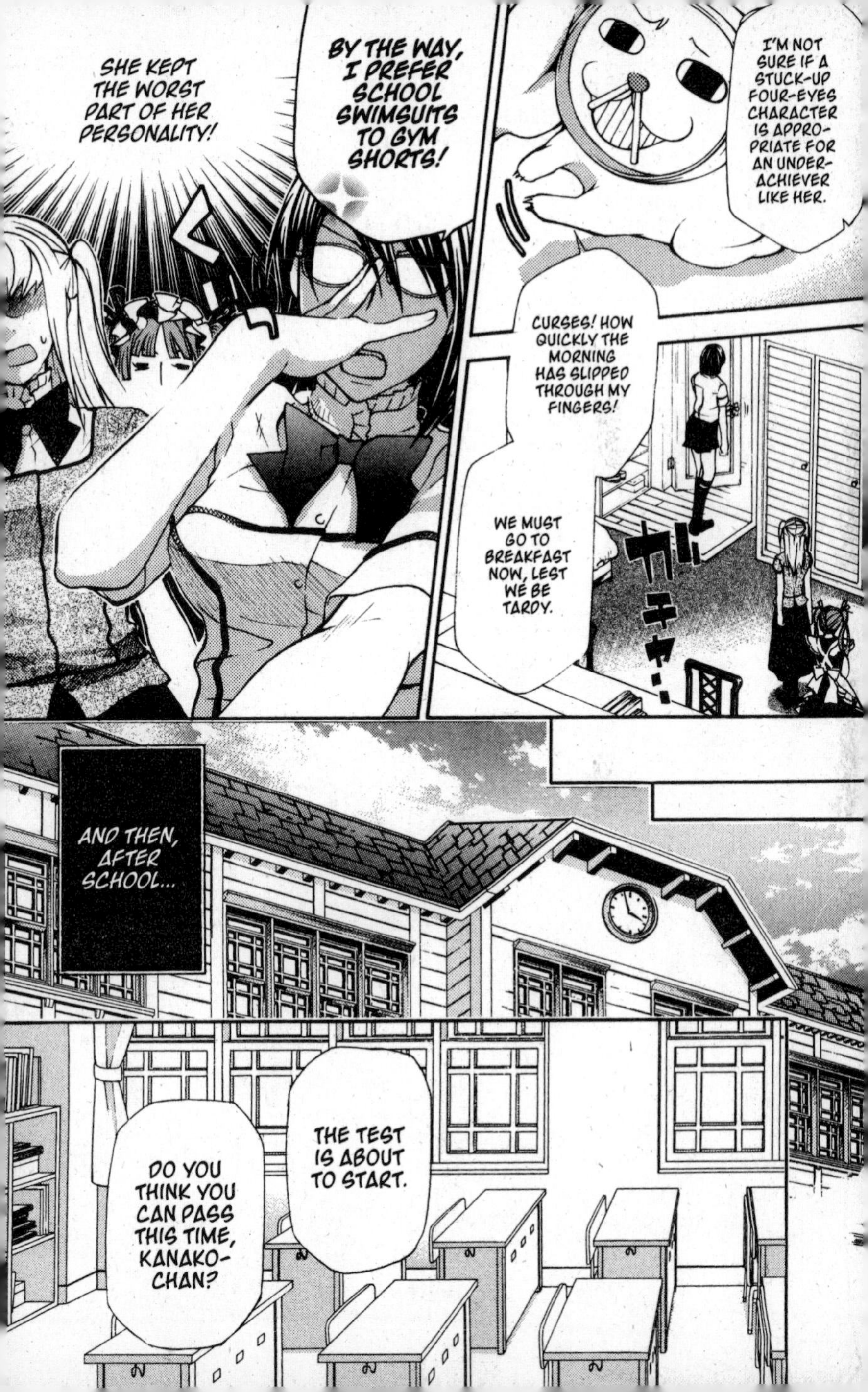
I'M NOT SURE IF A STUCK-UP FOUR-EYES CHARACTER IS APPROPRIATE FOR AN UNDER-ACHIEVER LIKE HER.
CURSES! HOW QUICKLY THE MORNING HAS SLIPPED THROUGH MY FINGERS!
WE MUST GO TO BREAKFAST NOW, LEST WE BE TARDY.
BY THE WAY, I PREFER SCHOOL SWIMSUITS TO GYM SHORTS!
SHE KEPT THE WORST PART OF HER PERSONALITY!
AND THEN, AFTER SCHOOL...
THE TEST IS ABOUT TO START.
DO YOU THINK YOU CAN PASS THIS TIME, KANAKO-CHAN?

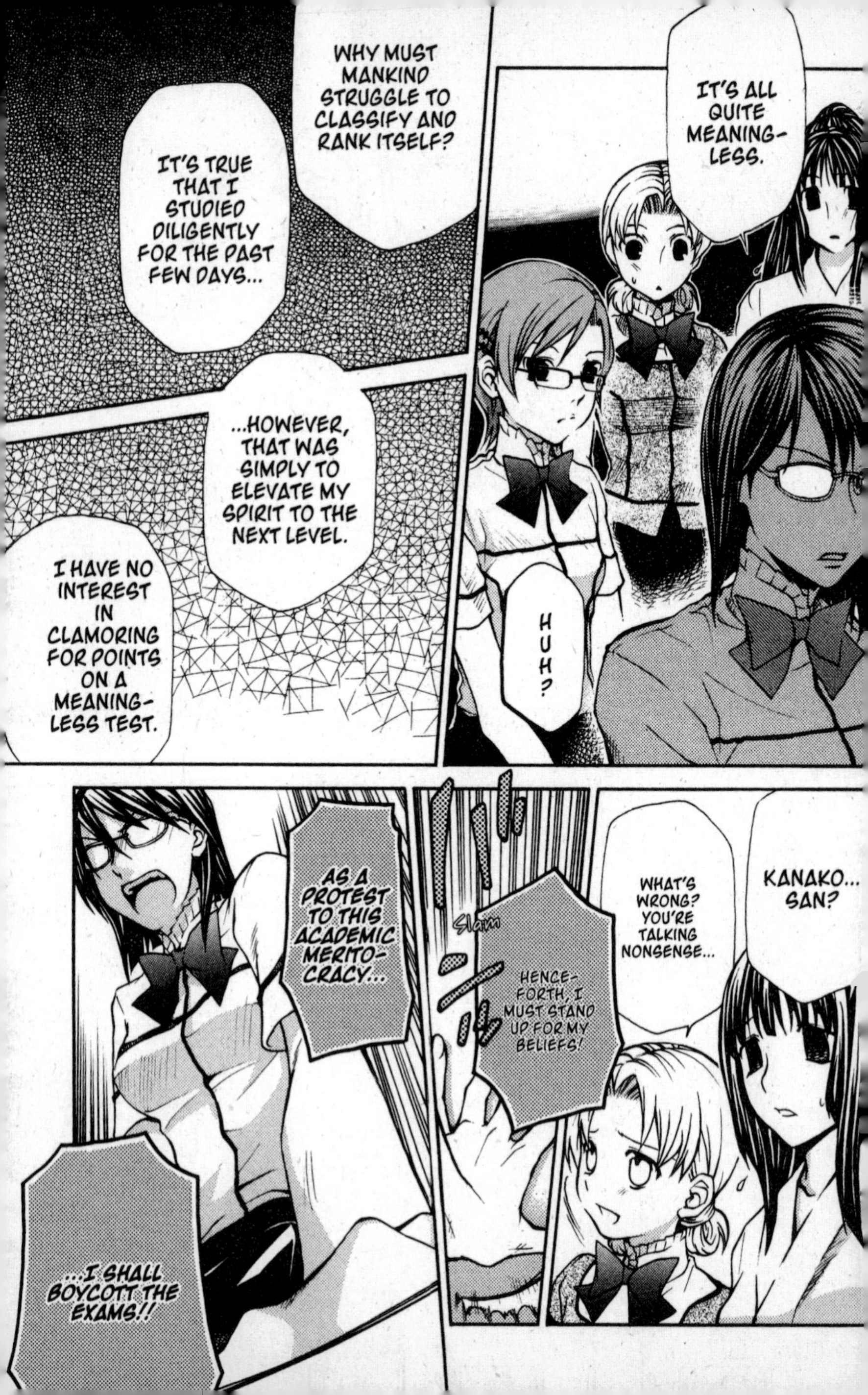
IT'S ALL QUITE MEANING-LESS.
HUH?
WHY MUST MANKIND STRUGGLE TO CLASSIFY AND RANK ITSELF?
IT'S TRUE THAT I STUDIED DILIGENTLY FOR THE PAST FEW DAYS...
...HOWEVER, THAT WAS SIMPLY TO ELEVATE MY SPIRIT TO THE NEXT LEVEL.
I HAVE NO INTEREST IN CLAMORING FOR POINTS ON A MEANING-LESS TEST.
KANAKO... SAN?
WHAT'S WRONG? YOU'RE TALKING NONSENSE...
HENCE-FORTH, I MUST STAND UP FOR MY BELIEFS!
Slam
AS A PROTEST TO THIS ACADEMIC MERITO-CRACY...
...I SHALL BOYCOTT THE EXAMS!!

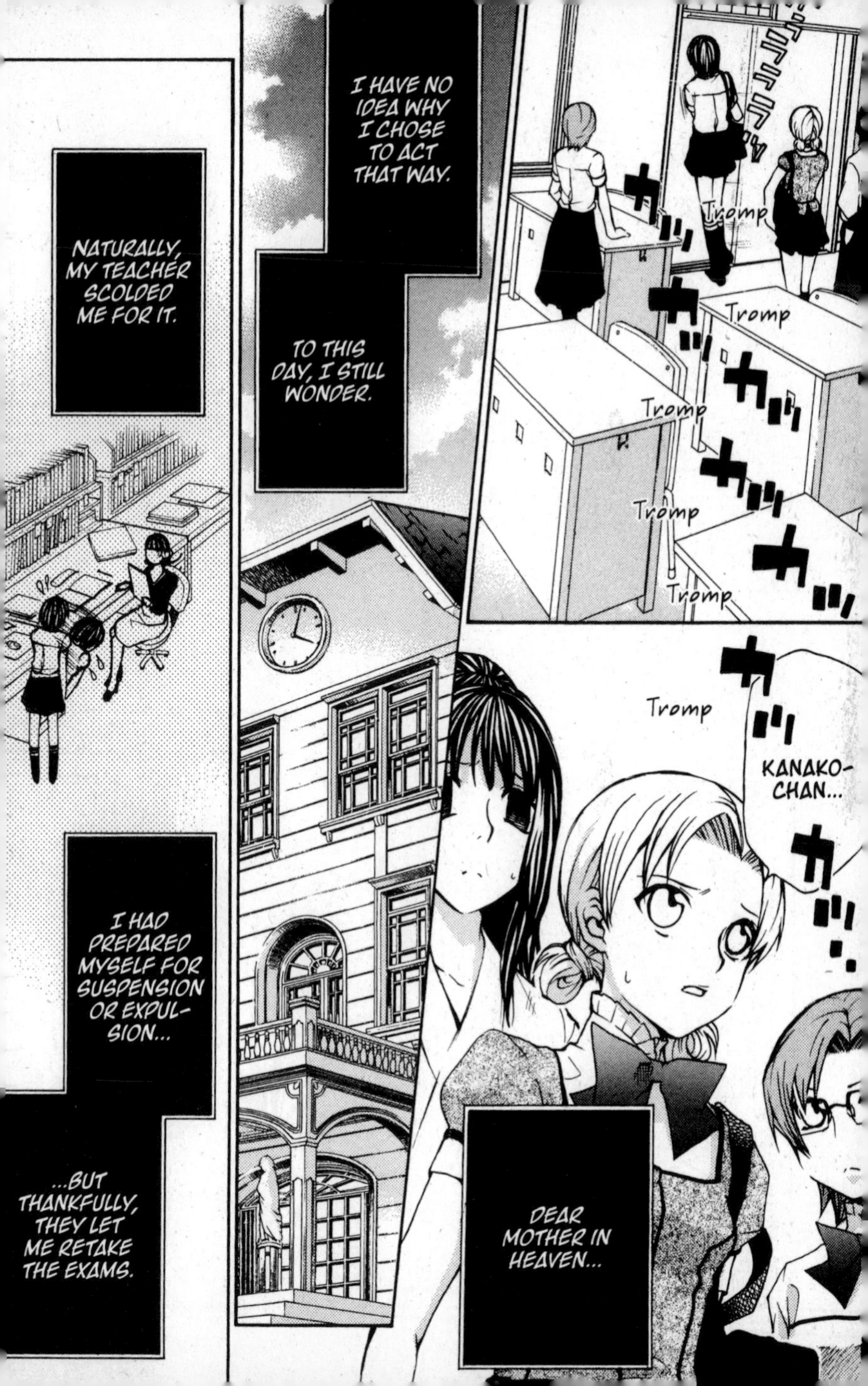
Tromp
Tromp
Tromp
Tromp
Tromp
Tromp
KANAKO-CHAN...
DEAR MOTHER IN HEAVEN...
I HAVE NO IDEA WHY I CHOSE TO ACT THAT WAY.
TO THIS DAY, I STILL WONDER.
NATURALLY, MY TEACHER SCOLDED ME FOR IT.
I HAD PREPARED MYSELF FOR SUSPENSION OR EXPUL-SION...
...BUT THANKFULLY, THEY LET ME RETAKE THE EXAMS.

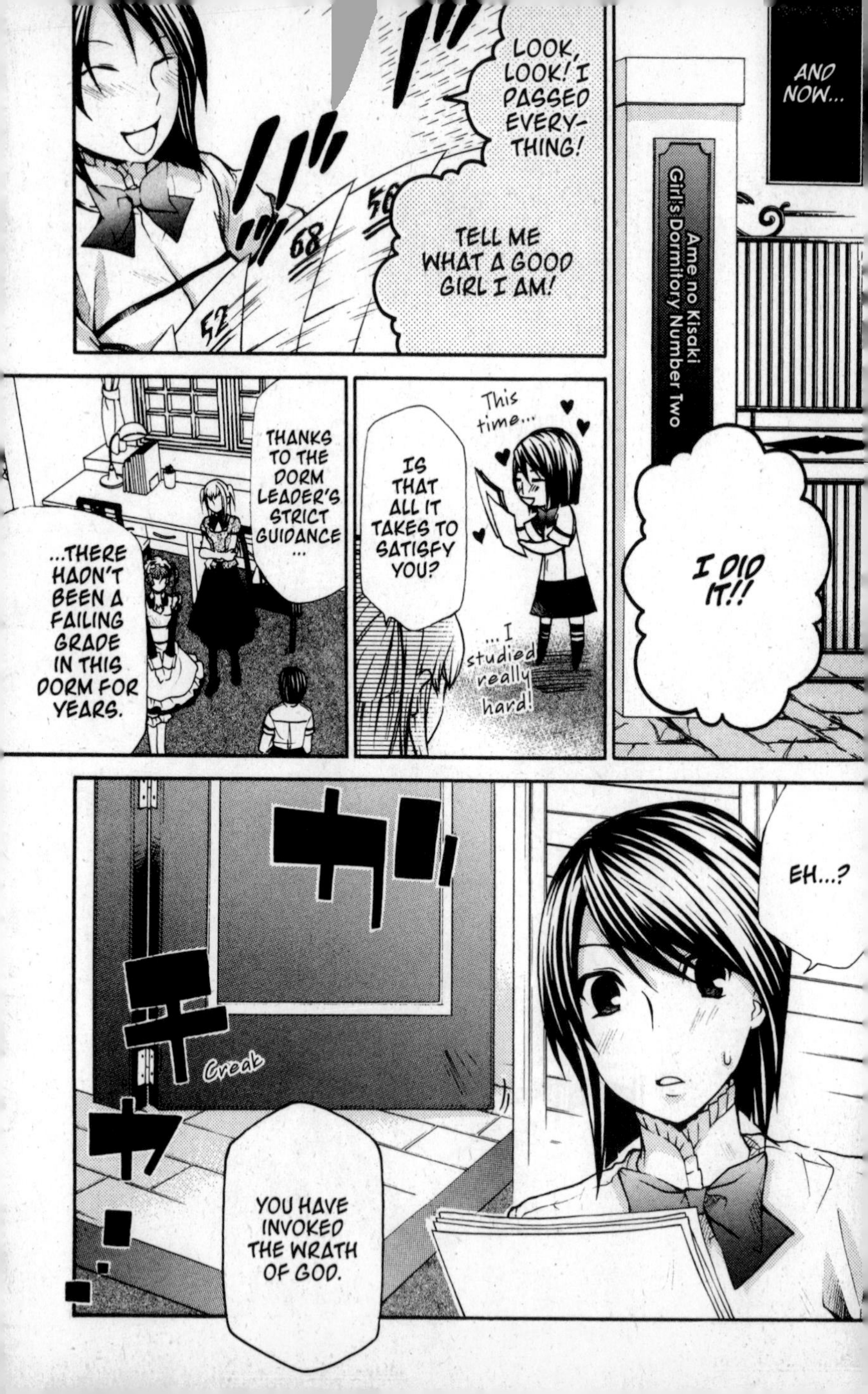
AND NOW...
Ame no Kisaki Girl's Dormitory Number Two
I DID IT!!
LOOK, LOOK! I PASSED EVERY-THING!
TELL ME WHAT A GOOD GIRL I AM!
This time...
...I studied really hard!
IS THAT ALL IT TAKES TO SATISFY YOU?
THANKS TO THE DORM LEADER'S STRICT GUIDANCE...
...THERE HADN'T BEEN A FAILING GRADE IN THIS DORM FOR YEARS.
EH...?
Creak
YOU HAVE INVOKED THE WRATH OF GOD.

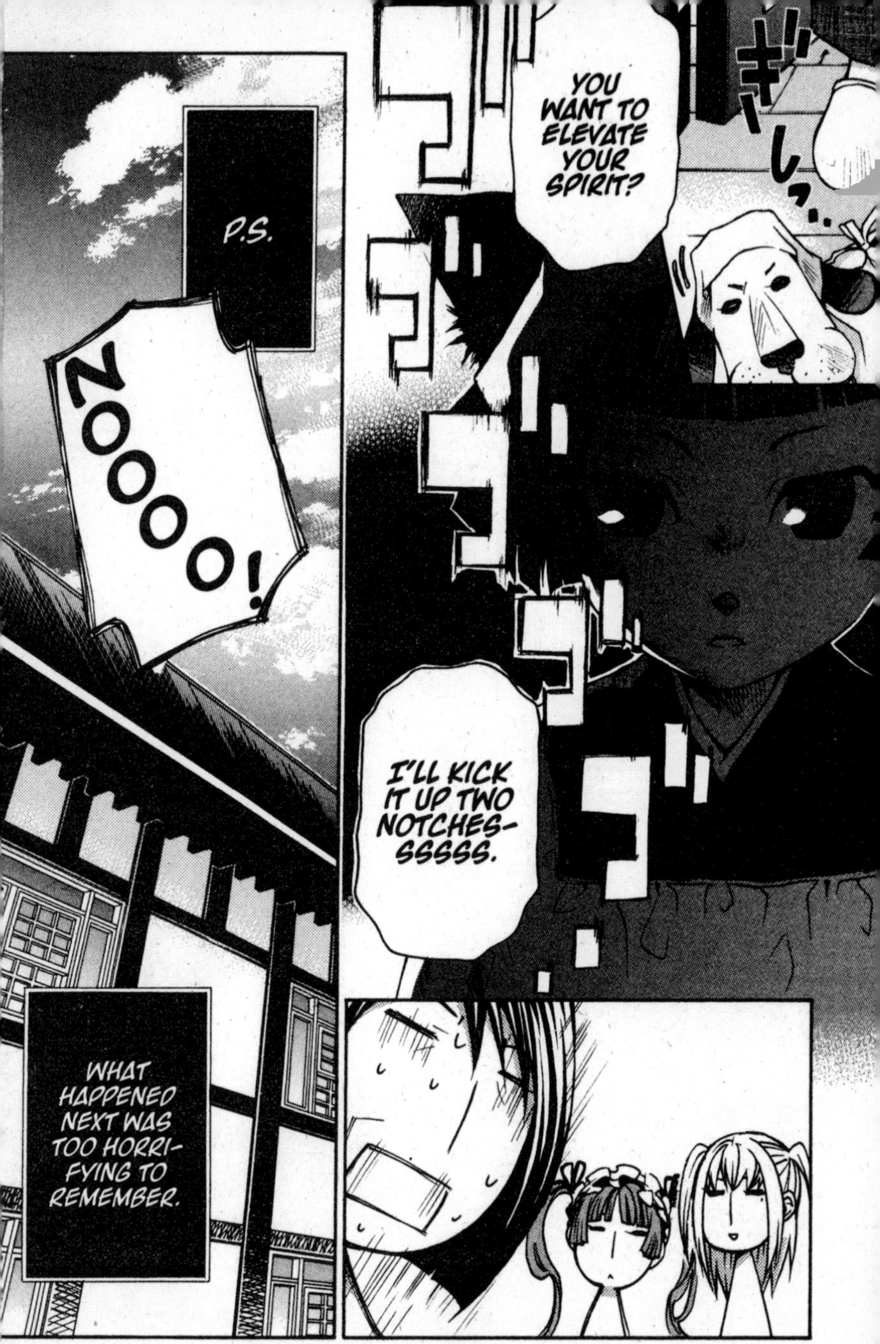
YOU WANT TO ELEVATE YOUR SPIRIT?
I'LL KICK IT UP TWO NOTCHES-SSSSS.
P.S.
ZOOOOO!
WHAT HAPPENED NEXT WAS TOO HORRI-FYING TO REMEMBER.

TONY AND MYTY

DISCOVER WORLD HERITAGE SITES

T: SAGRADA FAMILIA IS A ROMAN CATHOLIC CHURCH DESIGNED BY THE RENOWNED CATALAN ARCHITECT ANTONI GAUDI. IT HAS BEEN UNDER CONSTRUCTION FOR 120 YEARS BUT HAS YET TO BE COMPLETED. I CAN'T WAIT TO SEE IT FINISHED!

M: IN 120 YEARS, PIGEON POST HAS CHANGED TO MOBILE PHONES. THE MEMO TO HURRY UP AND FINISH MUST HAVE BEEN SENT BY PIGEON, TOO.

T: IN 120 YEARS, PARTS OF THE BUILDING HAVE ALREADY BEGUN TO SHOW AGE, SO THEY ARE FORCED TO BOTH REPAIR AND CONSTRUCT AT THE SAME TIME.

M: JUST LIKE THE FACE OF A MIDDLE-AGED ACTRESS.

M A R I A H O L I C

Maria Holic

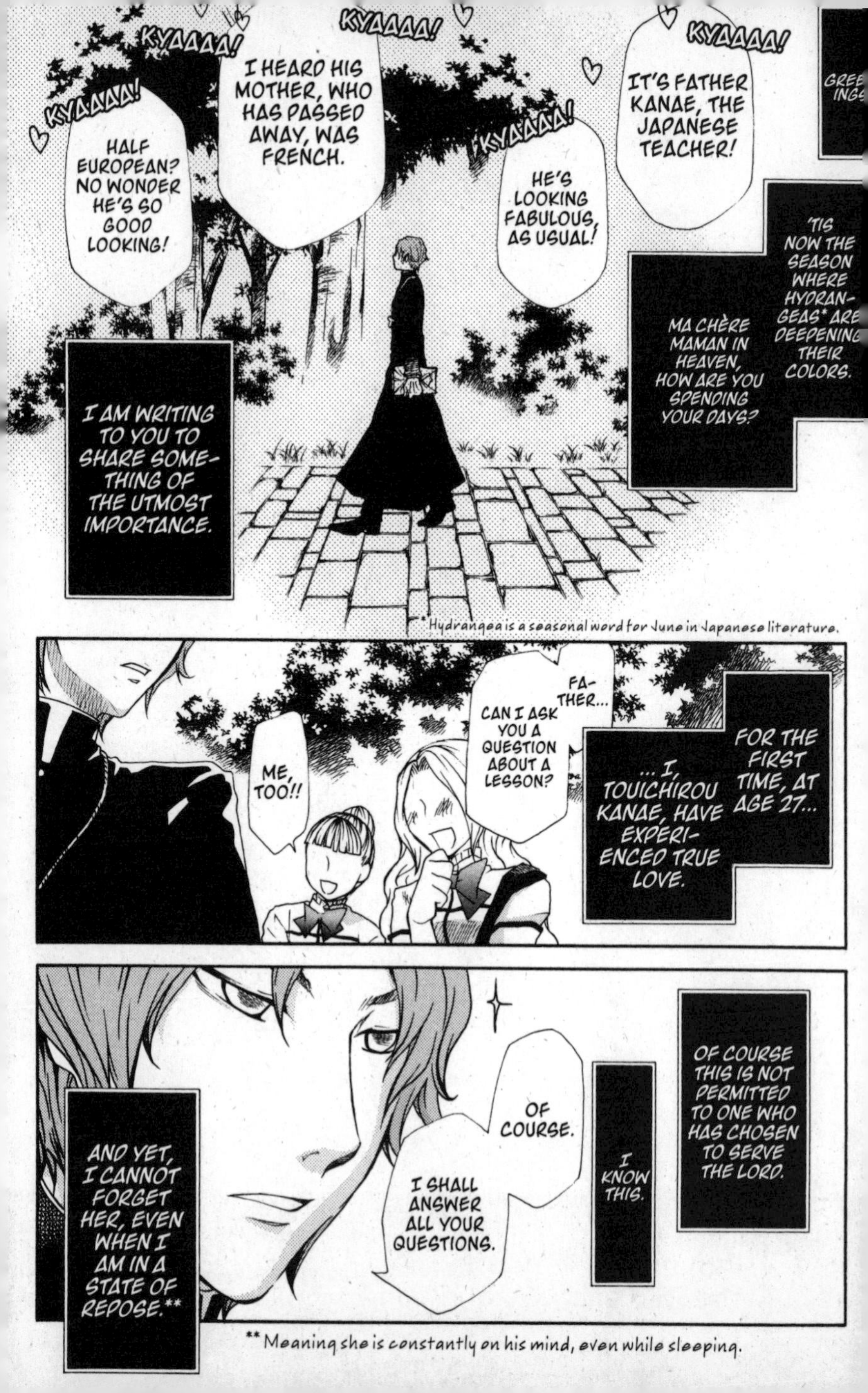
GREE INGS
'TIS NOW THE SEASON WHERE HYDRANGEAS* ARE DEEPENING THEIR COLORS.
MA CHÈRE MAMAN IN HEAVEN, HOW ARE YOU SPENDING YOUR DAYS?
KYAAAA!
IT'S FATHER KANAE, THE JAPANESE TEACHER!
KYAAAA!
HE'S LOOKING FABULOUS, AS USUAL!
KYAAAA!
I HEARD HIS MOTHER, WHO HAS PASSED AWAY, WAS FRENCH.
KYAAAA!
KYAAAA!
HALF EUROPEAN? NO WONDER HE'S SO GOOD LOOKING!
I AM WRITING TO YOU TO SHARE SOMETHING OF THE UTMOST IMPORTANCE.
FOR THE FIRST TIME, AT AGE 27...
... I, TOUICHIROU KANAE, HAVE EXPERIENCED TRUE LOVE.
FATHER...
CAN I ASK YOU A QUESTION ABOUT A LESSON?
ME, TOO!!
OF COURSE THIS IS NOT PERMITTED TO ONE WHO HAS CHOSEN TO SERVE THE LORD.
I KNOW THIS.
OF COURSE.
I SHALL ANSWER ALL YOUR QUESTIONS.
AND YET, I CANNOT FORGET HER, EVEN WHEN I AM IN A STATE OF REPOSE.**

*Hydrangea is a seasonal word for June in Japanese literature.

** Meaning she is constantly on his mind, even while sleeping.

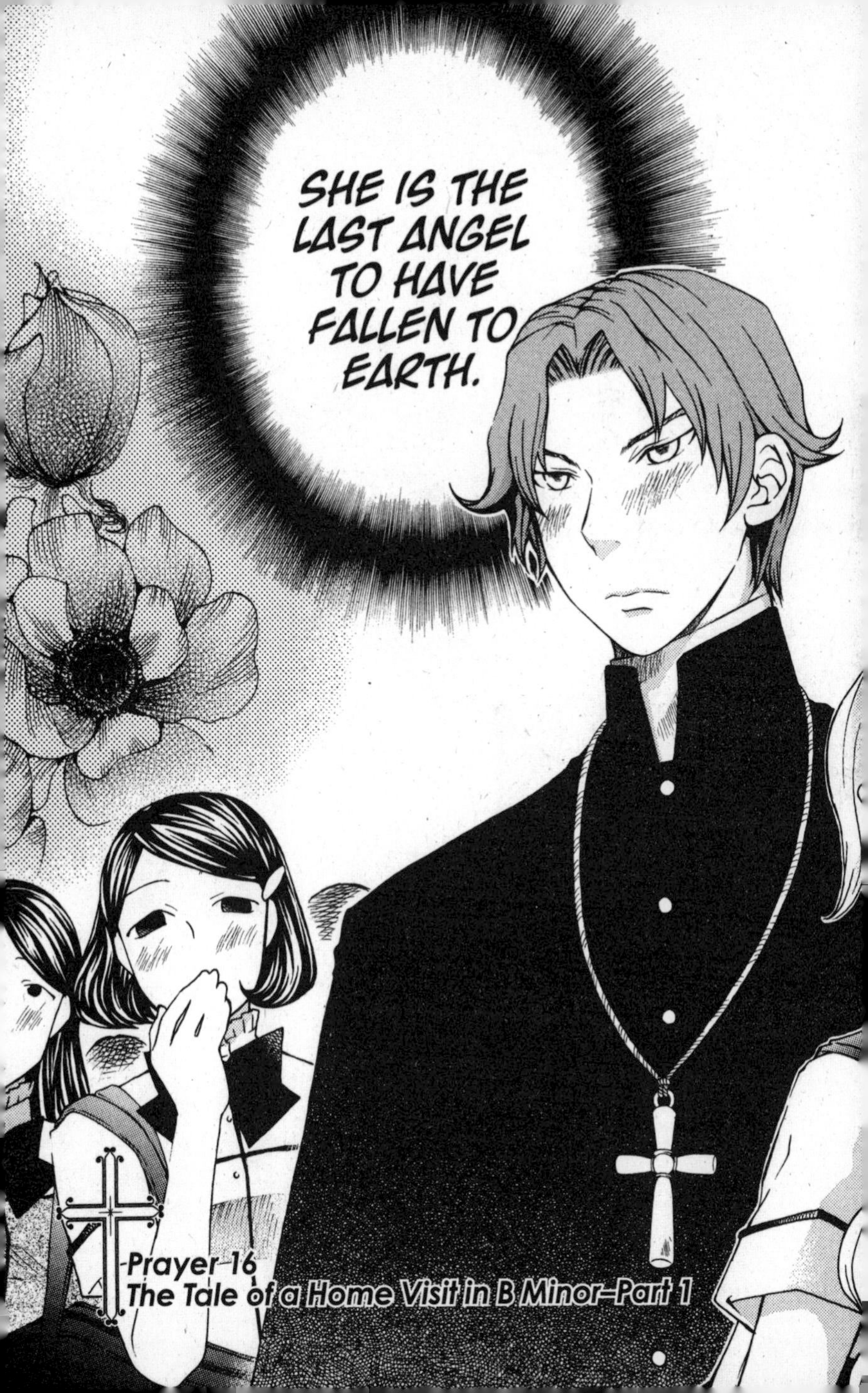
SHE IS THE LAST ANGEL TO HAVE FALLEN TO EARTH.
Prayer 16
The Tale of a Home Visit in B Minor—Part 1

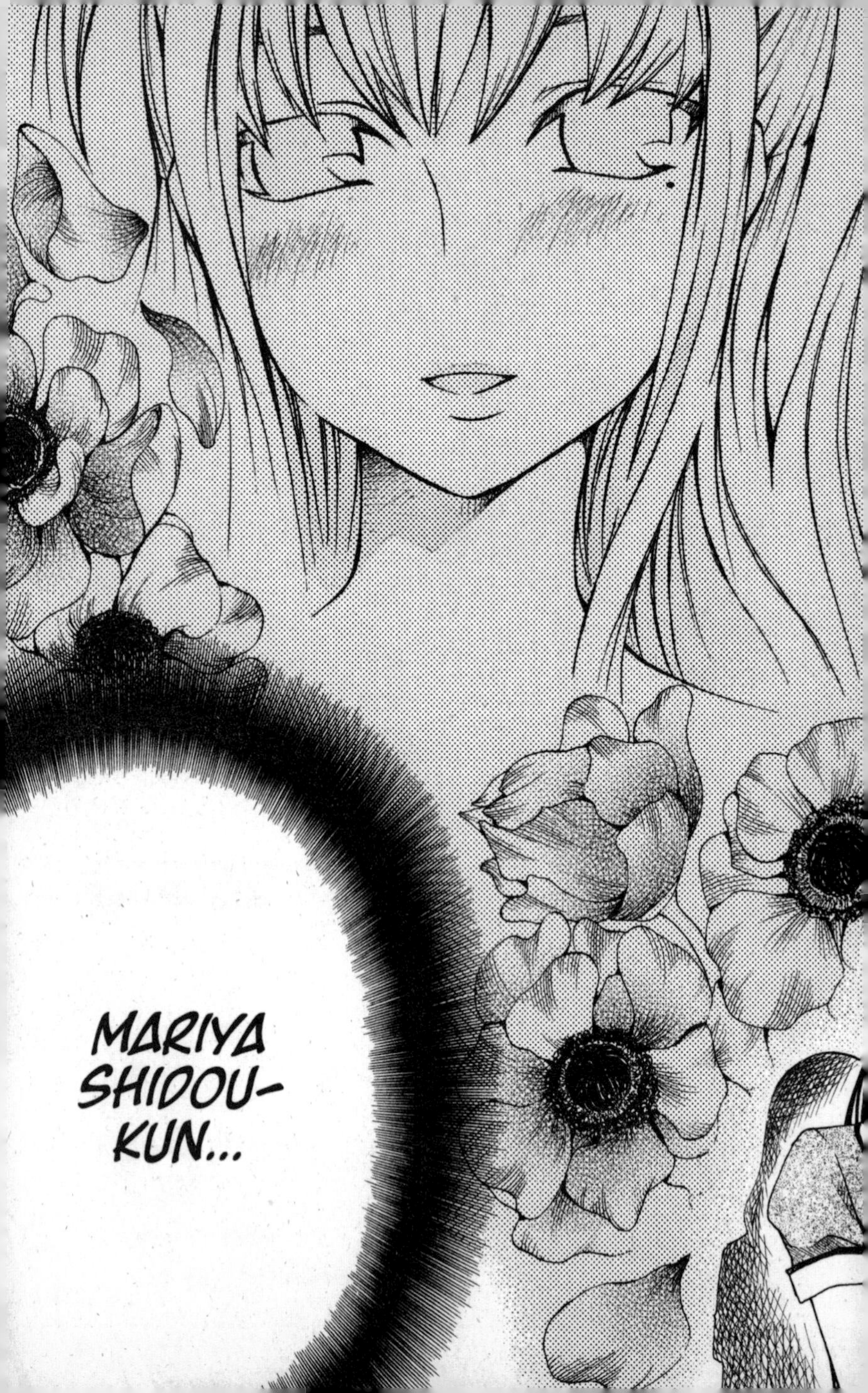
MARIYA SHIDOU-KUN...

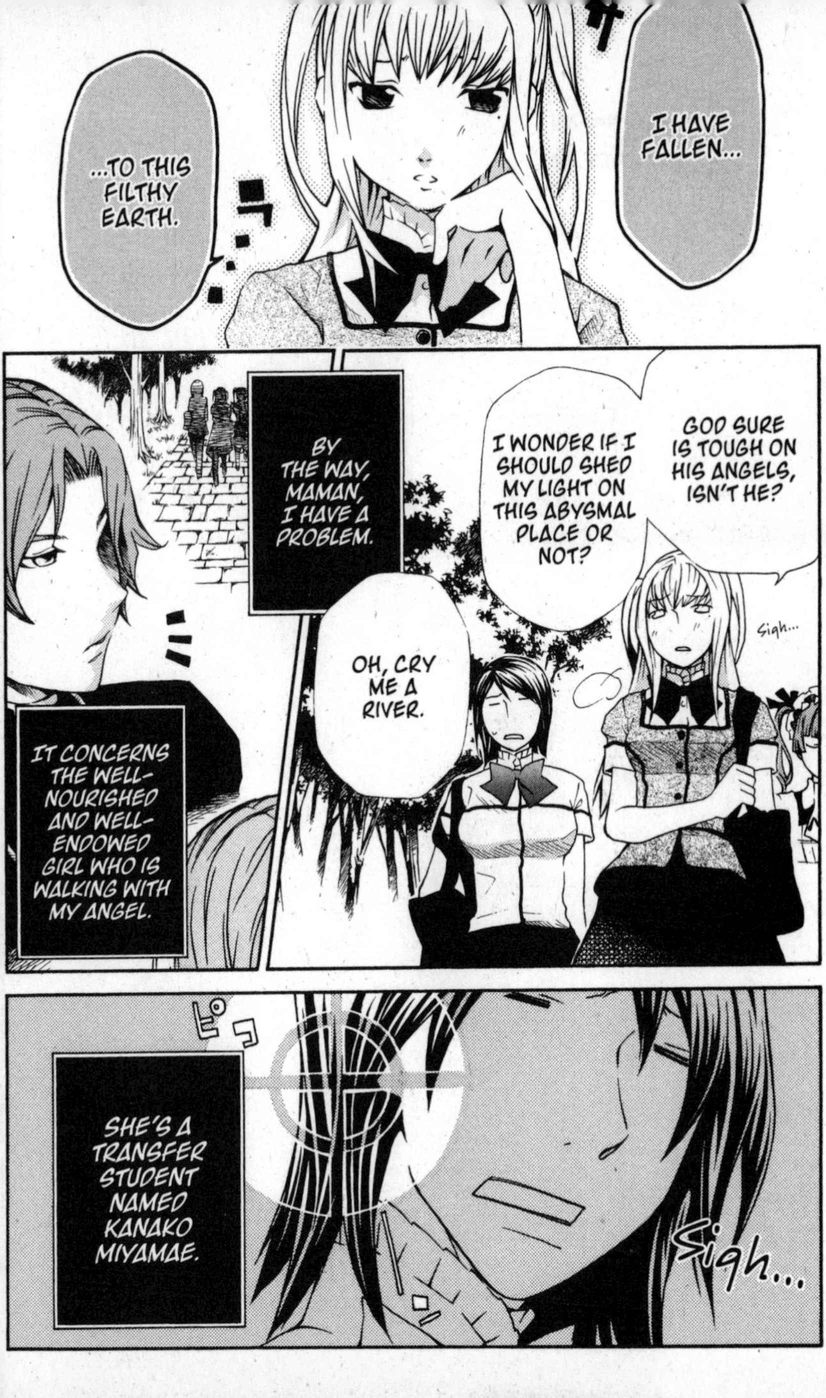
I HAVE FALLEN...
...TO THIS FILTHY EARTH.
GOD SURE IS TOUGH ON HIS ANGELS, ISN'T HE?
Sigh...
I WONDER IF I SHOULD SHED MY LIGHT ON THIS ABYSMAL PLACE OR NOT?
OH, CRY ME A RIVER.
BY THE WAY, MAMAN, I HAVE A PROBLEM.
IT CONCERNS THE WELL-NOURISHED AND WELL-ENDOWED GIRL WHO IS WALKING WITH MY ANGEL.
SHE'S A TRANSFER STUDENT NAMED KANAKO MIYAMAE.
Sigh...

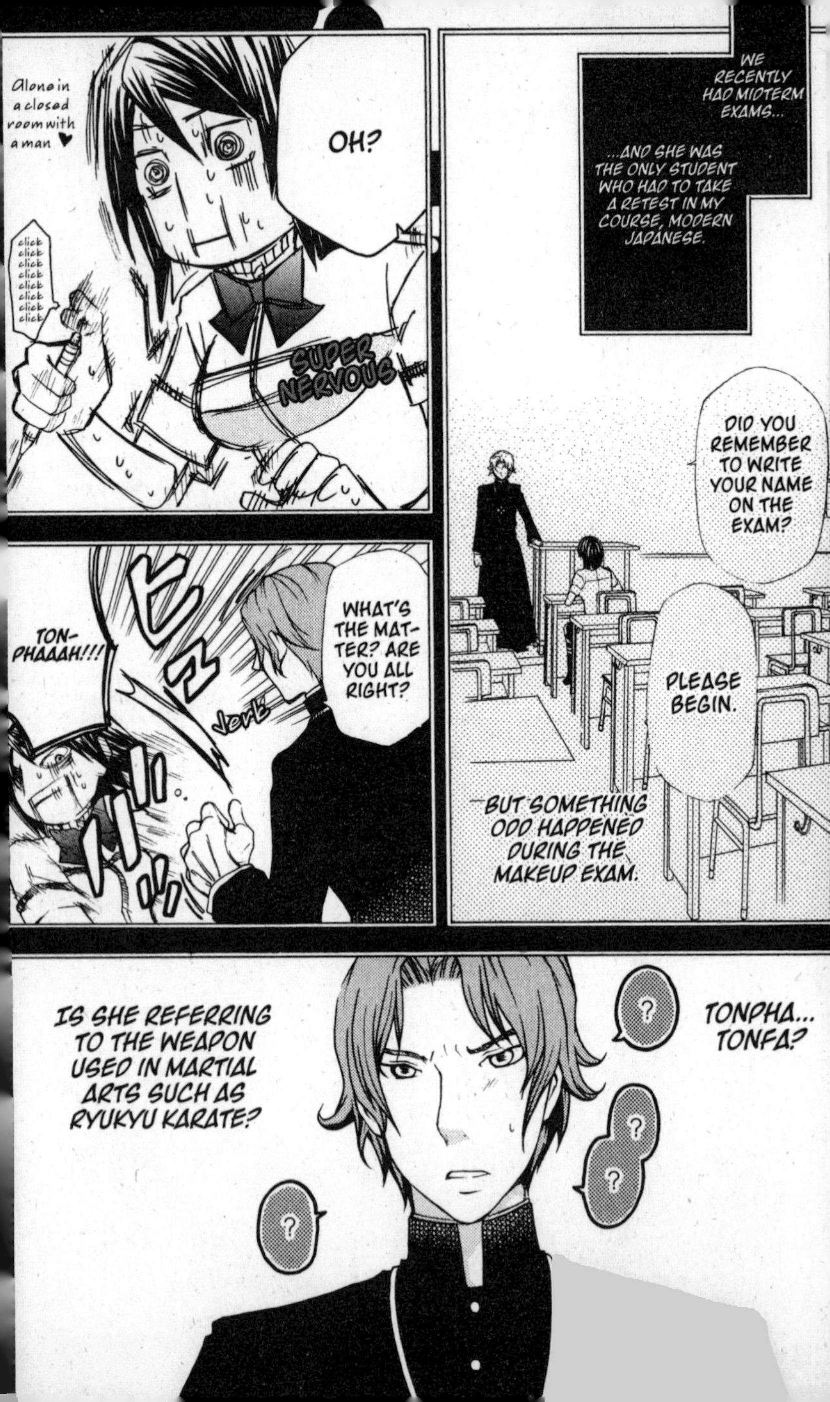
WE RECENTLY HAD MIDTERM EXAMS...
...AND SHE WAS THE ONLY STUDENT WHO HAD TO TAKE A RETEST IN MY COURSE, MODERN JAPANESE.
DID YOU REMEMBER TO WRITE YOUR NAME ON THE EXAM?
PLEASE BEGIN.
BUT SOMETHING ODD HAPPENED DURING THE MAKEUP EXAM.
OH?
Alone in a closed room with a man ♥
click click click click click click click click
SUPER NERVOUS
WHAT'S THE MATTER? ARE YOU ALL RIGHT?
TON-PHAAAH!!!
Jerk
TONPHA... TONFA?
?
?
?
?
IS SHE REFERRING TO THE WEAPON USED IN MARTIAL ARTS SUCH AS RYUKYU KARATE?

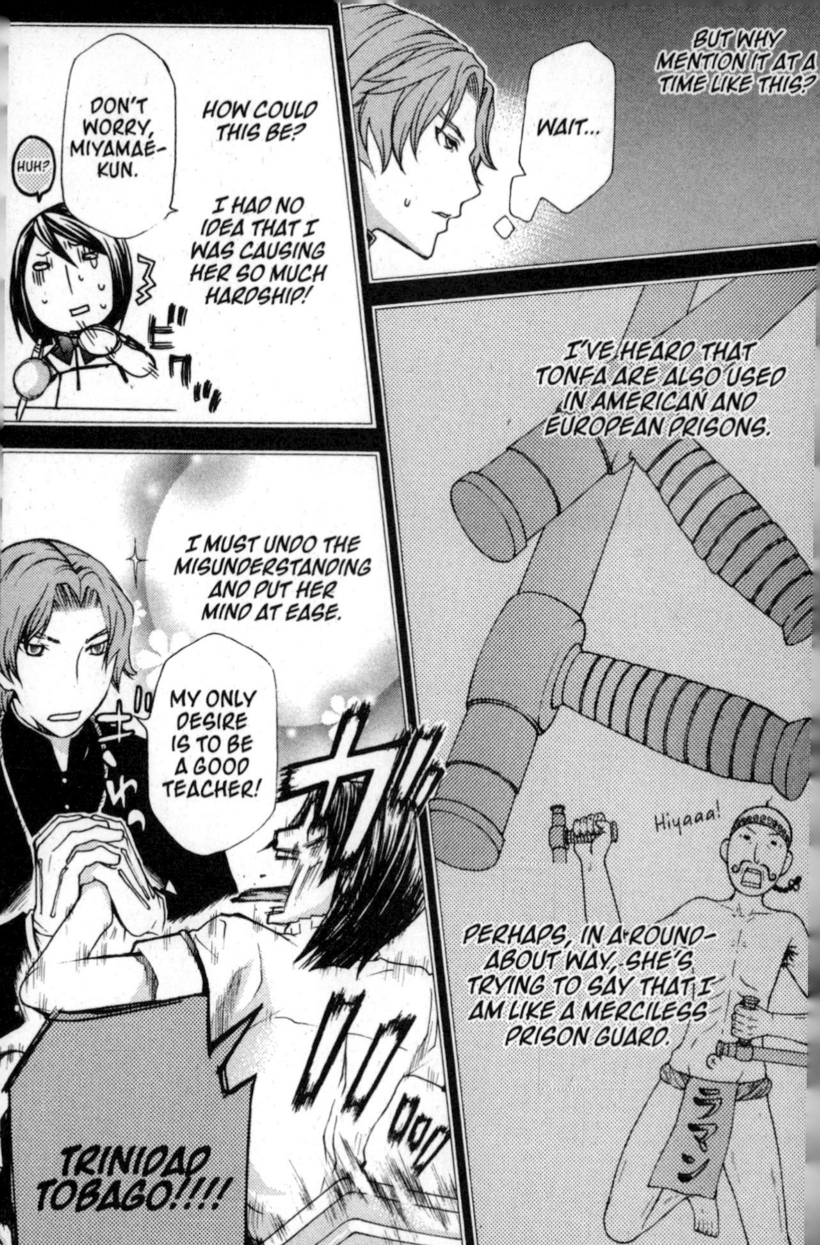
WAIT...
BUT WHY MENTION IT AT A TIME LIKE THIS?
DON'T WORRY, MIYAMAE-KUN.
HUH?
HOW COULD THIS BE?
I HAD NO IDEA THAT I WAS CAUSING HER SO MUCH HARDSHIP!
I'VE HEARD THAT TONFA ARE ALSO USED IN AMERICAN AND EUROPEAN PRISONS.
Hiyaaa!
PERHAPS, IN A ROUND-ABOUT WAY, SHE'S TRYING TO SAY THAT I AM LIKE A MERCILESS PRISON GUARD.
I MUST UNDO THE MISUNDERSTANDING AND PUT HER MIND AT EASE.
MY ONLY DESIRE IS TO BE A GOOD TEACHER!
TRINIDAD TOBAGO!!!!

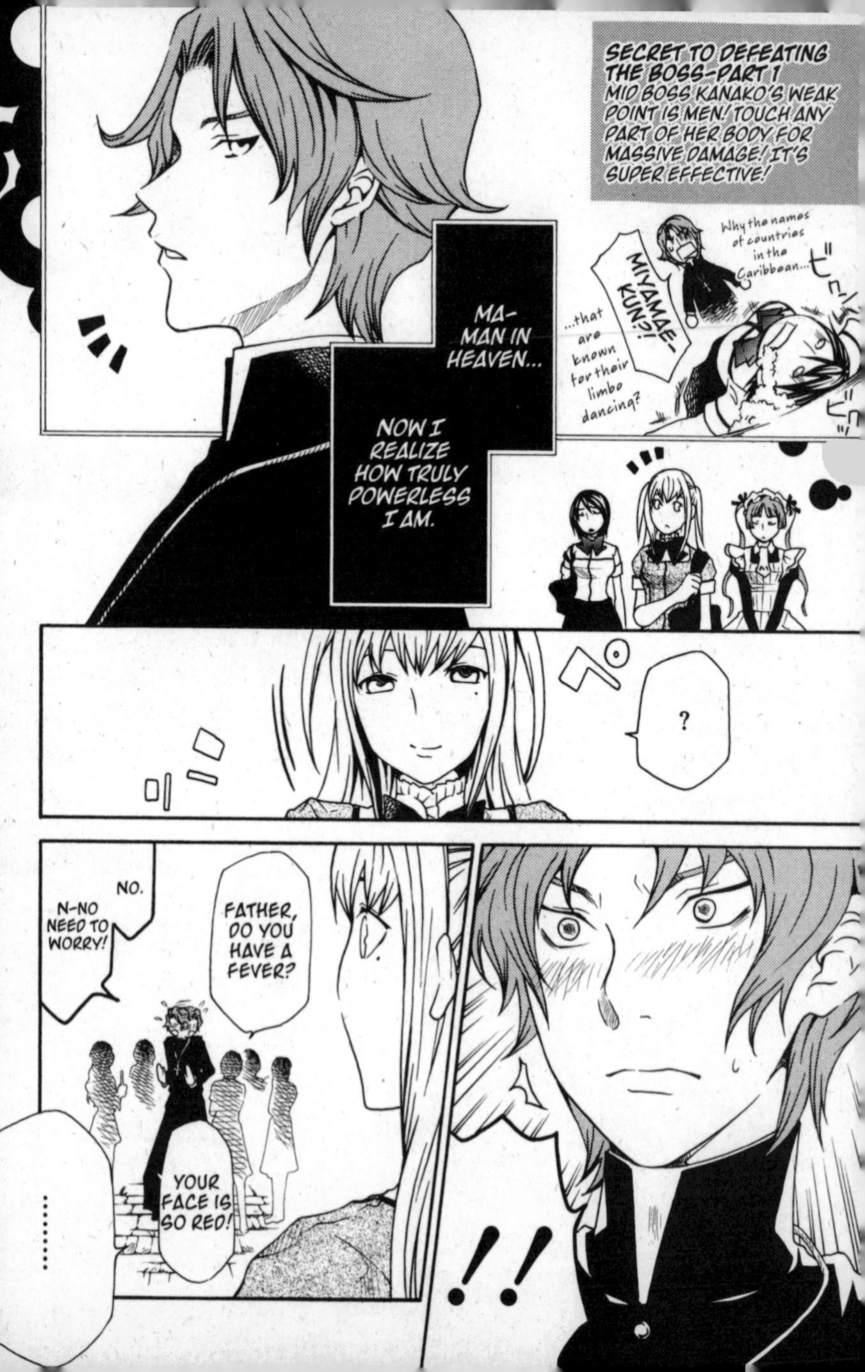
SECRET TO DEFEATING THE BOSS-PART 1
MID BOSS KANAKO'S WEAK POINT IS MEN! TOUCH ANY PART OF HER BODY FOR MASSIVE DAMAGE! IT'S SUPER EFFECTIVE!
Why the names of countries in the Caribbean...
...that are known for their limbo dancing?
MIYAMAE-KUN?!
MA-MAN IN HEAVEN...
NOW I REALIZE HOW TRULY POWERLESS I AM.
?
!!
FATHER, DO YOU HAVE A FEVER?
NO.
N-NO NEED TO WORRY!
YOUR FACE IS SO RED!
....

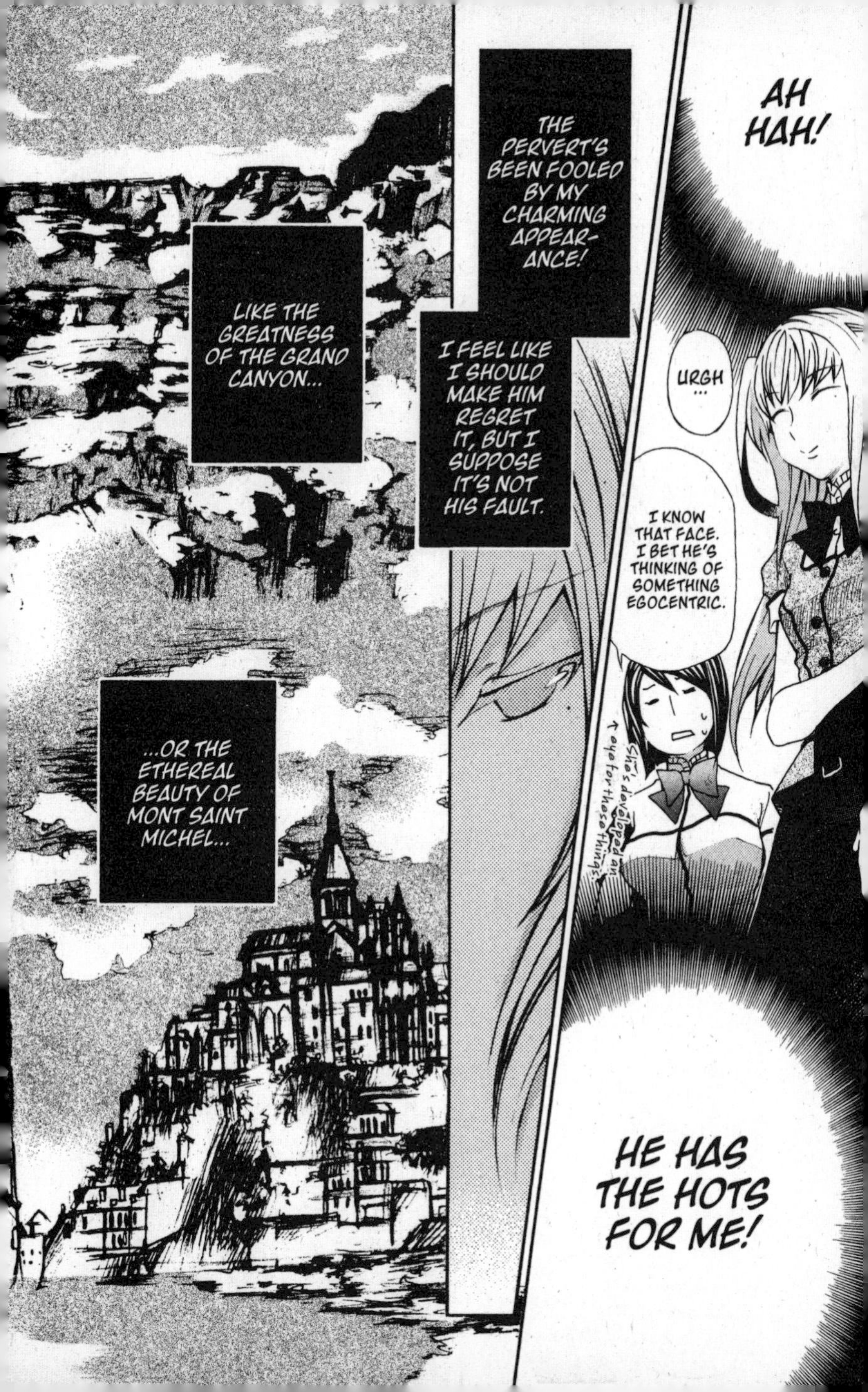
AH HAH!
URGH...
I KNOW THAT FACE. I BET HE'S THINKING OF SOMETHING EGOCENTRIC.
← She's developed an eye for those things.
HE HAS THE HOTS FOR ME!
THE PERVERT'S BEEN FOOLED BY MY CHARMING APPEAR-ANCE!
I FEEL LIKE I SHOULD MAKE HIM REGRET IT, BUT I SUPPOSE IT'S NOT HIS FAULT.
LIKE THE GREATNESS OF THE GRAND CANYON...
...OR THE ETHEREAL BEAUTY OF MONT SAINT MICHEL...

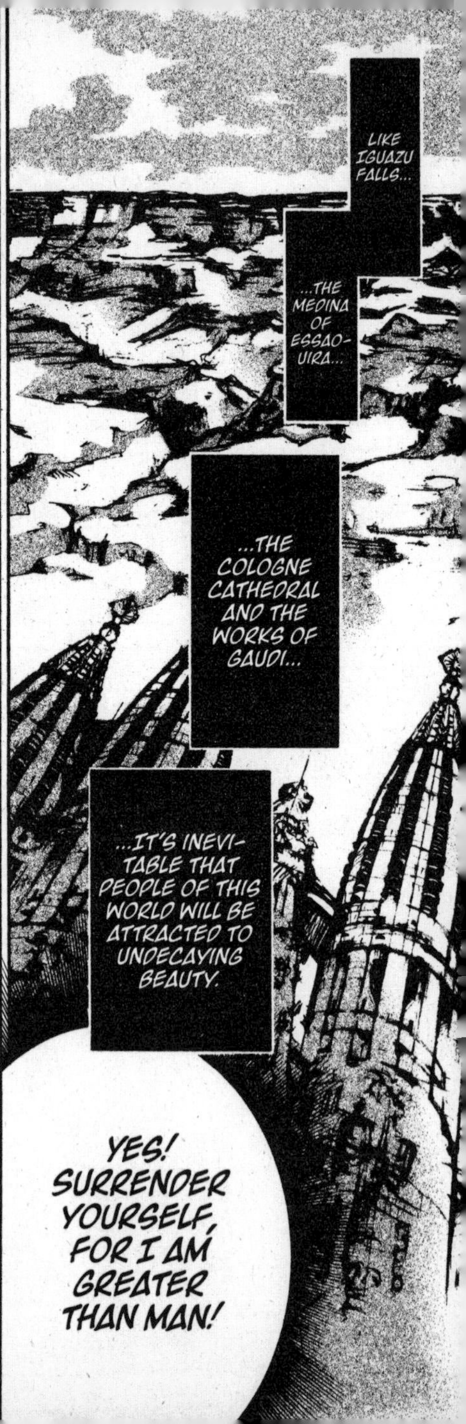
LIKE IGUAZU FALLS...
...THE MEDINA OF ESSAOUIRA...
...THE COLOGNE CATHEDRAL AND THE WORKS OF GAUDI...
...IT'S INEVITABLE THAT PEOPLE OF THIS WORLD WILL BE ATTRACTED TO UNDECAYING BEAUTY.
YES! SURRENDER YOURSELF, FOR I AM GREATER THAN MAN!
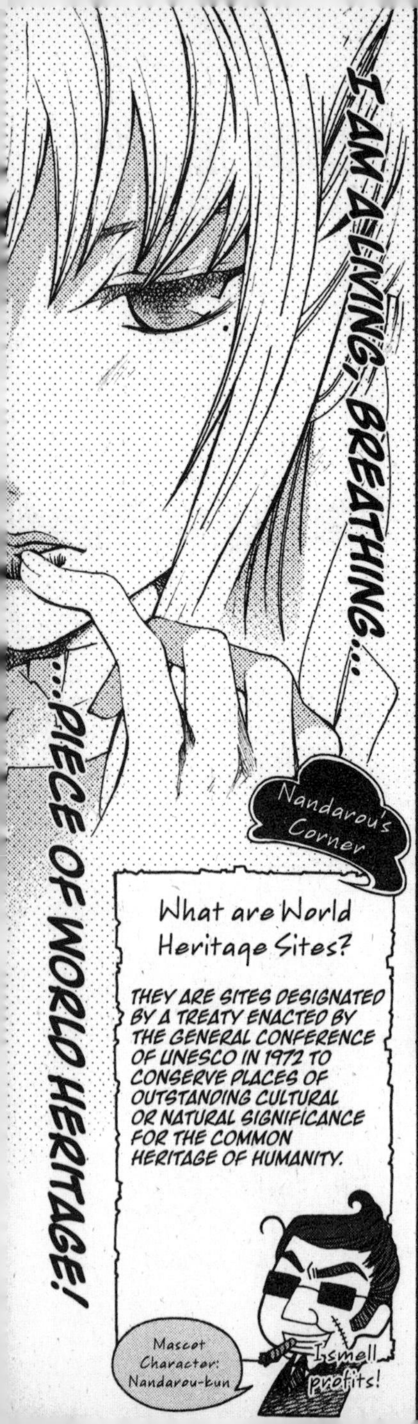
I AM A LIVING, BREATHING...
...PIECE OF WORLD HERITAGE!
Nandarou's Corner
What are World Heritage Sites?
THEY ARE SITES DESIGNATED BY A TREATY ENACTED BY THE GENERAL CONFERENCE OF UNESCO IN 1972 TO CONSERVE PLACES OF OUTSTANDING CULTURAL OR NATURAL SIGNIFICANCE FOR THE COMMON HERITAGE OF HUMANITY.
I smell profits!
Mascot Character: Nandarou-kun

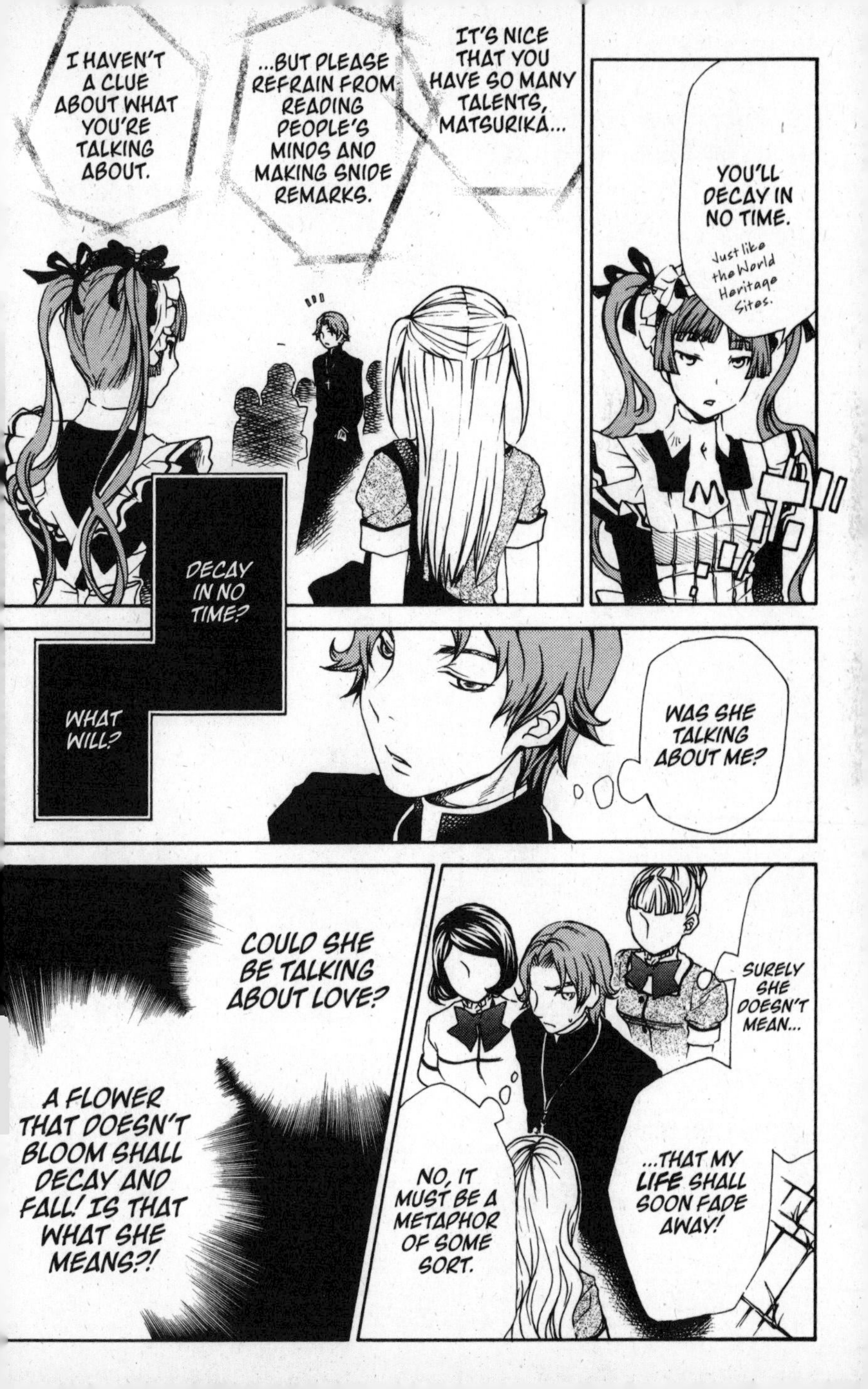
YOU'LL DECAY IN NO TIME.
Just like the World Heritage Sites.
IT'S NICE THAT YOU HAVE SO MANY TALENTS, MATSURIKA...
...BUT PLEASE REFRAIN FROM READING PEOPLE'S MINDS AND MAKING SNIDE REMARKS.
I HAVEN'T A CLUE ABOUT WHAT YOU'RE TALKING ABOUT.
DECAY IN NO TIME?
WHAT WILL?
WAS SHE TALKING ABOUT ME?
SURELY SHE DOESN'T MEAN...
...THAT MY LIFE SHALL SOON FADE AWAY!
NO, IT MUST BE A METAPHOR OF SOME SORT.
COULD SHE BE TALKING ABOUT LOVE?
A FLOWER THAT DOESN'T BLOOM SHALL DECAY AND FALL! IS THAT WHAT SHE MEANS?!

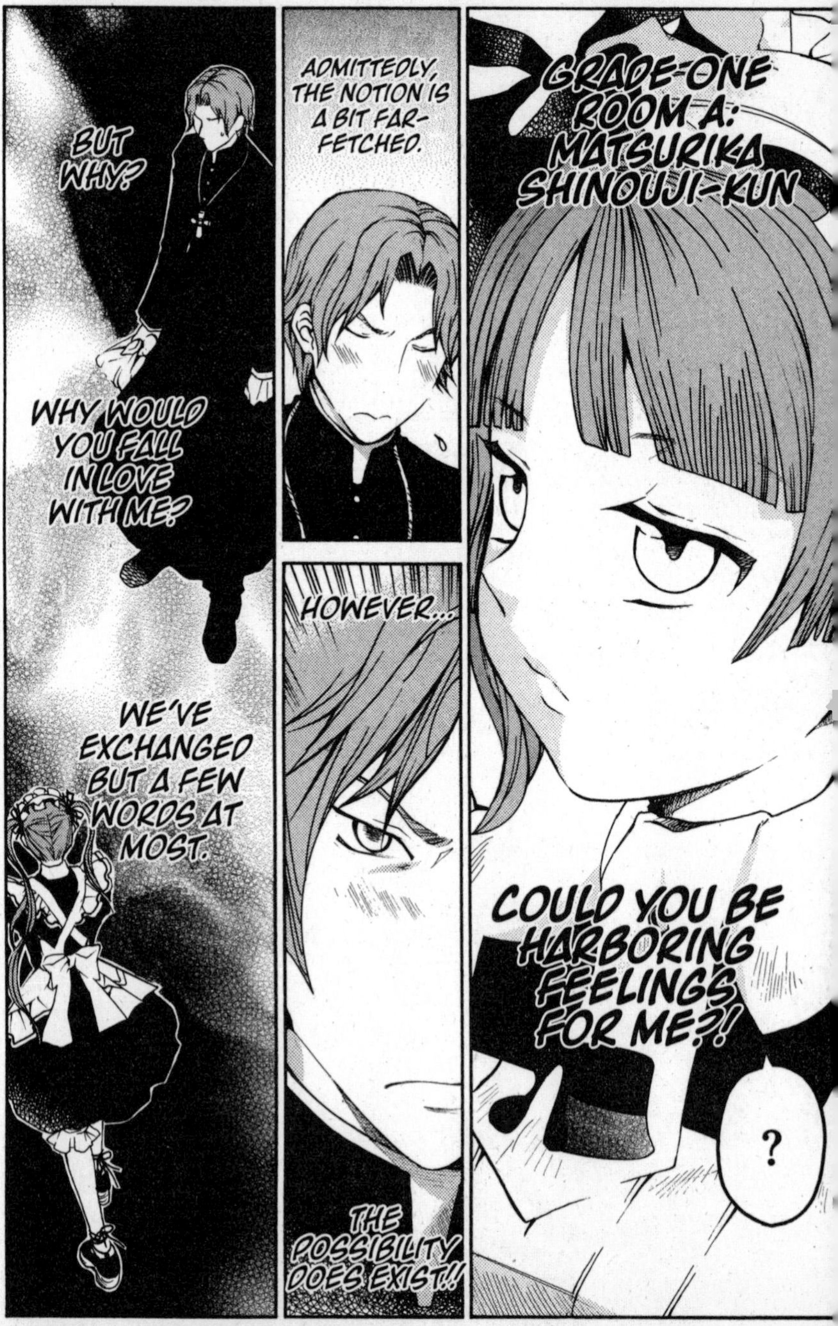
GRADE-ONE ROOM A: MATSURIKA SHINOUJI-KUN
COULD YOU BE HARBORING FEELINGS FOR ME?!
?
ADMITTEDLY, THE NOTION IS A BIT FAR-FETCHED.
HOWEVER...
THE POSSIBILITY DOES EXIST!!
BUT WHY?
WHY WOULD YOU FALL IN LOVE WITH ME?
WE'VE EXCHANGED BUT A FEW WORDS AT MOST.

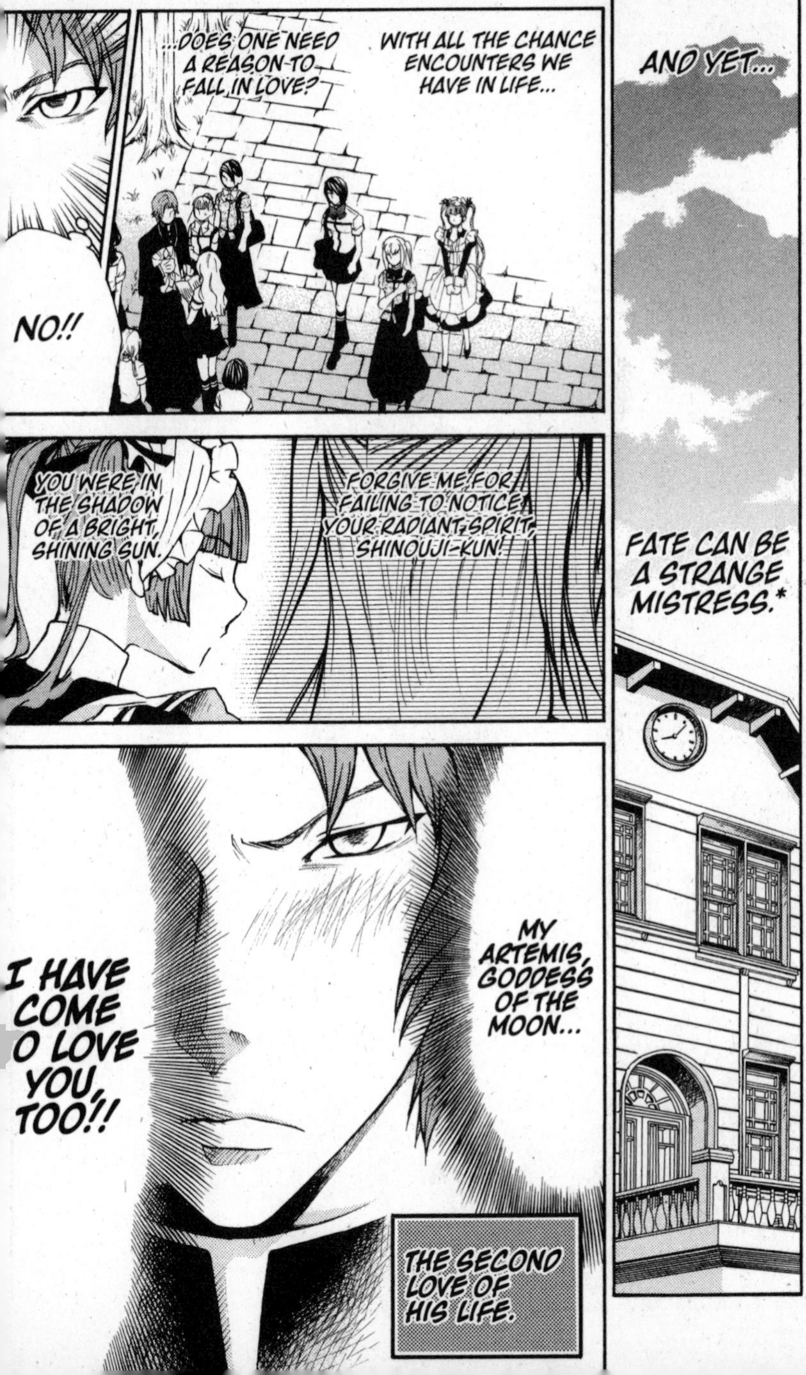
AND YET...
FATE CAN BE A STRANGE MISTRESS.*
WITH ALL THE CHANCE ENCOUNTERS WE HAVE IN LIFE...
...DOES ONE NEED A REASON TO FALL IN LOVE?
NO!!
FORGIVE ME FOR FAILING TO NOTICE YOUR RADIANT SPIRIT, SHINOUJI-KUN!
YOU WERE IN THE SHADOW OF A BRIGHT, SHINING SUN.
MY ARTEMIS, GODDESS OF THE MOON...
I HAVE COME O LOVE YOU, TOO!!
THE SECOND LOVE OF HIS LIFE.

*Meaning that you never know what might bring a man and a woman together.

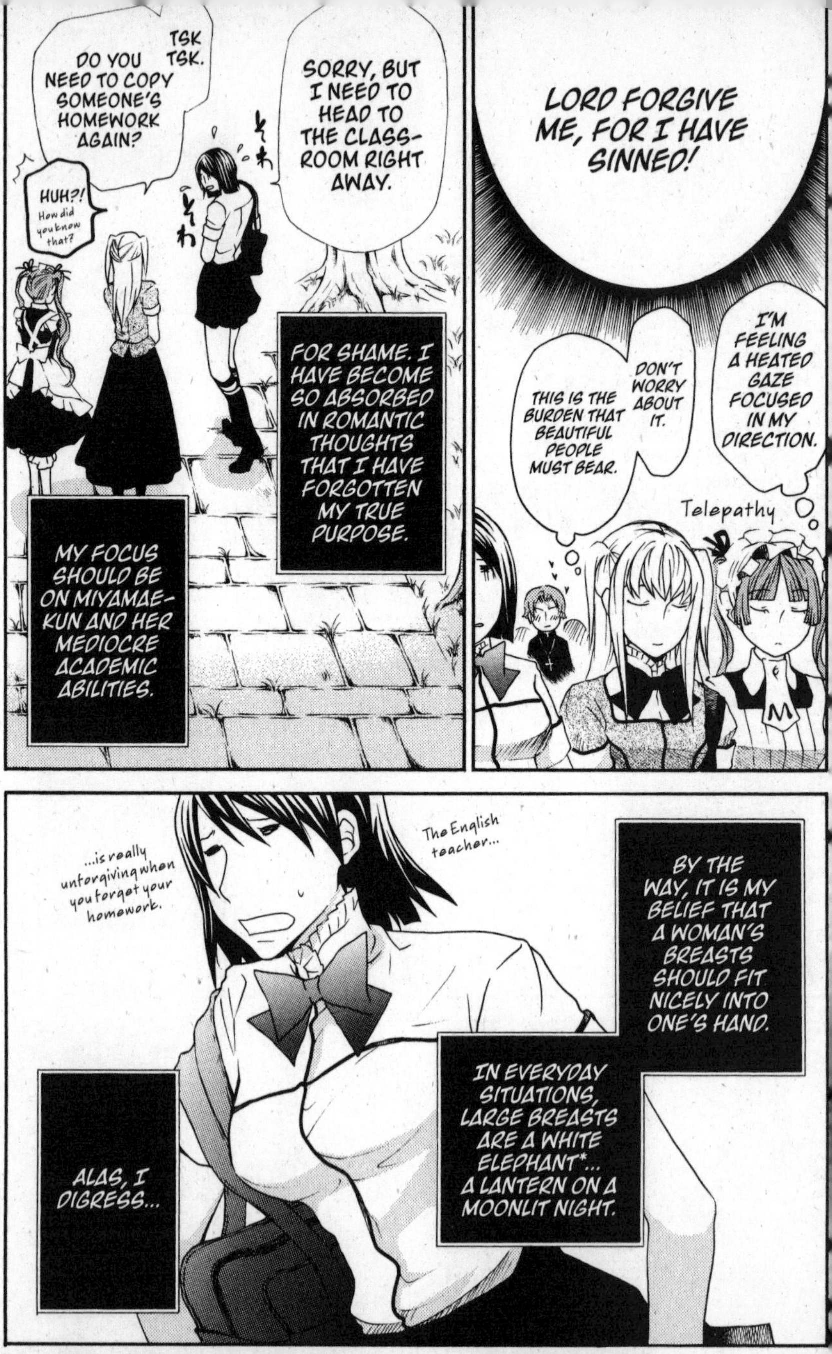
LORD FORGIVE ME, FOR I HAVE SINNED!
I'M FEELING A HEATED GAZE FOCUSED IN MY DIRECTION.
DON'T WORRY ABOUT IT.
THIS IS THE BURDEN THAT BEAUTIFUL PEOPLE MUST BEAR.
Telepathy
SORRY, BUT I NEED TO HEAD TO THE CLASS-ROOM RIGHT AWAY.
そわ そわ
TSK TSK.
DO YOU NEED TO COPY SOMEONE'S HOMEWORK AGAIN?
HUH?! How did you know that?
FOR SHAME. I HAVE BECOME SO ABSORBED IN ROMANTIC THOUGHTS THAT I HAVE FORGOTTEN MY TRUE PURPOSE.
MY FOCUS SHOULD BE ON MIYAMAE-KUN AND HER MEDIOCRE ACADEMIC ABILITIES.
BY THE WAY, IT IS MY BELIEF THAT A WOMAN'S BREASTS SHOULD FIT NICELY INTO ONE'S HAND.
The English teacher...
...is really unforgiving when you forget your homework.
IN EVERYDAY SITUATIONS, LARGE BREASTS ARE A WHITE ELEPHANT*... A LANTERN ON A MOONLIT NIGHT.
ALAS, I DIGRESS...

*White elephants and lanterns on a moonlit night both indicate something superfluous or useless.

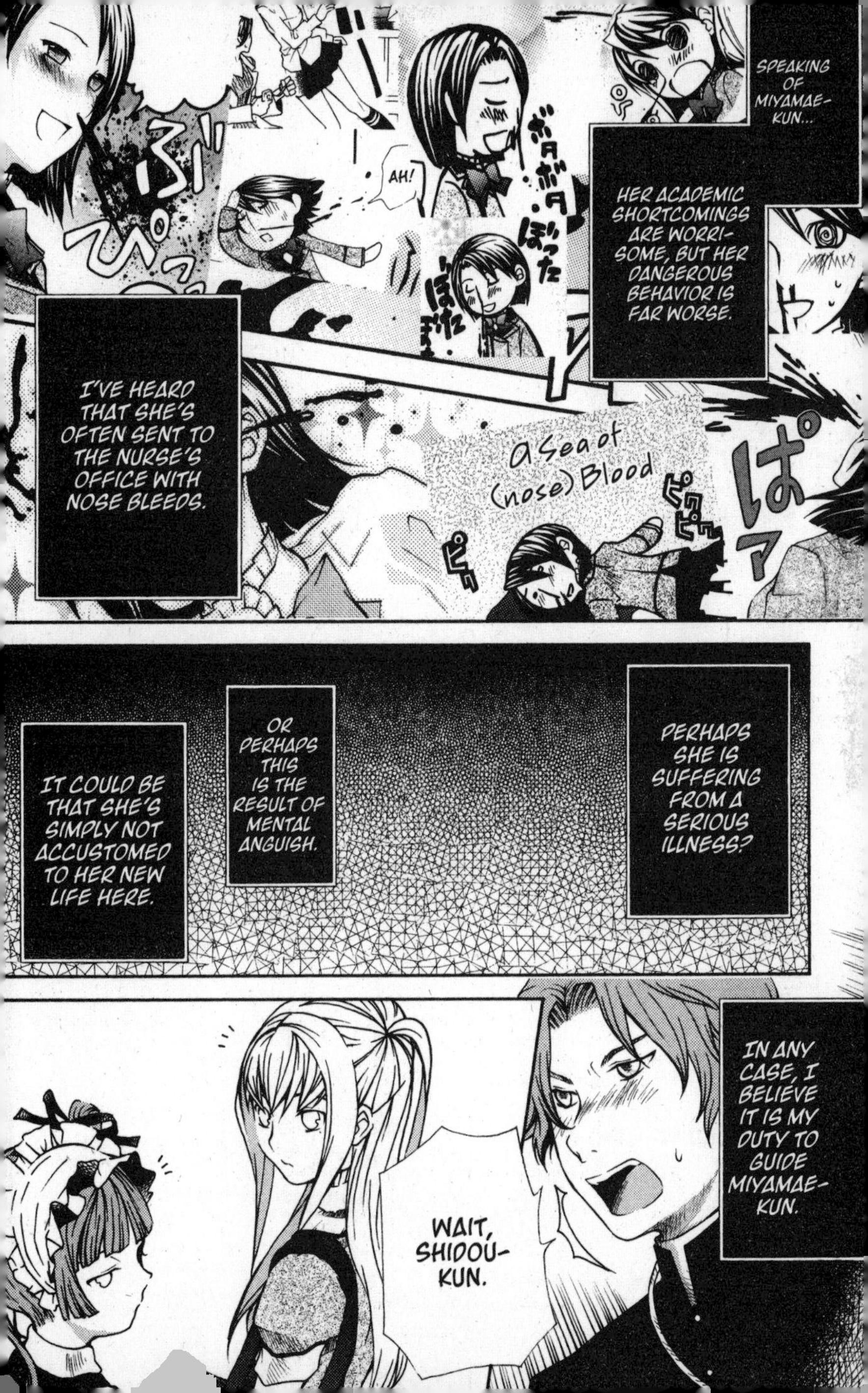
SPEAKING OF MIYAMAE-KUN...
HER ACADEMIC SHORTCOMINGS ARE WORRISOME, BUT HER DANGEROUS BEHAVIOR IS FAR WORSE.
AH!
I'VE HEARD THAT SHE'S OFTEN SENT TO THE NURSE'S OFFICE WITH NOSE BLEEDS.
A Sea of (nose) Blood
PERHAPS SHE IS SUFFERING FROM A SERIOUS ILLNESS?
OR PERHAPS THIS IS THE RESULT OF MENTAL ANGUISH.
IT COULD BE THAT SHE'S SIMPLY NOT ACCUSTOMED TO HER NEW LIFE HERE.
IN ANY CASE, I BELIEVE IT IS MY DUTY TO GUIDE MIYAMAE-KUN.
WAIT, SHIDOU-KUN.

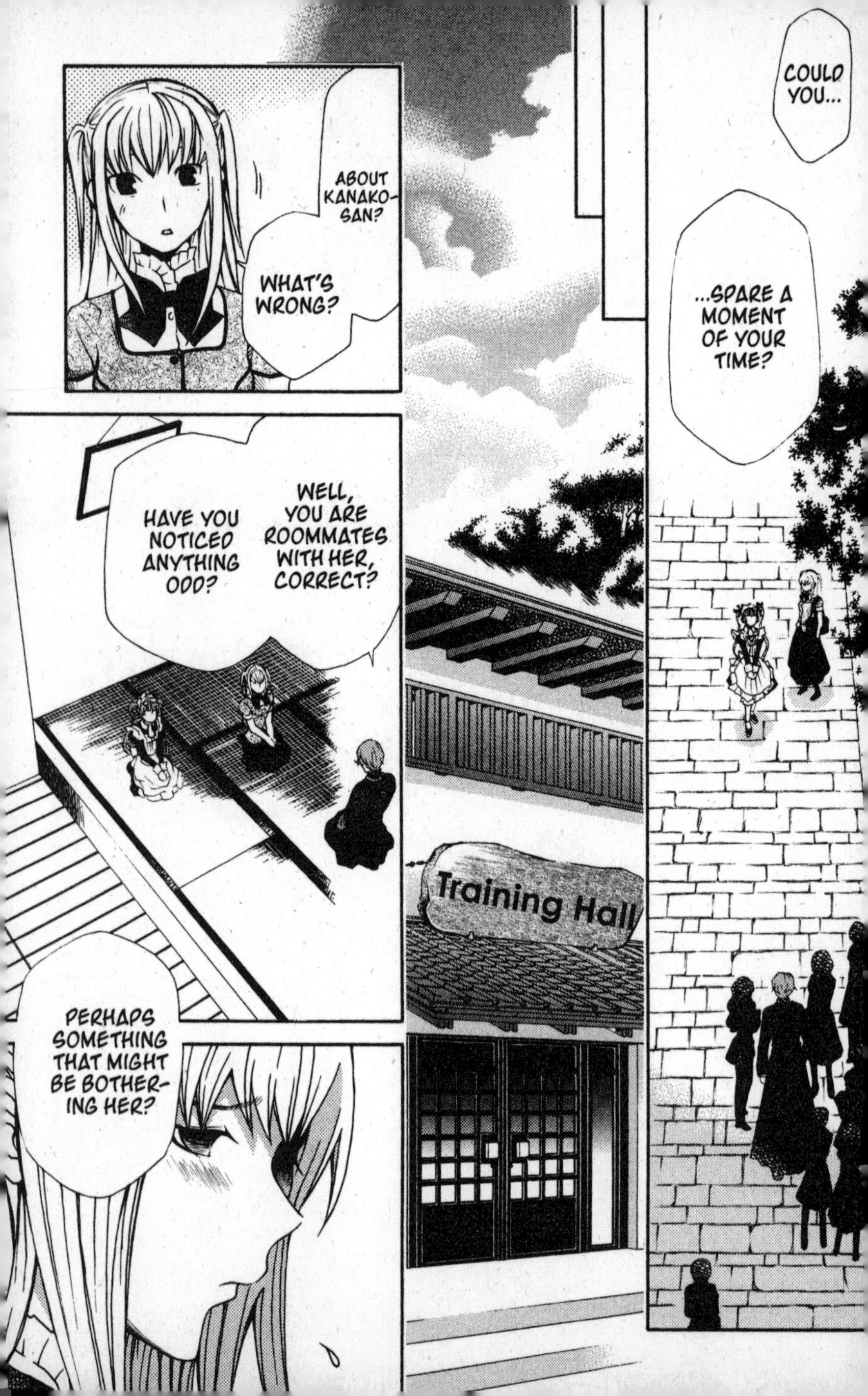
COULD YOU...
...SPARE A MOMENT OF YOUR TIME?
Training Hall
ABOUT KANAKO-SAN?
WHAT'S WRONG?
WELL, YOU ARE ROOMMATES WITH HER, CORRECT?
HAVE YOU NOTICED ANYTHING ODD?
PERHAPS SOMETHING THAT MIGHT BE BOTHERING HER?

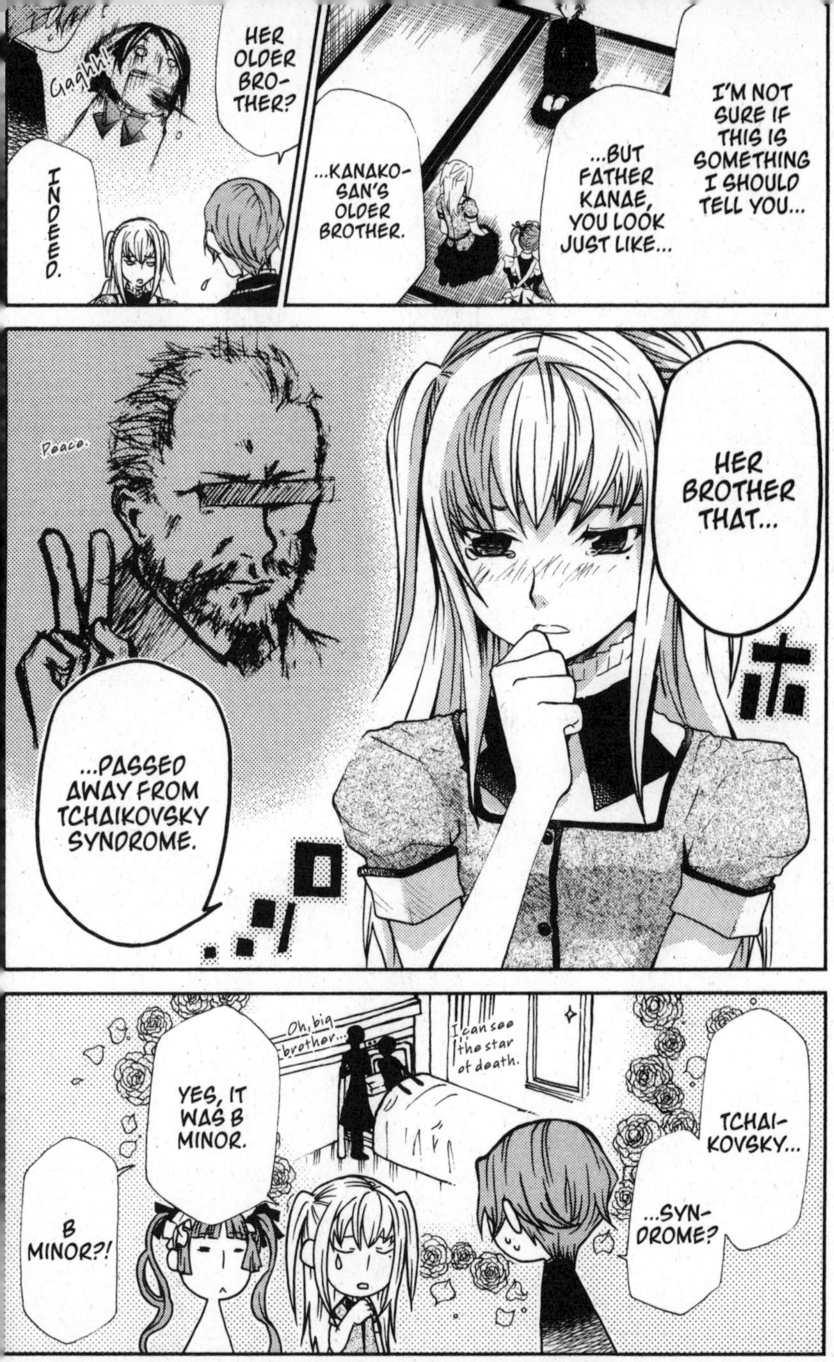
I'M NOT SURE IF THIS IS SOMETHING I SHOULD TELL YOU...
...BUT FATHER KANAE, YOU LOOK JUST LIKE...
...KANAKO-SAN'S OLDER BROTHER.
HER OLDER BRO-THER?
Gaghh!
INDEED.
HER BROTHER THAT...
Peace.
...PASSED AWAY FROM TCHAIKOVSKY SYNDROME.
TCHAI-KOVSKY...
...SYN-DROME?
I can see the star of death.
Oh, big brother...
YES, IT WAS B MINOR.
B MINOR?!

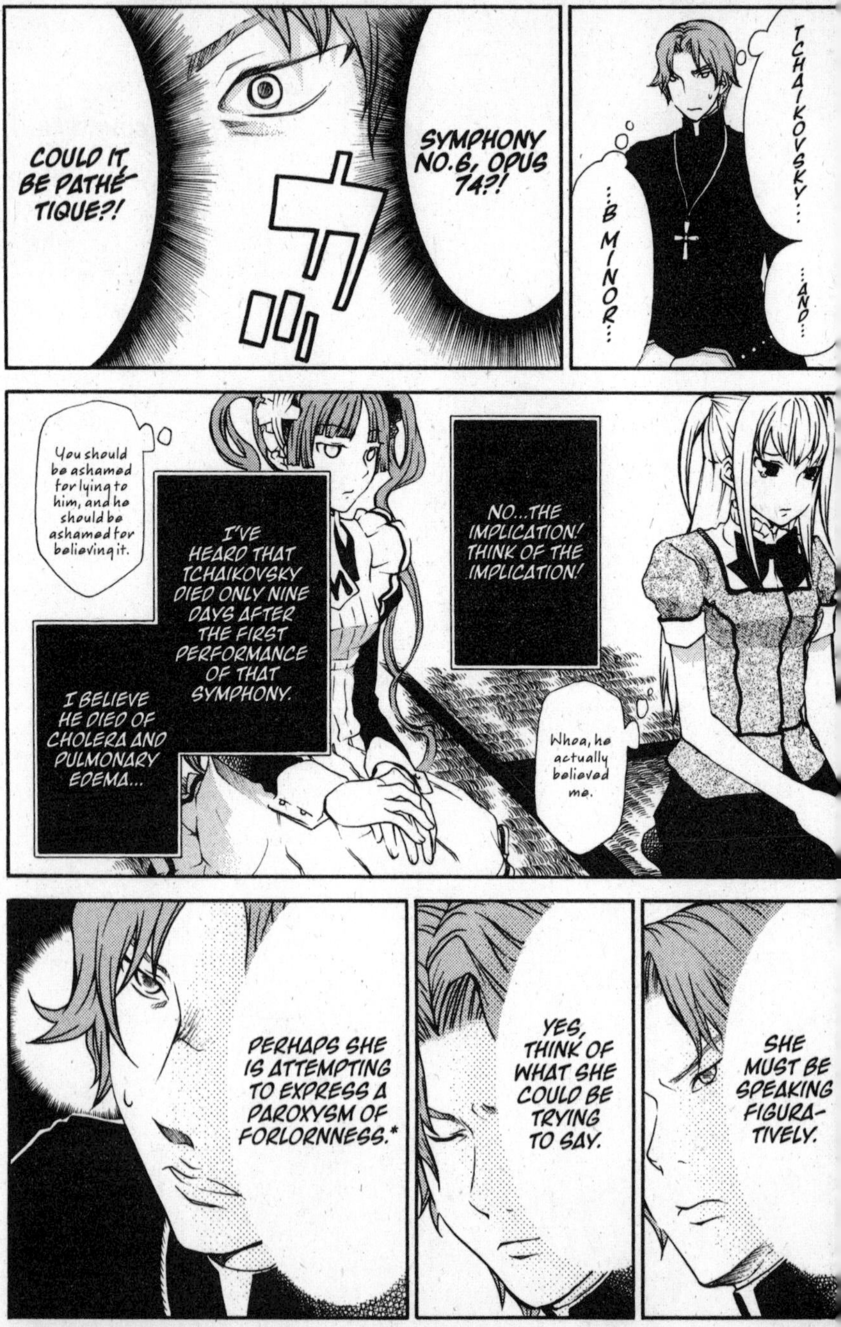
TCHAIKOVSKY...
...AND...
...B MINOR...
SYMPHONY NO.6, OPUS 74?!
COULD IT BE PATHÉTIQUE?!
NO...THE IMPLICATION! THINK OF THE IMPLICATION!
Whoa, he actually believed me.
I'VE HEARD THAT TCHAIKOVSKY DIED ONLY NINE DAYS AFTER THE FIRST PERFORMANCE OF THAT SYMPHONY.
You should be ashamed for lying to him, and he should be ashamed for believing it.
I BELIEVE HE DIED OF CHOLERA AND PULMONARY EDEMA...
SHE MUST BE SPEAKING FIGURATIVELY.
YES, THINK OF WHAT SHE COULD BE TRYING TO SAY.
PERHAPS SHE IS ATTEMPTING TO EXPRESS A PAROXYSM OF FORLORNNESS.*

*Meaning that she's lonely.

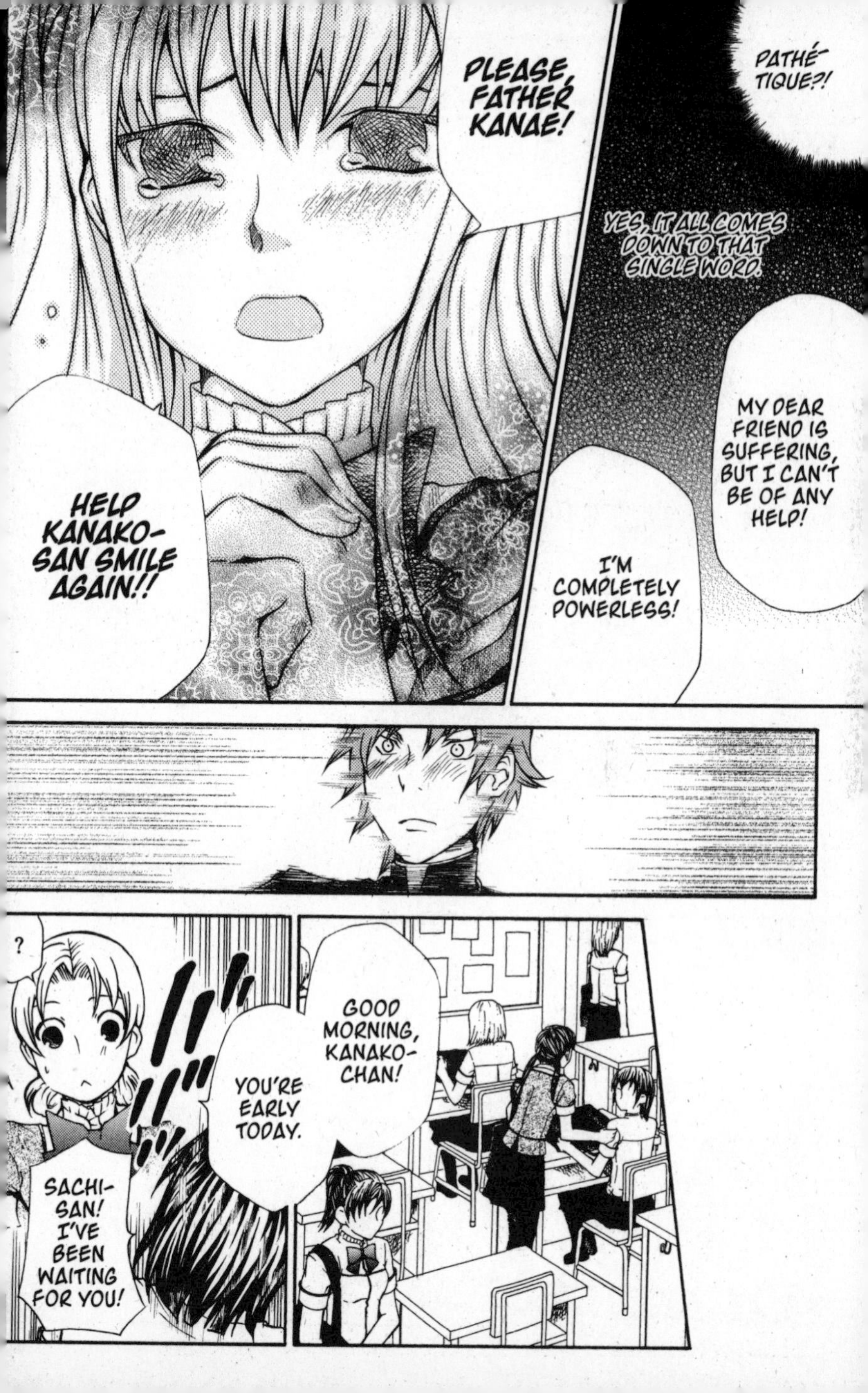
PATHÉ-TIQUE?!
YES, IT ALL COMES DOWN TO THAT SINGLE WORD.
MY DEAR FRIEND IS SUFFERING, BUT I CAN'T BE OF ANY HELP!
I'M COMPLETELY POWERLESS!
PLEASE, FATHER KANAE!
HELP KANAKO-SAN SMILE AGAIN!!
GOOD MORNING, KANAKO-CHAN!
YOU'RE EARLY TODAY.
?
SACHI-SAN! I'VE BEEN WAITING FOR YOU!

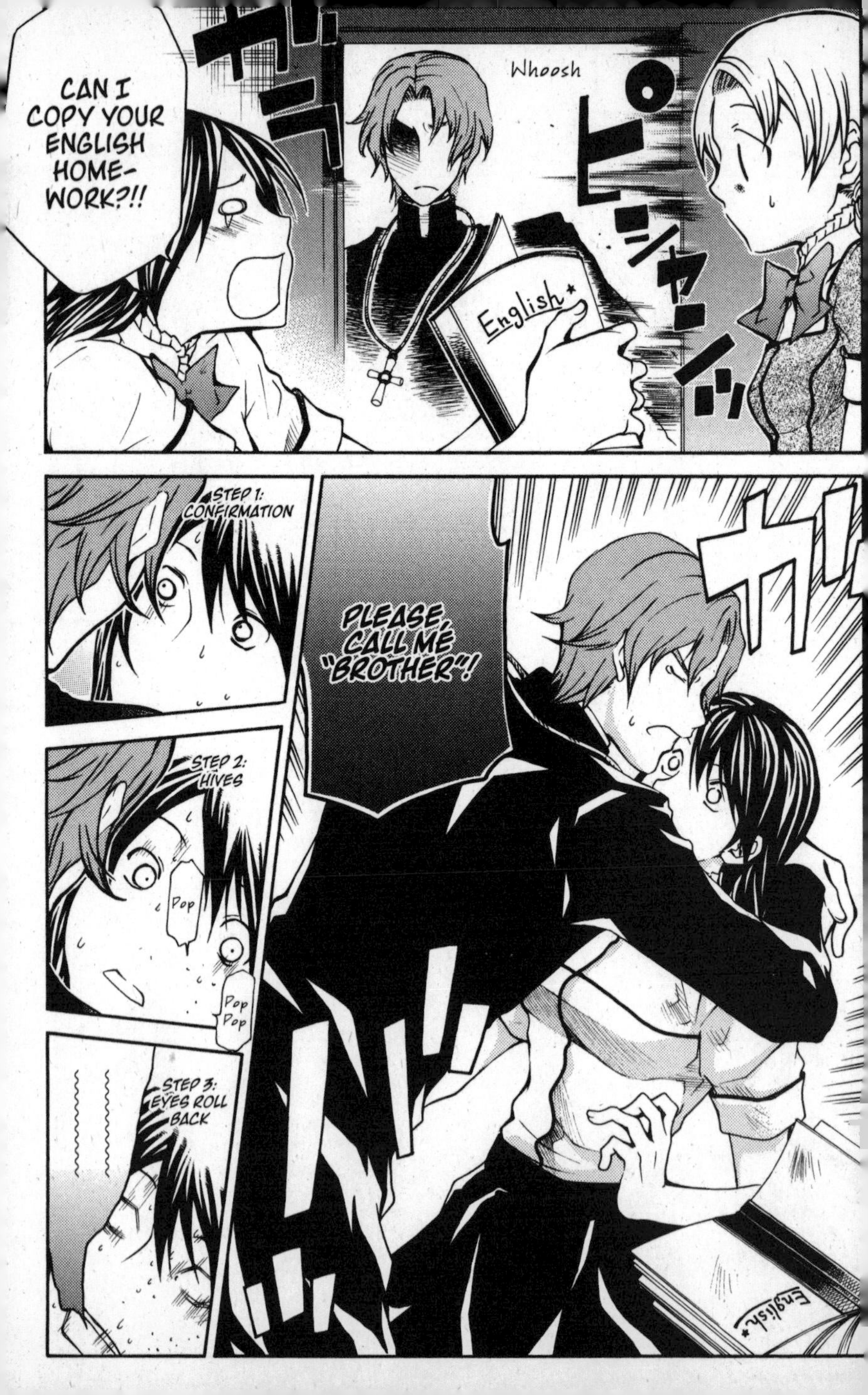
Whoosh
CAN I COPY YOUR ENGLISH HOME-WORK?!!
English
PLEASE, CALL ME "BROTHER"!
English
STEP 1: CONFIRMATION
STEP 2: HIVES
Pop
Pop Pop
STEP 3: EYES ROLL BACK

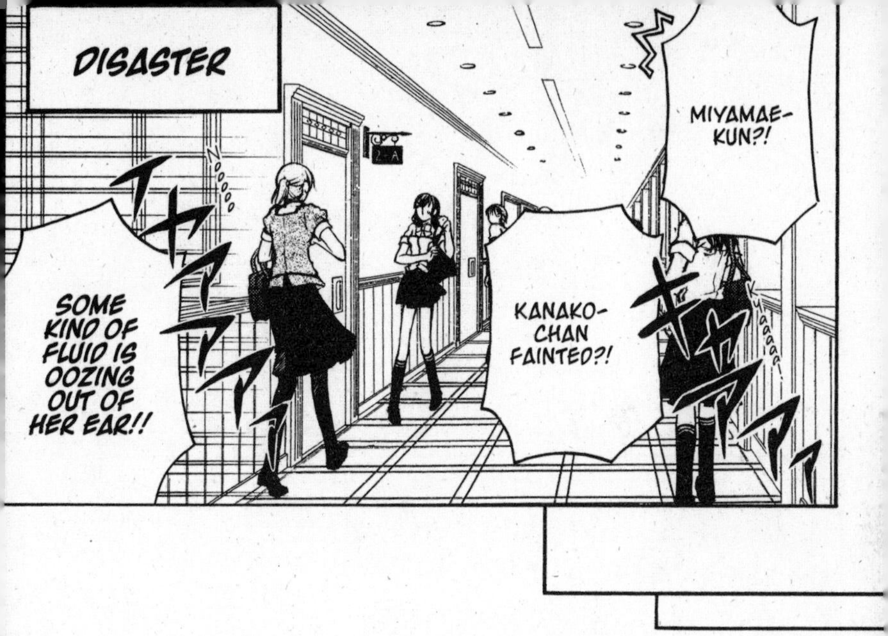
MIYAMAE-KUN?!
KANAKO-CHAN FAINTED?!
SOME KIND OF FLUID IS OOZING OUT OF HER EAR!!
DISASTER

*Meaning someone who has become weak and lost weight.

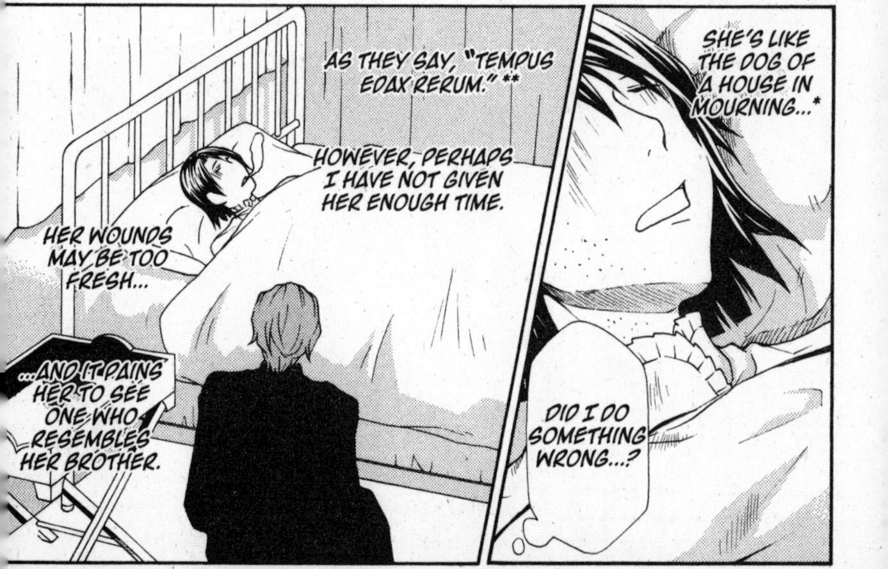
SHE'S LIKE THE DOG OF A HOUSE IN MOURNING...*
DID I DO SOMETHING WRONG...?
AS THEY SAY, "TEMPUS EDAX RERUM." **
HOWEVER, PERHAPS I HAVE NOT GIVEN HER ENOUGH TIME.
HER WOUNDS MAY BE TOO FRESH...
...AND IT PAINS HER TO SEE ONE WHO RESEMBLES HER BROTHER.

**Time devours all.

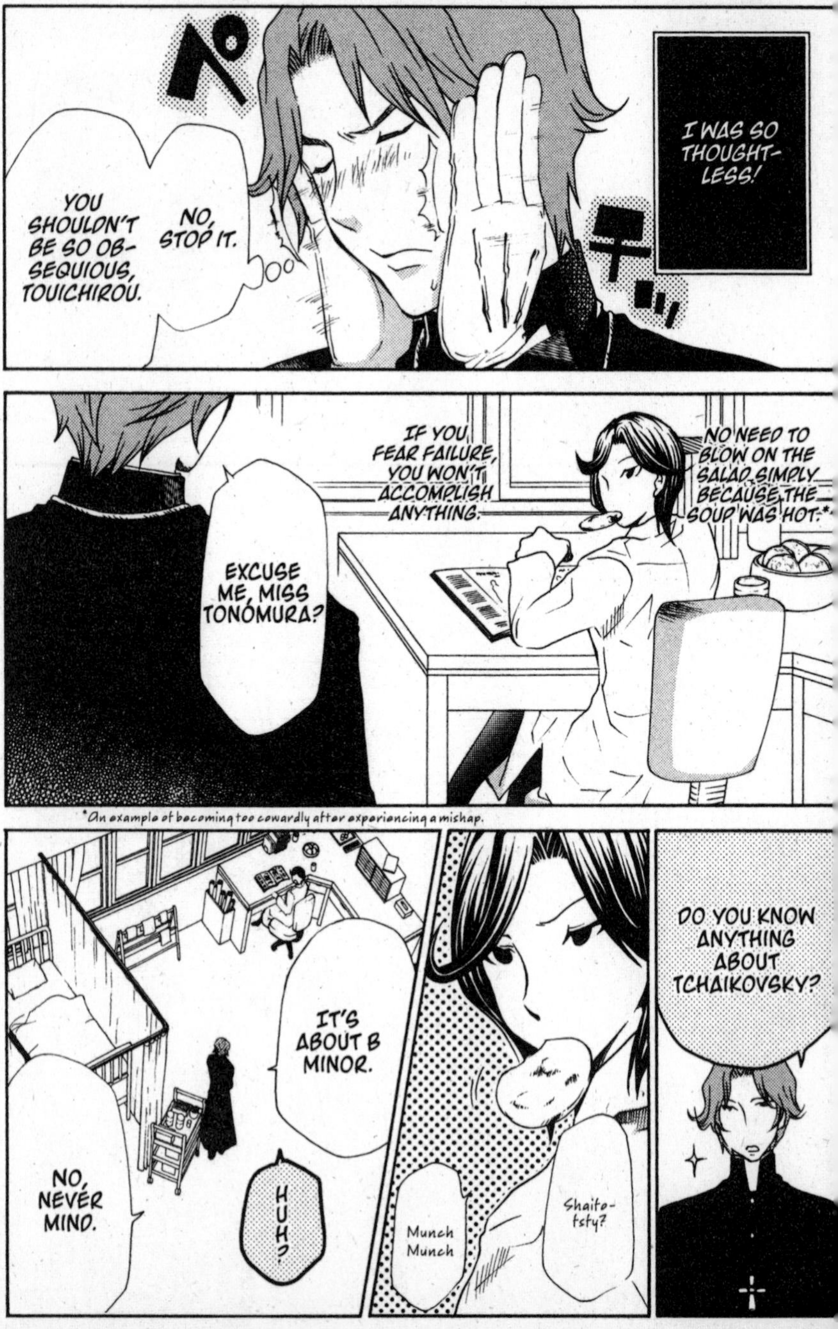
I WAS SO THOUGHT-LESS!
NO, STOP IT.
YOU SHOULDN'T BE SO OB-SEQUIOUS, TOUICHIROU.
NO NEED TO BLOW ON THE SALAD SIMPLY BECAUSE THE SOUP WAS HOT.*
IF YOU FEAR FAILURE, YOU WON'T ACCOMPLISH ANYTHING.
EXCUSE ME, MISS TONOMURA?
DO YOU KNOW ANYTHING ABOUT TCHAIKOVSKY?
Shaito-tsty?
Munch Munch
IT'S ABOUT B MINOR.
HUH?
NO, NEVER MIND.

*An example of becoming too cowardly after experiencing a mishap.

*The Japanese saying, "To ask is a shame of the moment, to not ask is a shame of a lifetime" means if you don't ask, you'll end up never knowing.

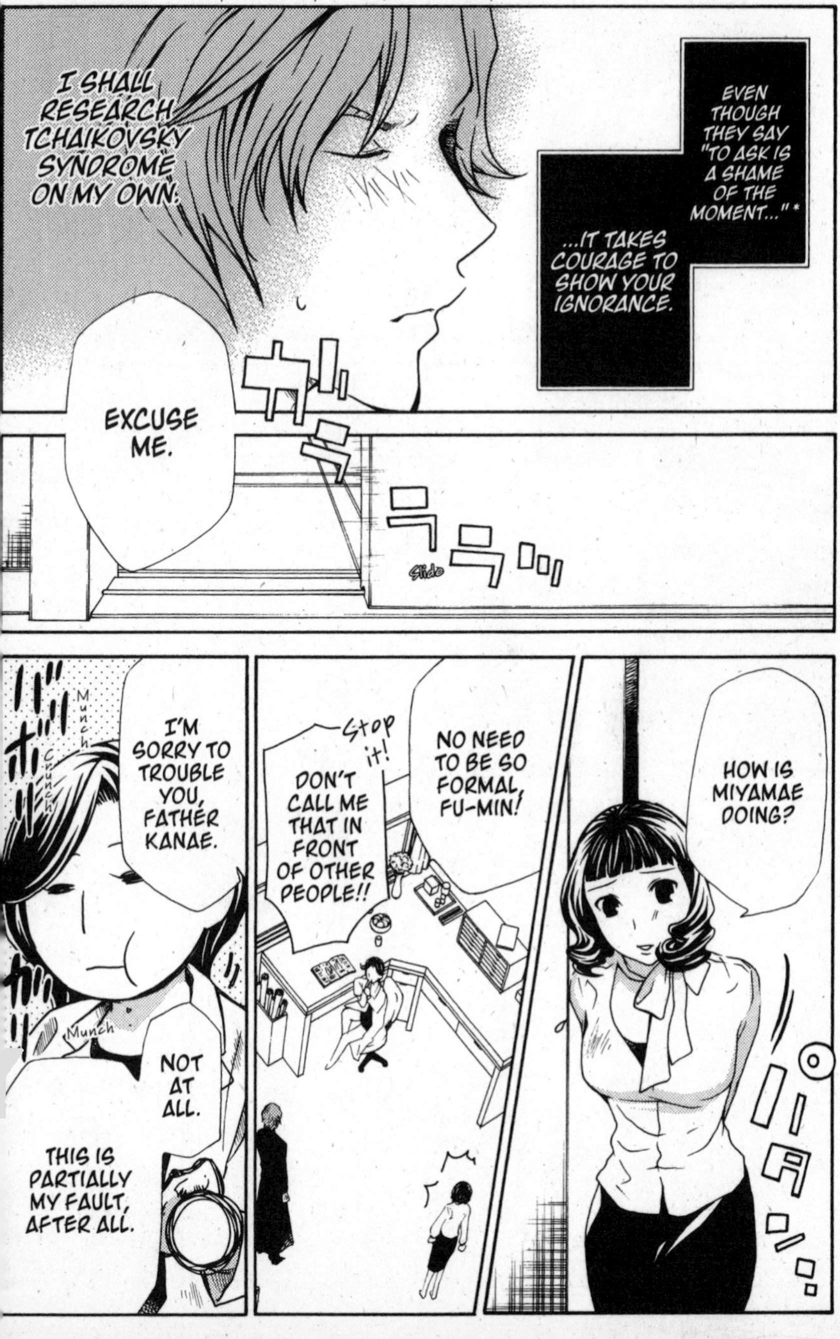
EVEN THOUGH THEY SAY "TO ASK IS A SHAME OF THE MOMENT..."*
...IT TAKES COURAGE TO SHOW YOUR IGNORANCE.
I SHALL RESEARCH TCHAIKOVSKY SYNDROME ON MY OWN.
EXCUSE ME.
Slide
HOW IS MIYAMAE DOING?
NO NEED TO BE SO FORMAL, FU-MIN!
Stop it!
DON'T CALL ME THAT IN FRONT OF OTHER PEOPLE!!
I'M SORRY TO TROUBLE YOU, FATHER KANAE.
Munch
Crunch
NOT AT ALL.
Munch
THIS IS PARTIALLY MY FAULT, AFTER ALL.

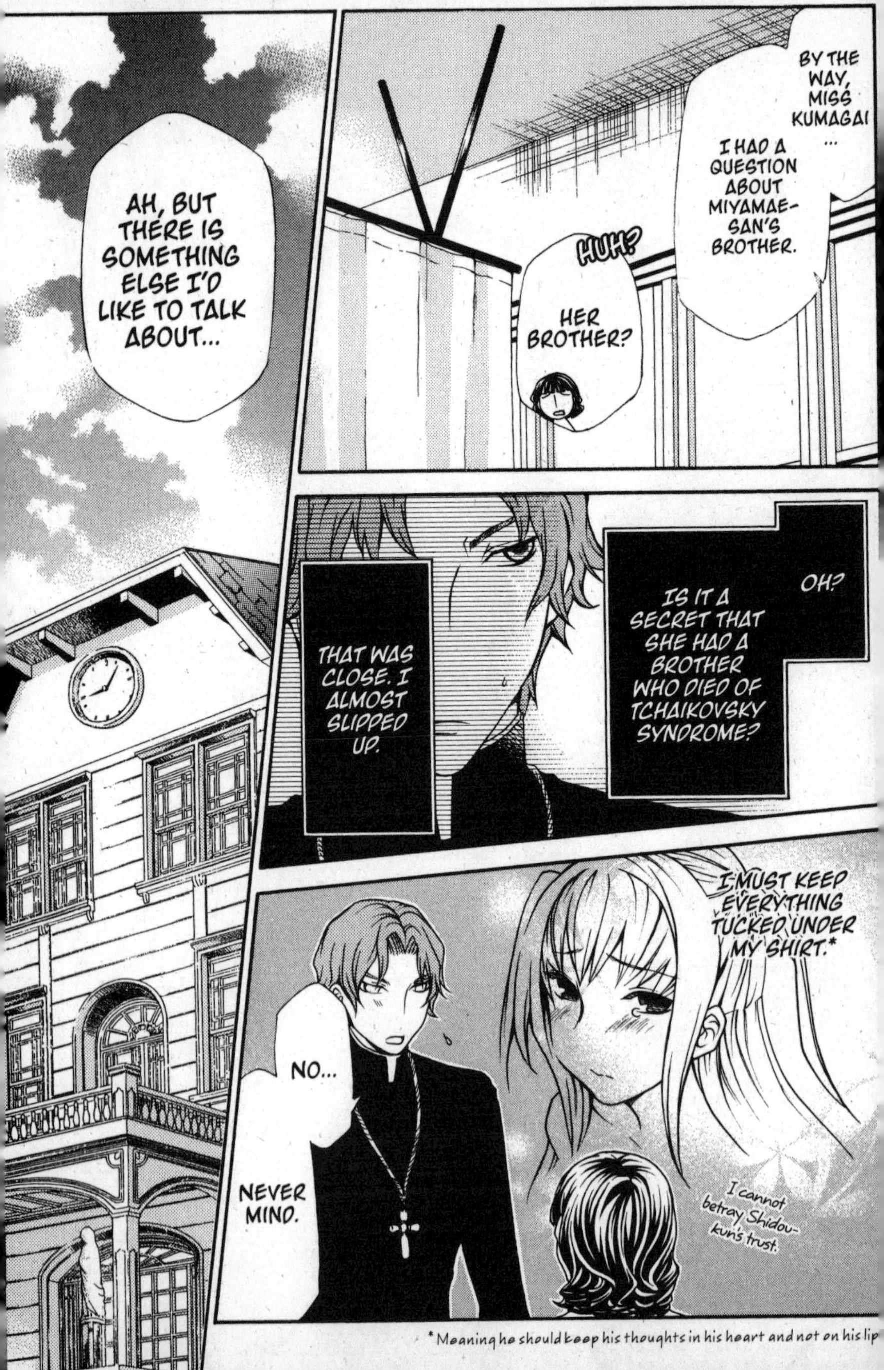
BY THE WAY, MISS KUMAGAI ...
I HAD A QUESTION ABOUT MIYAMAE-SAN'S BROTHER.
HUH?
HER BROTHER?
OH?
IS IT A SECRET THAT SHE HAD A BROTHER WHO DIED OF TCHAIKOVSKY SYNDROME?
THAT WAS CLOSE. I ALMOST SLIPPED UP.
I MUST KEEP EVERYTHING TUCKED UNDER MY SHIRT.*
I cannot betray Shidou-kun's trust.
NO...
NEVER MIND.
AH, BUT THERE IS SOMETHING ELSE I'D LIKE TO TALK ABOUT...

*Meaning he should keep his thoughts in his heart and not on his lip

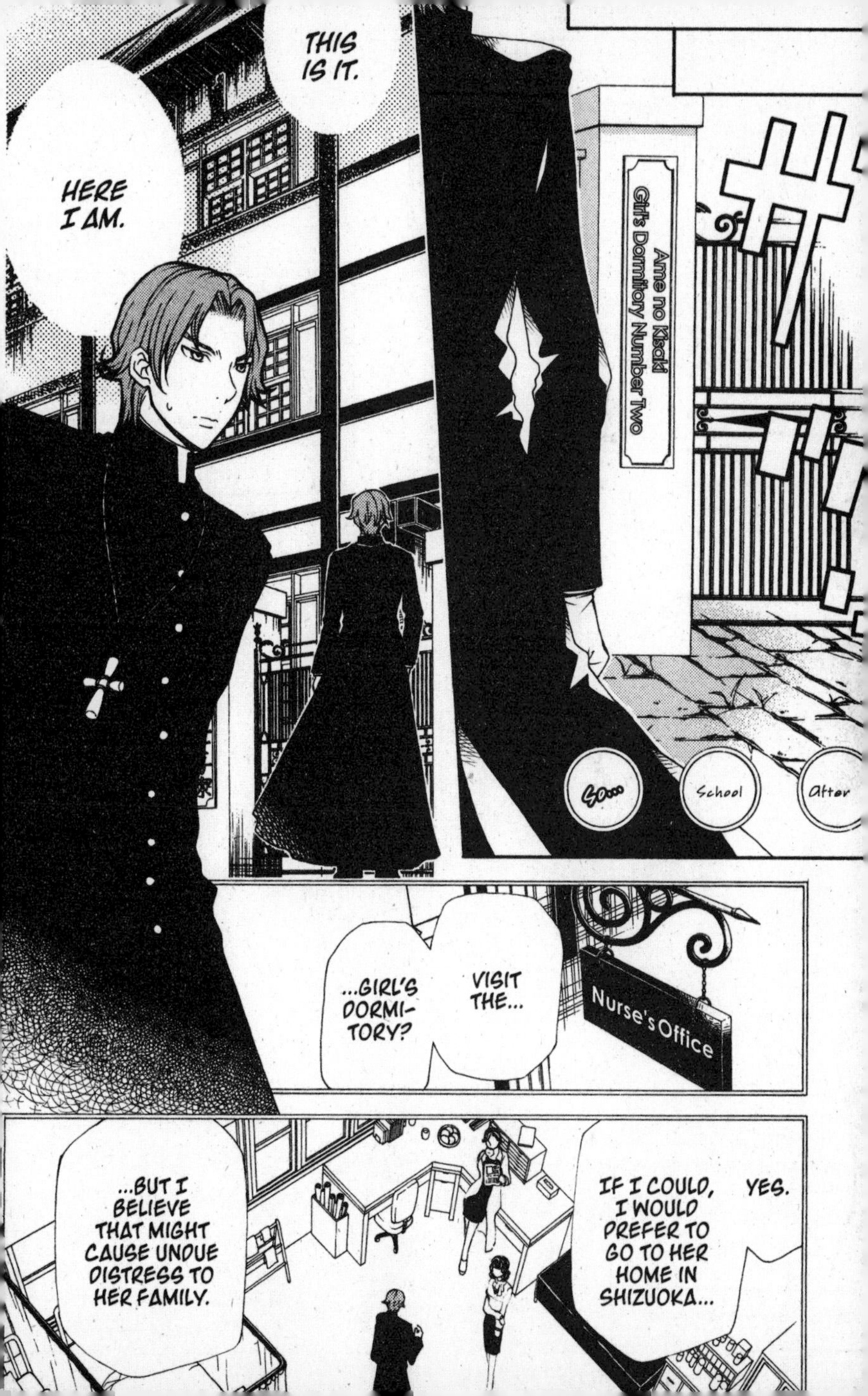
After
School
So...
Ame no Kisaki Girl's Dormitory Number Two
THIS IS IT.
HERE I AM.
Nurse's Office
VISIT THE...
...GIRL'S DORMITORY?
YES.
IF I COULD, I WOULD PREFER TO GO TO HER HOME IN SHIZUOKA...
...BUT I BELIEVE THAT MIGHT CAUSE UNDUE DISTRESS TO HER FAMILY.

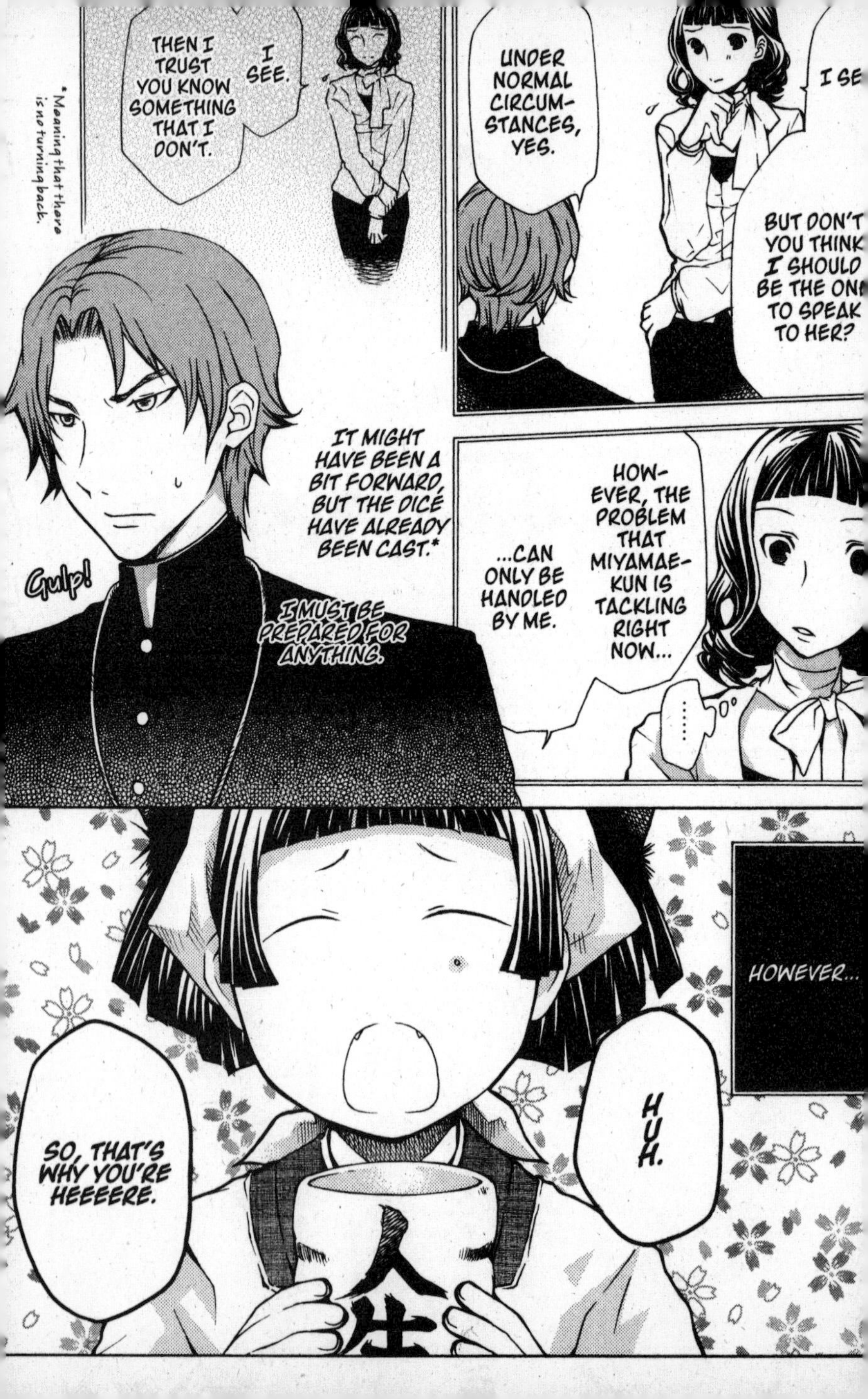
I SE
BUT DON'T YOU THINK I SHOULD BE THE ON TO SPEAK TO HER?
UNDER NORMAL CIRCUM-STANCES, YES.
I SEE.
THEN I TRUST YOU KNOW SOMETHING THAT I DON'T.
*Meaning that there is no turning back.
HOW-EVER, THE PROBLEM THAT MIYAMAE-KUN IS TACKLING RIGHT NOW...
...CAN ONLY BE HANDLED BY ME.
......
IT MIGHT HAVE BEEN A BIT FORWARD, BUT THE DICE HAVE ALREADY BEEN CAST.*
I MUST BE PREPARED FOR ANYTHING.
Gulp!
HOWEVER...
HUH.
SO, THAT'S WHY YOU'RE HEEEERE.

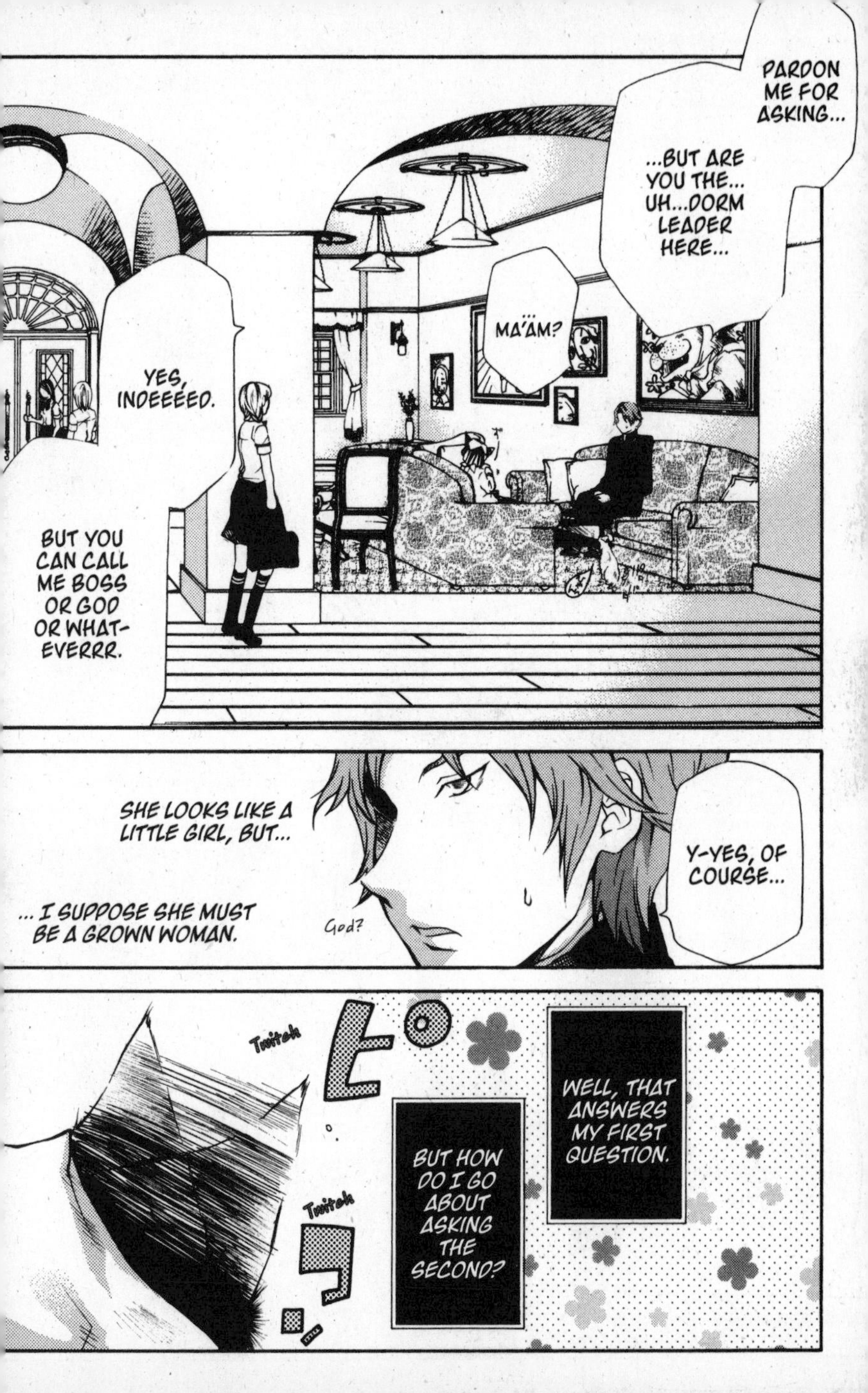
PARDON ME FOR ASKING...
...BUT ARE YOU THE... UH...DORM LEADER HERE...
...MA'AM?
YES, INDEEEEED.
BUT YOU CAN CALL ME BOSS OR GOD OR WHAT-EVERRR.
Y-YES, OF COURSE...
God?
SHE LOOKS LIKE A LITTLE GIRL, BUT...
... I SUPPOSE SHE MUST BE A GROWN WOMAN.
WELL, THAT ANSWERS MY FIRST QUESTION.
BUT HOW DO I GO ABOUT ASKING THE SECOND?
Twitch
Twitch

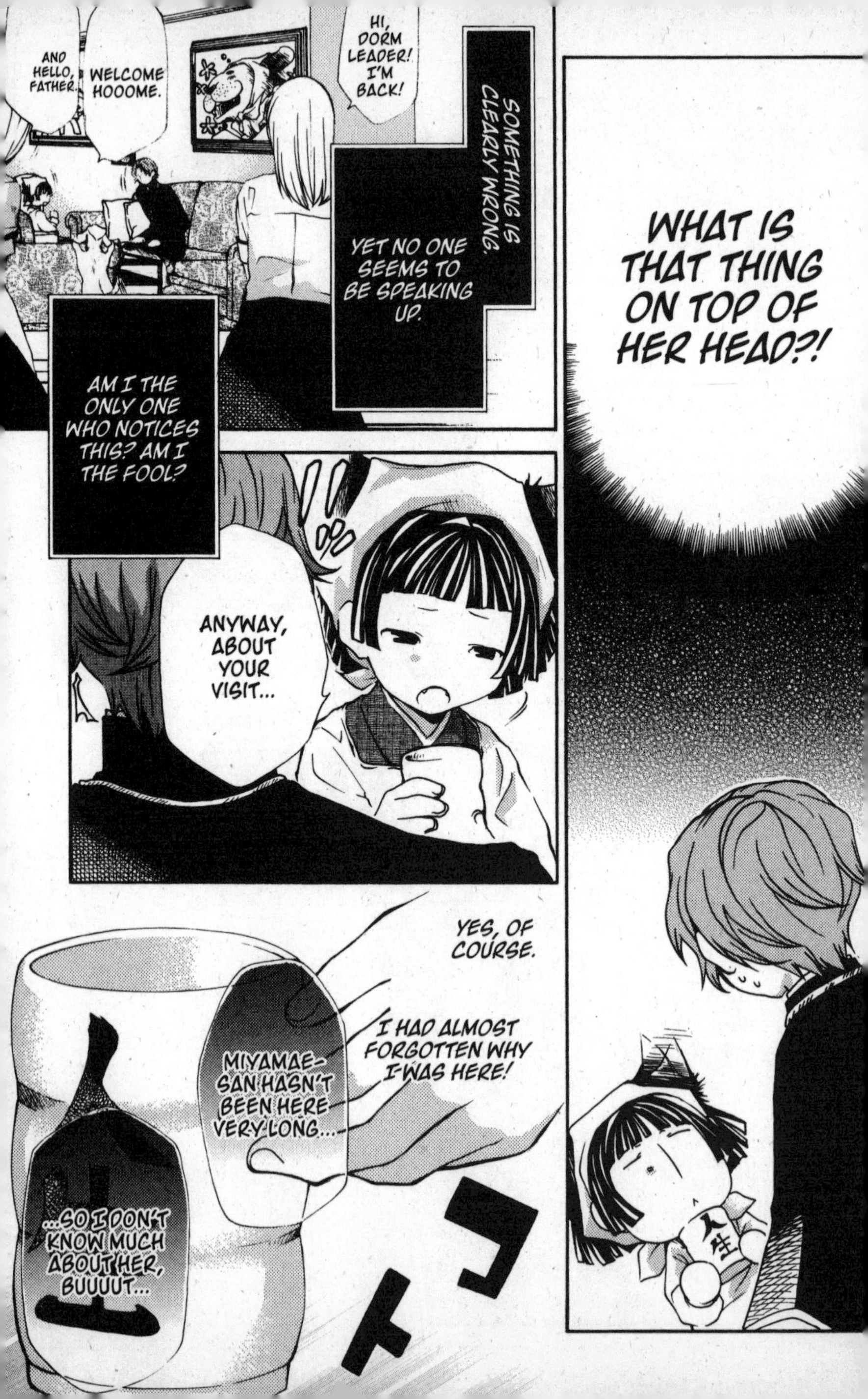
WHAT IS THAT THING ON TOP OF HER HEAD?!
HI, DORM LEADER! I'M BACK!
SOMETHING IS CLEARLY WRONG.
YET NO ONE SEEMS TO BE SPEAKING UP.
WELCOME HOOOME.
AND HELLO, FATHER.
AM I THE ONLY ONE WHO NOTICES THIS? AM I THE FOOL?
ANYWAY, ABOUT YOUR VISIT...
YES, OF COURSE.
I HAD ALMOST FORGOTTEN WHY I WAS HERE!
MIYAMAE-SAN HASN'T BEEN HERE VERY LONG...
...SO I DON'T KNOW MUCH ABOUT HER, BUUUUT...

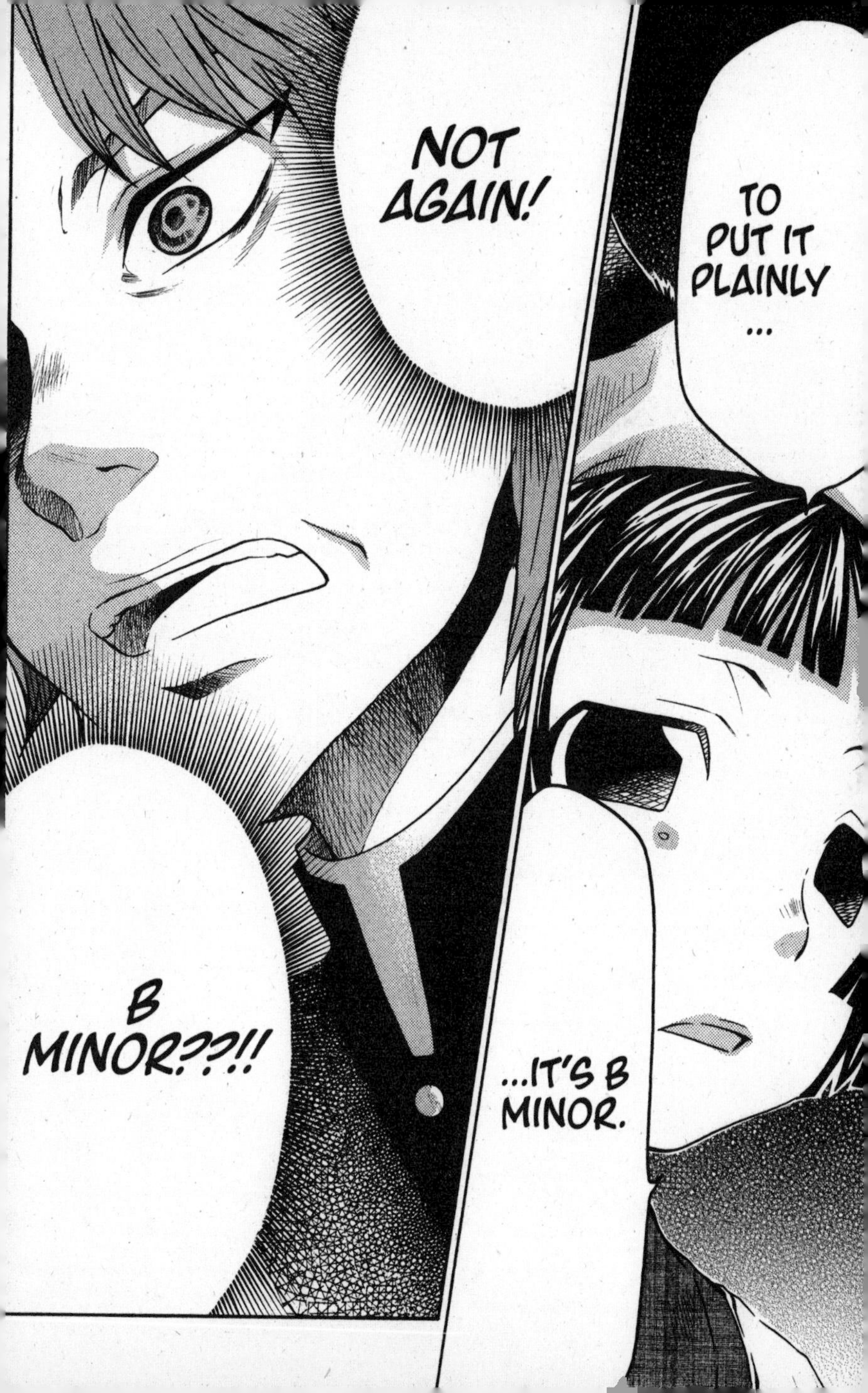
TO PUT IT PLAINLY ...
...IT'S B MINOR.
NOT AGAIN!
B MINOR??!!

TONY AND MYTY

DISCOVER WORLD HERITAGE SITES

T: WOOHOO! THIS VIEW MUST BE OF THE GRAND CANYON. AN UPLIFT OF THE COLORADO PLATEAU WAS CAUSED BY A TECTONIC MOVEMENT THAT BEGAN ABOUT 65 MILLION YEARS AGO.

M: IT'S GOT A SEXY FIGURE, DON'T YOU THINK?

T: SINCE ABOUT 40 MILLION YEARS AGO, THE COLORADO RIVER HAS CARVED AWAY THE AREA TO SHOW MORE STRATA.

M: I LIKE A GAL WHO'S NOT AFRAID TO SHOW A LITTLE STRATA.

Maria†Holic

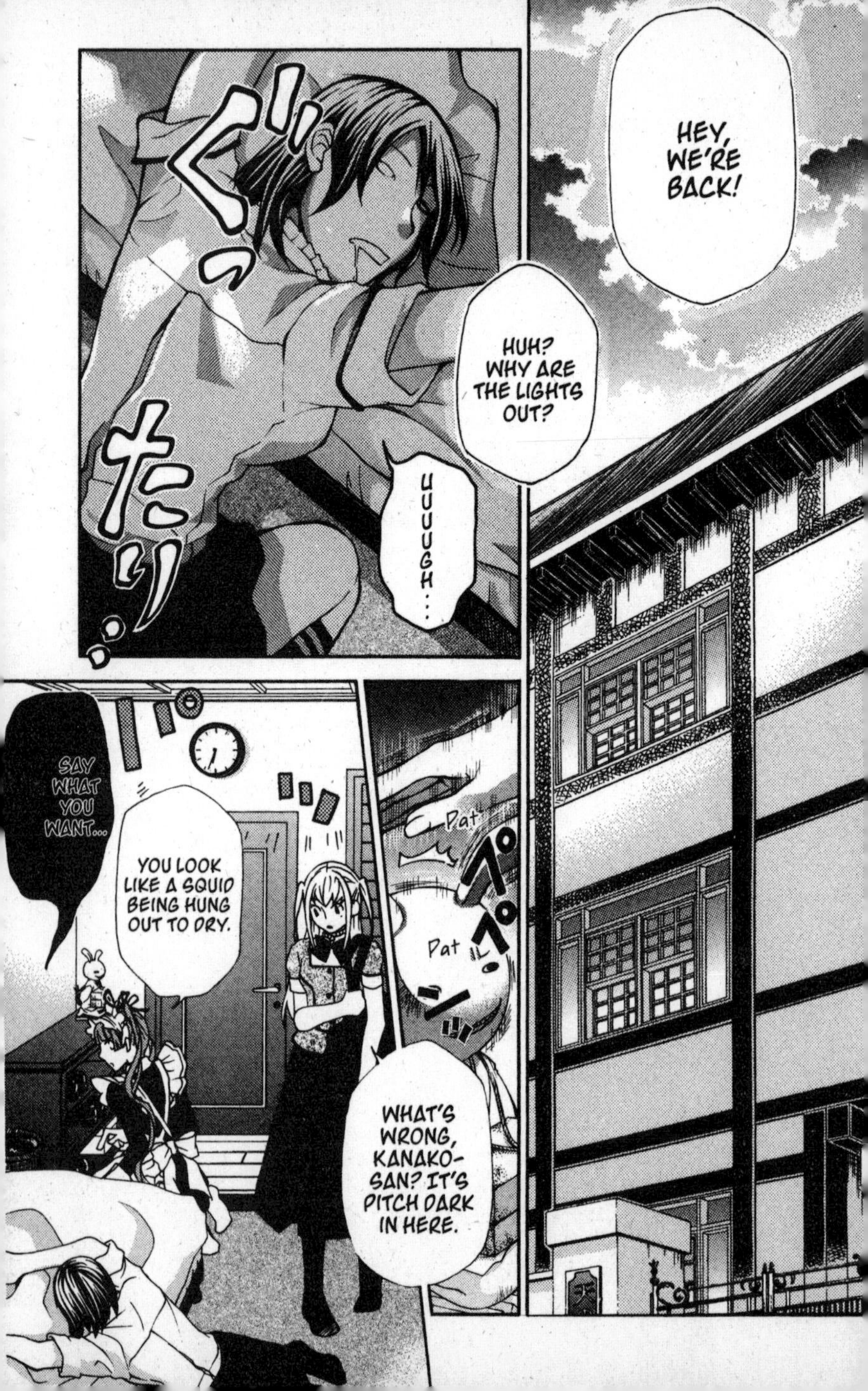
HEY, WE'RE BACK!
HUH? WHY ARE THE LIGHTS OUT?
UUUUGH...
Pat
Pat
WHAT'S WRONG, KANAKO-SAN? IT'S PITCH DARK IN HERE.
YOU LOOK LIKE A SQUID BEING HUNG OUT TO DRY.
SAY WHAT YOU WANT...

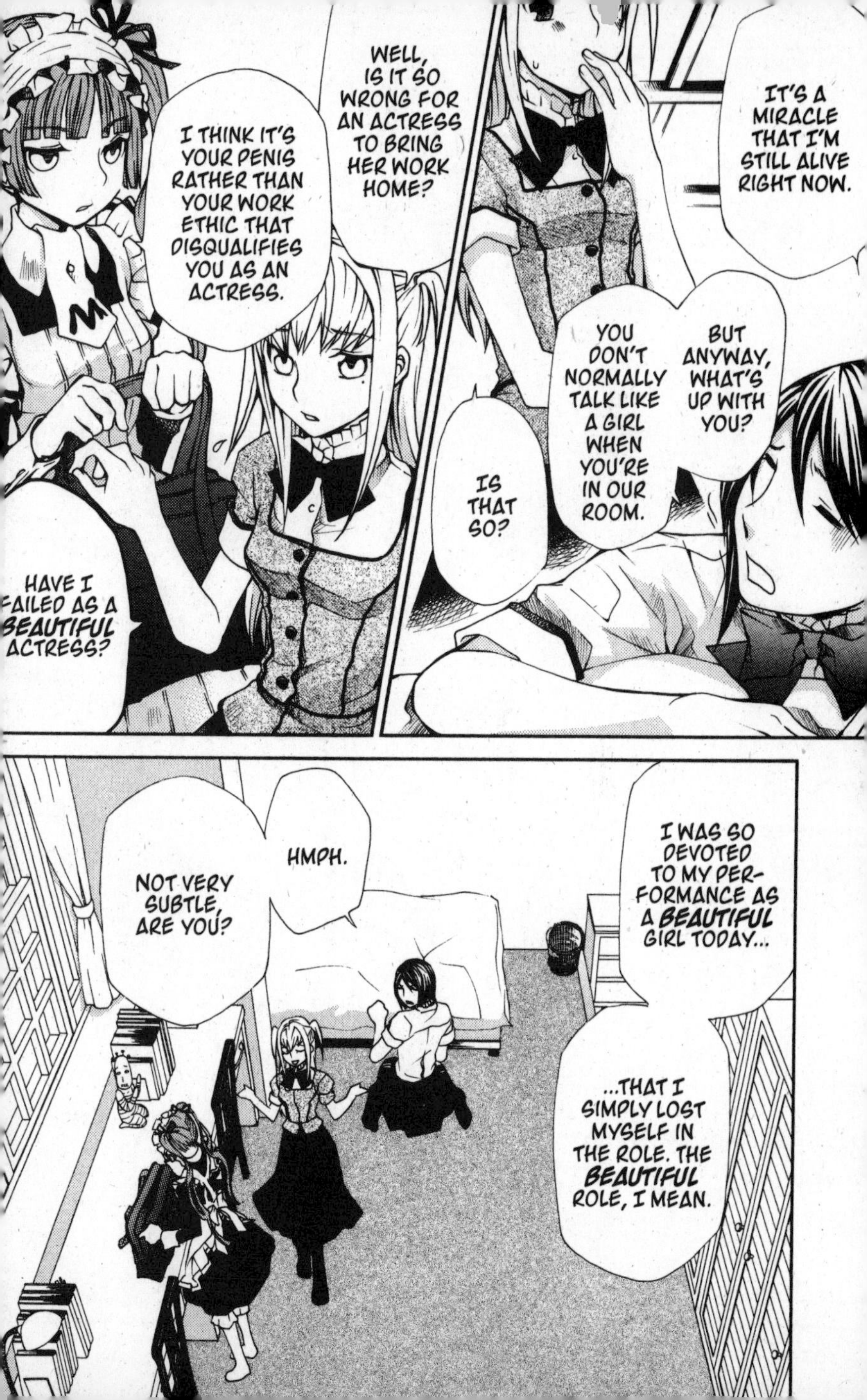
IT'S A MIRACLE THAT I'M STILL ALIVE RIGHT NOW.
BUT ANYWAY, WHAT'S UP WITH YOU?
YOU DON'T NORMALLY TALK LIKE A GIRL WHEN YOU'RE IN OUR ROOM.
IS THAT SO?
WELL, IS IT SO WRONG FOR AN ACTRESS TO BRING HER WORK HOME?
I THINK IT'S YOUR PENIS RATHER THAN YOUR WORK ETHIC THAT DISQUALIFIES YOU AS AN ACTRESS.
HAVE I FAILED AS A *BEAUTIFUL* ACTRESS?
I WAS SO DEVOTED TO MY PER-FORMANCE AS A *BEAUTIFUL* GIRL TODAY...
...THAT I SIMPLY LOST MYSELF IN THE ROLE. THE *BEAUTIFUL* ROLE, I MEAN.
HMPH.
NOT VERY SUBTLE, ARE YOU?

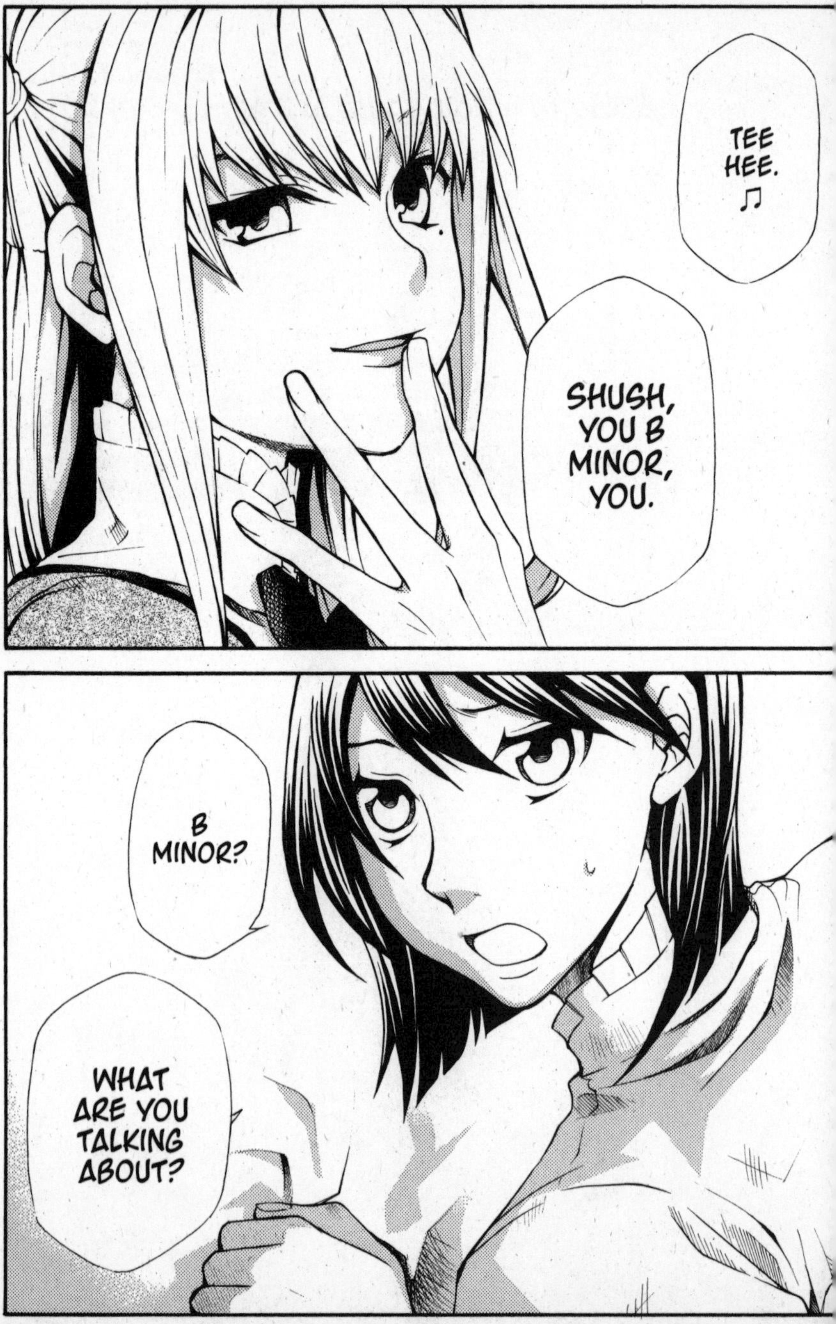
TEE HEE. ♫
SHUSH, YOU B MINOR, YOU.
B MINOR?
WHAT ARE YOU TALKING ABOUT?

Prayer 17
The Tale of a Home Visit in B Minor–Part 2

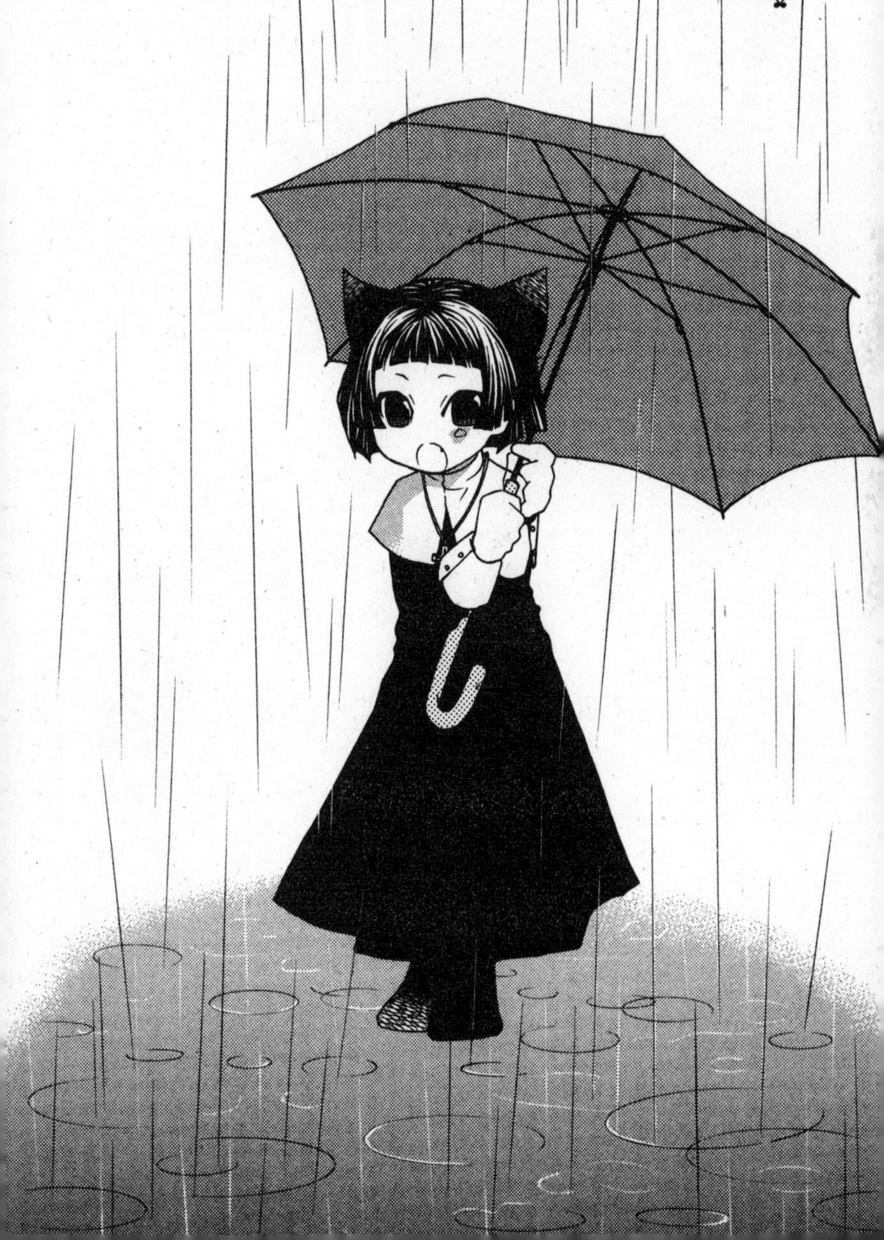

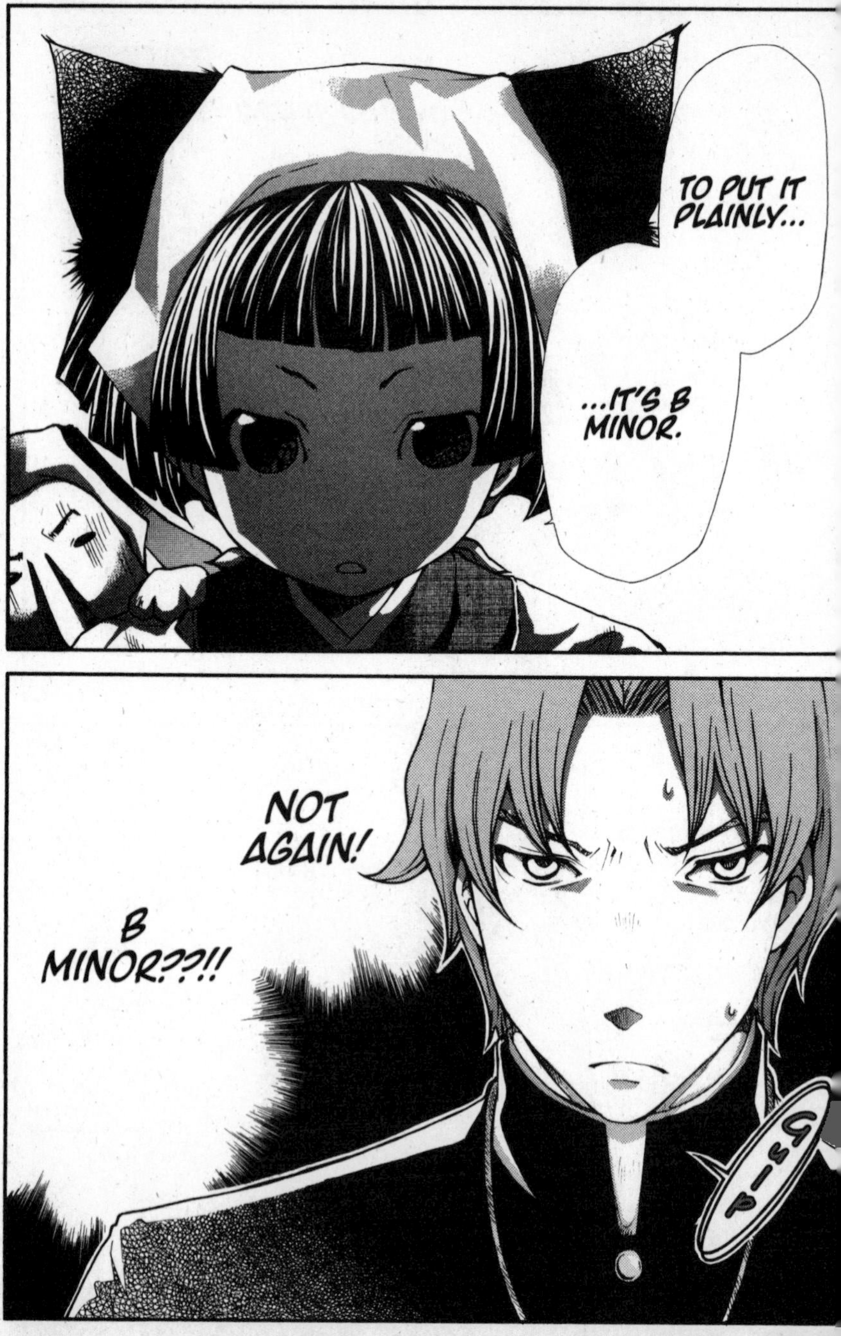
TO PUT IT PLAINLY...
...IT'S B MINOR.
NOT AGAIN!
B MINOR??!!

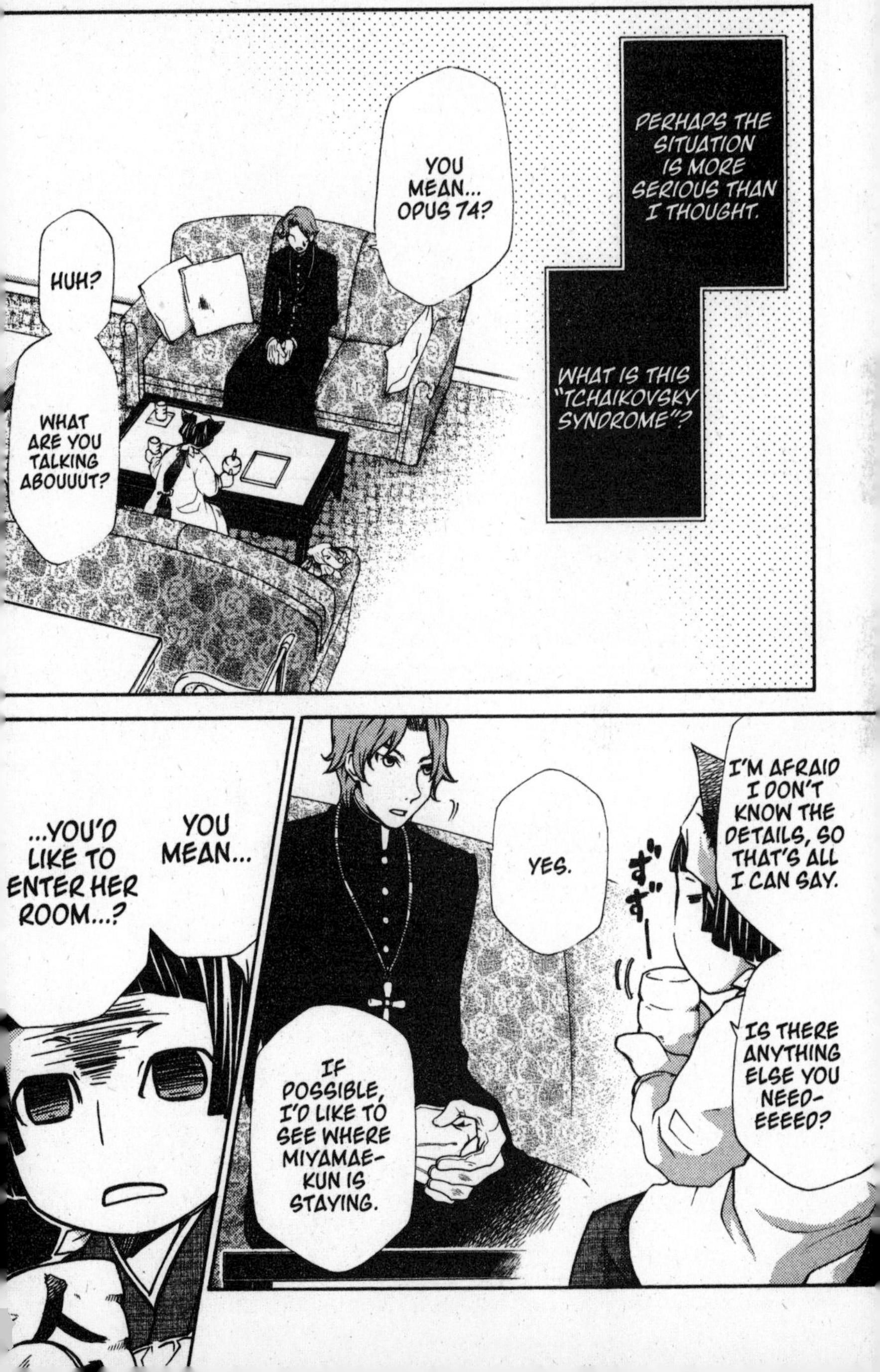
PERHAPS THE SITUATION IS MORE SERIOUS THAN I THOUGHT.
WHAT IS THIS "TCHAIKOVSKY SYNDROME"?
YOU MEAN... OPUS 74?
HUH?
WHAT ARE YOU TALKING ABOUUUT?
I'M AFRAID I DON'T KNOW THE DETAILS, SO THAT'S ALL I CAN SAY.
ずずー
YES.
IS THERE ANYTHING ELSE YOU NEED-EEEED?
IF POSSIBLE, I'D LIKE TO SEE WHERE MIYAMAE-KUN IS STAYING.
YOU MEAN...
...YOU'D LIKE TO ENTER HER ROOM...?

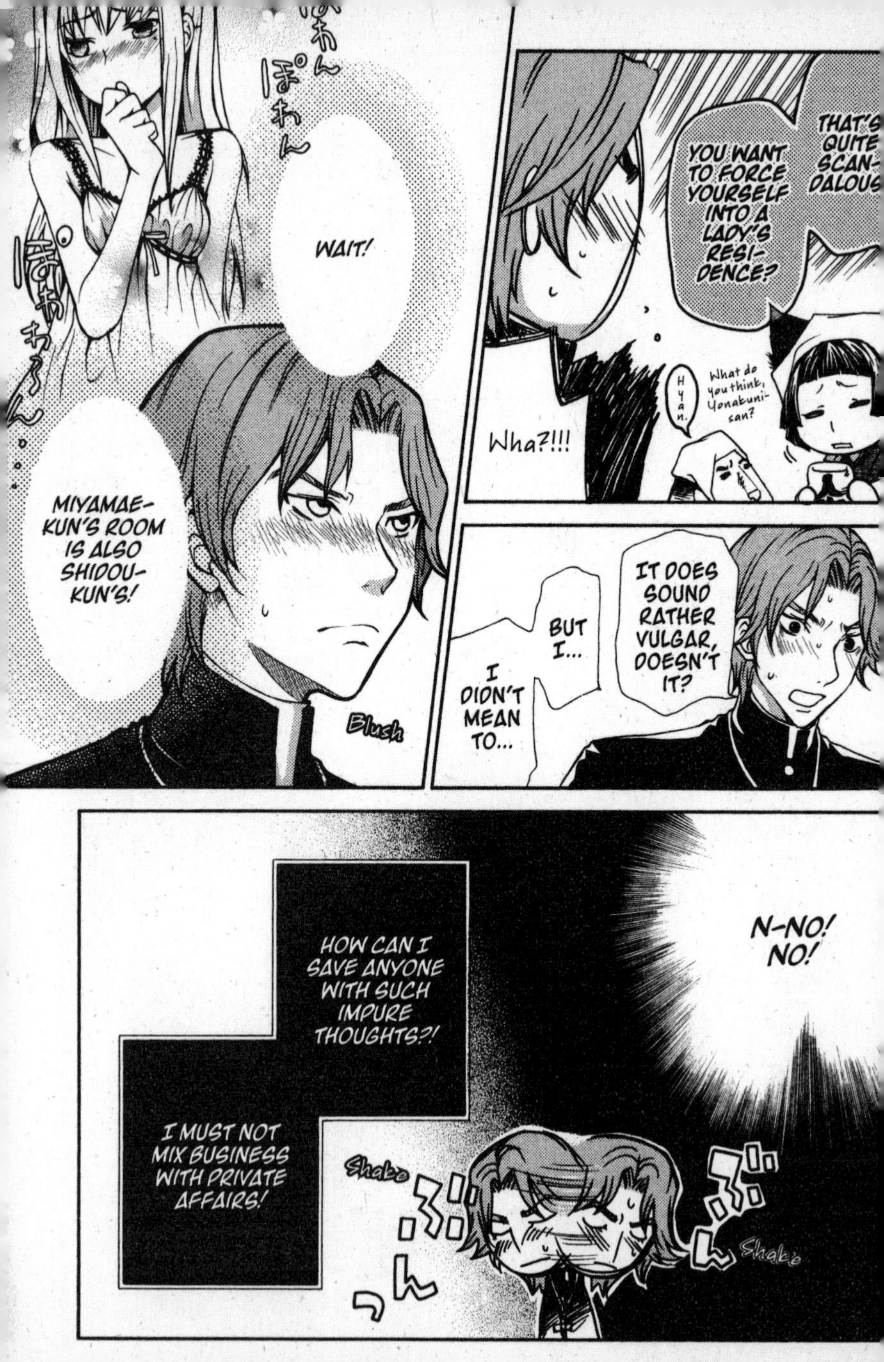
THAT'S QUITE SCAN-DALOUS
YOU WANT TO FORCE YOURSELF INTO A LADY'S RESI-DENCE?
What do you think, Yonakuni-san?
Hyan.
Wha?!!!
IT DOES SOUND RATHER VULGAR, DOESN'T IT?
BUT I...
I DIDN'T MEAN TO...
WAIT!
MIYAMAE-KUN'S ROOM IS ALSO SHIDOU-KUN'S!
Blush
N-NO! NO!
HOW CAN I SAVE ANYONE WITH SUCH IMPURE THOUGHTS?!
I MUST NOT MIX BUSINESS WITH PRIVATE AFFAIRS!
Shake
Shake

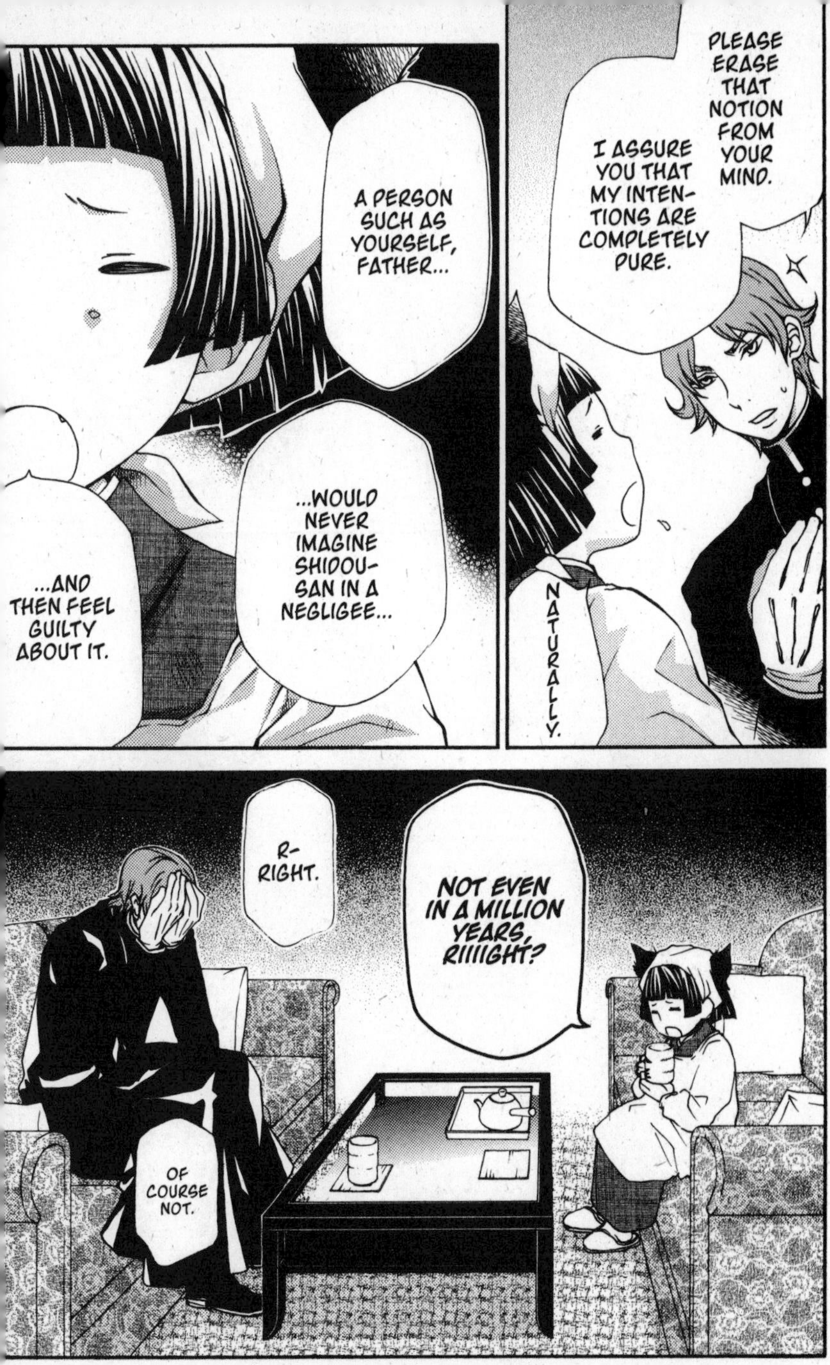
PLEASE ERASE THAT NOTION FROM YOUR MIND.
I ASSURE YOU THAT MY INTEN-TIONS ARE COMPLETELY PURE.
NATURALLY.
A PERSON SUCH AS YOURSELF, FATHER...
...WOULD NEVER IMAGINE SHIDOU-SAN IN A NEGLIGEE...
...AND THEN FEEL GUILTY ABOUT IT.
NOT EVEN IN A MILLION YEARS, RIIIIGHT?
R-RIGHT.
OF COURSE NOT.

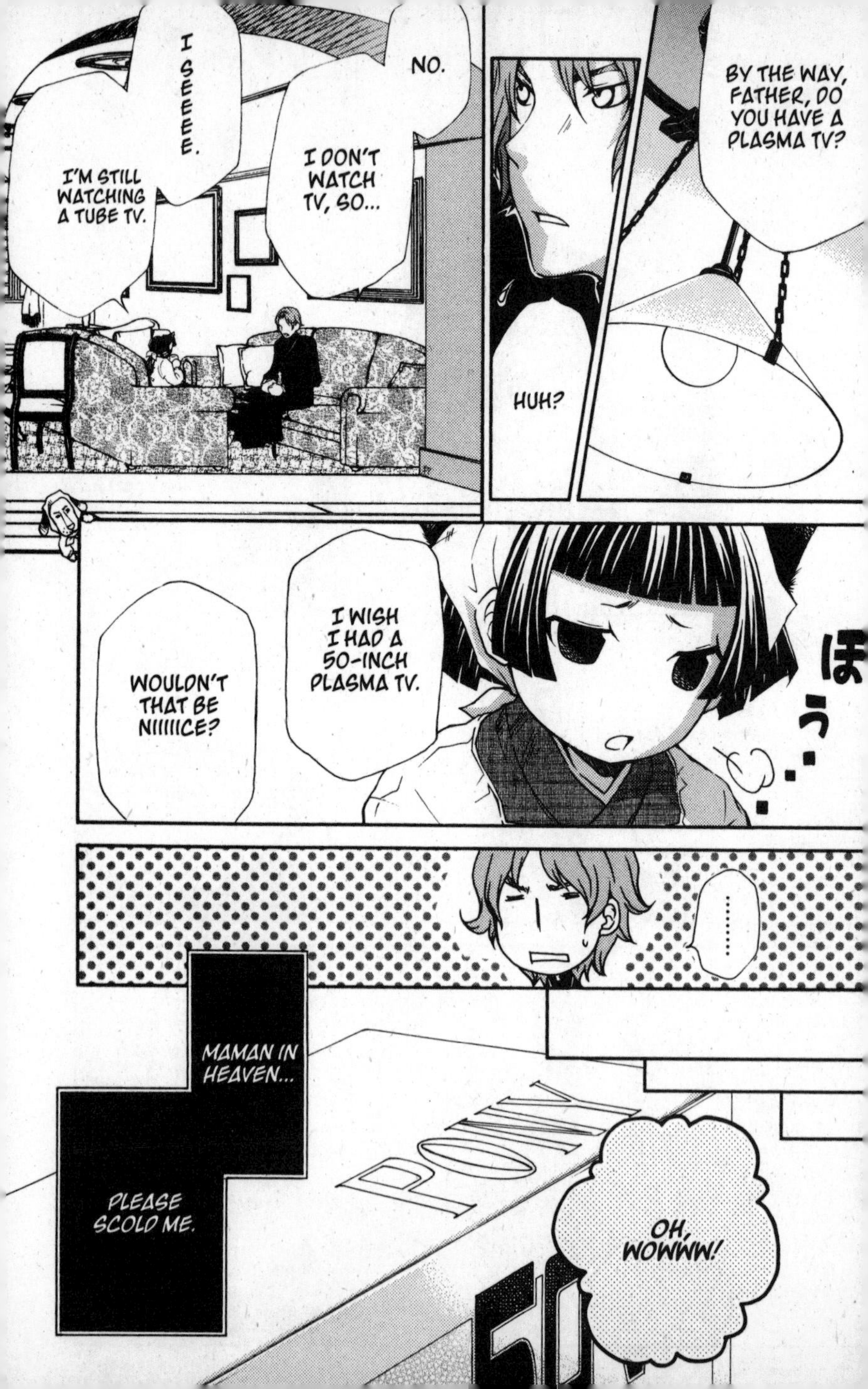

BY THE WAY, FATHER, DO YOU HAVE A PLASMA TV?
HUH?
NO.
I DON'T WATCH TV, SO...
I SEEEE.
I'M STILL WATCHING A TUBE TV.
ほう…
I WISH I HAD A 50-INCH PLASMA TV.
WOULDN'T THAT BE NIIIIICE?
......
PONY
OH, WOWWW!
MAMAN IN HEAVEN...
PLEASE SCOLD ME.

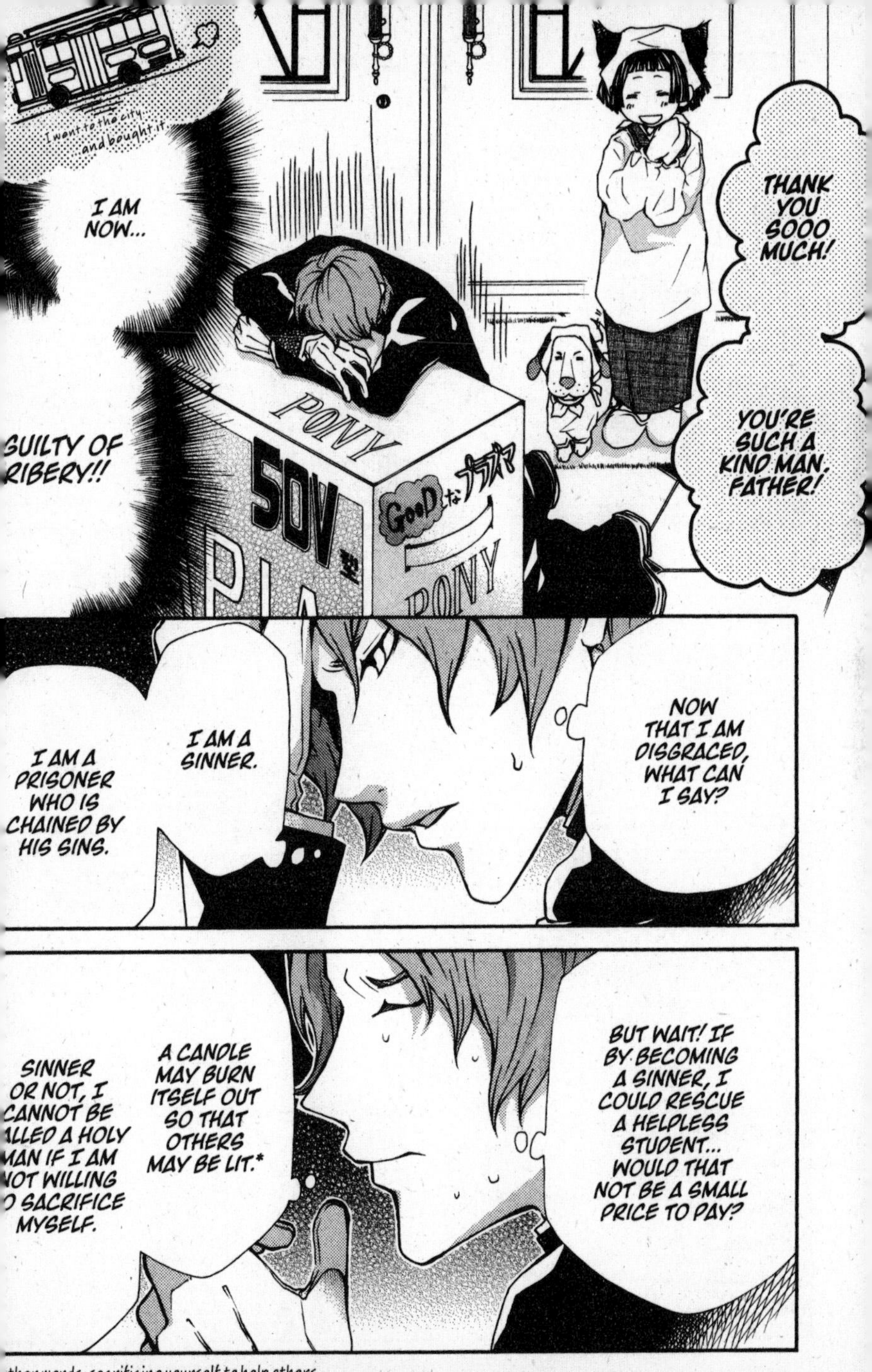
THANK YOU SOOO MUCH!
YOU'RE SUCH A KIND MAN, FATHER!
I went to the city and bought it.
I AM NOW...
UILTY OF RIBERY!!
NOW THAT I AM DISGRACED, WHAT CAN I SAY?
I AM A SINNER.
I AM A PRISONER WHO IS CHAINED BY HIS SINS.
BUT WAIT! IF BY BECOMING A SINNER, I COULD RESCUE A HELPLESS STUDENT... WOULD THAT NOT BE A SMALL PRICE TO PAY?
A CANDLE MAY BURN ITSELF OUT SO THAT OTHERS MAY BE LIT.*
SINNER OR NOT, I CANNOT BE ALLED A HOLY MAN IF I AM NOT WILLING O SACRIFICE MYSELF.

ther words, sacrificing yourself to help others.

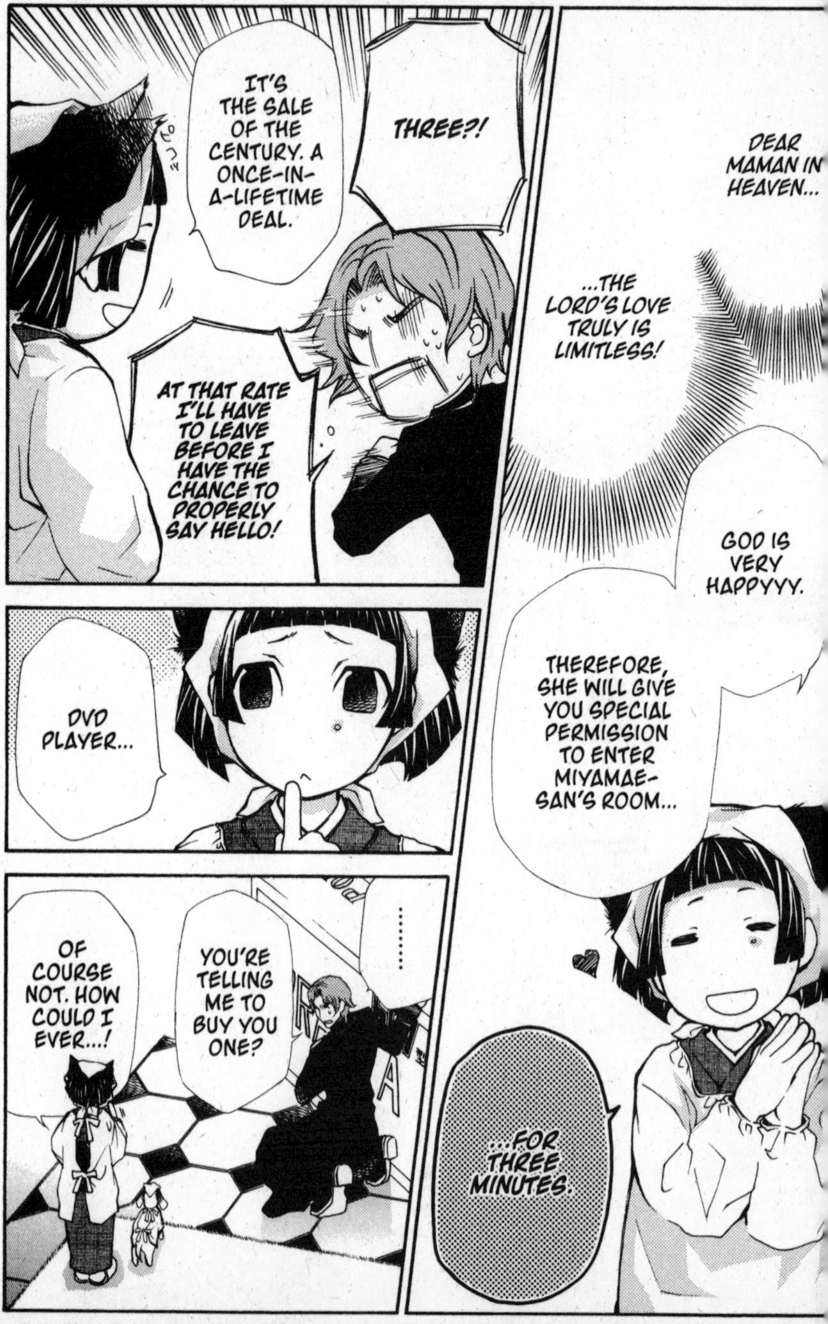
DEAR MAMAN IN HEAVEN...
...THE LORD'S LOVE TRULY IS LIMITLESS!
GOD IS VERY HAPPYYY.
THEREFORE, SHE WILL GIVE YOU SPECIAL PERMISSION TO ENTER MIYAMAE-SAN'S ROOM...
...FOR THREE MINUTES.
THREE?!
IT'S THE SALE OF THE CENTURY. A ONCE-IN-A-LIFETIME DEAL.
AT THAT RATE I'LL HAVE TO LEAVE BEFORE I HAVE THE CHANCE TO PROPERLY SAY HELLO!
DVD PLAYER...
......
YOU'RE TELLING ME TO BUY YOU ONE?
OF COURSE NOT. HOW COULD I EVER...!

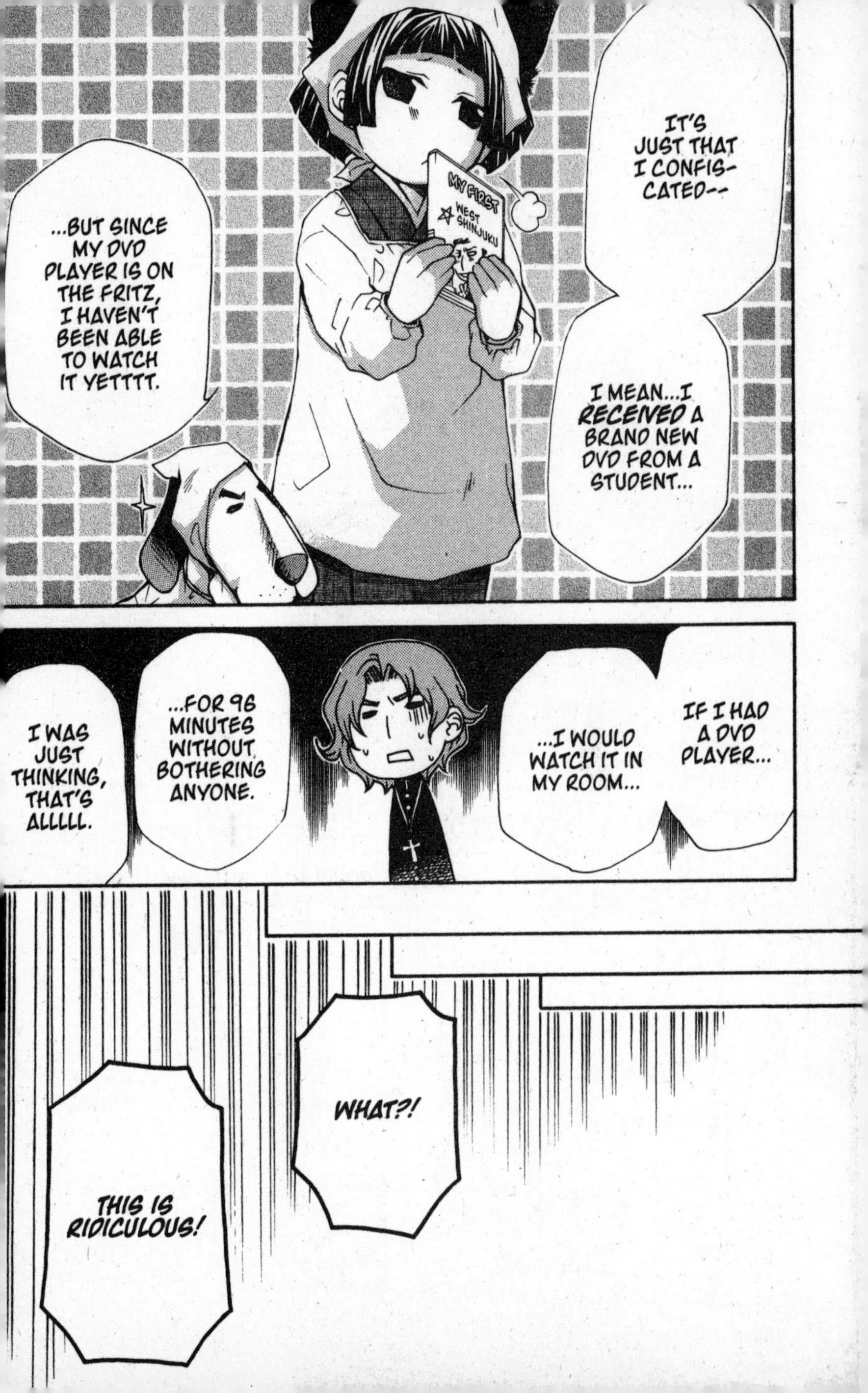
IT'S JUST THAT I CONFIS-CATED--
MY FIRST WEST SHINJUKU
I MEAN...I RECEIVED A BRAND NEW DVD FROM A STUDENT...
...BUT SINCE MY DVD PLAYER IS ON THE FRITZ, I HAVEN'T BEEN ABLE TO WATCH IT YETTTT.
IF I HAD A DVD PLAYER...
...I WOULD WATCH IT IN MY ROOM...
...FOR 96 MINUTES WITHOUT BOTHERING ANYONE.
I WAS JUST THINKING, THAT'S ALLLLL.
WHAT?!
THIS IS RIDICULOUS!

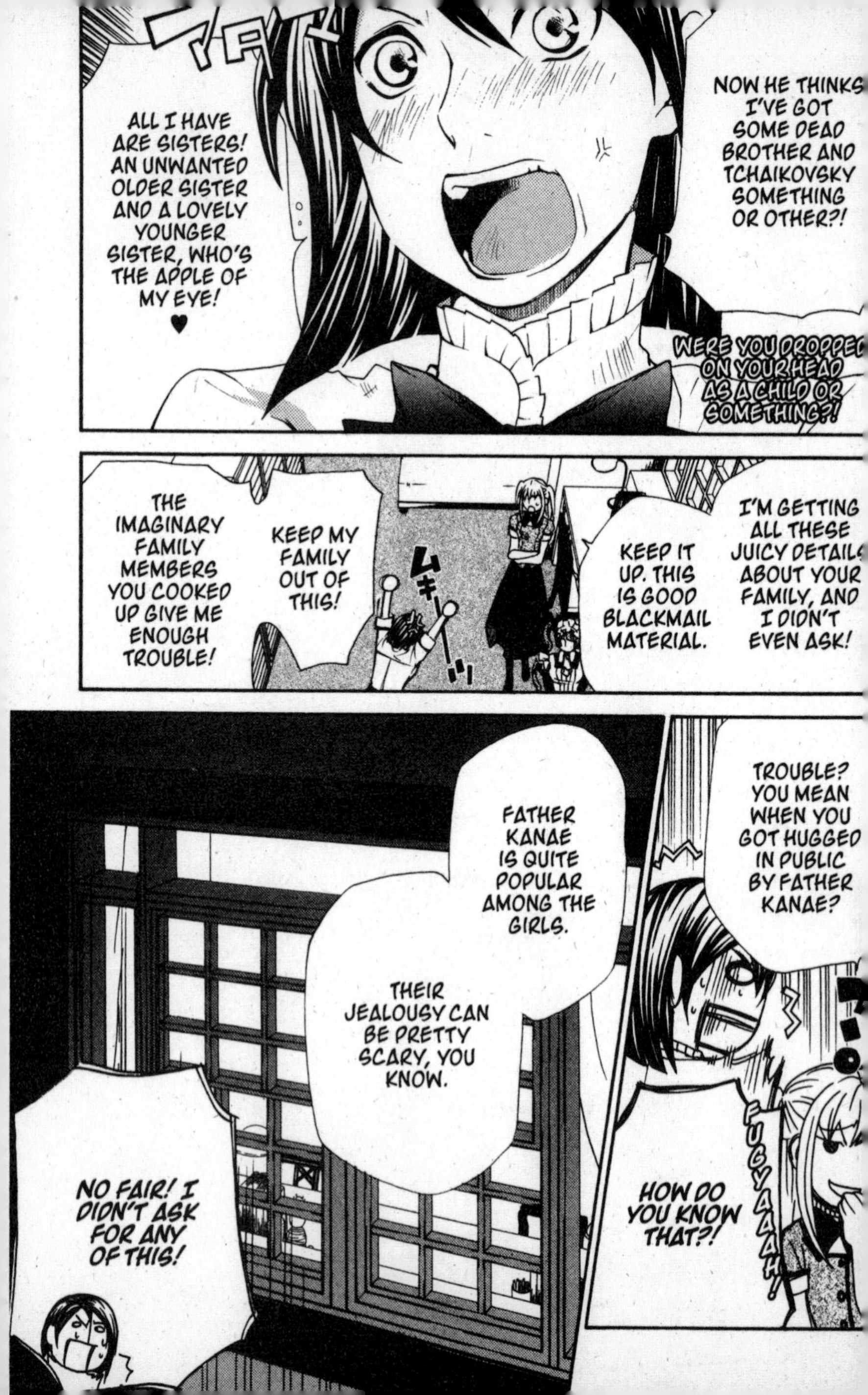
NOW HE THINKS I'VE GOT SOME DEAD BROTHER AND TCHAIKOVSKY SOMETHING OR OTHER?!
ALL I HAVE ARE SISTERS! AN UNWANTED OLDER SISTER AND A LOVELY YOUNGER SISTER, WHO'S THE APPLE OF MY EYE! ♥
WERE YOU DROPPED ON YOUR HEAD AS A CHILD OR SOMETHING?!
I'M GETTING ALL THESE JUICY DETAIL ABOUT YOUR FAMILY, AND I DIDN'T EVEN ASK!
KEEP IT UP. THIS IS GOOD BLACKMAIL MATERIAL.
KEEP MY FAMILY OUT OF THIS!
THE IMAGINARY FAMILY MEMBERS YOU COOKED UP GIVE ME ENOUGH TROUBLE!
TROUBLE? YOU MEAN WHEN YOU GOT HUGGED IN PUBLIC BY FATHER KANAE?
FUGYAAAH!
HOW DO YOU KNOW THAT?!
FATHER KANAE IS QUITE POPULAR AMONG THE GIRLS.
THEIR JEALOUSY CAN BE PRETTY SCARY, YOU KNOW.
NO FAIR! I DIDN'T ASK FOR ANY OF THIS!

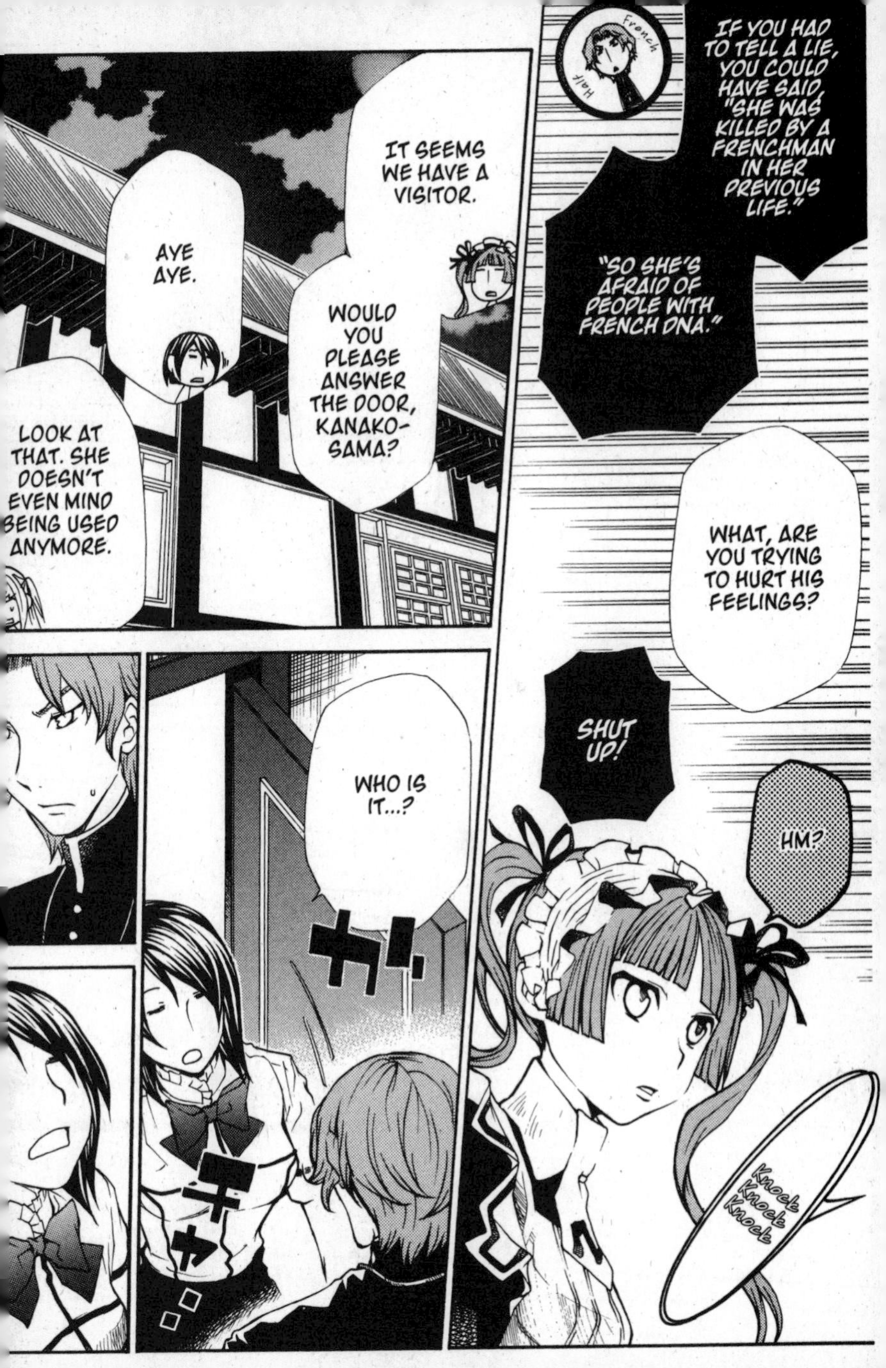
Half French
IF YOU HAD TO TELL A LIE, YOU COULD HAVE SAID, "SHE WAS KILLED BY A FRENCHMAN IN HER PREVIOUS LIFE."
"SO SHE'S AFRAID OF PEOPLE WITH FRENCH DNA."
WHAT, ARE YOU TRYING TO HURT HIS FEELINGS?
SHUT UP!
HM?
Knock Knock Knock
IT SEEMS WE HAVE A VISITOR.
WOULD YOU PLEASE ANSWER THE DOOR, KANAKO-SAMA?
AYE AYE.
LOOK AT THAT. SHE DOESN'T EVEN MIND BEING USED ANYMORE.
WHO IS IT...?

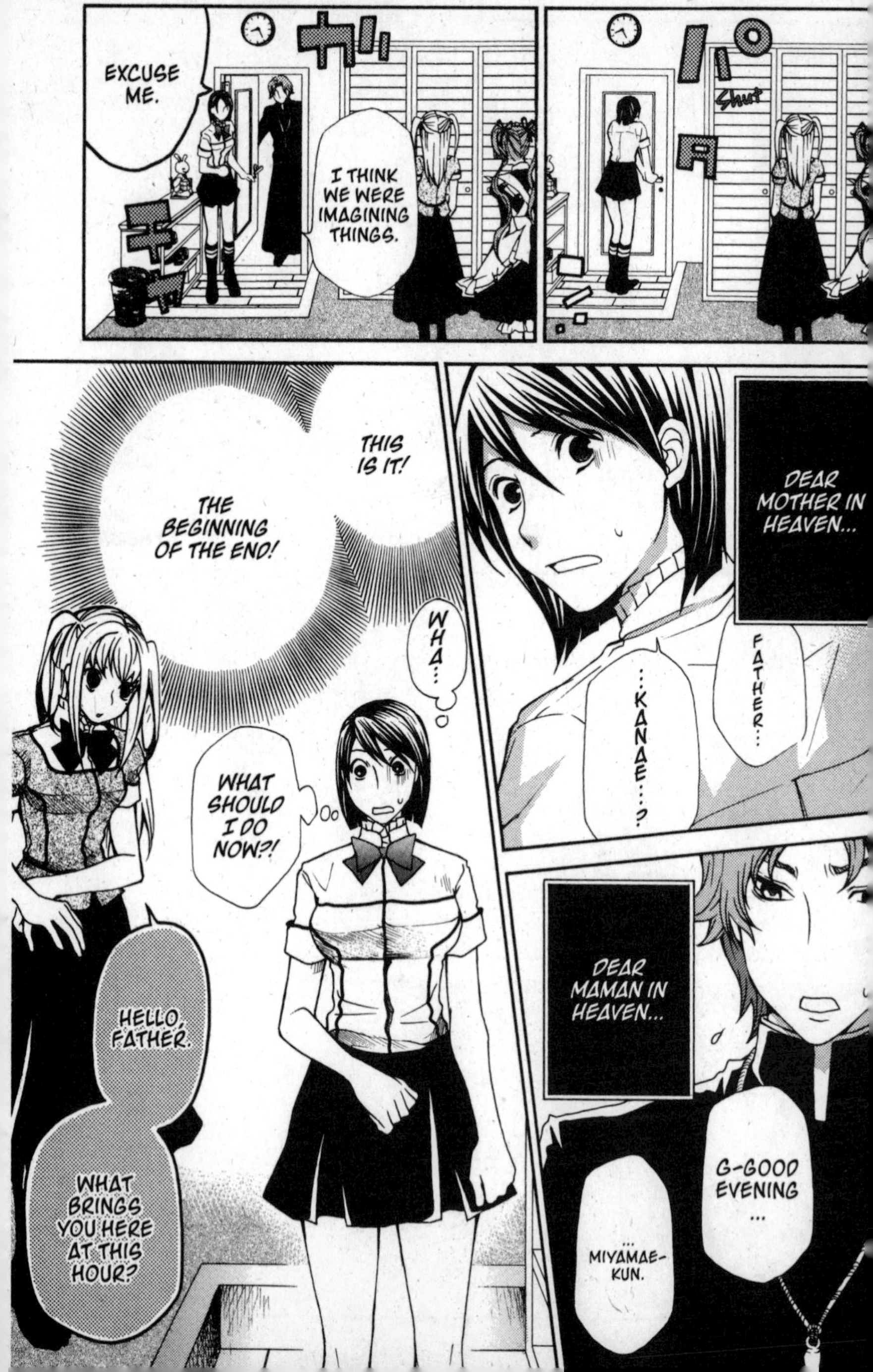
Shut
I THINK WE WERE IMAGINING THINGS.
EXCUSE ME.
DEAR MOTHER IN HEAVEN...
FATHER...
...KANAE...?
DEAR MAMAN IN HEAVEN...
G-GOOD EVENING ...
... MIYAMAE-KUN.
THIS IS IT!
THE BEGINNING OF THE END!
WHA...
WHAT SHOULD I DO NOW?!
HELLO, FATHER.
WHAT BRINGS YOU HERE AT THIS HOUR?

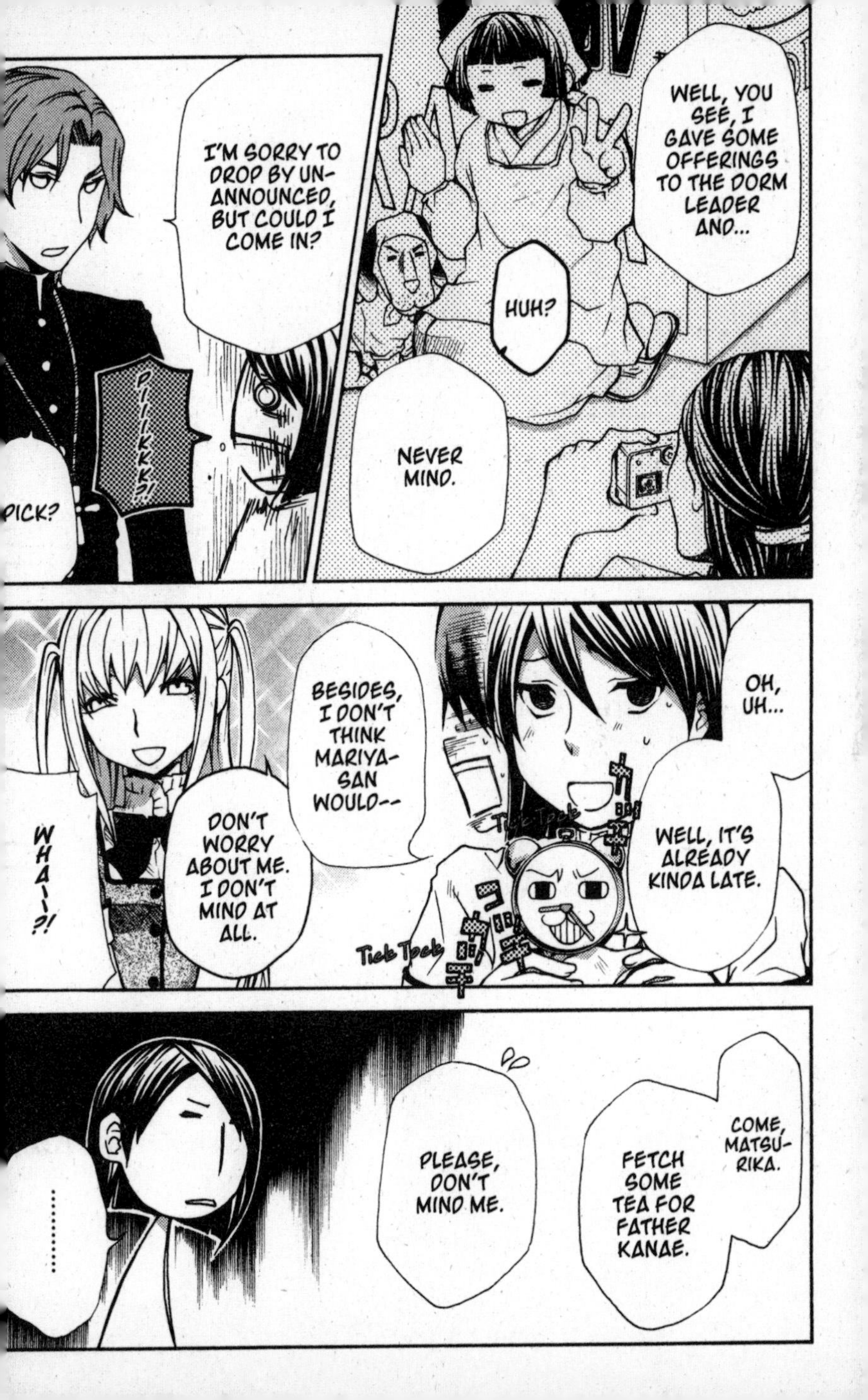
WELL, YOU SEE, I GAVE SOME OFFERINGS TO THE DORM LEADER AND...
HUH?
NEVER MIND.
I'M SORRY TO DROP BY UN-ANNOUNCED, BUT COULD I COME IN?
PIIIKKK?!
PICK?
OH, UH...
WELL, IT'S ALREADY KINDA LATE.
Tick Tock
Tick Tock
BESIDES, I DON'T THINK MARIYA-SAN WOULD--
DON'T WORRY ABOUT ME. I DON'T MIND AT ALL.
WHA--?!
COME, MATSURIKA.
FETCH SOME TEA FOR FATHER KANAE.
PLEASE, DON'T MIND ME.
....

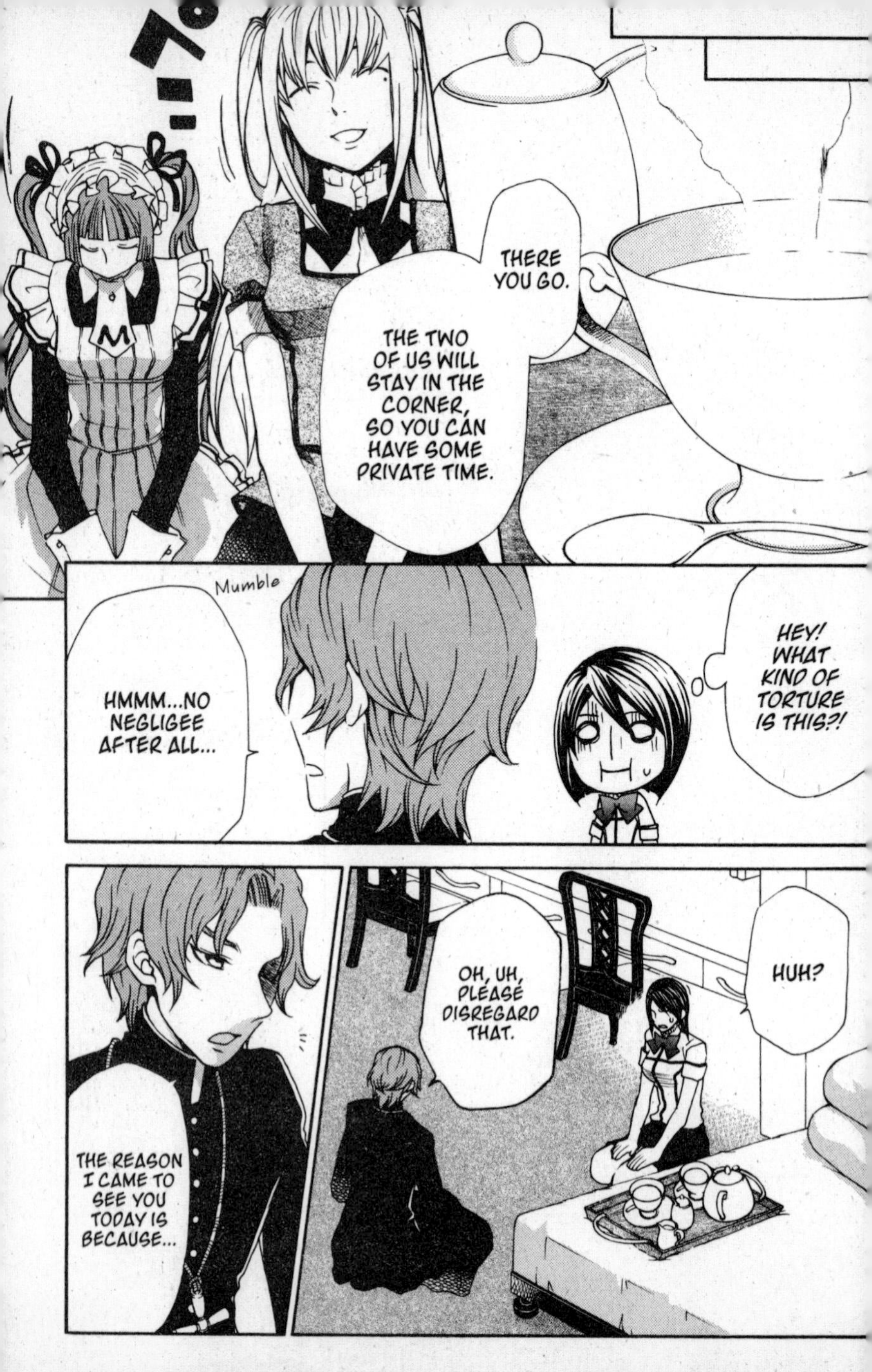
THERE YOU GO.
THE TWO OF US WILL STAY IN THE CORNER, SO YOU CAN HAVE SOME PRIVATE TIME.
HEY! WHAT KIND OF TORTURE IS THIS?!
Mumble
HMMM...NO NEGLIGEE AFTER ALL...
HUH?
OH, UH, PLEASE DISREGARD THAT.
THE REASON I CAME TO SEE YOU TODAY IS BECAUSE...

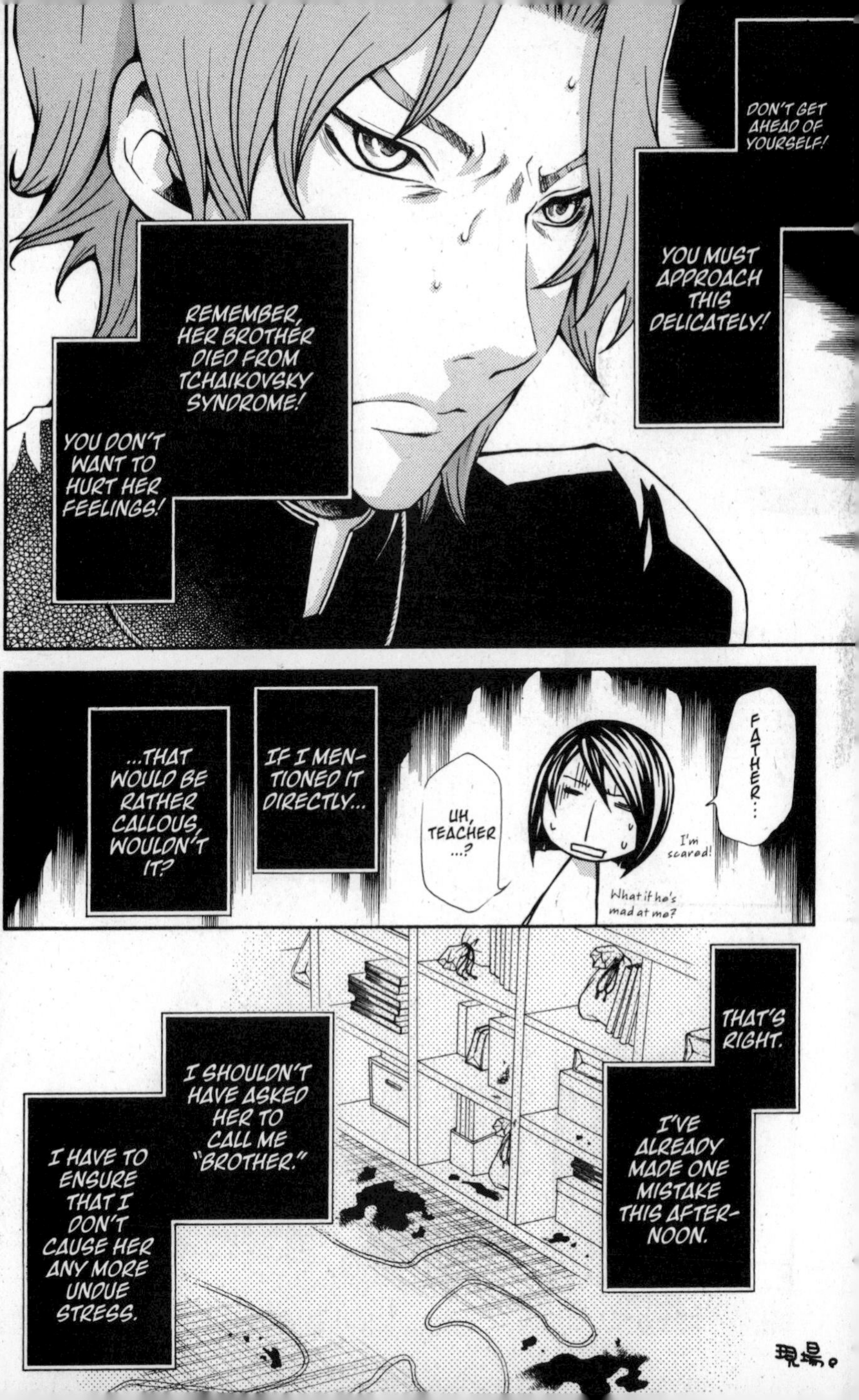
DON'T GET AHEAD OF YOURSELF!
YOU MUST APPROACH THIS DELICATELY!
REMEMBER, HER BROTHER DIED FROM TCHAIKOVSKY SYNDROME!
YOU DON'T WANT TO HURT HER FEELINGS!
FATHER...
I'm scared!
What if he's mad at me?
UH, TEACHER ...?
IF I MENTIONED IT DIRECTLY...
...THAT WOULD BE RATHER CALLOUS, WOULDN'T IT?
THAT'S RIGHT.
I'VE ALREADY MADE ONE MISTAKE THIS AFTERNOON.
I SHOULDN'T HAVE ASKED HER TO CALL ME "BROTHER."
I HAVE TO ENSURE THAT I DON'T CAUSE HER ANY MORE UNDUE STRESS.
現場。

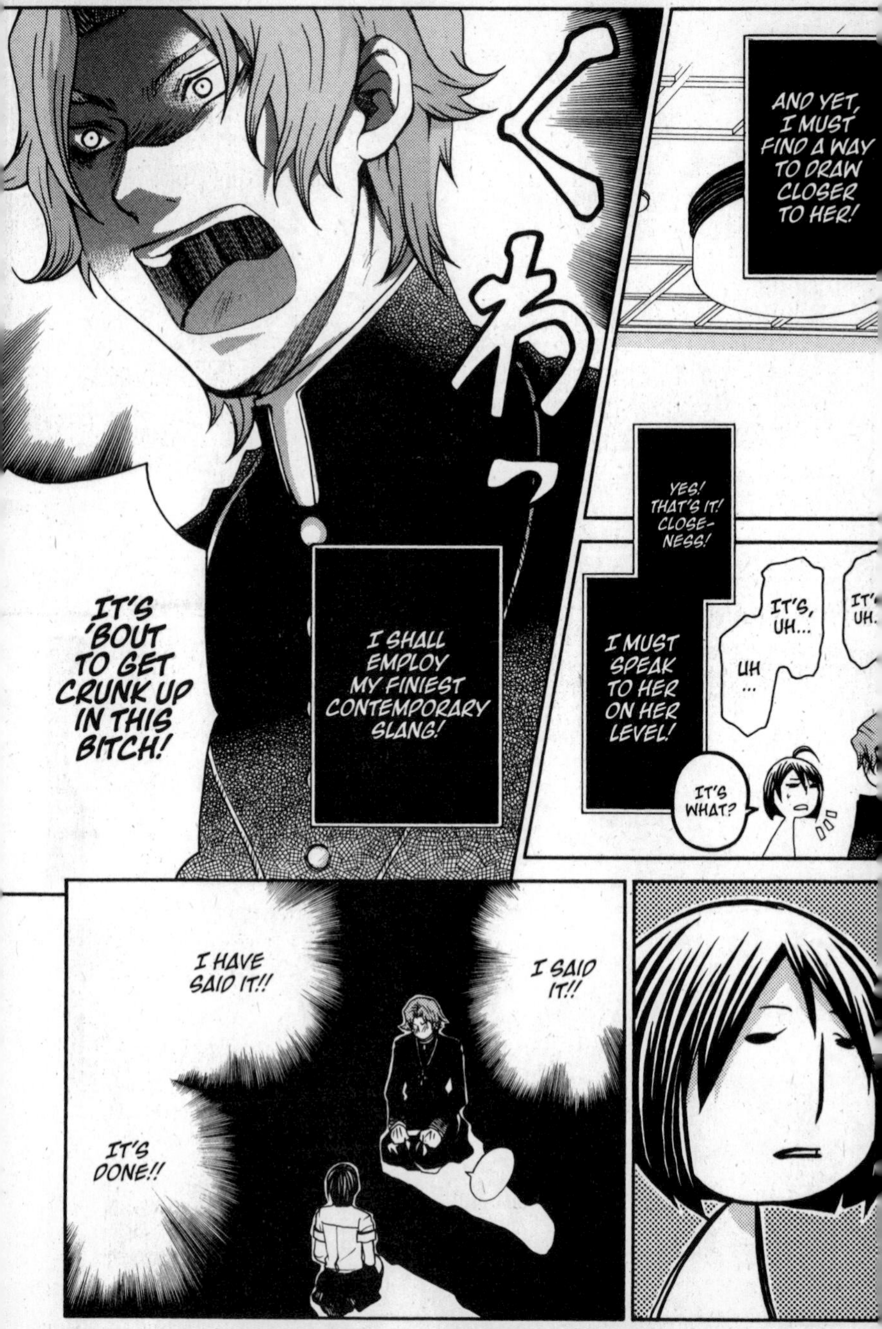
AND YET, I MUST FIND A WAY TO DRAW CLOSER TO HER!
YES! THAT'S IT! CLOSE-NESS!
IT'S, UH...
UH ...
I MUST SPEAK TO HER ON HER LEVEL!
IT'S WHAT?
くわっ
I SHALL EMPLOY MY FINIEST CONTEMPORARY SLANG!
IT'S 'BOUT TO GET CRUNK UP IN THIS BITCH!
I SAID IT!!
I HAVE SAID IT!!
IT'S DONE!!

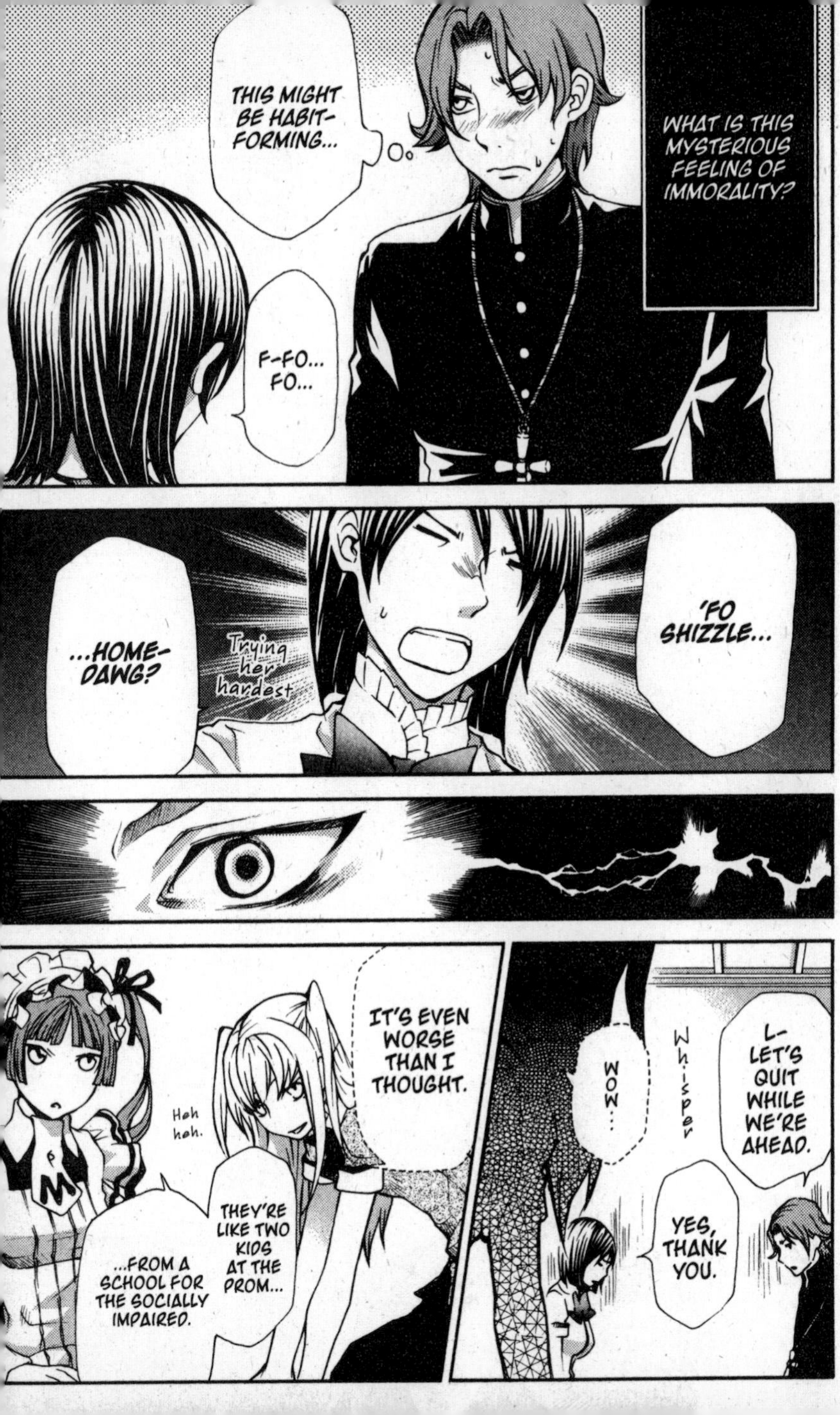
WHAT IS THIS MYSTERIOUS FEELING OF IMMORALITY?
THIS MIGHT BE HABIT-FORMING...
F-FO... FO...
'FO SHIZZLE...
Trying her hardest
...HOME-DAWG?
L-LET'S QUIT WHILE WE'RE AHEAD.
Whisper
WOW...
YES, THANK YOU.
IT'S EVEN WORSE THAN I THOUGHT.
Heh heh.
THEY'RE LIKE TWO KIDS AT THE PROM...
...FROM A SCHOOL FOR THE SOCIALLY IMPAIRED.

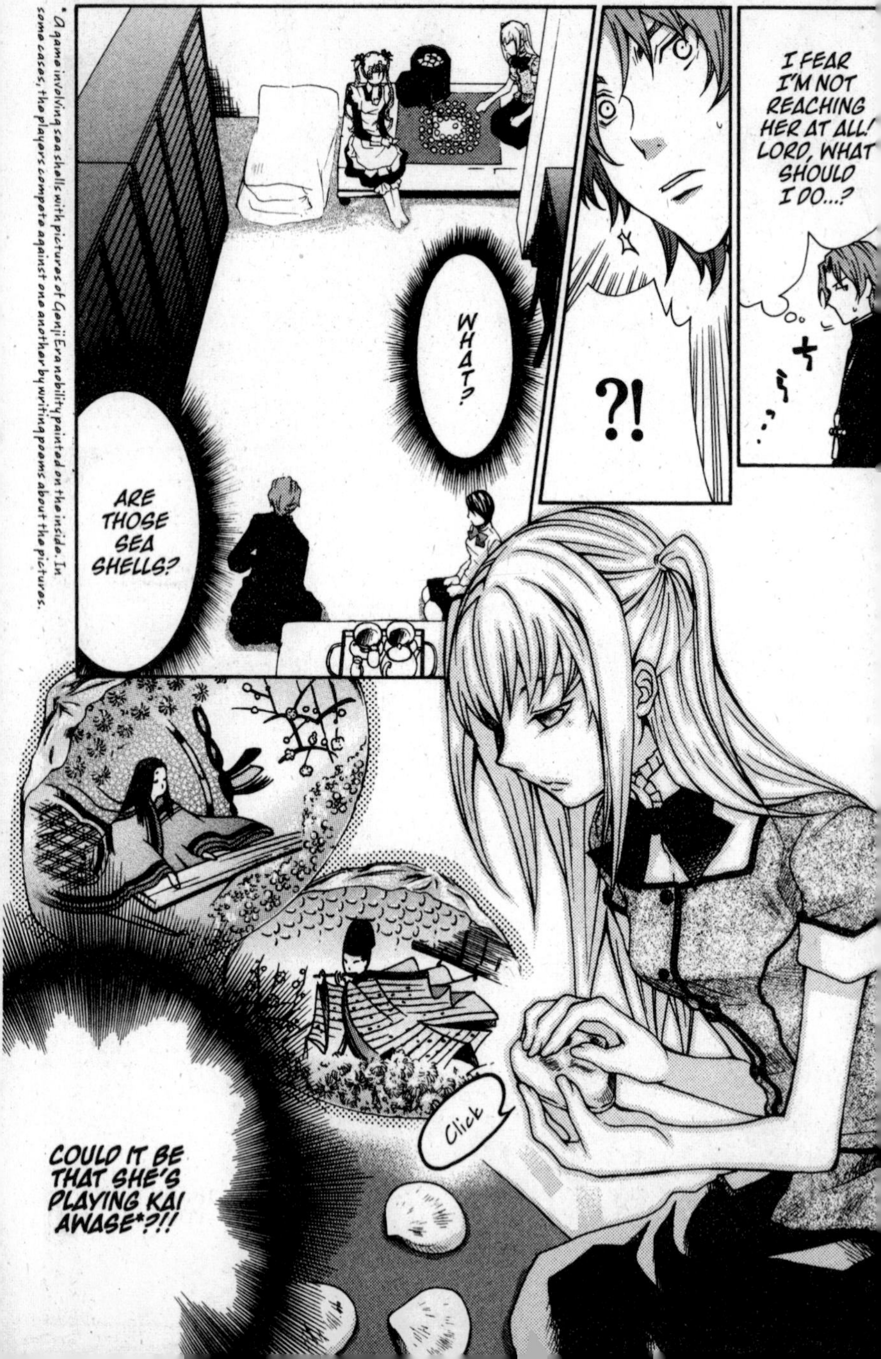
I FEAR I'M NOT REACHING HER AT ALL! LORD, WHAT SHOULD I DO...?
?!
WHAT?
ARE THOSE SEA SHELLS?
Click
COULD IT BE THAT SHE'S PLAYING KAI AWASE*?!!

* A game involving sea shells with pictures of Genji Era nobility painted on the inside. In some cases, the players compete against one another by writing poems about the pictures.

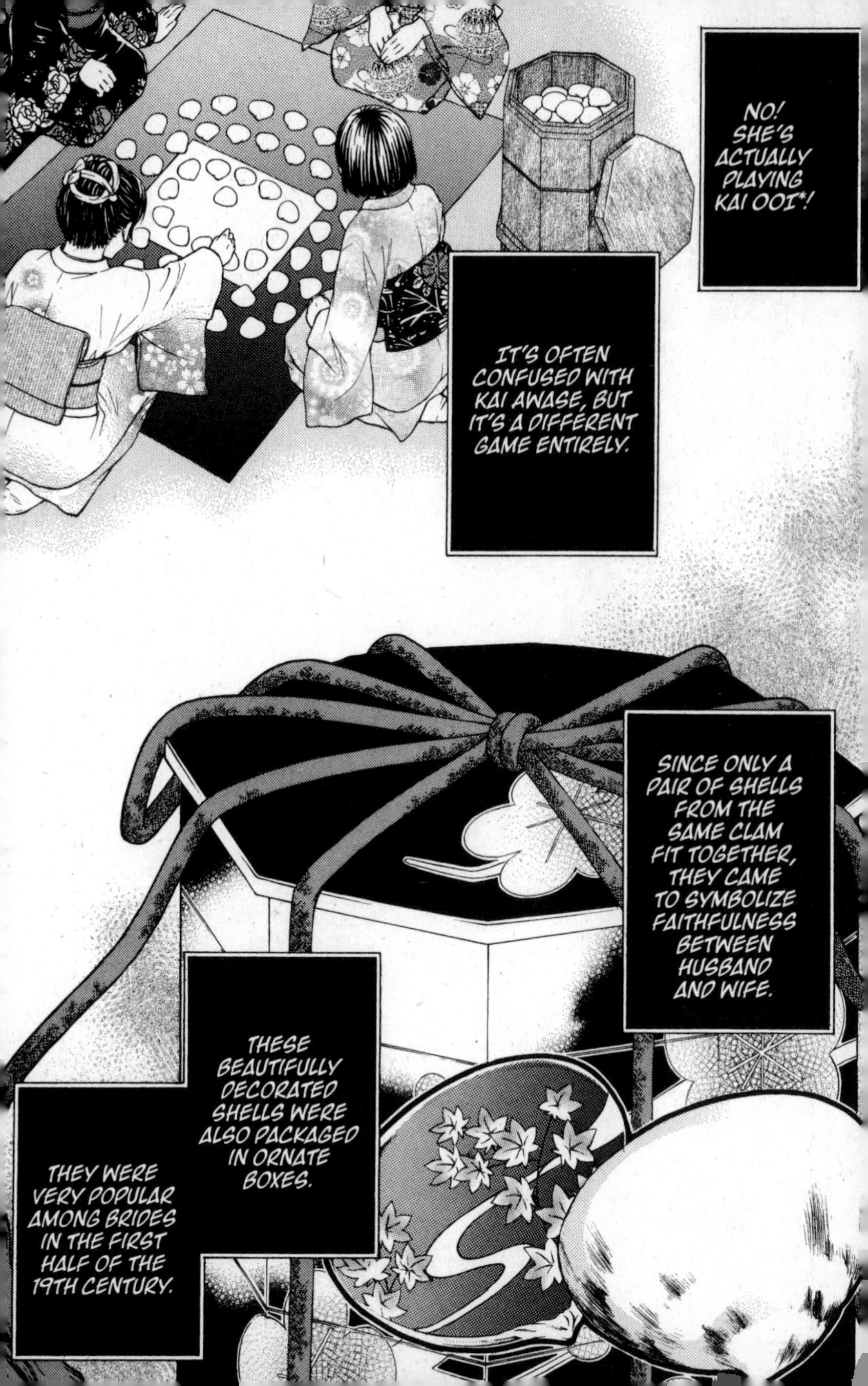
NO! SHE'S ACTUALLY PLAYING KAI OOI*!
IT'S OFTEN CONFUSED WITH KAI AWASE, BUT IT'S A DIFFERENT GAME ENTIRELY.
SINCE ONLY A PAIR OF SHELLS FROM THE SAME CLAM FIT TOGETHER, THEY CAME TO SYMBOLIZE FAITHFULNESS BETWEEN HUSBAND AND WIFE.
THESE BEAUTIFULLY DECORATED SHELLS WERE ALSO PACKAGED IN ORNATE BOXES.
THEY WERE VERY POPULAR AMONG BRIDES IN THE FIRST HALF OF THE 19TH CENTURY.

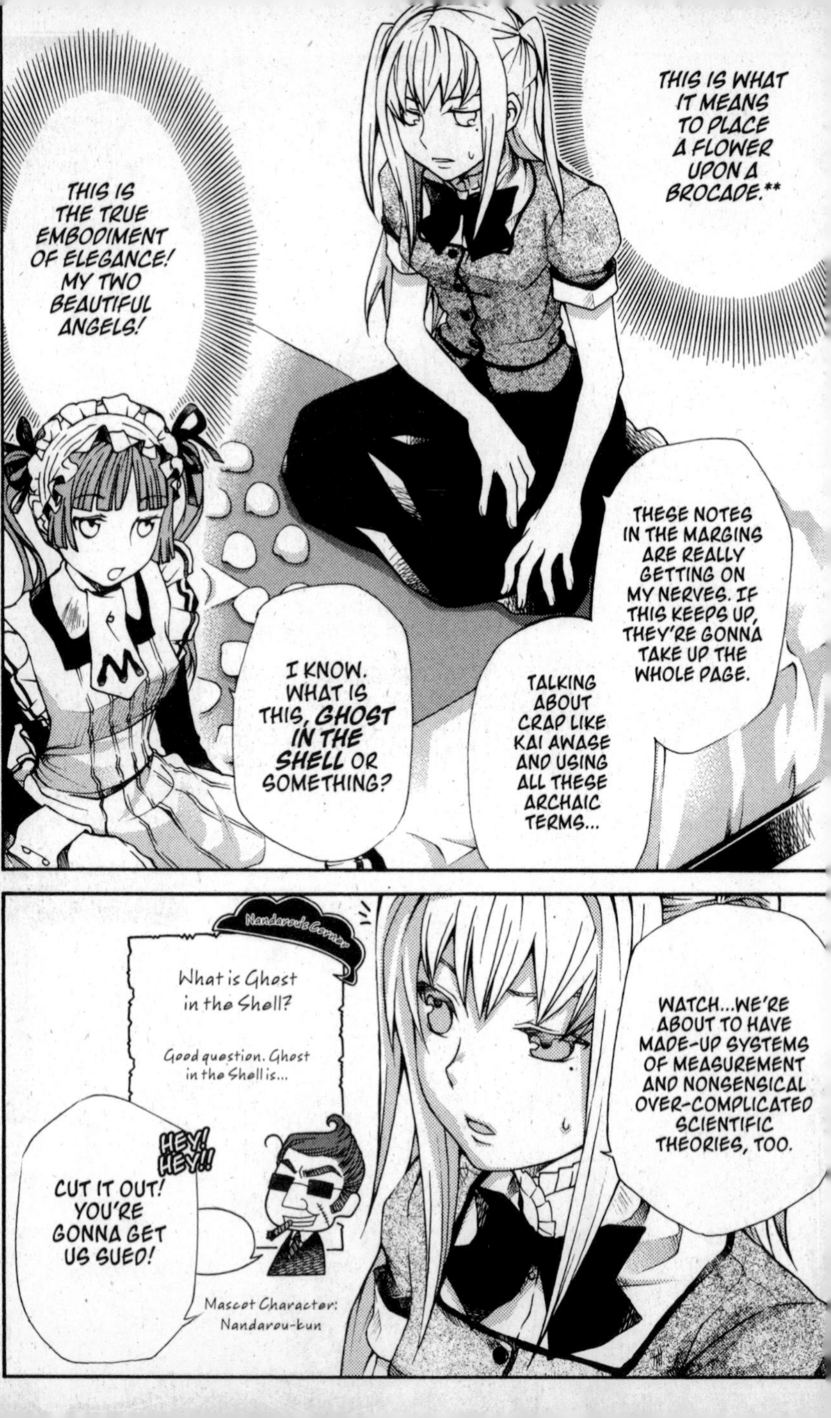
THIS IS WHAT IT MEANS TO PLACE A FLOWER UPON A BROCADE.**
THIS IS THE TRUE EMBODIMENT OF ELEGANCE! MY TWO BEAUTIFUL ANGELS!
THESE NOTES IN THE MARGINS ARE REALLY GETTING ON MY NERVES. IF THIS KEEPS UP, THEY'RE GONNA TAKE UP THE WHOLE PAGE.
TALKING ABOUT CRAP LIKE KAI AWASE AND USING ALL THESE ARCHAIC TERMS...
I KNOW. WHAT IS THIS, GHOST IN THE SHELL OR SOMETHING?
WATCH...WE'RE ABOUT TO HAVE MADE-UP SYSTEMS OF MEASUREMENT AND NONSENSICAL OVER-COMPLICATED SCIENTIFIC THEORIES, TOO.
Nandarou's Corner
What is Ghost in the Shell?
Good question. Ghost in the Shell is...
HEY! HEY!!
CUT IT OUT! YOU'RE GONNA GET US SUED!
Mascot Character: Nandarou-kun

* A game in which you match shells by looking at their different patterns.

** Indicating something very beautiful (i.e., piling beauty on top of beauty).

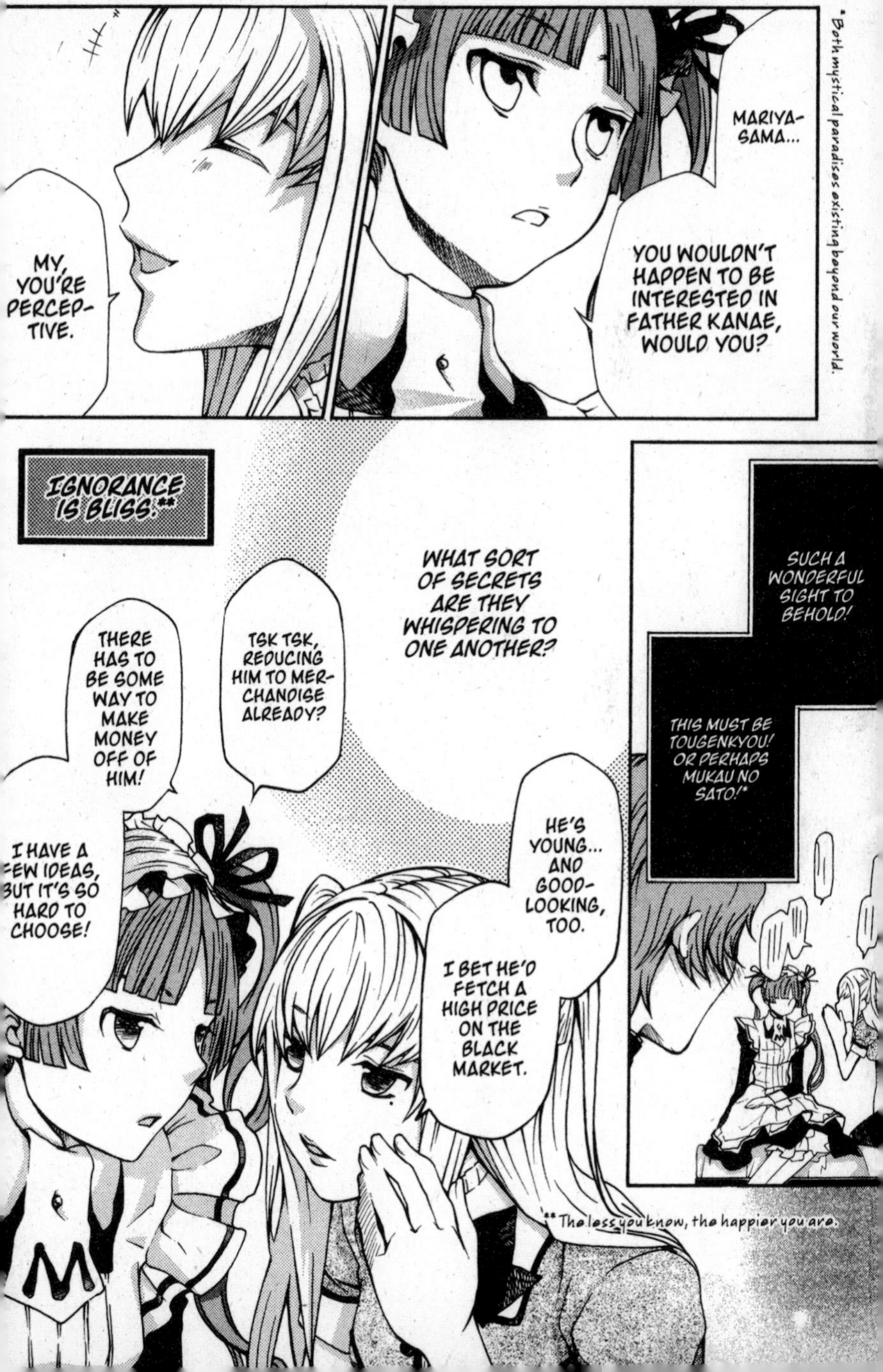
MARIYA-SAMA...
YOU WOULDN'T HAPPEN TO BE INTERESTED IN FATHER KANAE, WOULD YOU?
MY, YOU'RE PERCEPTIVE.
SUCH A WONDERFUL SIGHT TO BEHOLD!
THIS MUST BE TOUGENKYOU! OR PERHAPS MUKAU NO SATO!*
WHAT SORT OF SECRETS ARE THEY WHISPERING TO ONE ANOTHER?
IGNORANCE IS BLISS.**
HE'S YOUNG... AND GOOD-LOOKING, TOO.
I BET HE'D FETCH A HIGH PRICE ON THE BLACK MARKET.
TSK TSK, REDUCING HIM TO MER-CHANDISE ALREADY?
THERE HAS TO BE SOME WAY TO MAKE MONEY OFF OF HIM!
I HAVE A FEW IDEAS, BUT IT'S SO HARD TO CHOOSE!

*Both mystical paradises existing beyond our world.

**The less you know, the happier you are.

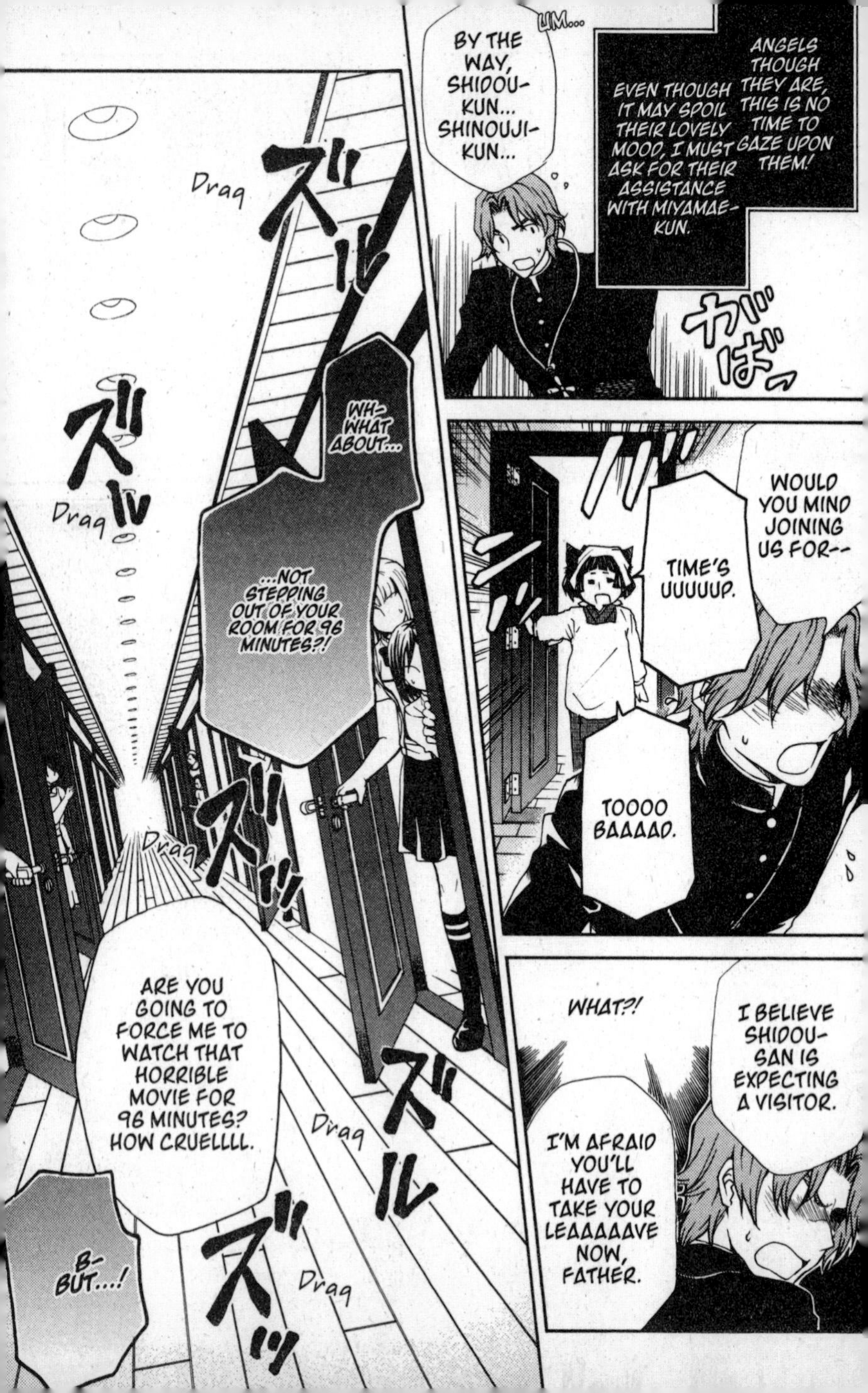
ANGELS THOUGH THEY ARE, THIS IS NO TIME TO GAZE UPON THEM!
EVEN THOUGH IT MAY SPOIL THEIR LOVELY MOOD, I MUST ASK FOR THEIR ASSISTANCE WITH MIYAMAE-KUN.
UM...
BY THE WAY, SHIDOU-KUN... SHINOUJI-KUN...
WOULD YOU MIND JOINING US FOR--
TIME'S UUUUUP.
TOOOO BAAAAAD.
I BELIEVE SHIDOU-SAN IS EXPECTING A VISITOR.
WHAT?!
I'M AFRAID YOU'LL HAVE TO TAKE YOUR LEAAAAAVE NOW, FATHER.
Drag
Drag
WH-WHAT ABOUT...
...NOT STEPPING OUT OF YOUR ROOM FOR 96 MINUTES?!
Drag
ARE YOU GOING TO FORCE ME TO WATCH THAT HORRIBLE MOVIE FOR 96 MINUTES? HOW CRUELLLL.
Drag
B-BUT...!
Drag

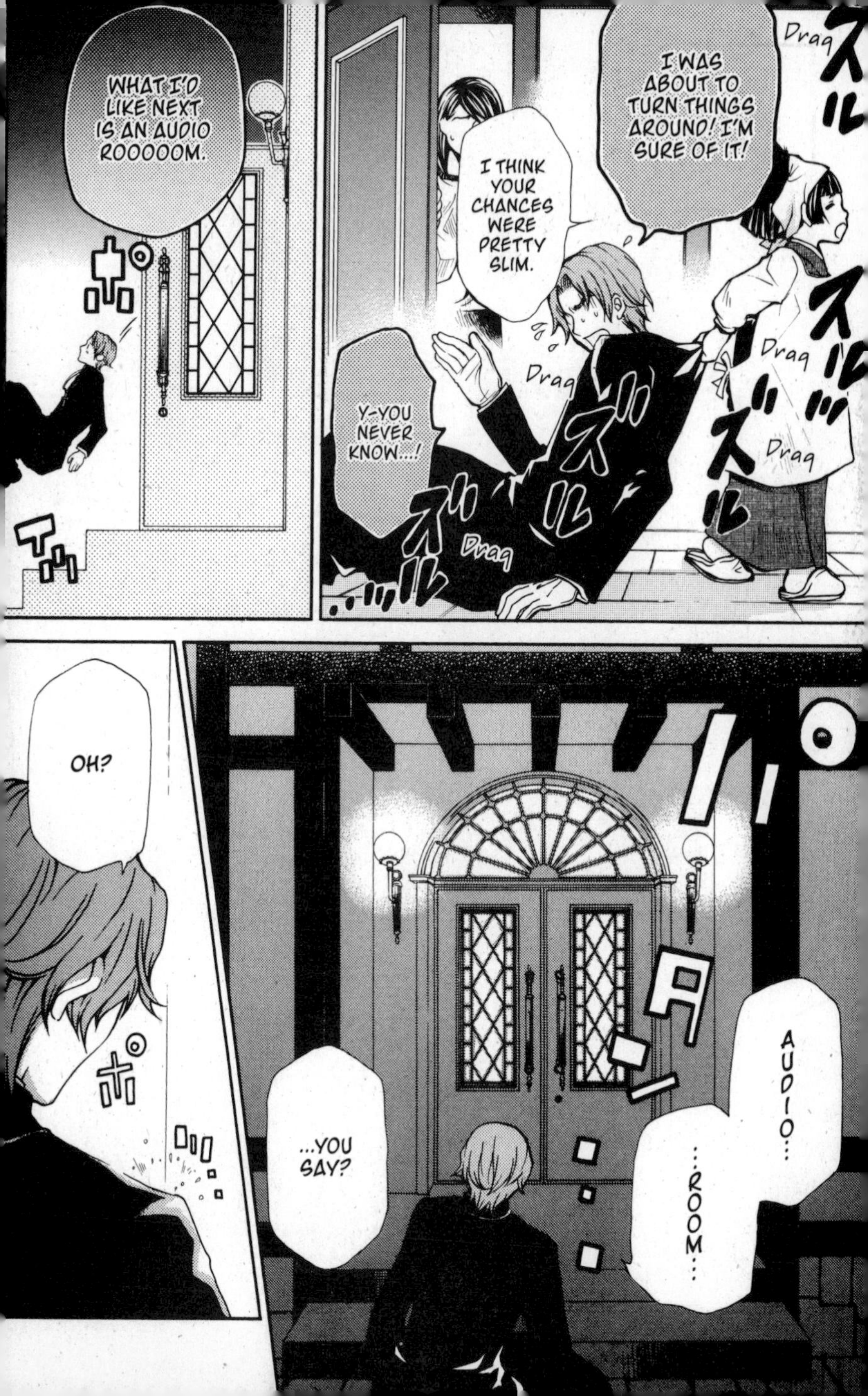
Drag
I WAS ABOUT TO TURN THINGS AROUND! I'M SURE OF IT!
I THINK YOUR CHANCES WERE PRETTY SLIM.
Drag
Drag
Drag
Y-YOU NEVER KNOW...!
Drag
WHAT I'D LIKE NEXT IS AN AUDIO ROOOOOM.
AUDIO...
...ROOM...
...YOU SAY?
OH?

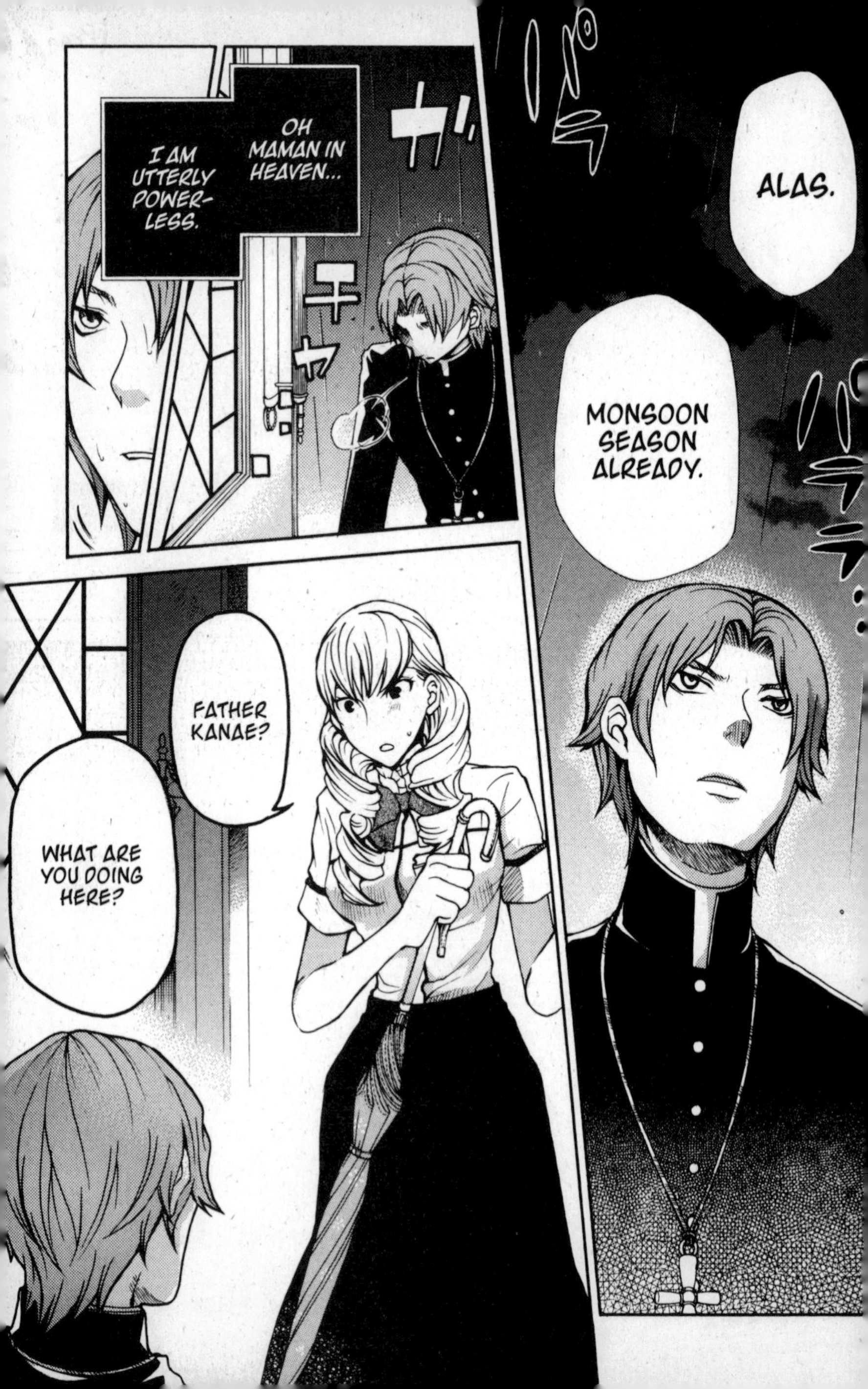
ALAS.
MONSOON SEASON ALREADY.
OH MAMAN IN HEAVEN...
I AM UTTERLY POWER-LESS.
FATHER KANAE?
WHAT ARE YOU DOING HERE?

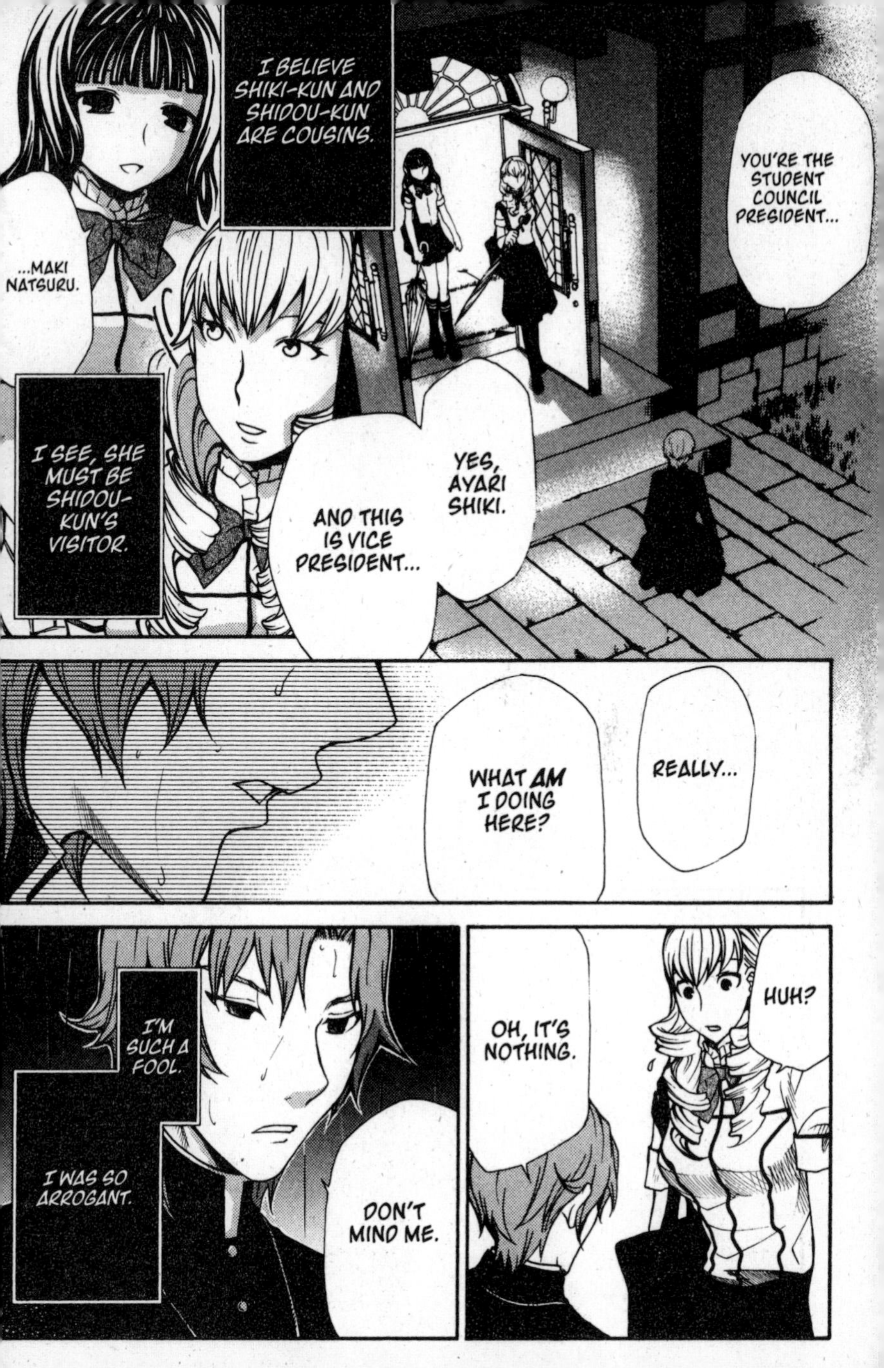
YOU'RE THE STUDENT COUNCIL PRESIDENT...
YES, AYARI SHIKI.
AND THIS IS VICE PRESIDENT...
...MAKI NATSURU.
I BELIEVE SHIKI-KUN AND SHIDOU-KUN ARE COUSINS.
I SEE, SHE MUST BE SHIDOU-KUN'S VISITOR.
REALLY...
WHAT AM I DOING HERE?
HUH?
OH, IT'S NOTHING.
DON'T MIND ME.
I'M SUCH A FOOL.
I WAS SO ARROGANT.

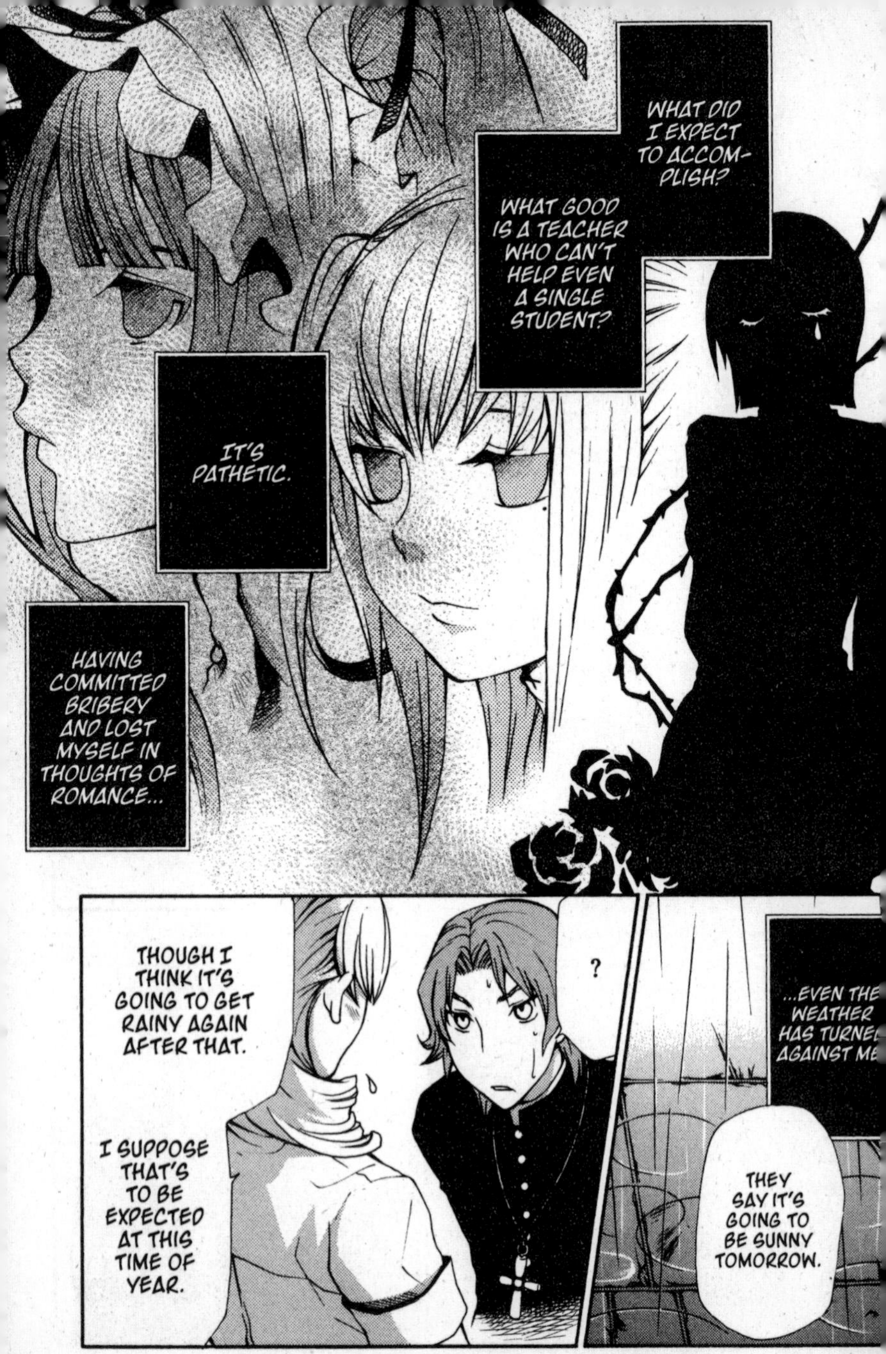
WHAT DID I EXPECT TO ACCOMPLISH?
WHAT GOOD IS A TEACHER WHO CAN'T HELP EVEN A SINGLE STUDENT?
IT'S PATHETIC.
HAVING COMMITTED BRIBERY AND LOST MYSELF IN THOUGHTS OF ROMANCE...
...EVEN THE WEATHER HAS TURNED AGAINST ME
THEY SAY IT'S GOING TO BE SUNNY TOMORROW.
?
THOUGH I THINK IT'S GOING TO GET RAINY AGAIN AFTER THAT.
I SUPPOSE THAT'S TO BE EXPECTED AT THIS TIME OF YEAR.

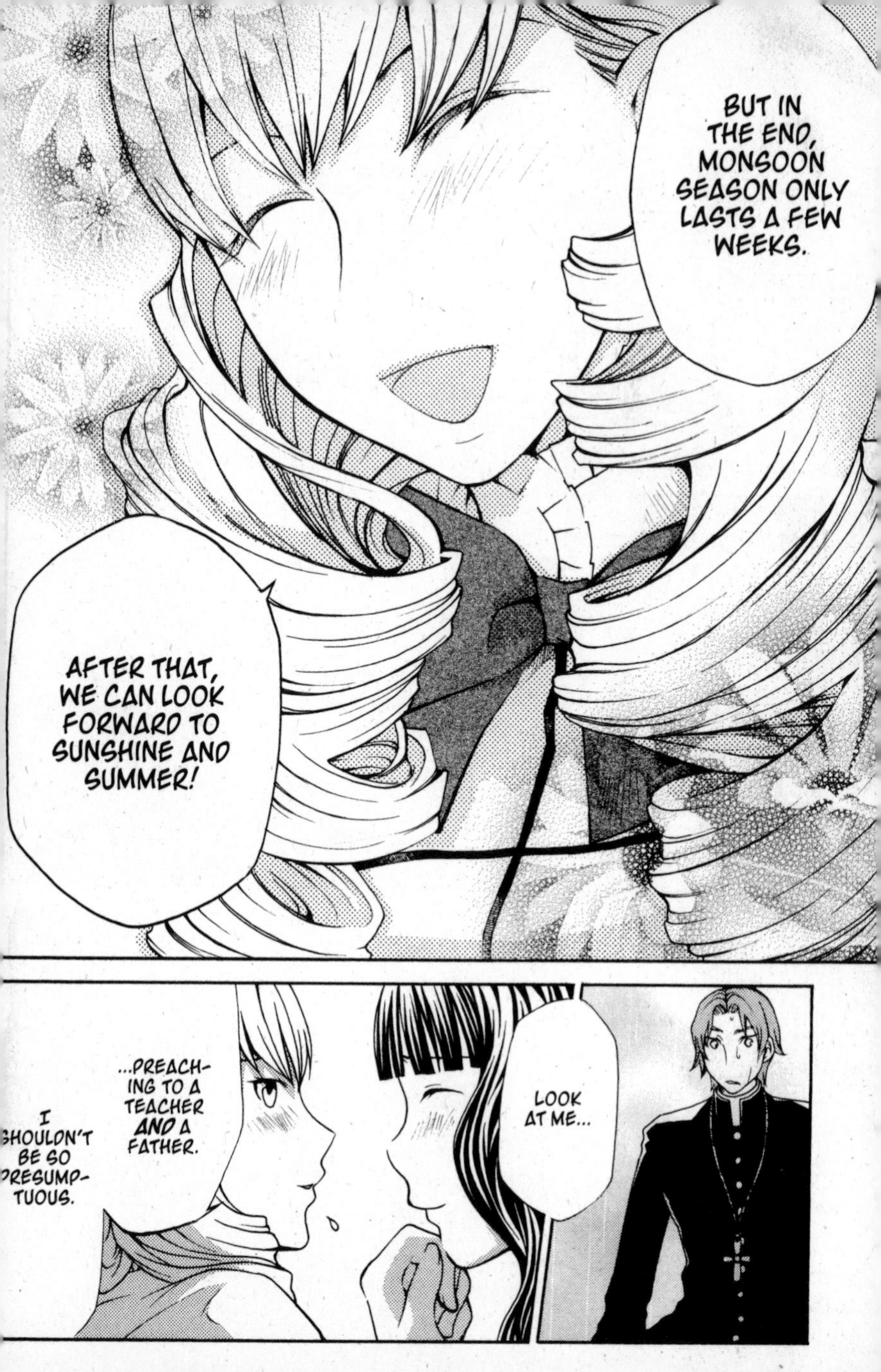
BUT IN THE END, MONSOON SEASON ONLY LASTS A FEW WEEKS.
AFTER THAT, WE CAN LOOK FORWARD TO SUNSHINE AND SUMMER!
LOOK AT ME...
...PREACHING TO A TEACHER AND A FATHER.
I SHOULDN'T BE SO PRESUMPTUOUS.

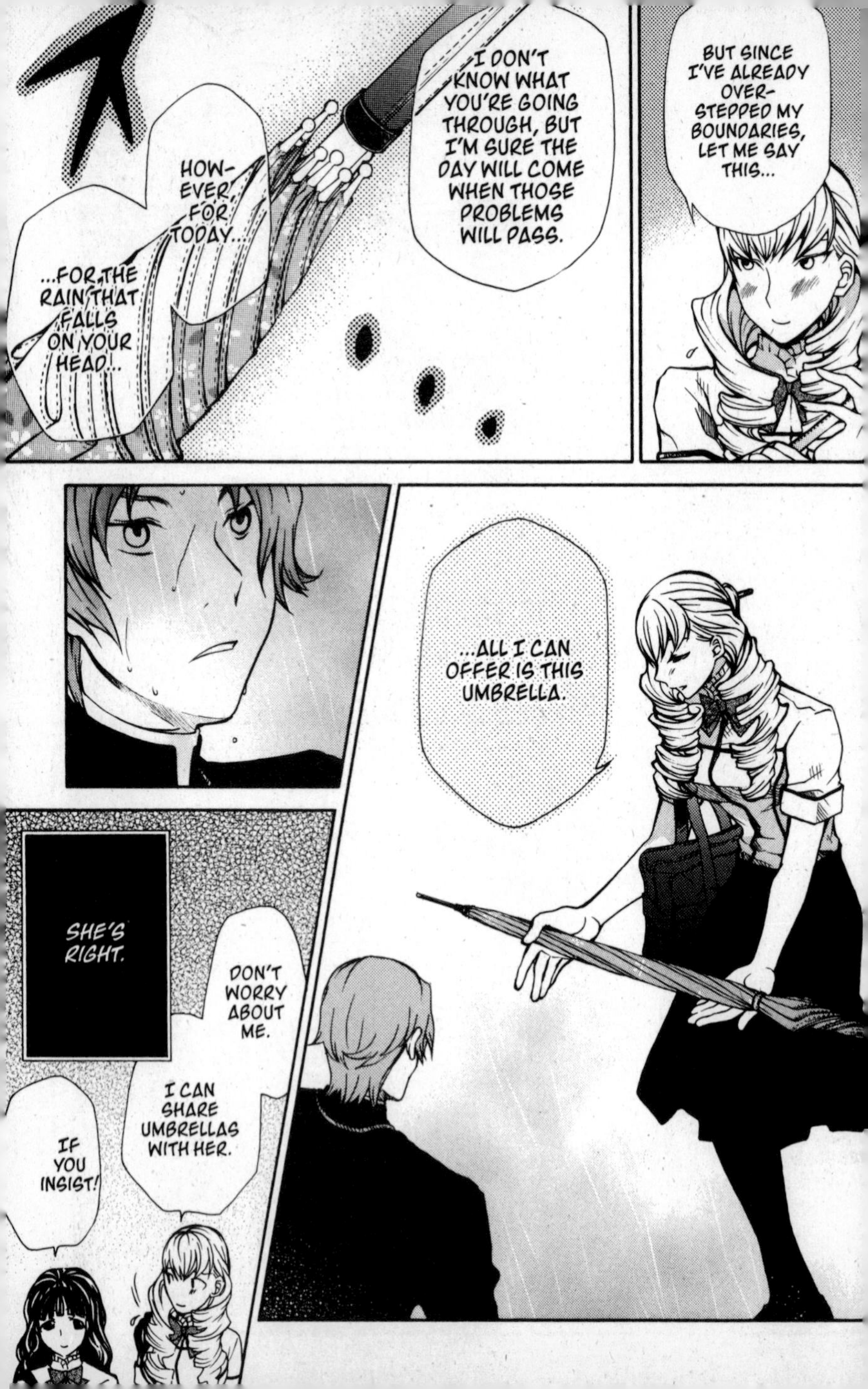
BUT SINCE I'VE ALREADY OVER-STEPPED MY BOUNDARIES, LET ME SAY THIS...
I DON'T KNOW WHAT YOU'RE GOING THROUGH, BUT I'M SURE THE DAY WILL COME WHEN THOSE PROBLEMS WILL PASS.
HOW-EVER, FOR TODAY...
...FOR THE RAIN THAT FALLS ON YOUR HEAD...
...ALL I CAN OFFER IS THIS UMBRELLA.
SHE'S RIGHT.
DON'T WORRY ABOUT ME.
I CAN SHARE UMBRELLAS WITH HER.
IF YOU INSIST!

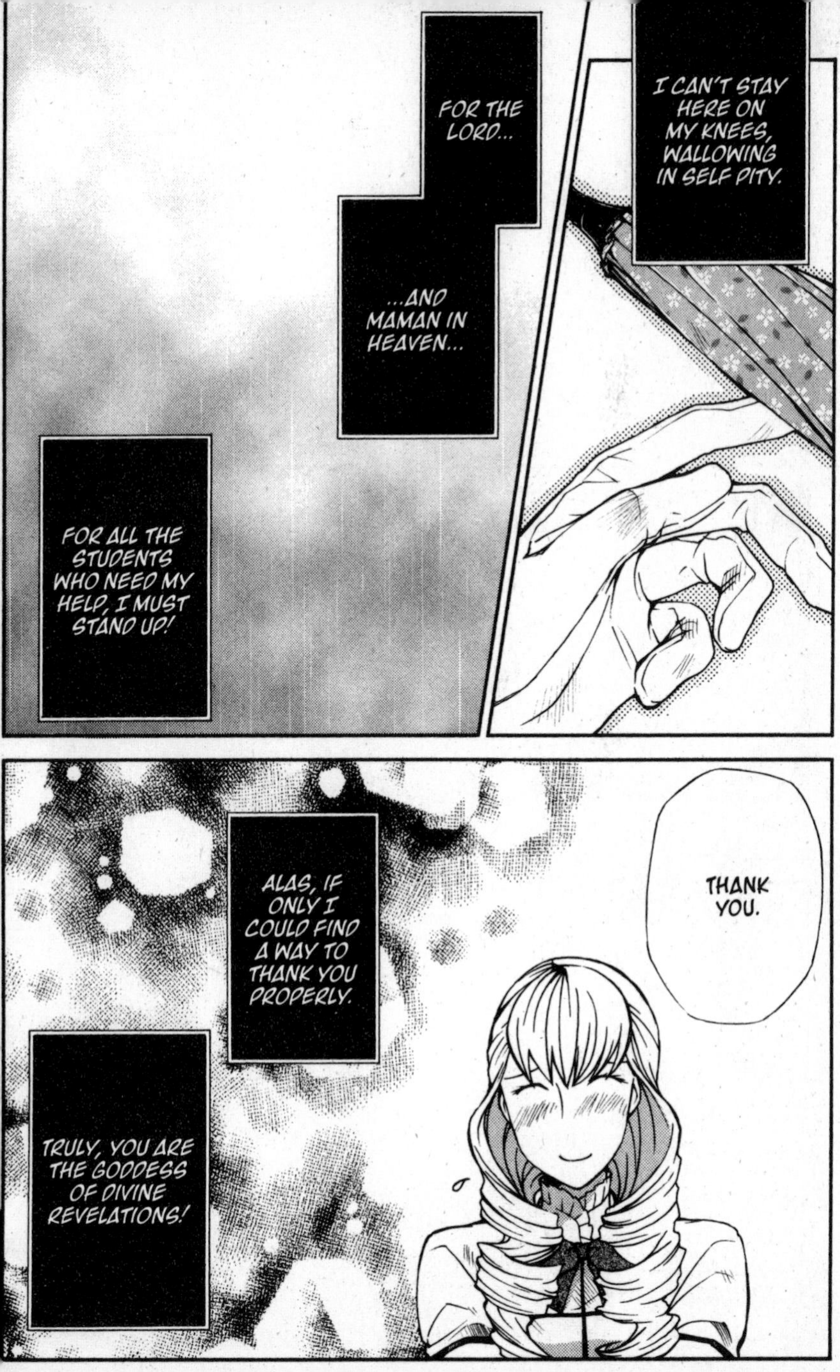
I CAN'T STAY HERE ON MY KNEES, WALLOWING IN SELF PITY.
FOR THE LORD...
...AND MAMAN IN HEAVEN...
FOR ALL THE STUDENTS WHO NEED MY HELP, I MUST STAND UP!
THANK YOU.
ALAS, IF ONLY I COULD FIND A WAY TO THANK YOU PROPERLY.
TRULY, YOU ARE THE GODDESS OF DIVINE REVELATIONS!

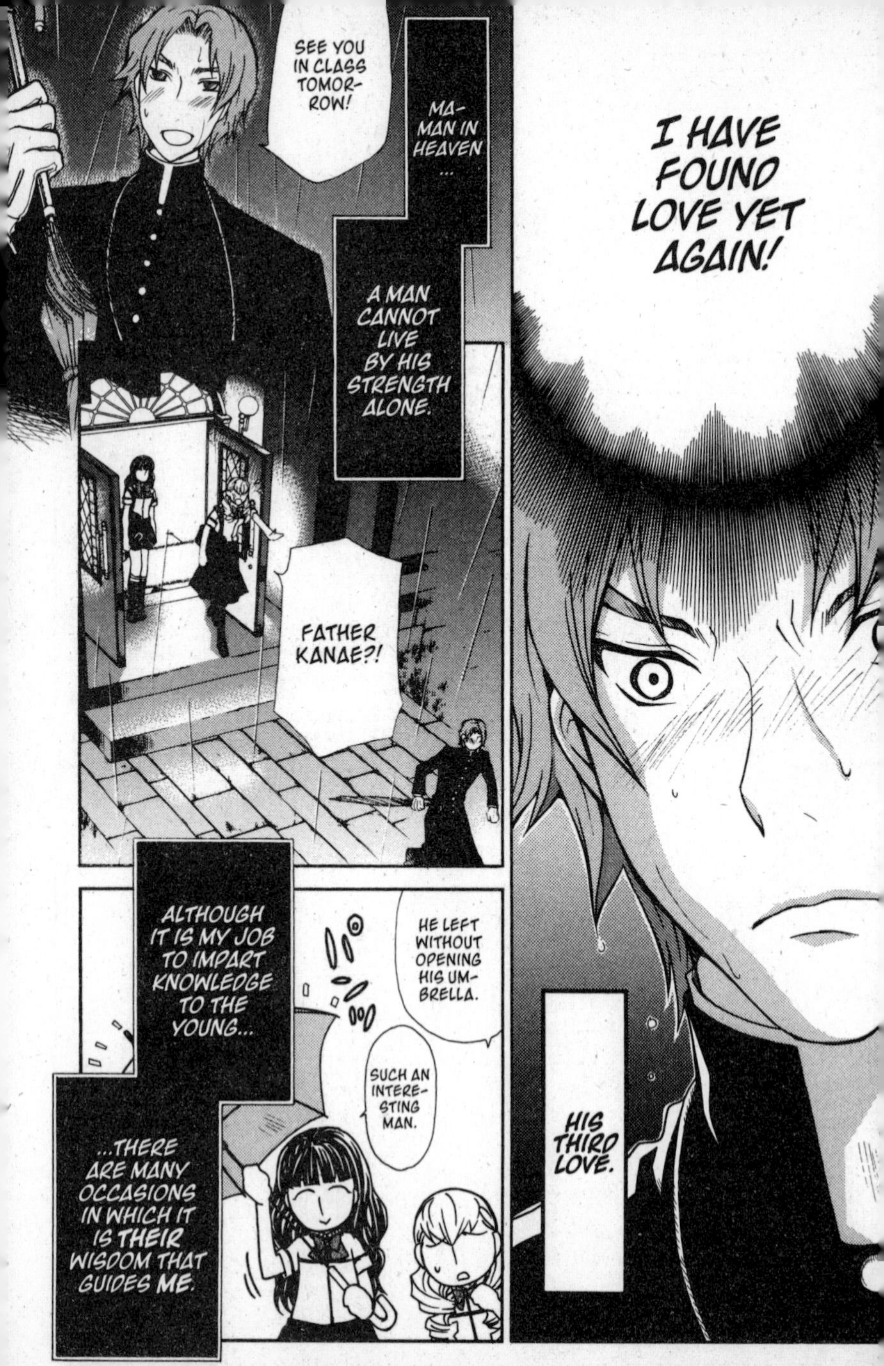
I HAVE FOUND LOVE YET AGAIN!
HIS THIRD LOVE.
MA-MAN IN HEAVEN...
SEE YOU IN CLASS TOMORROW!
A MAN CANNOT LIVE BY HIS STRENGTH ALONE.
FATHER KANAE?!
HE LEFT WITHOUT OPENING HIS UMBRELLA.
SUCH AN INTERESTING MAN.
ALTHOUGH IT IS MY JOB TO IMPART KNOWLEDGE TO THE YOUNG...
...THERE ARE MANY OCCASIONS IN WHICH IT IS THEIR WISDOM THAT GUIDES ME.

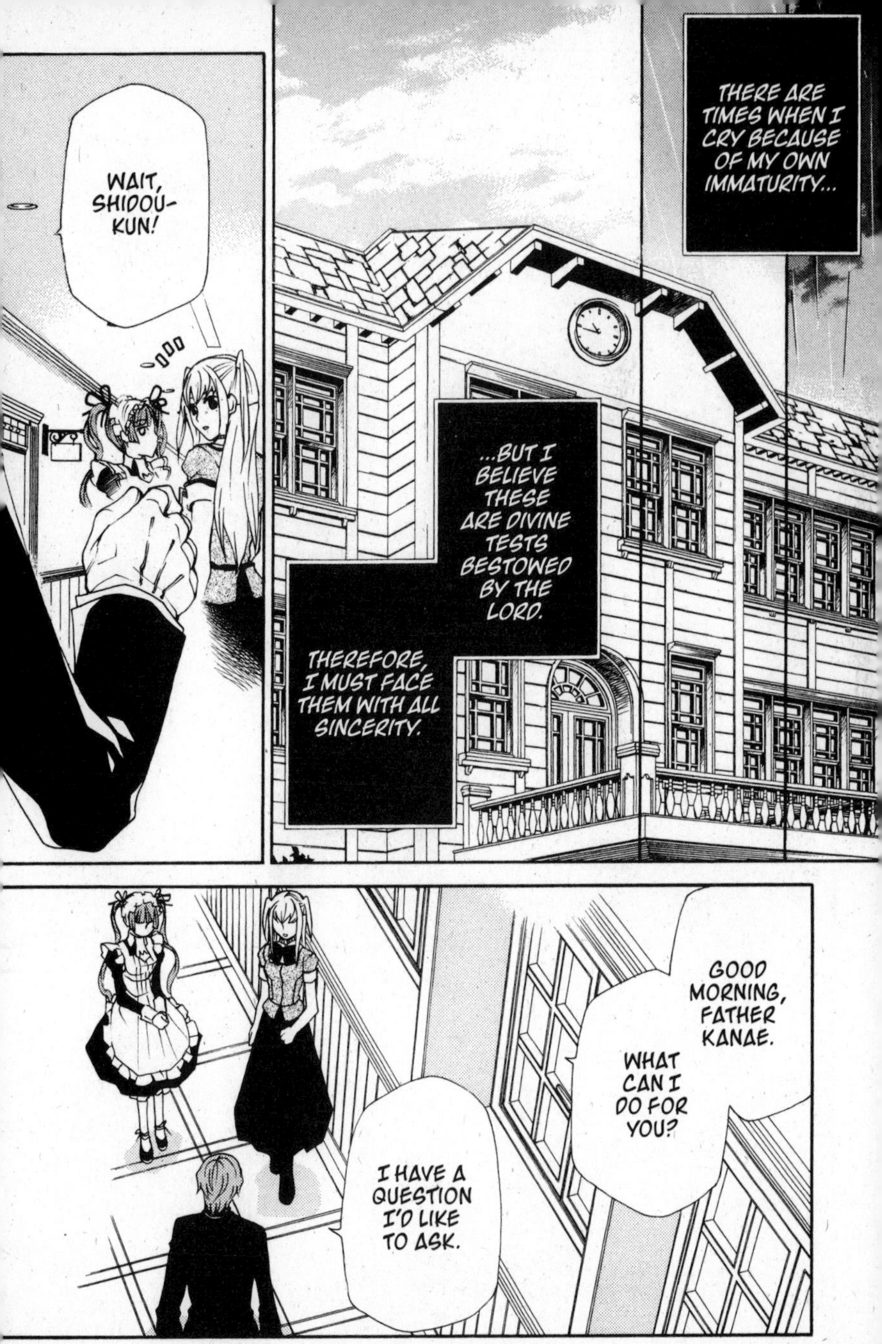
THERE ARE TIMES WHEN I CRY BECAUSE OF MY OWN IMMATURITY...
...BUT I BELIEVE THESE ARE DIVINE TESTS BESTOWED BY THE LORD.
THEREFORE, I MUST FACE THEM WITH ALL SINCERITY.
WAIT, SHIDOU-KUN!
GOOD MORNING, FATHER KANAE.
WHAT CAN I DO FOR YOU?
I HAVE A QUESTION I'D LIKE TO ASK.

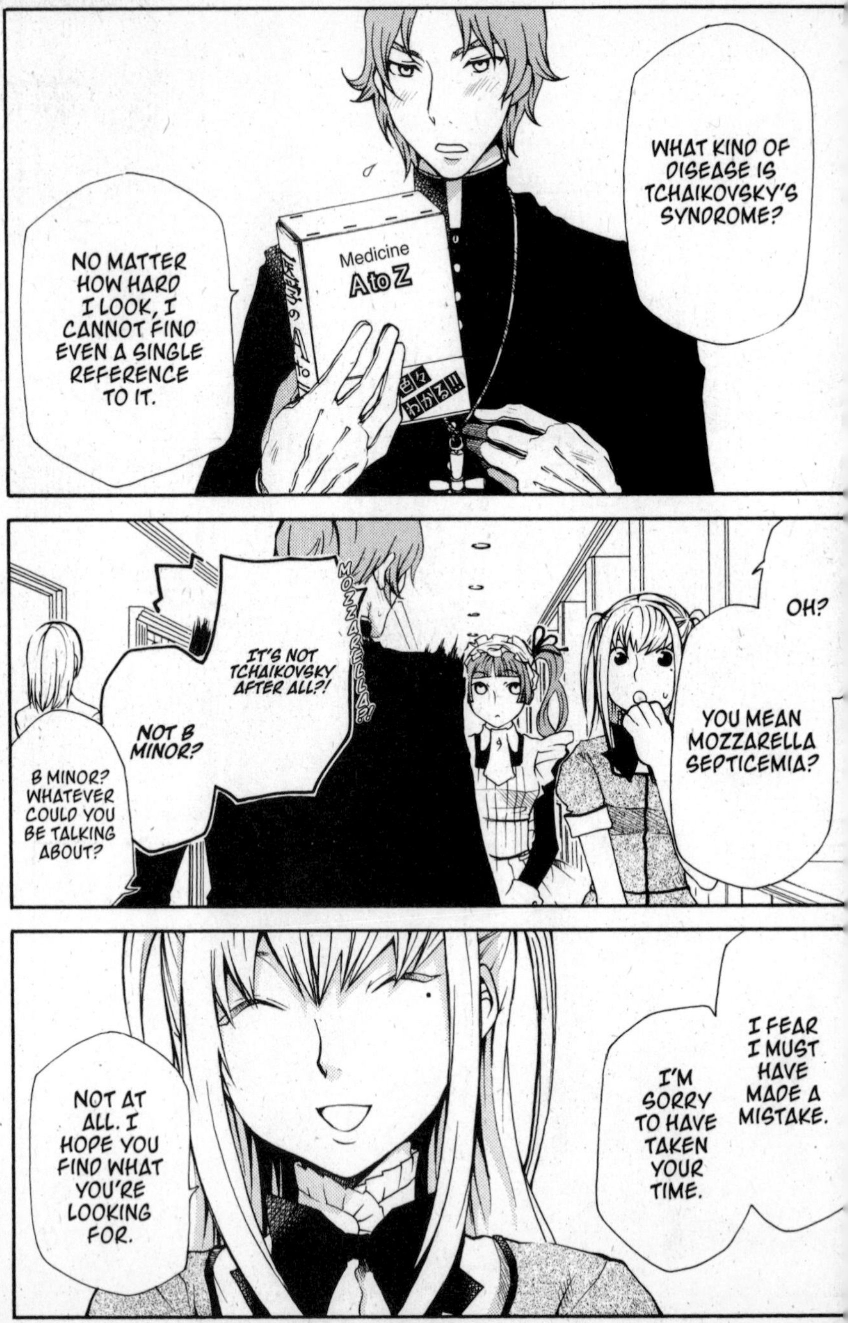
WHAT KIND OF DISEASE IS TCHAIKOVSKY'S SYNDROME?
Medicine A to Z
NO MATTER HOW HARD I LOOK, I CANNOT FIND EVEN A SINGLE REFERENCE TO IT.
OH?
YOU MEAN MOZZARELLA SEPTICEMIA?
MOZZARELLA?!
IT'S NOT TCHAIKOVSKY AFTER ALL?!
NOT B MINOR?
B MINOR? WHATEVER COULD YOU BE TALKING ABOUT?
I FEAR I MUST HAVE MADE A MISTAKE.
I'M SORRY TO HAVE TAKEN YOUR TIME.
NOT AT ALL. I HOPE YOU FIND WHAT YOU'RE LOOKING FOR.

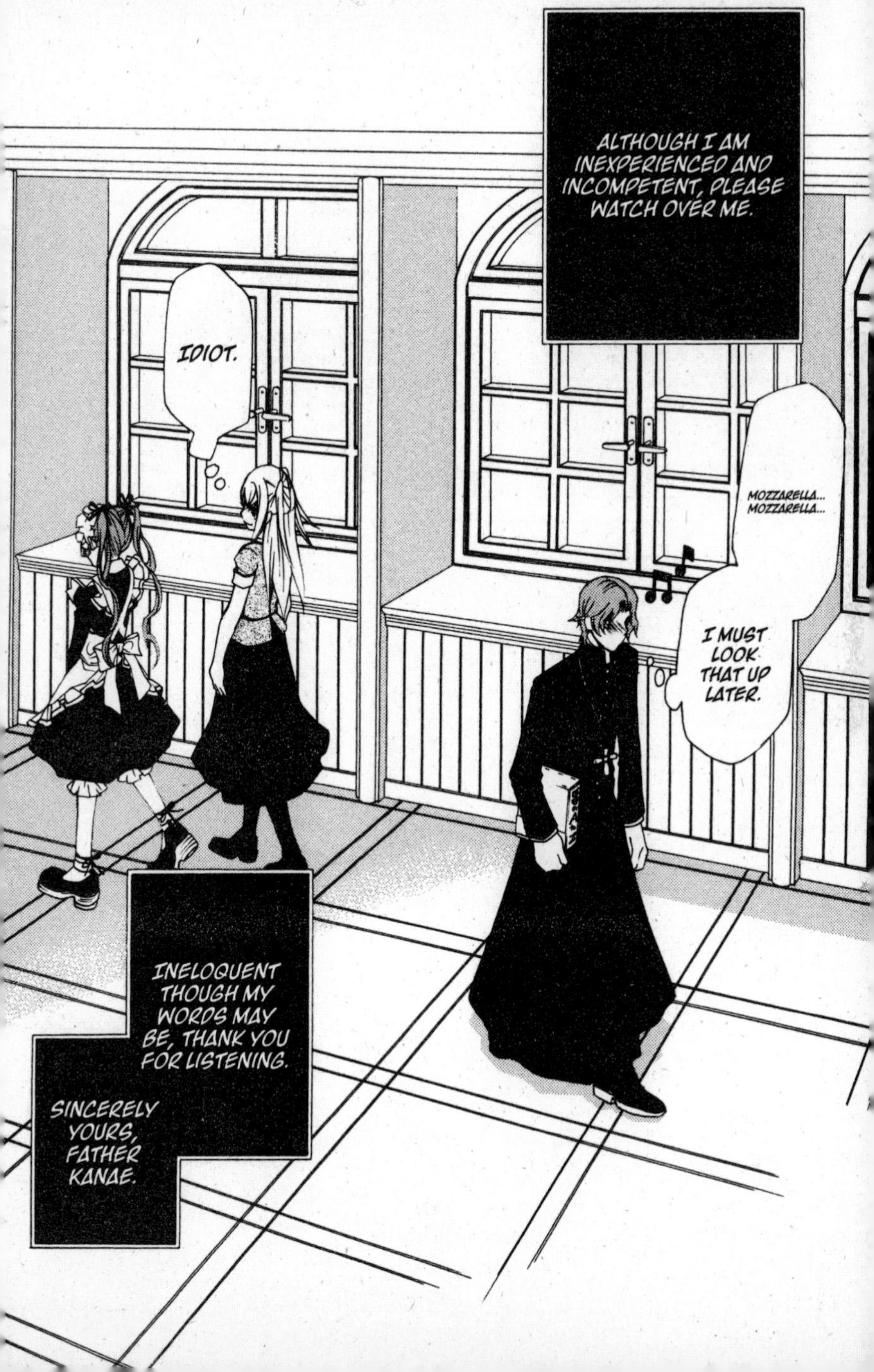
ALTHOUGH I AM INEXPERIENCED AND INCOMPETENT, PLEASE WATCH OVER ME.
IDIOT.
MOZZARELLA... MOZZARELLA...
I MUST LOOK THAT UP LATER.
INELOQUENT THOUGH MY WORDS MAY BE, THANK YOU FOR LISTENING.
SINCERELY YOURS, FATHER KANAE.

TONY AND MYTY

DISCOVER WORLD HERITAGE SITES

T: MONT SAINT MICHEL IS AN ABBEY BUILT ON A ROCKY ISLAND IN THE GULF OF SAINT MALO ALONG THE NORMANDY COAST IN WESTERN FRANCE.

M: YEAH, I KNOW. THE MUSSELS THERE ARE GREAT.

T: THOUGH IT WAS ORIGINALLY BUILT AS AN ABBEY, IT WAS USED AS A FORT DURING THE HUNDRED YEARS' WAR AND BECAME A PRISON DURING THE FRENCH REVOLUTION.

M: THIS PLACE HAS GOT MORE TWISTS THAN A BAG OF PRETZELS!

T: IT'S BEEN RESTORED AS AN ABBEY AGAIN, AND IS NOW VISITED BY MANY TOURISTS. TO GET THERE, TAKE THE TGV FROM MONTPARNASSE STATION TO RENNES, (WHICH TAKES ABOUT TWO HOURS), THEN HOP ON A BUS THAT LEAVES FROM THE NORTH EXIT OF RENNES STATION. AFTER THAT, THE BUS TO MONT SAINT MICHEL TAKES ABOUT AN HOUR.

M: THINK YOU COULD REPEAT THOSE DIRECTIONS WITHOUT LOOKING AT THE GUIDEBOOK?

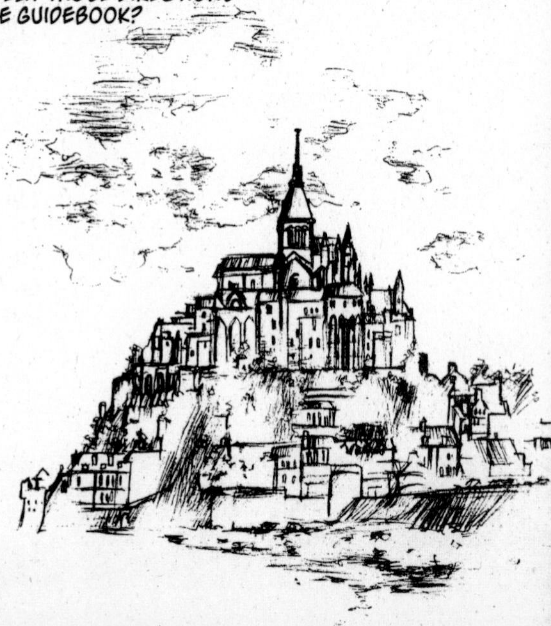

M A R I A H O L I C

Maria Holic

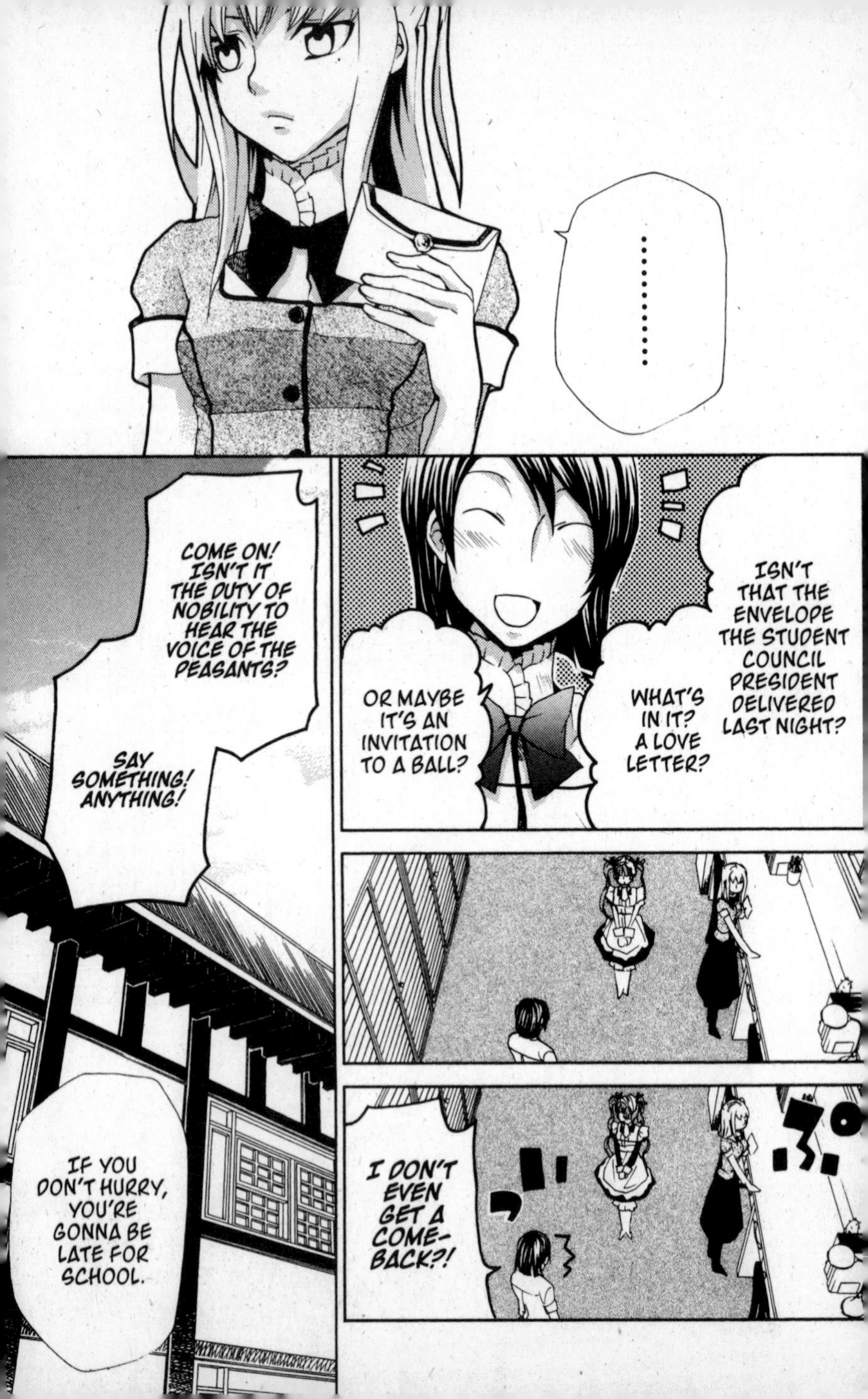

……
ISN'T THAT THE ENVELOPE THE STUDENT COUNCIL PRESIDENT DELIVERED LAST NIGHT?
WHAT'S IN IT? A LOVE LETTER?
OR MAYBE IT'S AN INVITATION TO A BALL?
I DON'T EVEN GET A COME-BACK?!
COME ON! ISN'T IT THE DUTY OF NOBILITY TO HEAR THE VOICE OF THE PEASANTS?
SAY SOMETHING! ANYTHING!
IF YOU DON'T HURRY, YOU'RE GONNA BE LATE FOR SCHOOL.

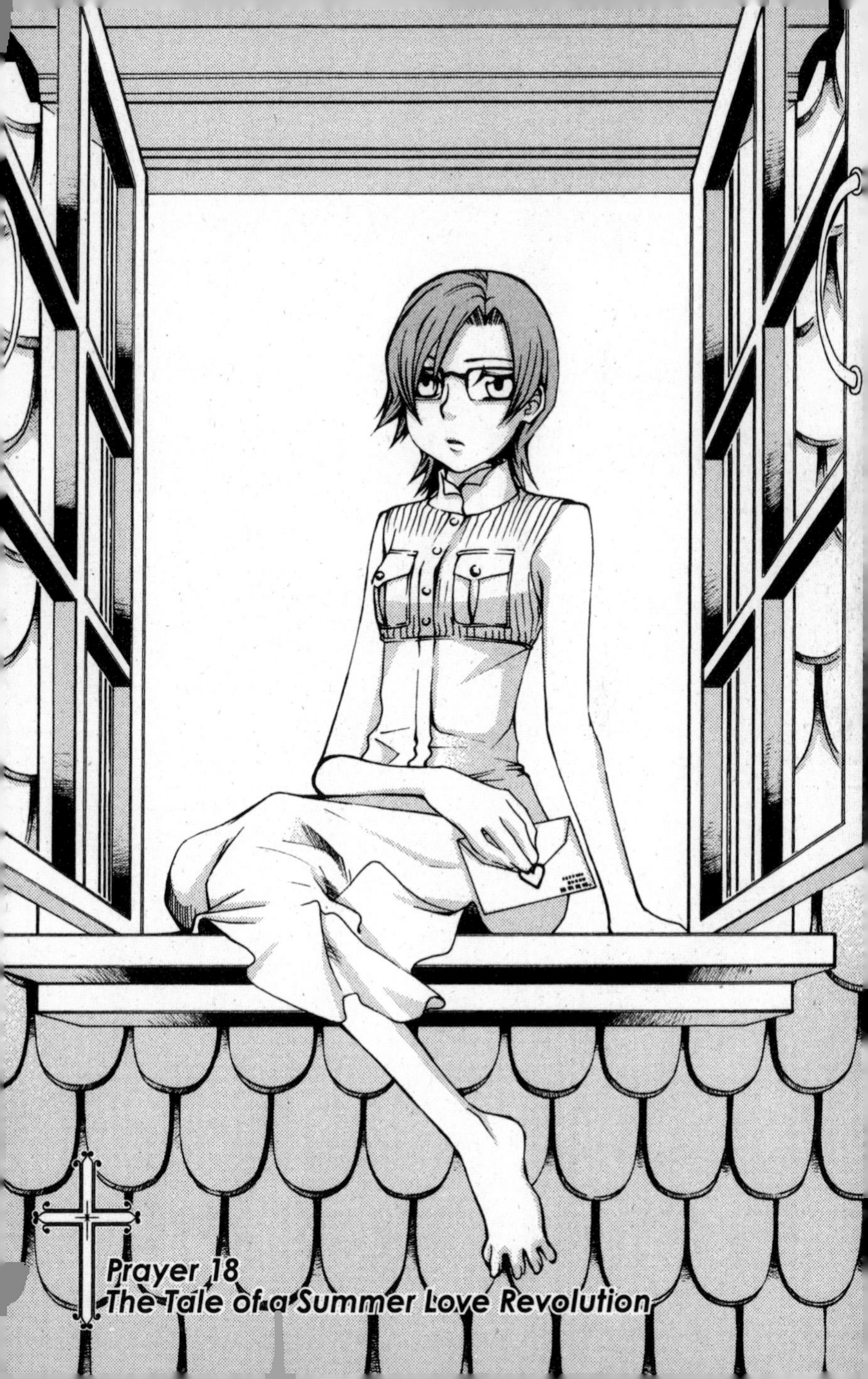
Prayer 18
The Tale of a Summer Love Revolution

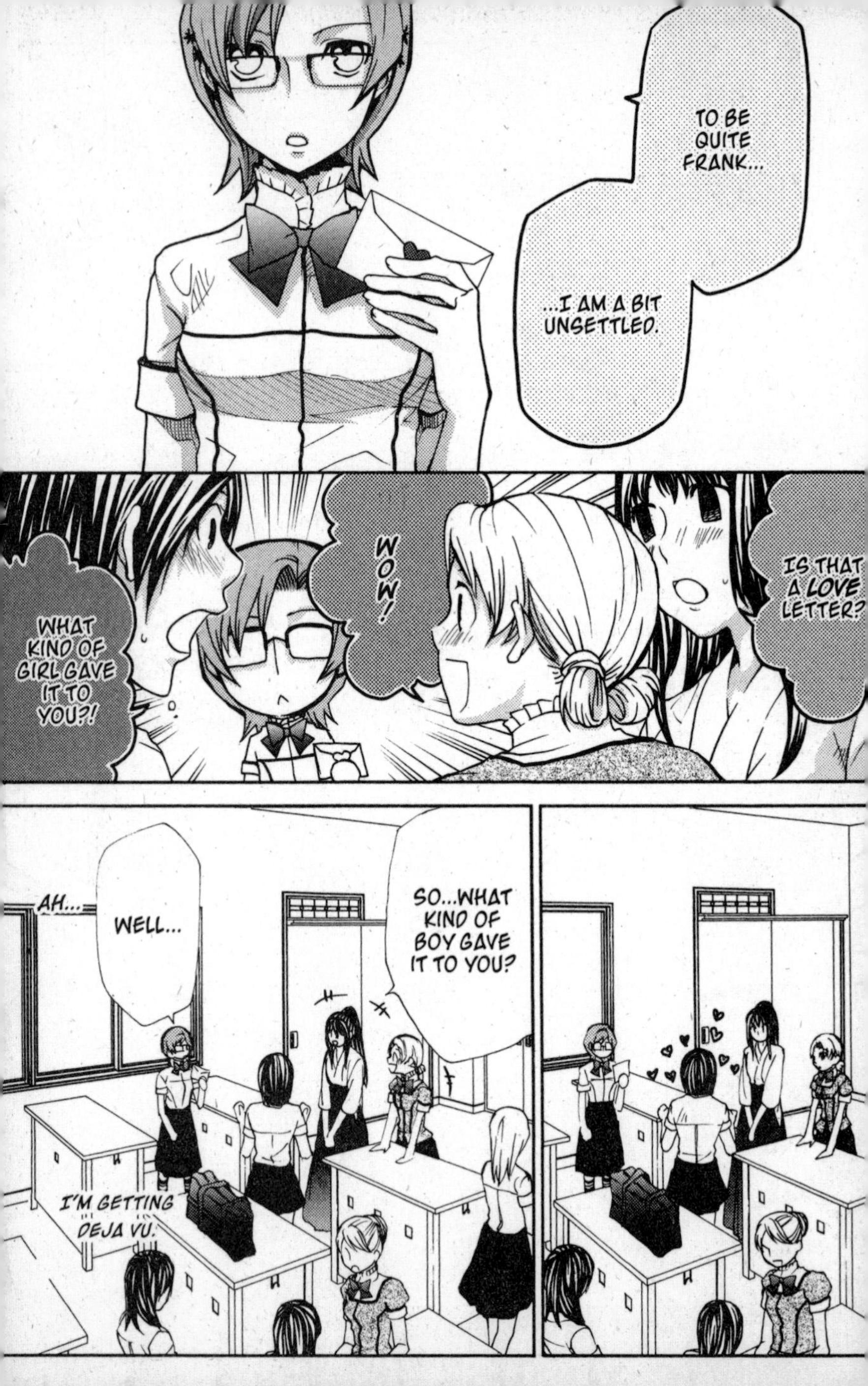
TO BE QUITE FRANK...
...I AM A BIT UNSETTLED.
IS THAT A LOVE LETTER?
WOW!
WHAT KIND OF GIRL GAVE IT TO YOU?!
SO...WHAT KIND OF BOY GAVE IT TO YOU?
WELL...
AH...
I'M GETTING DEJA VU.

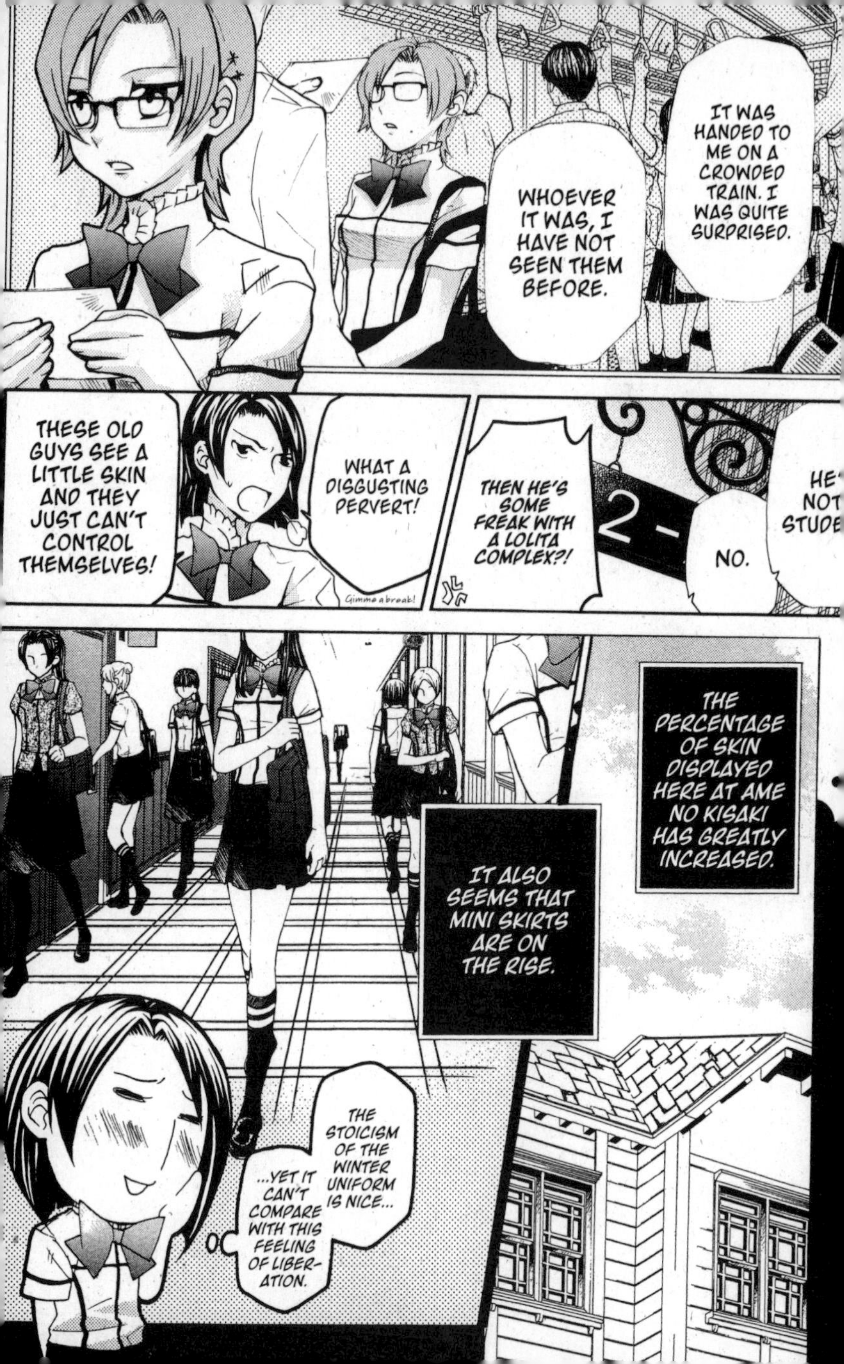

IT WAS HANDED TO ME ON A CROWDED TRAIN. I WAS QUITE SURPRISED.
WHOEVER IT WAS, I HAVE NOT SEEN THEM BEFORE.
NO.
THEN HE'S SOME FREAK WITH A LOLITA COMPLEX?!
WHAT A DISGUSTING PERVERT!
Gimme a break!
THESE OLD GUYS SEE A LITTLE SKIN AND THEY JUST CAN'T CONTROL THEMSELVES!
THE PERCENTAGE OF SKIN DISPLAYED HERE AT AME NO KISAKI HAS GREATLY INCREASED.
IT ALSO SEEMS THAT MINI SKIRTS ARE ON THE RISE.
THE STOICISM OF THE WINTER UNIFORM IS NICE...
...YET IT CAN'T COMPARE WITH THIS FEELING OF LIBERATION.

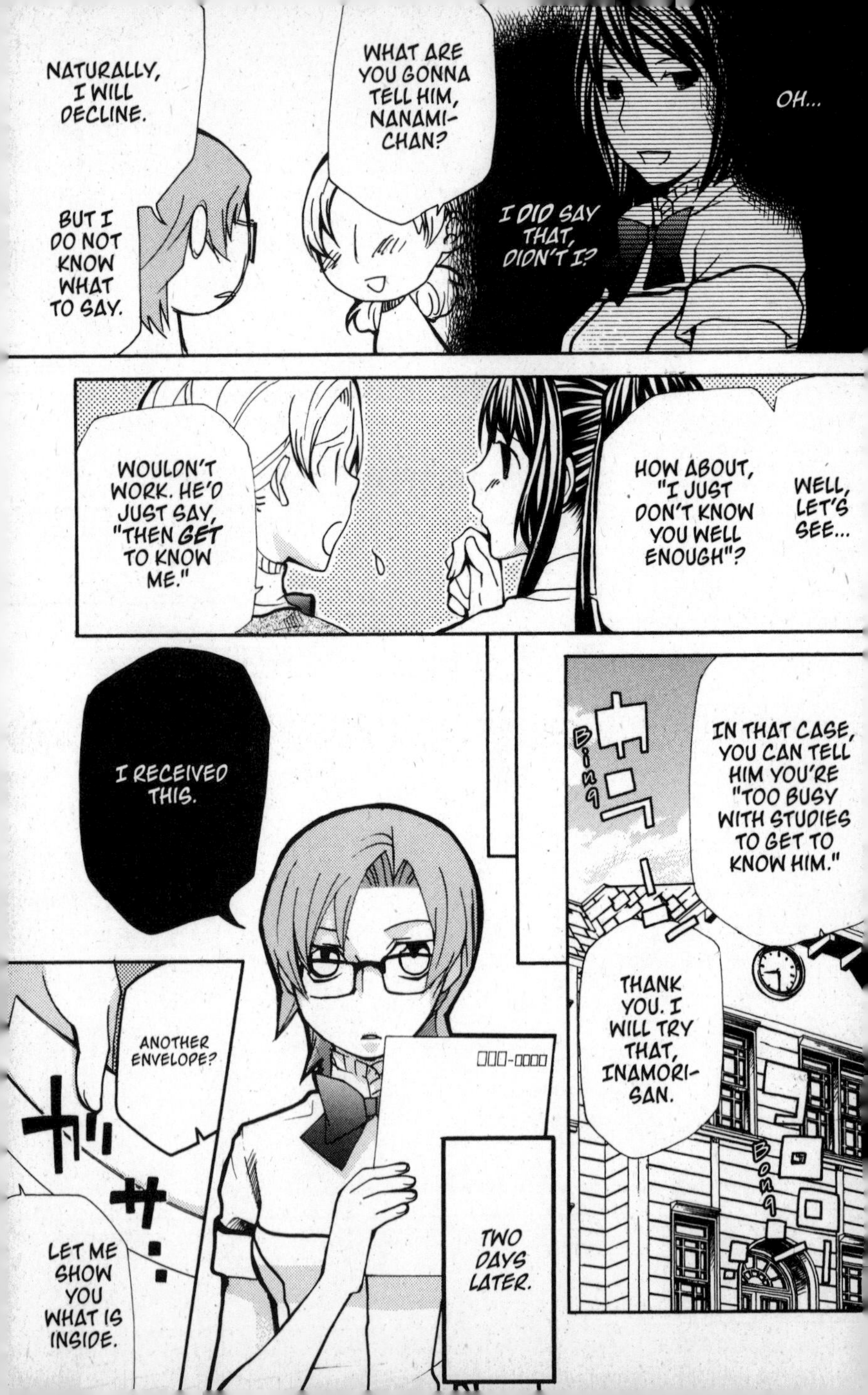
OH...
I DID SAY THAT, DIDN'T I?
WHAT ARE YOU GONNA TELL HIM, NANAMI-CHAN?
NATURALLY, I WILL DECLINE.
BUT I DO NOT KNOW WHAT TO SAY.
WELL, LET'S SEE...
HOW ABOUT, "I JUST DON'T KNOW YOU WELL ENOUGH"?
WOULDN'T WORK. HE'D JUST SAY, "THEN GET TO KNOW ME."
IN THAT CASE, YOU CAN TELL HIM YOU'RE "TOO BUSY WITH STUDIES TO GET TO KNOW HIM."
Bing
Bong
THANK YOU. I WILL TRY THAT, INAMORI-SAN.
TWO DAYS LATER.
I RECEIVED THIS.
ANOTHER ENVELOPE?
LET ME SHOW YOU WHAT IS INSIDE.

Era name	Year	Month	Education and Work Experience
	3	8	Finished special education for operation of compaction equipment
	6	1	Type 3 official softball referee
	7	13	Type 4 small marine vessel pilot license
	9	17	Finished special education for chainsaw logging operation
	11	13	Food Sanitation Inspector license
	2	8	Competition License Japan Automobile Federation (Domestic A)
	3	15	Competition License Japan Automobile Federation (Domestic B)
	4	24	Small construction equipment license (for site work, transportation, loading and excavation) operation (less than 3 tons)
	7	2	Official referee for Japan Tug of War Association (Singles A)
	11	10	Class 1 small marine vessel pilot license
	11	24	Boiler handling technician seminar
			Please see attached sheet for additional information

Reason for application

I had decided upon first glance.

Please write something about yourself (Your achievements, personality, hobbies, etc.)

I am a positive person. An English magazine said,

"The stress of riding on a Japanese train during rush hour is equal to that of a

soldier on the battlefield," but even then, when

I see the soft morning sun reflected off your glasses,

I feel as relaxed as I would in a garden full of flowers.

Commute time	Dependents	Spouse	Support for spouse
About 1 hour 20 minutes	0	※ Yes No	※ Yes No

Resume 6/27/200X Date

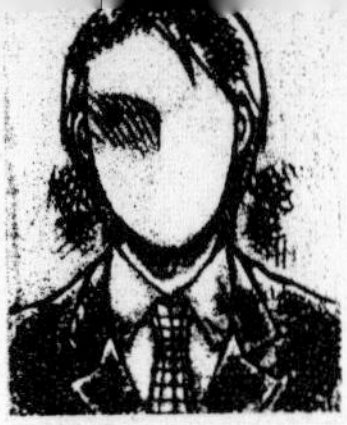

Name: Hideo Tsunoda	Gender: Male
Birthdate: June 6, 1985 (23 years old)	
Current Address: 2-4 Inoshishi, Koto-ku, Tokyo	Telephone: xxx-9696
E-mail: tsunoda★hero@gahoo.co.jp	Cell phone: 090-xxx-640
Mailing address: See above	Telephone at mailing address: See above

Era	Year	Month	Education and Employment History
			Education
Heisei	10	3	Graduated from Koto-ku Inoshishi Public Grade School
Heisei	13	3	Graduated from Koto-ku Inoshishi Public Junior High School
Heisei	13	4	Entered Zetsumeikan University (Tomakomai High School Division)
Heisei	16	3	Graduated from Zetsumeikan University (Tomakomai High School Division)
Heisei	16	4	Entered Zetsumeikan University (Industrial Social Studies Department)
Heisei	20	3	Graduated from Zetsumeikan University (Industrial Social Studies Department)
			Employment History
Heisei	20	4	Kamei Corporation
			To present
			Rewards and Punishments
			None

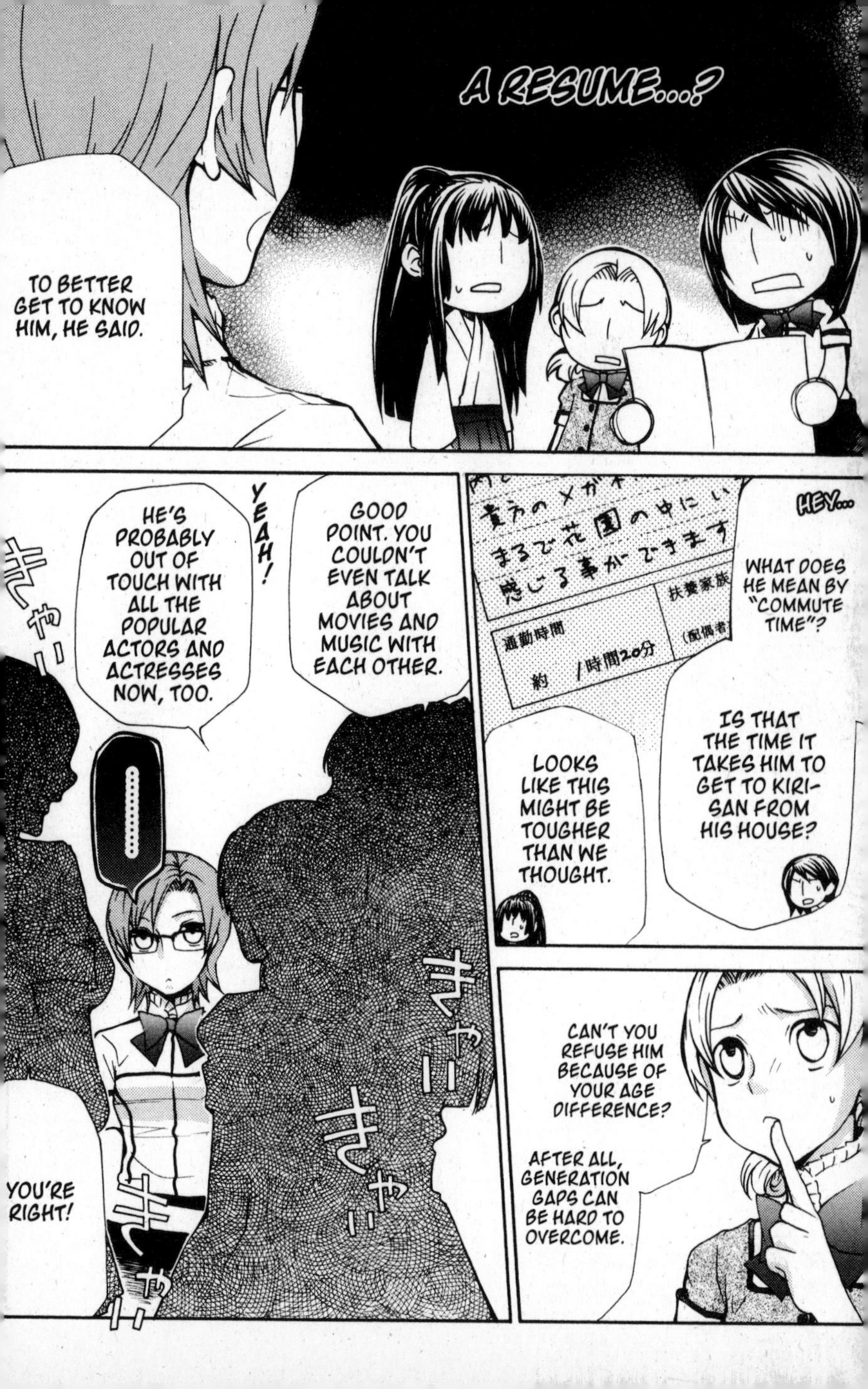
A RESUME...?
TO BETTER GET TO KNOW HIM, HE SAID.
扶養家族
(配偶者
通勤時間
約 1時間20分
HEY...
WHAT DOES HE MEAN BY "COMMUTE TIME"?
IS THAT THE TIME IT TAKES HIM TO GET TO KIRI-SAN FROM HIS HOUSE?
LOOKS LIKE THIS MIGHT BE TOUGHER THAN WE THOUGHT.
CAN'T YOU REFUSE HIM BECAUSE OF YOUR AGE DIFFERENCE?
AFTER ALL, GENERATION GAPS CAN BE HARD TO OVERCOME.
GOOD POINT. YOU COULDN'T EVEN TALK ABOUT MOVIES AND MUSIC WITH EACH OTHER.
YEAH!
HE'S PROBABLY OUT OF TOUCH WITH ALL THE POPULAR ACTORS AND ACTRESSES NOW, TOO.
きゃー
......
きゃー
きゃー
きゃー
YOU'RE RIGHT!

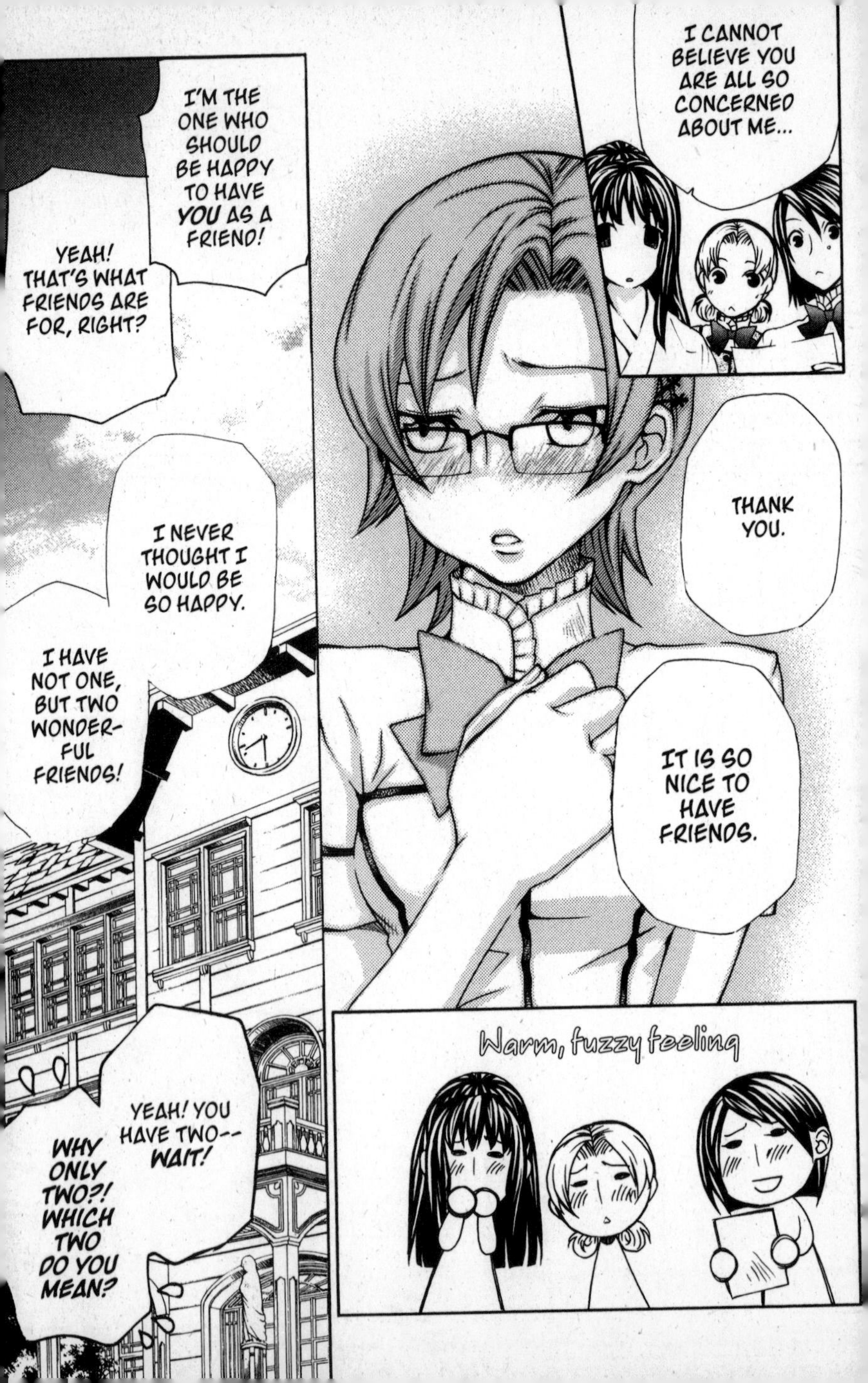
I CANNOT BELIEVE YOU ARE ALL SO CONCERNED ABOUT ME...
THANK YOU.
IT IS SO NICE TO HAVE FRIENDS.
I'M THE ONE WHO SHOULD BE HAPPY TO HAVE *YOU* AS A FRIEND!
YEAH! THAT'S WHAT FRIENDS ARE FOR, RIGHT?
I NEVER THOUGHT I WOULD BE SO HAPPY.
I HAVE NOT ONE, BUT TWO WONDER-FUL FRIENDS!
Warm, fuzzy feeling
YEAH! YOU HAVE TWO-- **WAIT!**
WHY ONLY TWO?! WHICH TWO DO YOU MEAN?

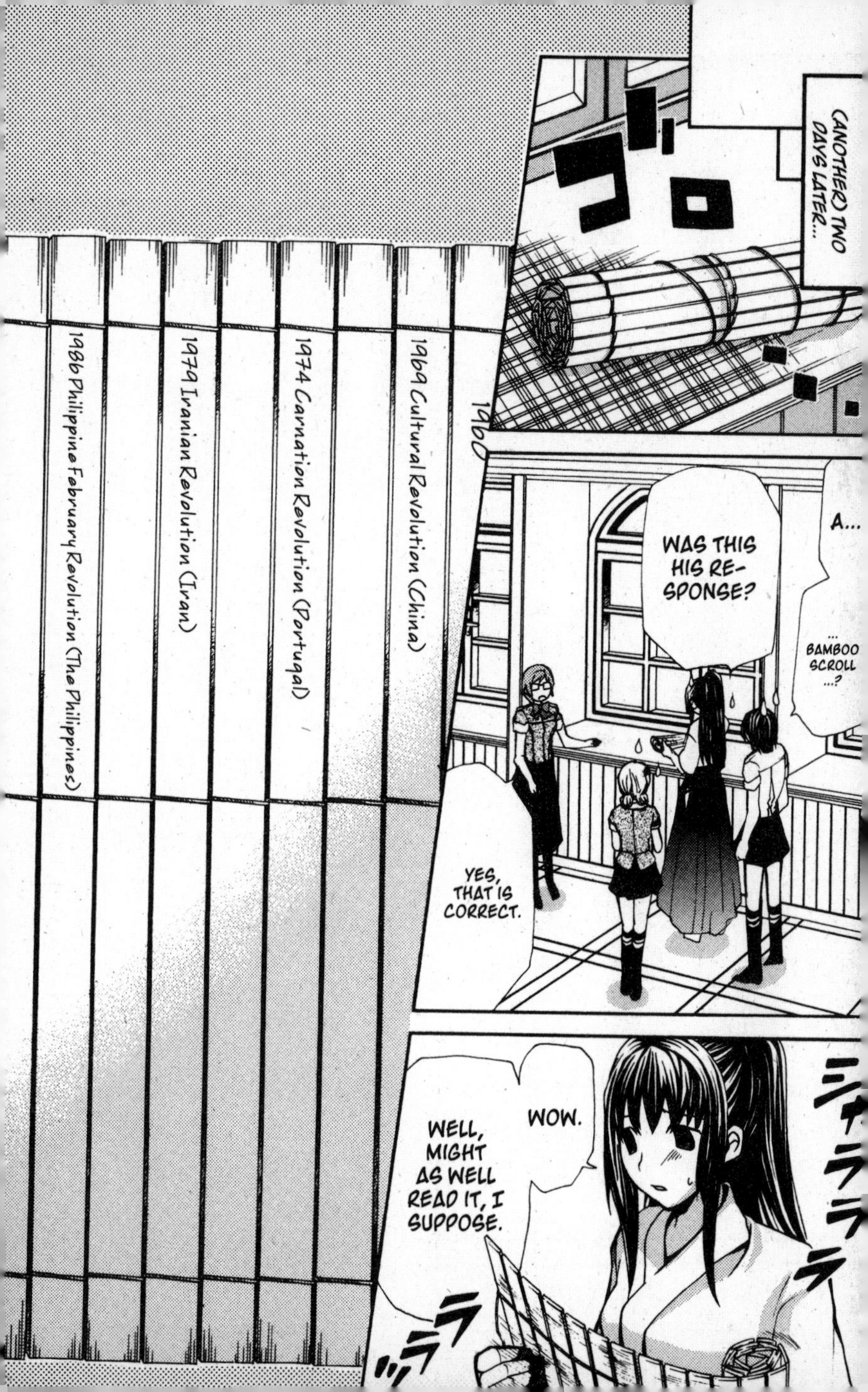
(ANOTHER) TWO DAYS LATER...
ゴロ
A...
... BAMBOO SCROLL ...?
WAS THIS HIS RE-SPONSE?
YES, THAT IS CORRECT.
WOW.
WELL, MIGHT AS WELL READ IT, I SUPPOSE.
シャラララ
1969 Cultural Revolution (China)
1974 Carnation Revolution (Portugal)
1979 Iranian Revolution (Iran)
1986 Philippine February Revolution (The Philippines)

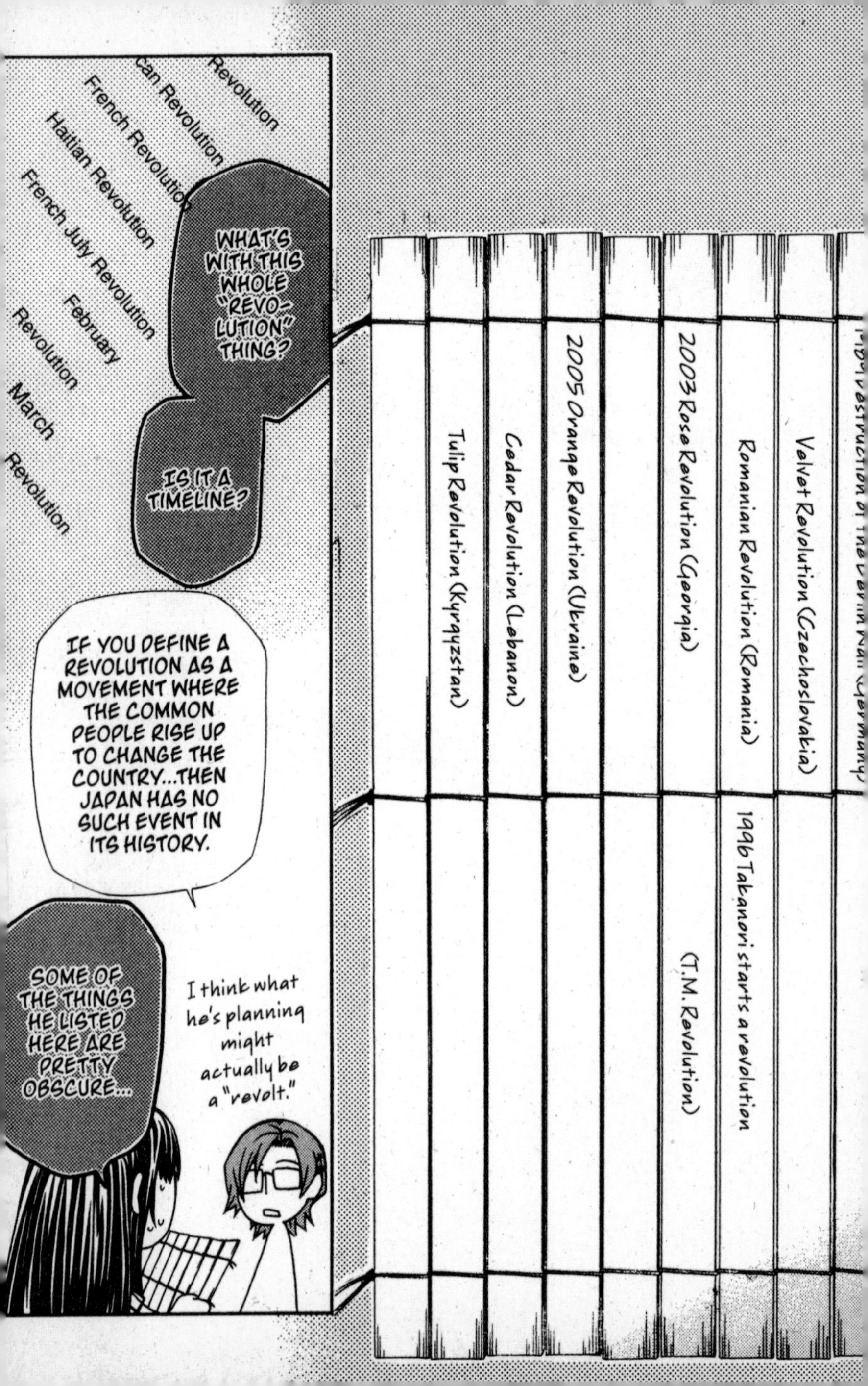

Velvet Revolution (Czechoslovakia)
Romanian Revolution (Romania)
1996 Takanori starts a revolution
2003 Rose Revolution (Georgia)
(T.M. Revolution)
2005 Orange Revolution (Ukraine)
Cedar Revolution (Lebanon)
Tulip Revolution (Kyrgyzstan)
Revolution
can Revolution
French Revolution
Haitian Revolution
French July Revolution
February Revolution
March Revolution
WHAT'S WITH THIS WHOLE "REVOLUTION" THING?
IS IT A TIMELINE?
IF YOU DEFINE A REVOLUTION AS A MOVEMENT WHERE THE COMMON PEOPLE RISE UP TO CHANGE THE COUNTRY...THEN JAPAN HAS NO SUCH EVENT IN ITS HISTORY.
I think what he's planning might actually be a "revolt."
SOME OF THE THINGS HE LISTED HERE ARE PRETTY OBSCURE...

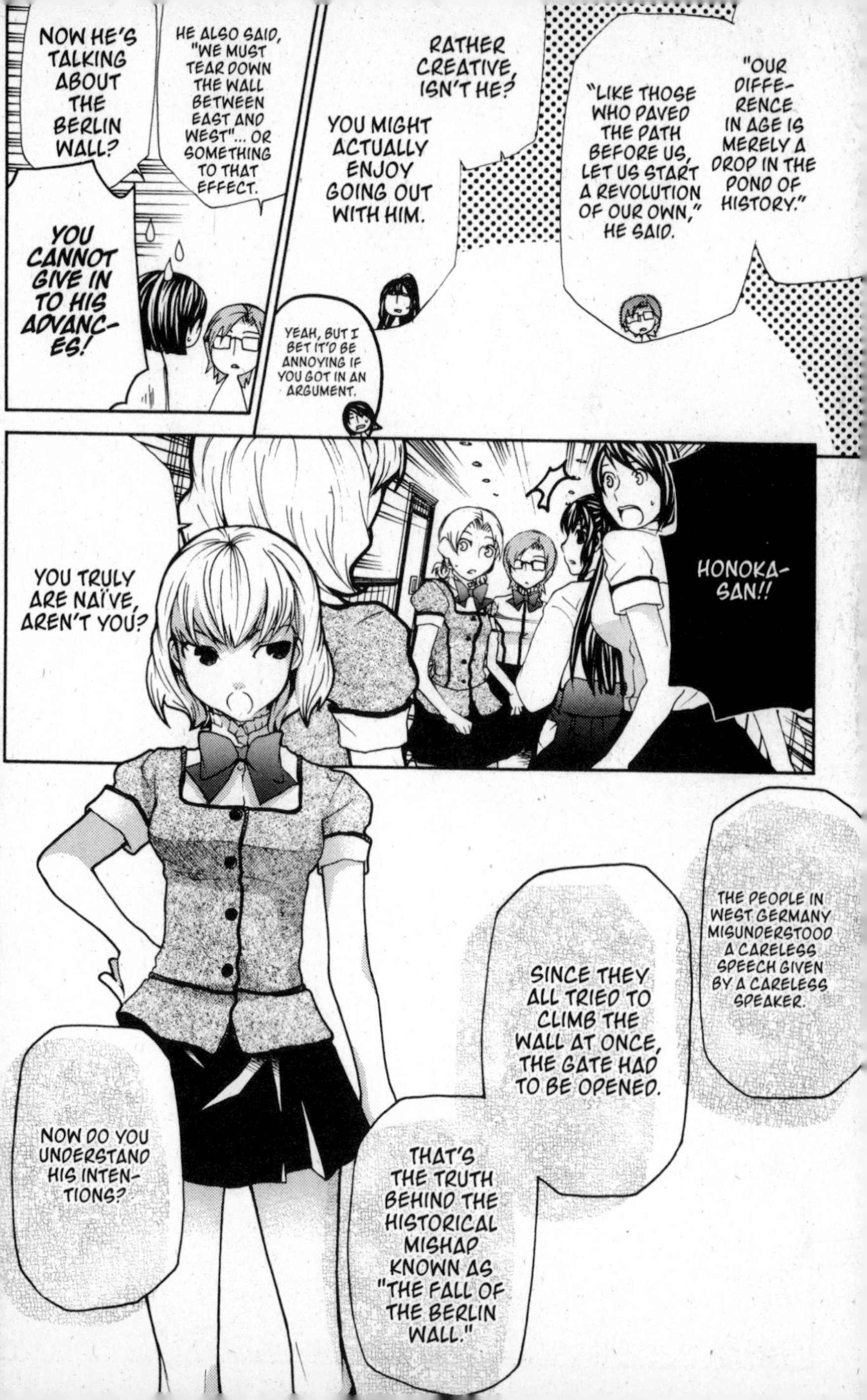
"OUR DIFFERENCE IN AGE IS MERELY A DROP IN THE POND OF HISTORY."
"LIKE THOSE WHO PAVED THE PATH BEFORE US, LET US START A REVOLUTION OF OUR OWN," HE SAID.
RATHER CREATIVE, ISN'T HE?
YOU MIGHT ACTUALLY ENJOY GOING OUT WITH HIM.
YEAH, BUT I BET IT'D BE ANNOYING IF YOU GOT IN AN ARGUMENT.
HE ALSO SAID, "WE MUST TEAR DOWN THE WALL BETWEEN EAST AND WEST"... OR SOMETHING TO THAT EFFECT.
NOW HE'S TALKING ABOUT THE BERLIN WALL?
YOU CANNOT GIVE IN TO HIS ADVANCES!
HONOKA-SAN!!
YOU TRULY ARE NAÏVE, AREN'T YOU?
THE PEOPLE IN WEST GERMANY MISUNDERSTOOD A CARELESS SPEECH GIVEN BY A CARELESS SPEAKER.
SINCE THEY ALL TRIED TO CLIMB THE WALL AT ONCE, THE GATE HAD TO BE OPENED.
THAT'S THE TRUTH BEHIND THE HISTORICAL MISHAP KNOWN AS "THE FALL OF THE BERLIN WALL."
NOW DO YOU UNDERSTAND HIS INTENTIONS?

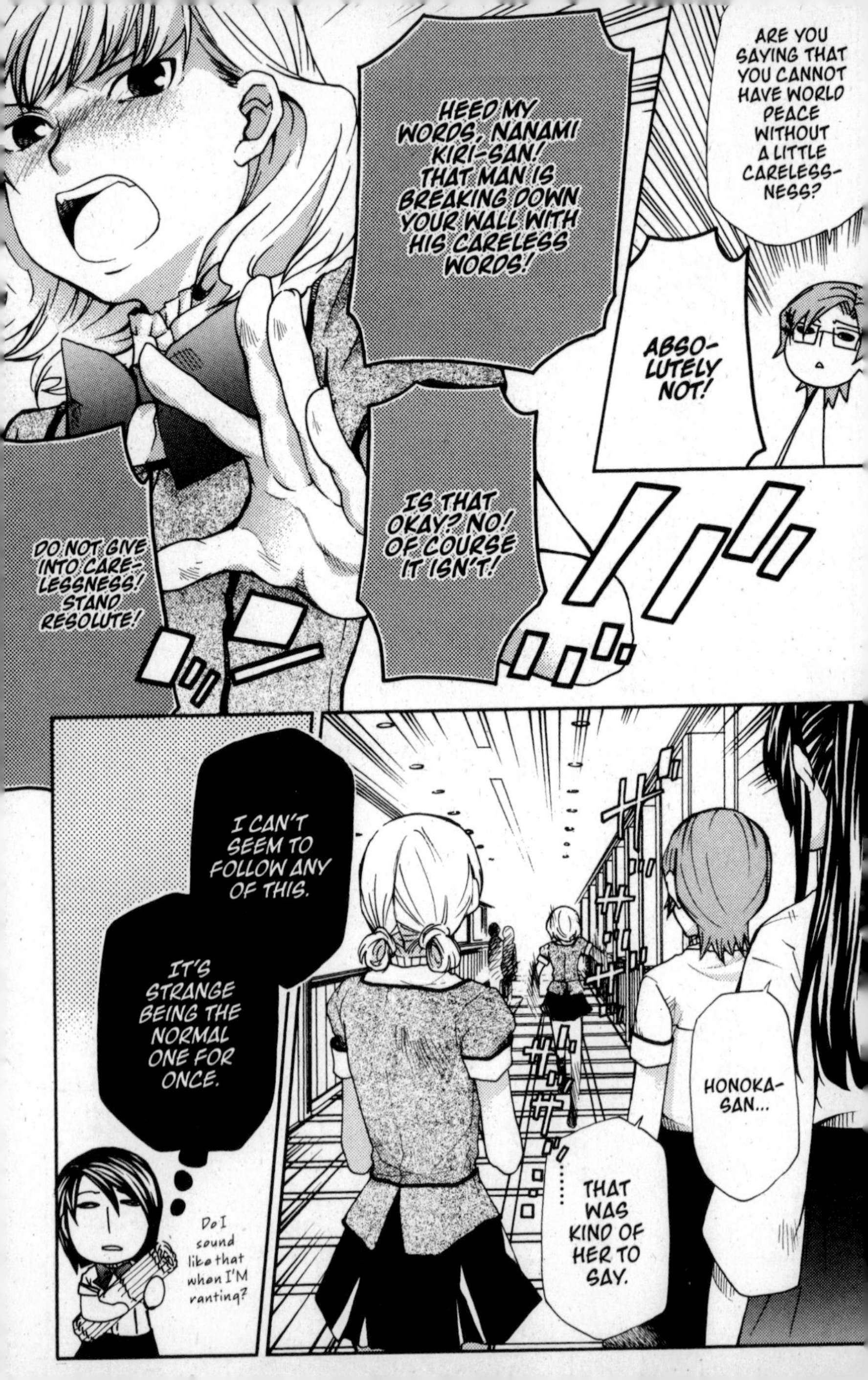
ARE YOU SAYING THAT YOU CANNOT HAVE WORLD PEACE WITHOUT A LITTLE CARELESS-NESS?
ABSO-LUTELY NOT!
HEED MY WORDS, NANAMI KIRI-SAN! THAT MAN IS BREAKING DOWN YOUR WALL WITH HIS CARELESS WORDS!
IS THAT OKAY? NO! OF COURSE IT ISN'T!
DO NOT GIVE INTO CARE-LESSNESS! STAND RESOLUTE!
HONOKA-SAN...
......
THAT WAS KIND OF HER TO SAY.
I CAN'T SEEM TO FOLLOW ANY OF THIS.
IT'S STRANGE BEING THE NORMAL ONE FOR ONCE.
Do I sound like that when I'M ranting?

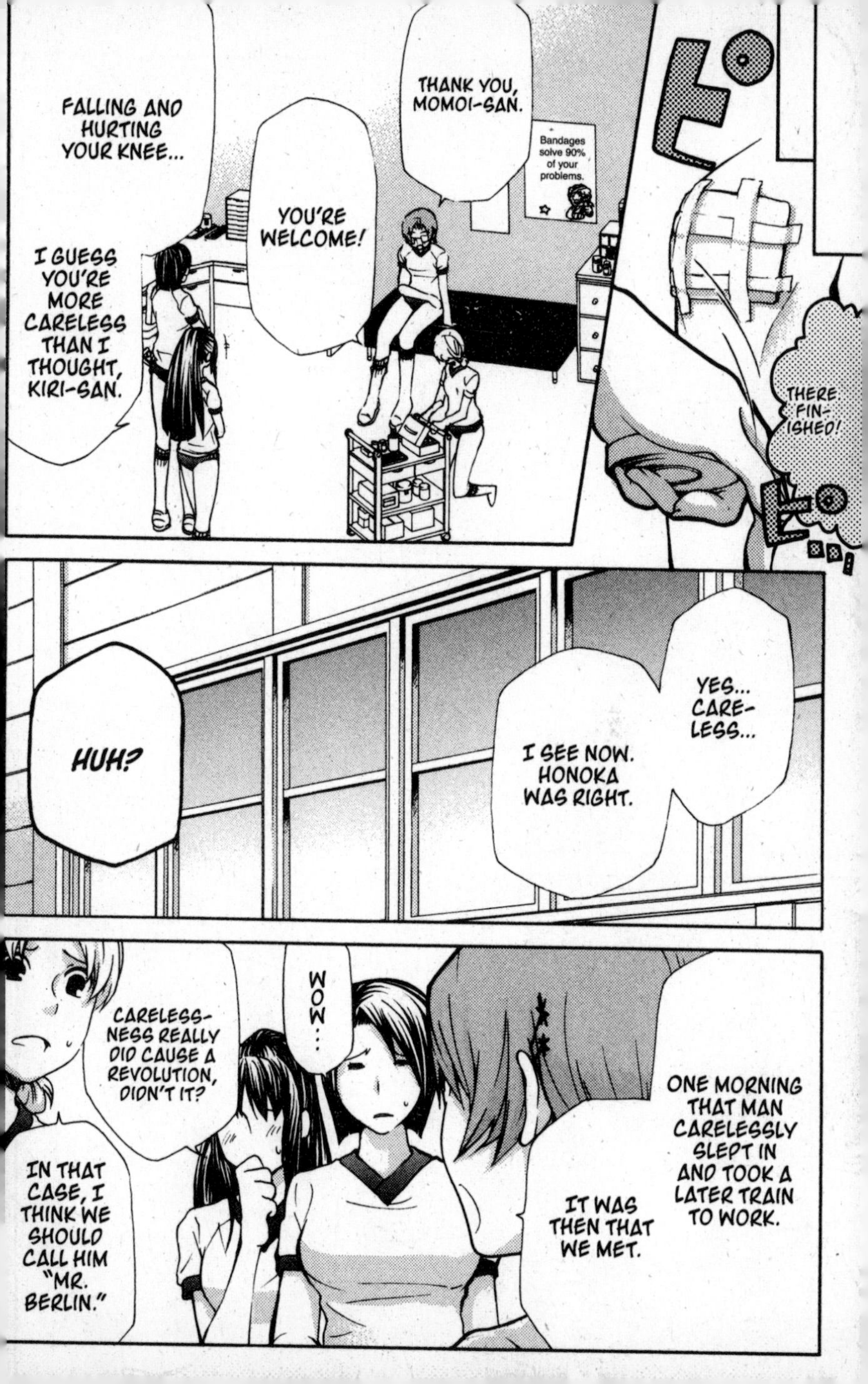
THERE. FIN-ISHED!
THANK YOU, MOMOI-SAN.
Bandages solve 90% of your problems.
YOU'RE WELCOME!
FALLING AND HURTING YOUR KNEE...
I GUESS YOU'RE MORE CARELESS THAN I THOUGHT, KIRI-SAN.
YES... CARE-LESS...
I SEE NOW. HONOKA WAS RIGHT.
HUH?
ONE MORNING THAT MAN CARELESSLY SLEPT IN AND TOOK A LATER TRAIN TO WORK.
IT WAS THEN THAT WE MET.
WOW...
CARELESS-NESS REALLY DID CAUSE A REVOLUTION, DIDN'T IT?
IN THAT CASE, I THINK WE SHOULD CALL HIM "MR. BERLIN."

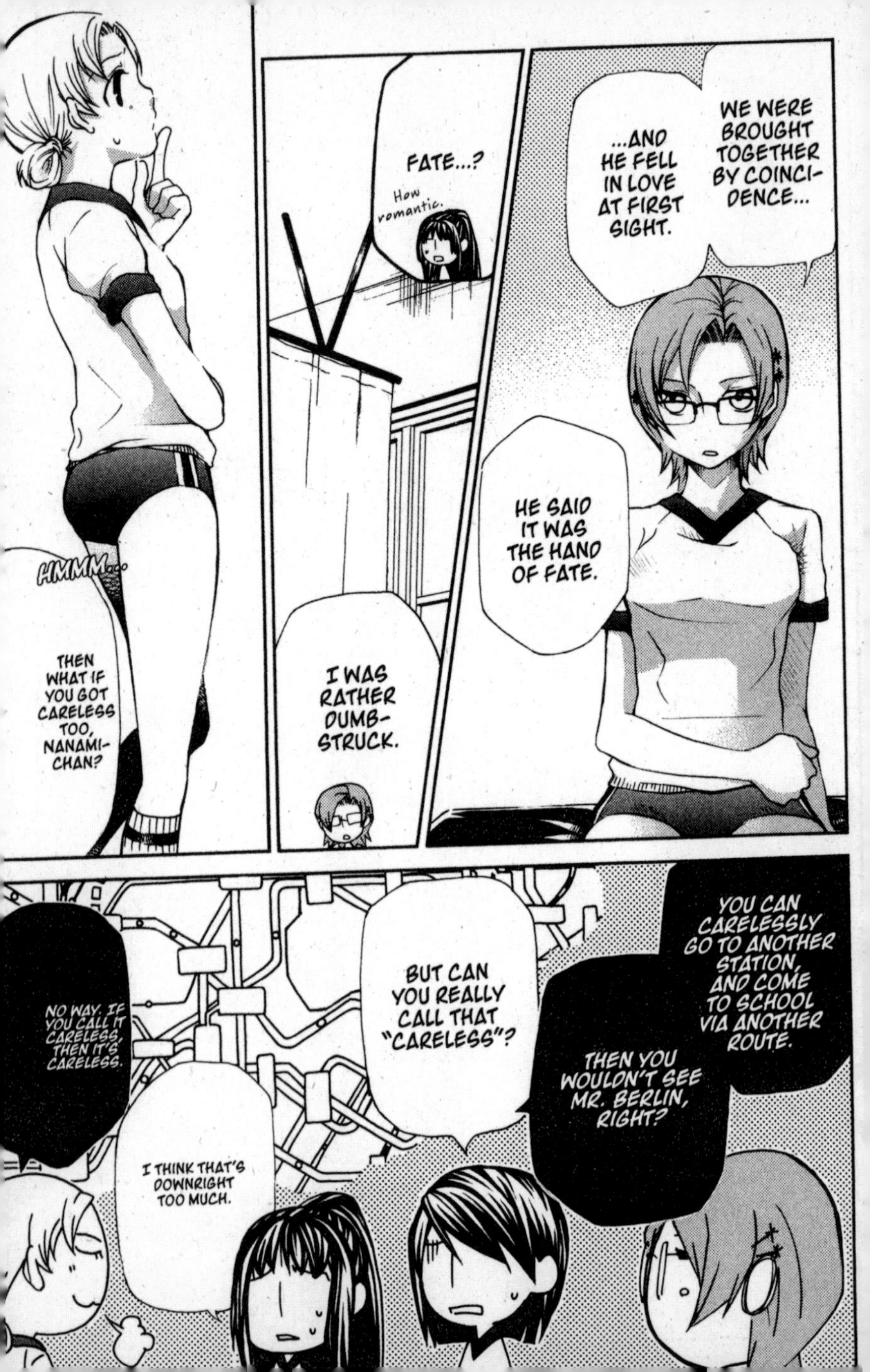
WE WERE BROUGHT TOGETHER BY COINCI-DENCE...
...AND HE FELL IN LOVE AT FIRST SIGHT.
HE SAID IT WAS THE HAND OF FATE.
FATE...?
How romantic.
I WAS RATHER DUMB-STRUCK.
HMMM...
THEN WHAT IF YOU GOT CARELESS TOO, NANAMI-CHAN?
YOU CAN CARELESSLY GO TO ANOTHER STATION, AND COME TO SCHOOL VIA ANOTHER ROUTE.
THEN YOU WOULDN'T SEE MR. BERLIN, RIGHT?
BUT CAN YOU REALLY CALL THAT "CARELESS"?
I THINK THAT'S DOWNRIGHT TOO MUCH.
NO WAY. IF YOU CALL IT CARELESS, THEN IT'S CARELESS.

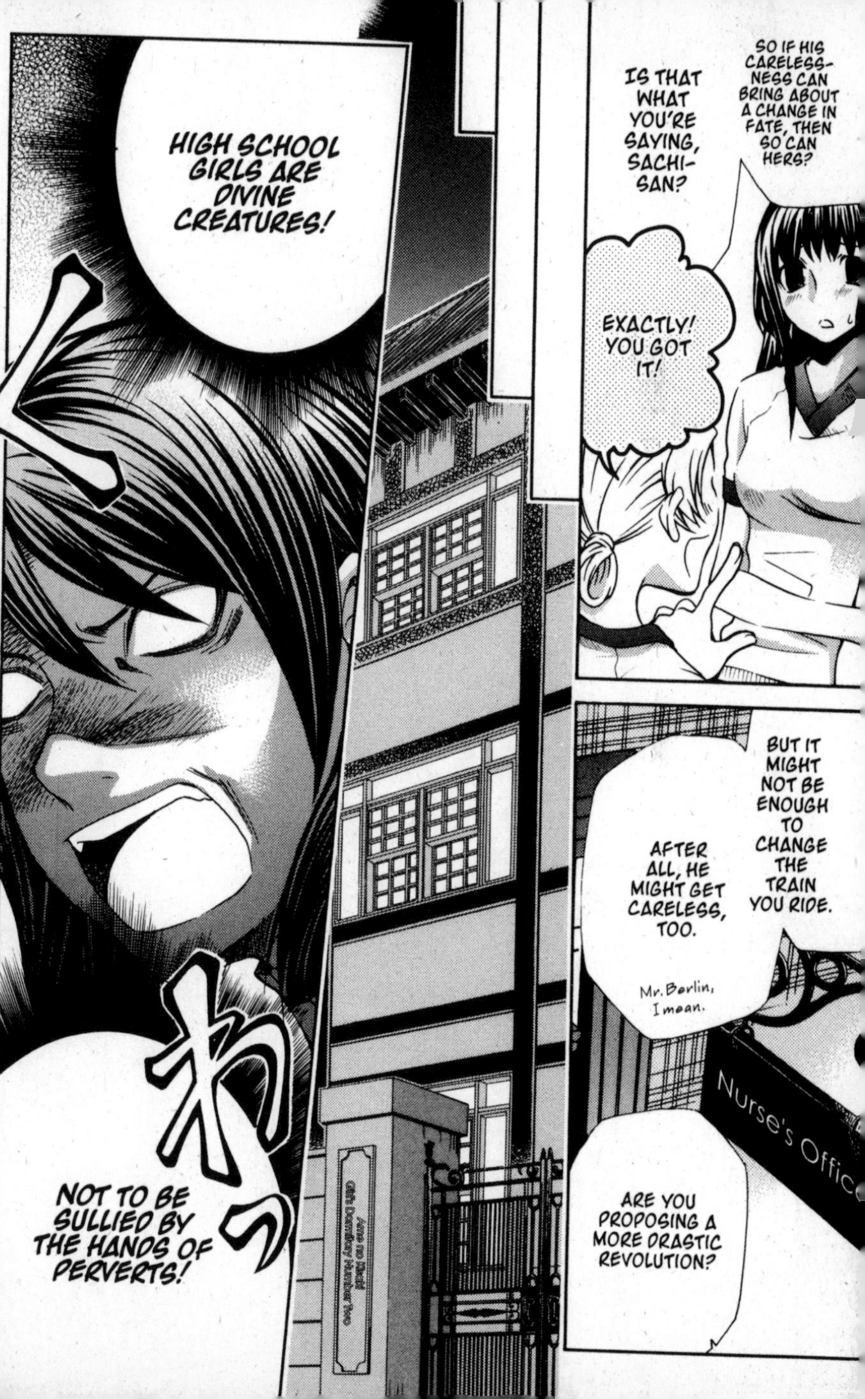
SO IF HIS CARELESSNESS CAN BRING ABOUT A CHANGE IN FATE, THEN SO CAN HERS?
IS THAT WHAT YOU'RE SAYING, SACHI-SAN?
EXACTLY! YOU GOT IT!
BUT IT MIGHT NOT BE ENOUGH TO CHANGE THE TRAIN YOU RIDE.
AFTER ALL, HE MIGHT GET CARELESS, TOO.
Mr. Berlin, I mean.
Nurse's Office
ARE YOU PROPOSING A MORE DRASTIC REVOLUTION?
Girl's Dormitory Number Two
HIGH SCHOOL GIRLS ARE DIVINE CREATURES!
NOT TO BE SULLIED BY THE HANDS OF PERVERTS!

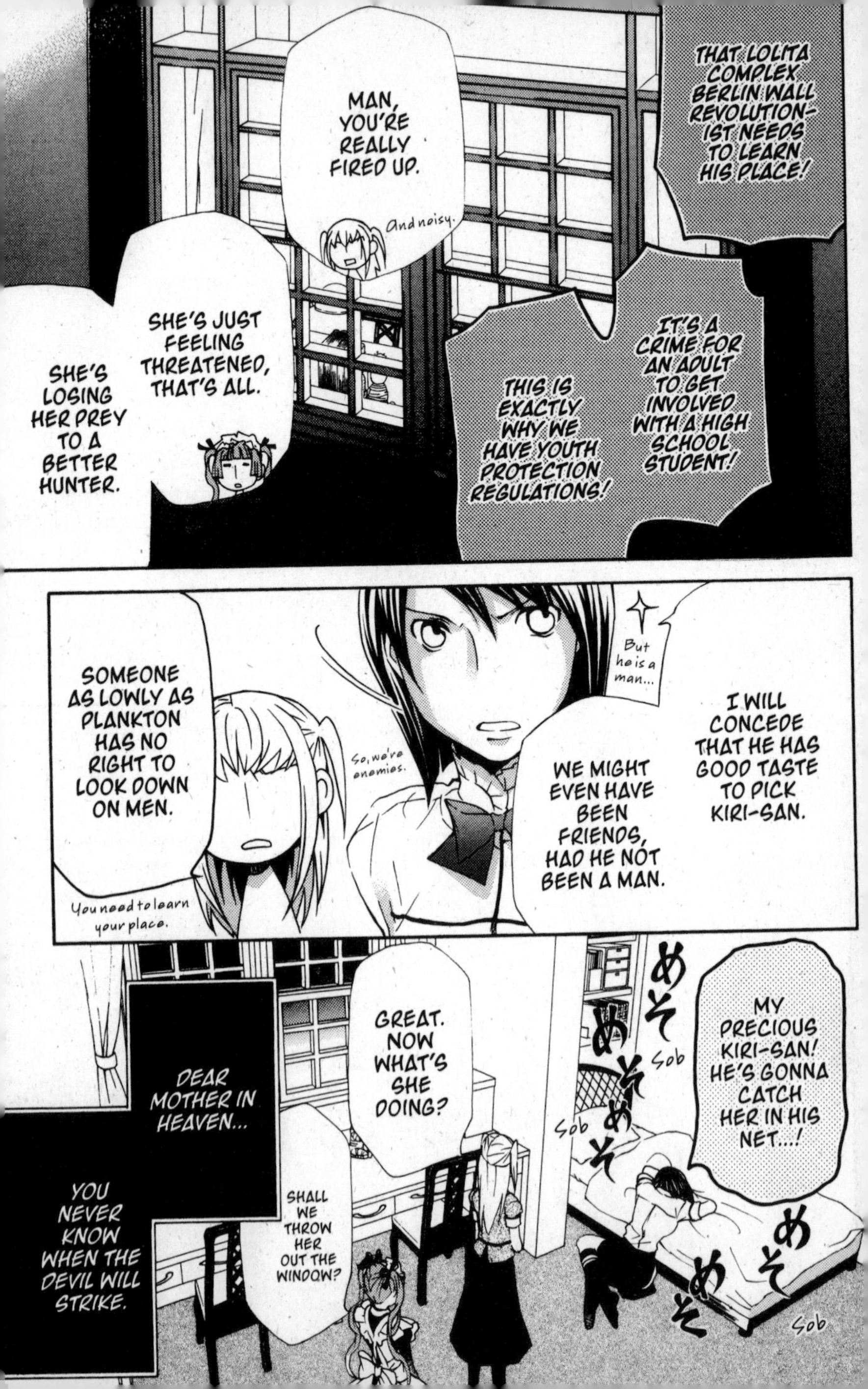
THAT LOLITA COMPLEX BERLIN WALL REVOLUTION-IST NEEDS TO LEARN HIS PLACE!
IT'S A CRIME FOR AN ADULT TO GET INVOLVED WITH A HIGH SCHOOL STUDENT!
THIS IS EXACTLY WHY WE HAVE YOUTH PROTECTION REGULATIONS!
MAN, YOU'RE REALLY FIRED UP.
And noisy.
SHE'S JUST FEELING THREATENED, THAT'S ALL.
SHE'S LOSING HER PREY TO A BETTER HUNTER.
I WILL CONCEDE THAT HE HAS GOOD TASTE TO PICK KIRI-SAN.
But he is a man...
WE MIGHT EVEN HAVE BEEN FRIENDS, HAD HE NOT BEEN A MAN.
So, we're enemies.
SOMEONE AS LOWLY AS PLANKTON HAS NO RIGHT TO LOOK DOWN ON MEN.
You need to learn your place.
MY PRECIOUS KIRI-SAN! HE'S GONNA CATCH HER IN HIS NET...!
めそ
Sob
めそ
Sob
めそ
めそ
Sob
GREAT. NOW WHAT'S SHE DOING?
SHALL WE THROW HER OUT THE WINDOW?
DEAR MOTHER IN HEAVEN...
YOU NEVER KNOW WHEN THE DEVIL WILL STRIKE.

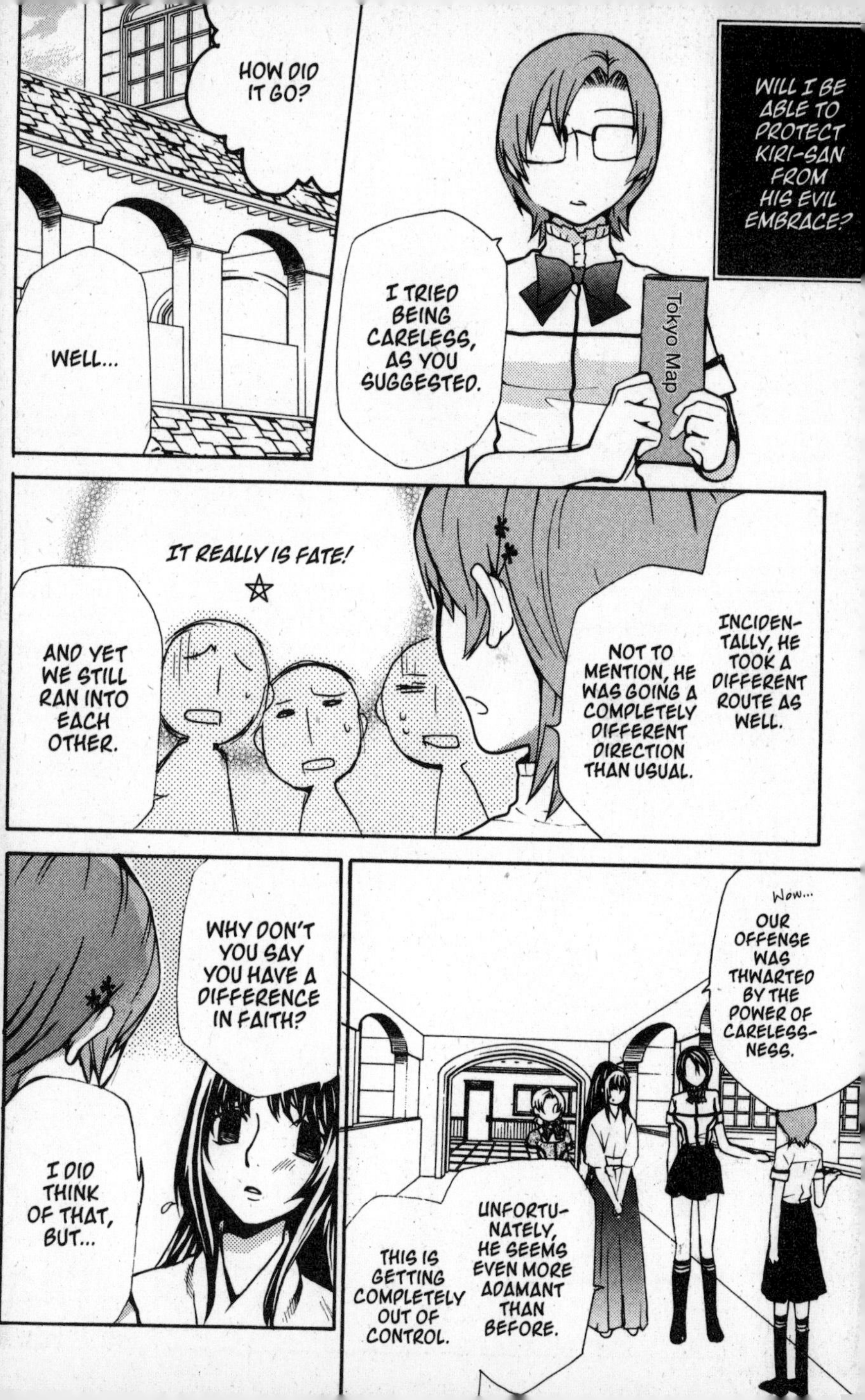
WILL I BE ABLE TO PROTECT KIRI-SAN FROM HIS EVIL EMBRACE?
Tokyo Map
I TRIED BEING CARELESS, AS YOU SUGGESTED.
HOW DID IT GO?
WELL...
INCIDEN-TALLY, HE TOOK A DIFFERENT ROUTE AS WELL.
NOT TO MENTION, HE WAS GOING A COMPLETELY DIFFERENT DIRECTION THAN USUAL.
IT REALLY IS FATE! ☆
AND YET WE STILL RAN INTO EACH OTHER.
Wow...
OUR OFFENSE WAS THWARTED BY THE POWER OF CARELESS-NESS.
UNFORTU-NATELY, HE SEEMS EVEN MORE ADAMANT THAN BEFORE.
THIS IS GETTING COMPLETELY OUT OF CONTROL.
WHY DON'T YOU SAY YOU HAVE A DIFFERENCE IN FAITH?
I DID THINK OF THAT, BUT...

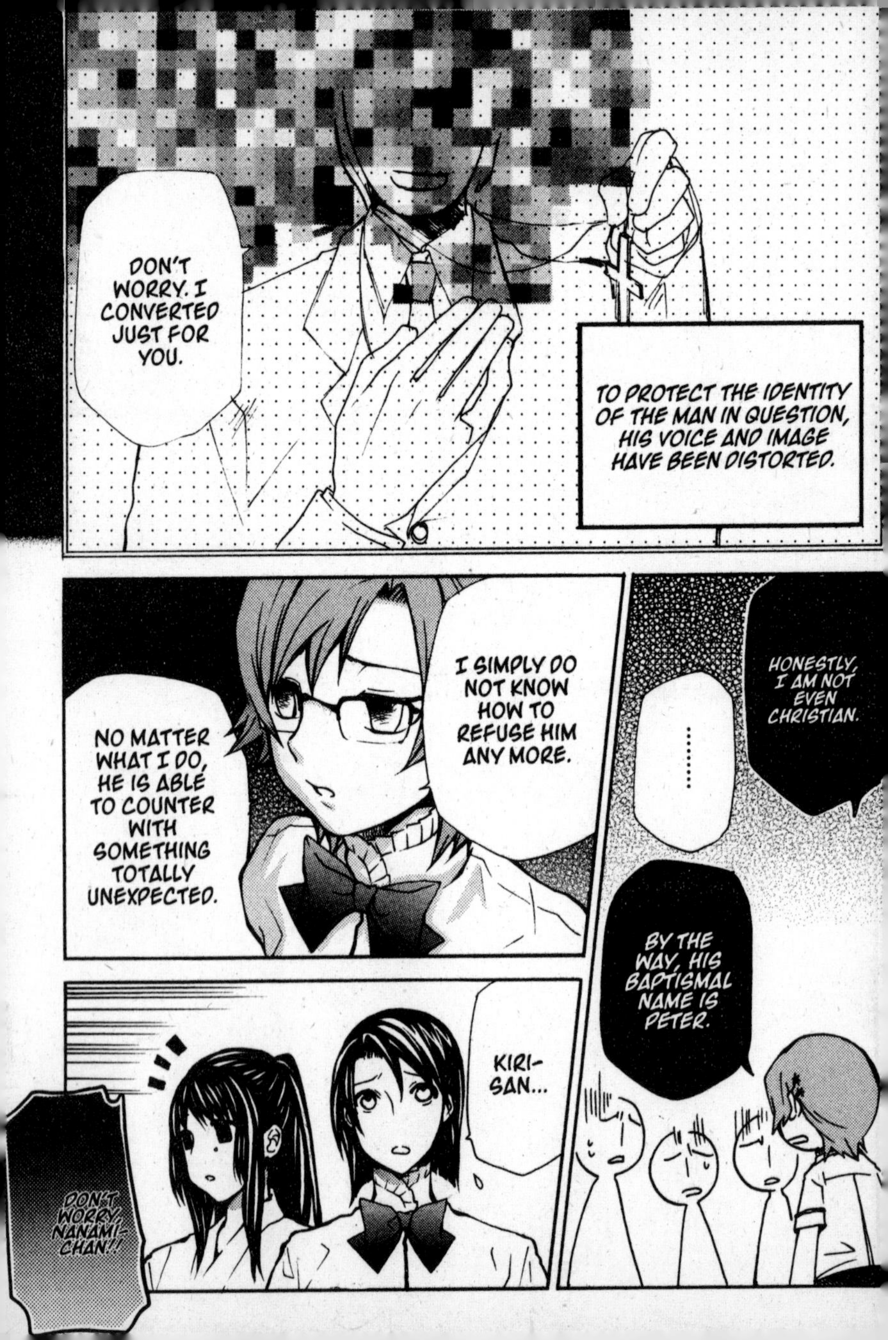
DON'T WORRY. I CONVERTED JUST FOR YOU.
TO PROTECT THE IDENTITY OF THE MAN IN QUESTION, HIS VOICE AND IMAGE HAVE BEEN DISTORTED.
HONESTLY, I AM NOT EVEN CHRISTIAN.
……
BY THE WAY, HIS BAPTISMAL NAME IS PETER.
I SIMPLY DO NOT KNOW HOW TO REFUSE HIM ANY MORE.
NO MATTER WHAT I DO, HE IS ABLE TO COUNTER WITH SOMETHING TOTALLY UNEXPECTED.
KIRI-SAN...
DON'T WORRY, NANAMI-CHAN!!

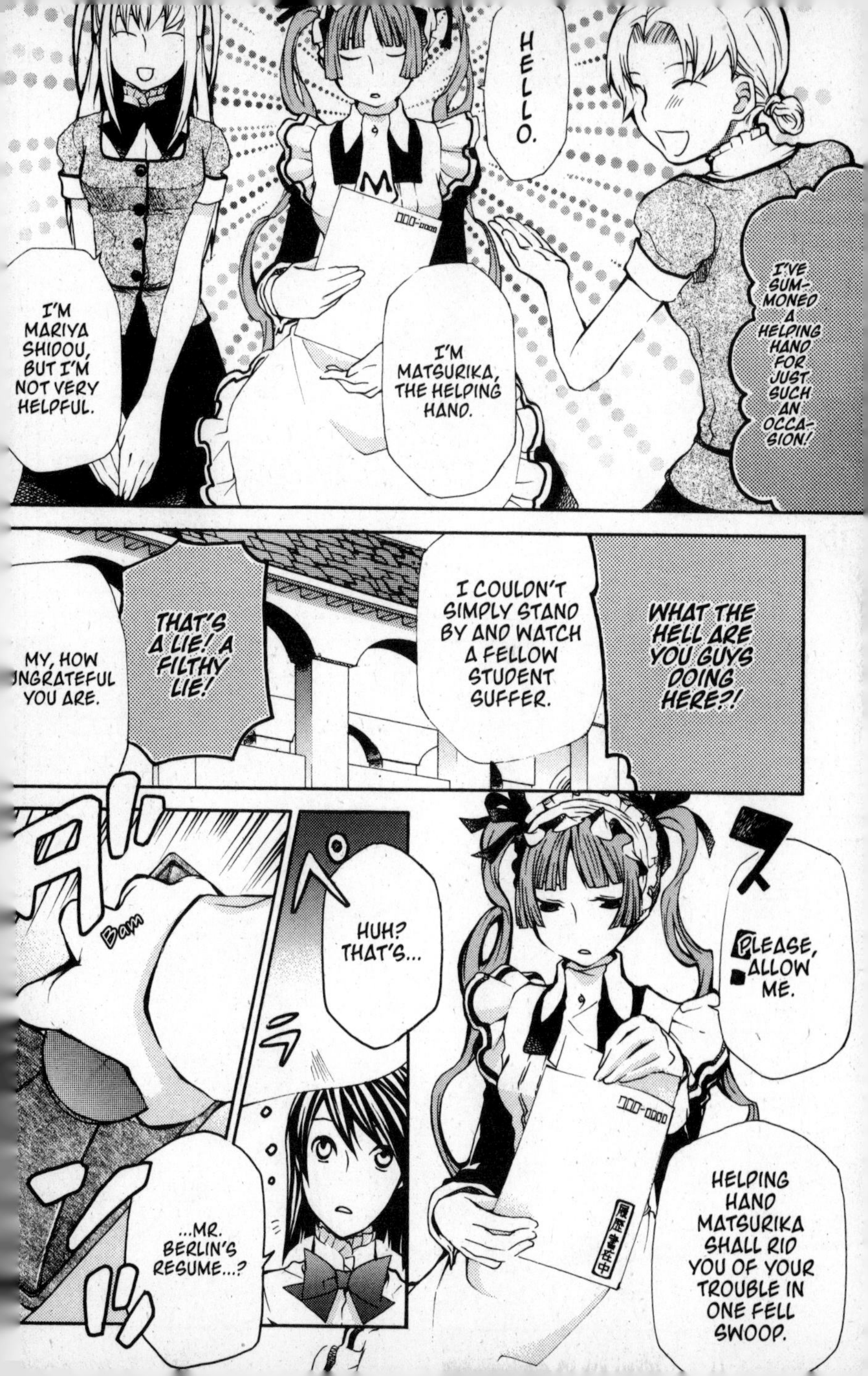
I'VE SUMMONED A HELPING HAND FOR JUST SUCH AN OCCASION!
HELLO.
I'M MATSURIKA, THE HELPING HAND.
I'M MARIYA SHIDOU, BUT I'M NOT VERY HELPFUL.
WHAT THE HELL ARE YOU GUYS DOING HERE?!
I COULDN'T SIMPLY STAND BY AND WATCH A FELLOW STUDENT SUFFER.
THAT'S A LIE! A FILTHY LIE!
MY, HOW UNGRATEFUL YOU ARE.
PLEASE, ALLOW ME.
HELPING HAND MATSURIKA SHALL RID YOU OF YOUR TROUBLE IN ONE FELL SWOOP.
HUH? THAT'S...
...MR. BERLIN'S RESUME...?
Bam

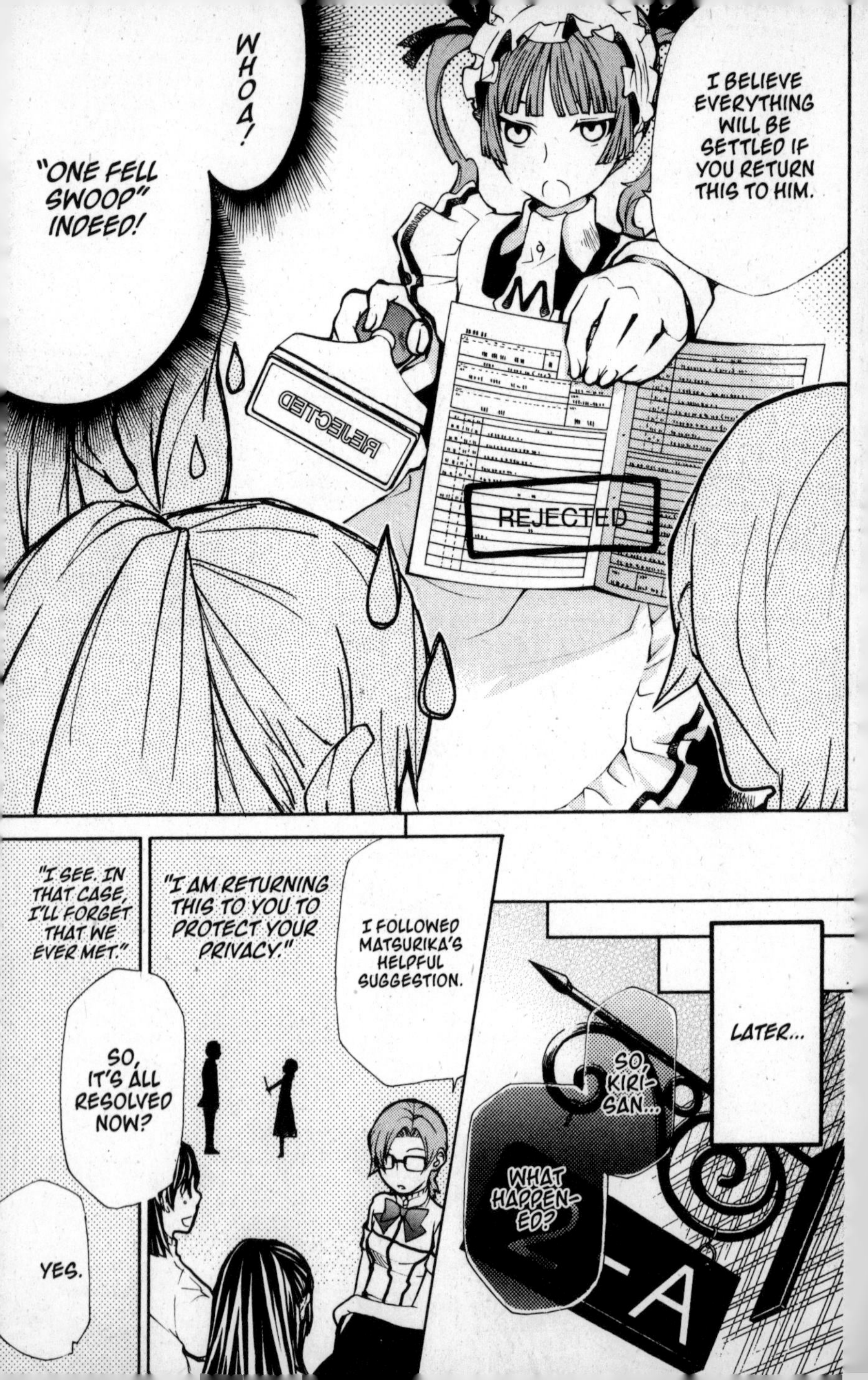
I BELIEVE EVERYTHING WILL BE SETTLED IF YOU RETURN THIS TO HIM.
WHOA!
"ONE FELL SWOOP" INDEED!
REJECTED
REJECTED
LATER...
SO, KIRI-SAN...
WHAT HAPPEN-ED?
I FOLLOWED MATSURIKA'S HELPFUL SUGGESTION.
"I AM RETURNING THIS TO YOU TO PROTECT YOUR PRIVACY."
"I SEE. IN THAT CASE, I'LL FORGET THAT WE EVER MET."
SO, IT'S ALL RESOLVED NOW?
YES.

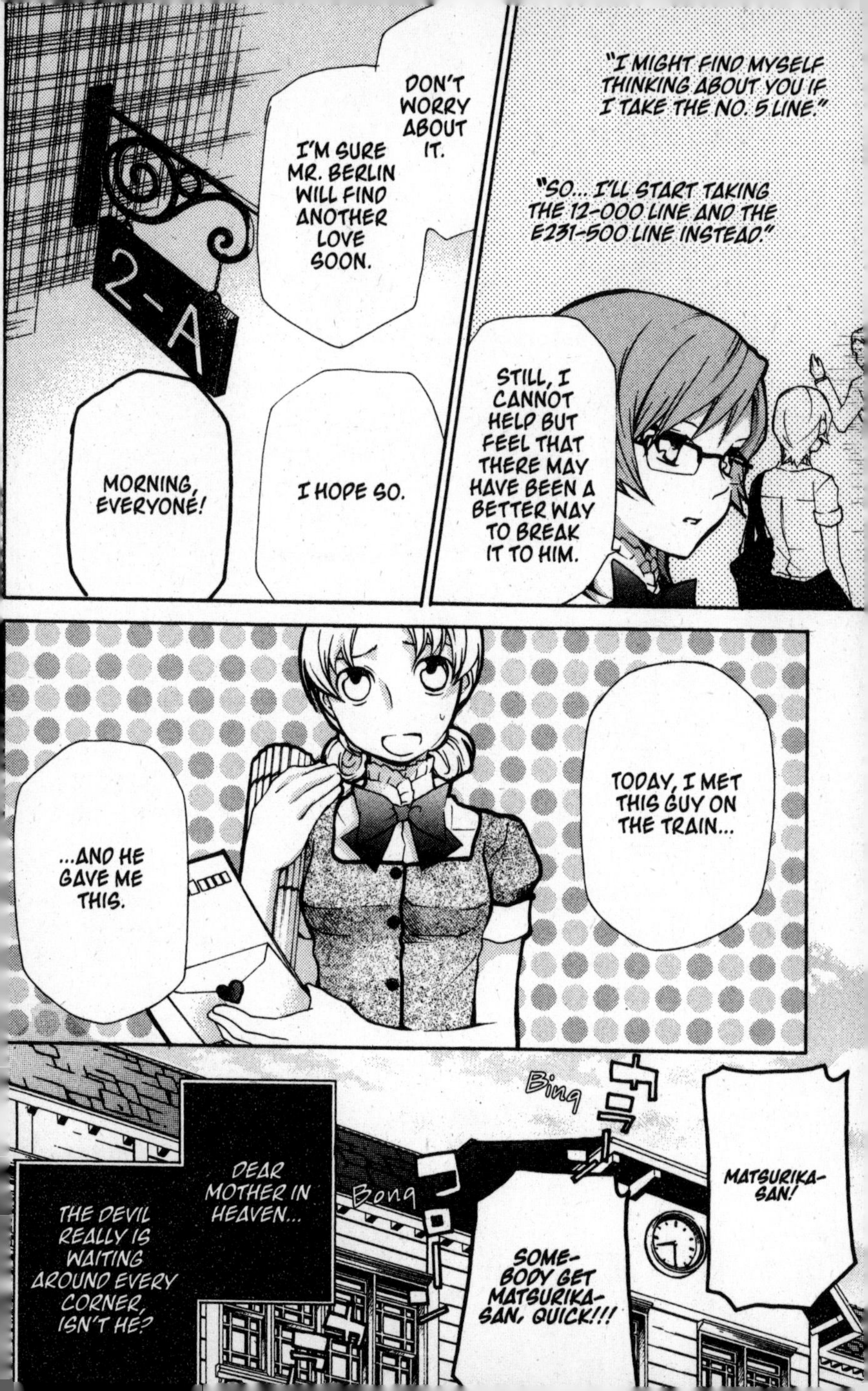
"I MIGHT FIND MYSELF THINKING ABOUT YOU IF I TAKE THE NO. 5 LINE."
"SO... I'LL START TAKING THE 12-000 LINE AND THE E231-500 LINE INSTEAD."
STILL, I CANNOT HELP BUT FEEL THAT THERE MAY HAVE BEEN A BETTER WAY TO BREAK IT TO HIM.
DON'T WORRY ABOUT IT.
I'M SURE MR. BERLIN WILL FIND ANOTHER LOVE SOON.
I HOPE SO.
MORNING, EVERYONE!
TODAY, I MET THIS GUY ON THE TRAIN...
...AND HE GAVE ME THIS.
Bing
MATSURIKA-SAN!
SOME-BODY GET MATSURIKA-SAN, QUICK!!!
Bong
DEAR MOTHER IN HEAVEN...
THE DEVIL REALLY IS WAITING AROUND EVERY CORNER, ISN'T HE?

TONY AND MYTY

DISCOVER WORLD HERITAGE SITES

M: OKAY, TONY, OKAY. I UNDERSTAND WHAT YOU'RE SAYING. JUST PLEASE...PUT THE GUN DOWN!

M A R I A H O L I C

Maria Holic

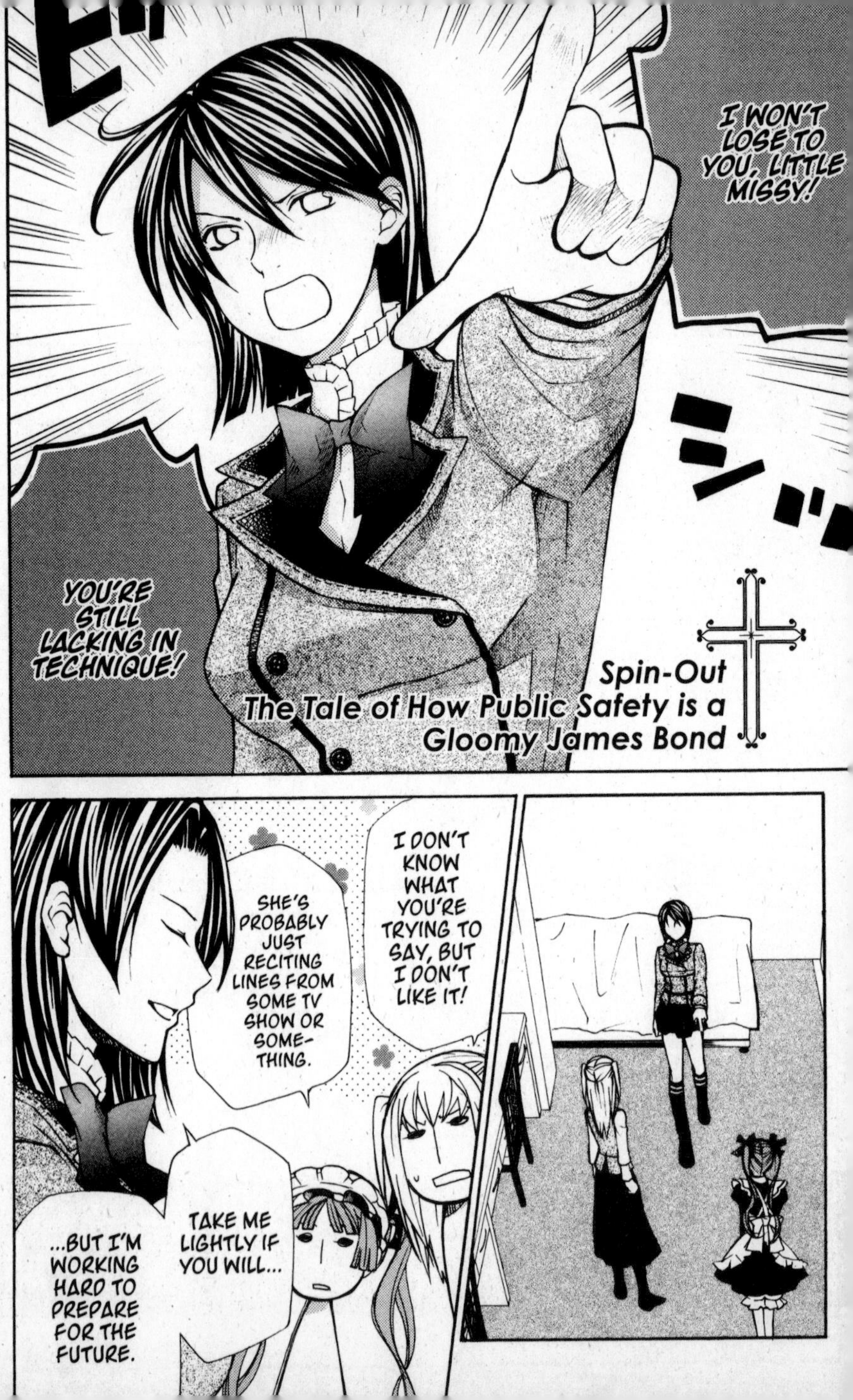
I WON'T LOSE TO YOU, LITTLE MISSY!
YOU'RE STILL LACKING IN TECHNIQUE!
Spin-Out
The Tale of How Public Safety is a Gloomy James Bond
I DON'T KNOW WHAT YOU'RE TRYING TO SAY, BUT I DON'T LIKE IT!
SHE'S PROBABLY JUST RECITING LINES FROM SOME TV SHOW OR SOME-THING.
TAKE ME LIGHTLY IF YOU WILL...
...BUT I'M WORKING HARD TO PREPARE FOR THE FUTURE.

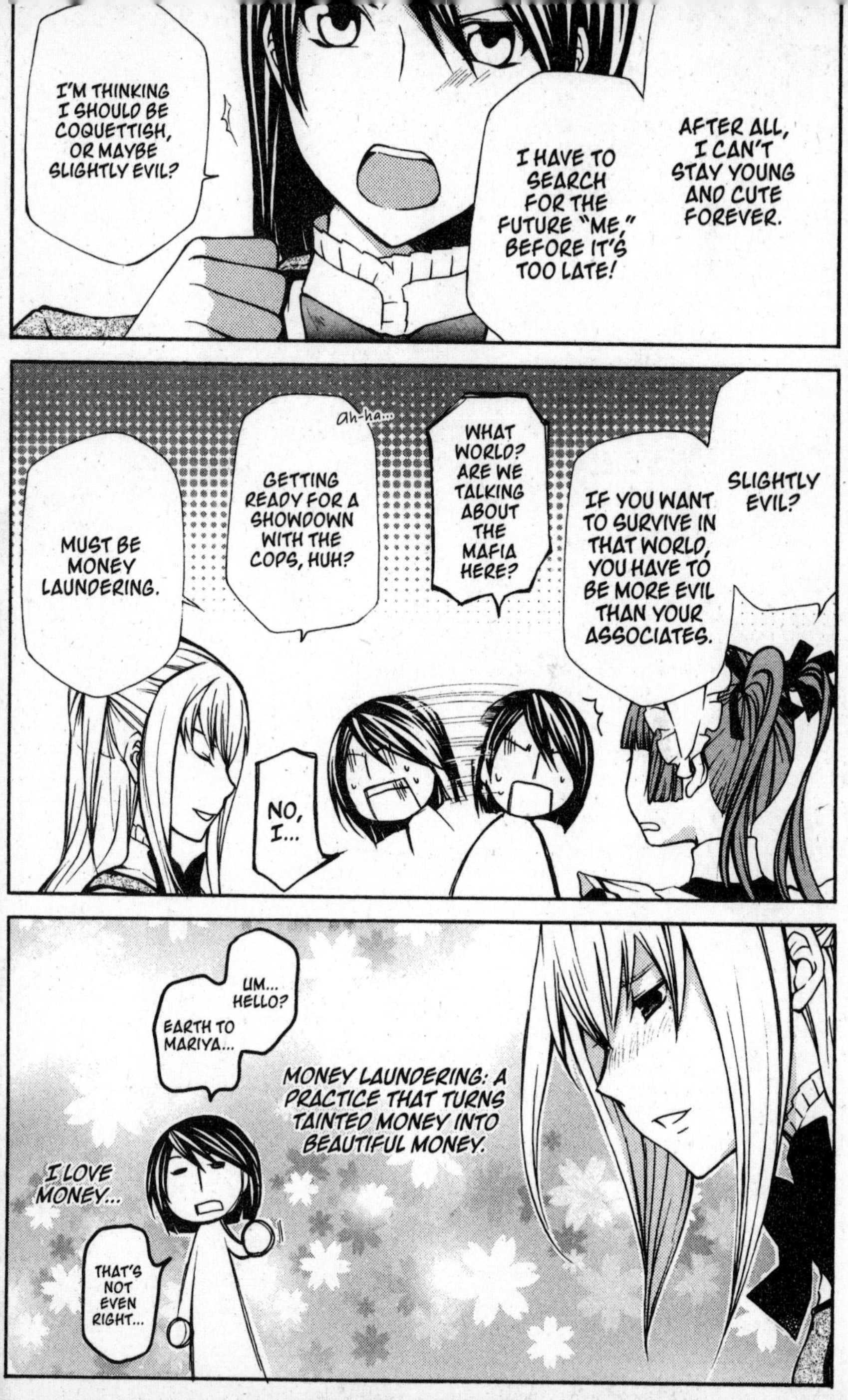
AFTER ALL, I CAN'T STAY YOUNG AND CUTE FOREVER.
I HAVE TO SEARCH FOR THE FUTURE "ME," BEFORE IT'S TOO LATE!
I'M THINKING I SHOULD BE COQUETTISH, OR MAYBE SLIGHTLY EVIL?
SLIGHTLY EVIL?
IF YOU WANT TO SURVIVE IN THAT WORLD, YOU HAVE TO BE MORE EVIL THAN YOUR ASSOCIATES.
WHAT WORLD? ARE WE TALKING ABOUT THE MAFIA HERE?
Ah-ha...
GETTING READY FOR A SHOWDOWN WITH THE COPS, HUH?
MUST BE MONEY LAUNDERING.
NO, I...
MONEY LAUNDERING: A PRACTICE THAT TURNS TAINTED MONEY INTO BEAUTIFUL MONEY.
UM... HELLO?
EARTH TO MARIYA...
I LOVE MONEY...
THAT'S NOT EVEN RIGHT...

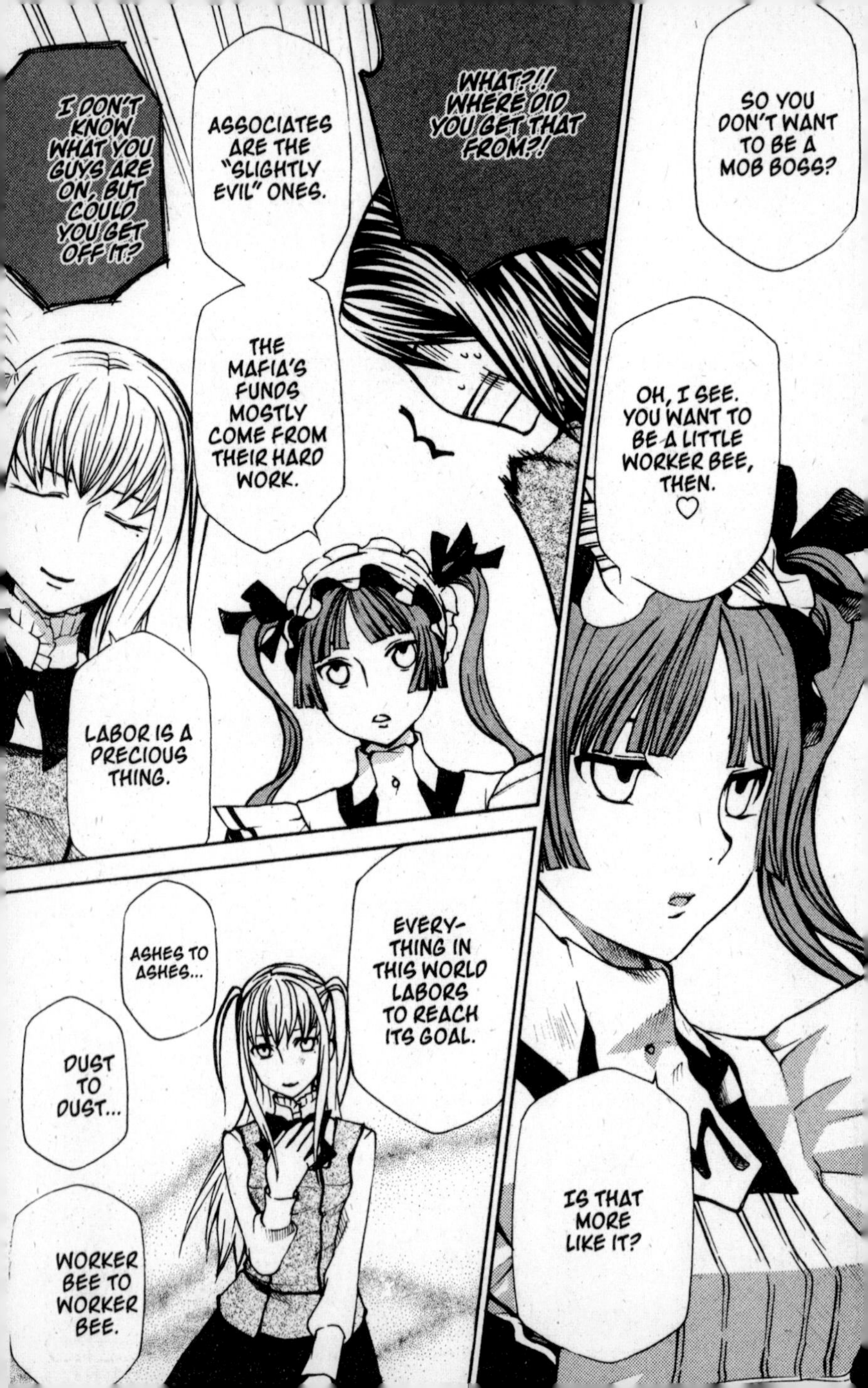
SO YOU DON'T WANT TO BE A MOB BOSS?
OH, I SEE. YOU WANT TO BE A LITTLE WORKER BEE, THEN. ♡
IS THAT MORE LIKE IT?
WHAT?!! WHERE DID YOU GET THAT FROM?!
ASSOCIATES ARE THE "SLIGHTLY EVIL" ONES.
I DON'T KNOW WHAT YOU GUYS ARE ON, BUT COULD YOU GET OFF IT?
THE MAFIA'S FUNDS MOSTLY COME FROM THEIR HARD WORK.
LABOR IS A PRECIOUS THING.
EVERYTHING IN THIS WORLD LABORS TO REACH ITS GOAL.
ASHES TO ASHES...
DUST TO DUST...
WORKER BEE TO WORKER BEE.

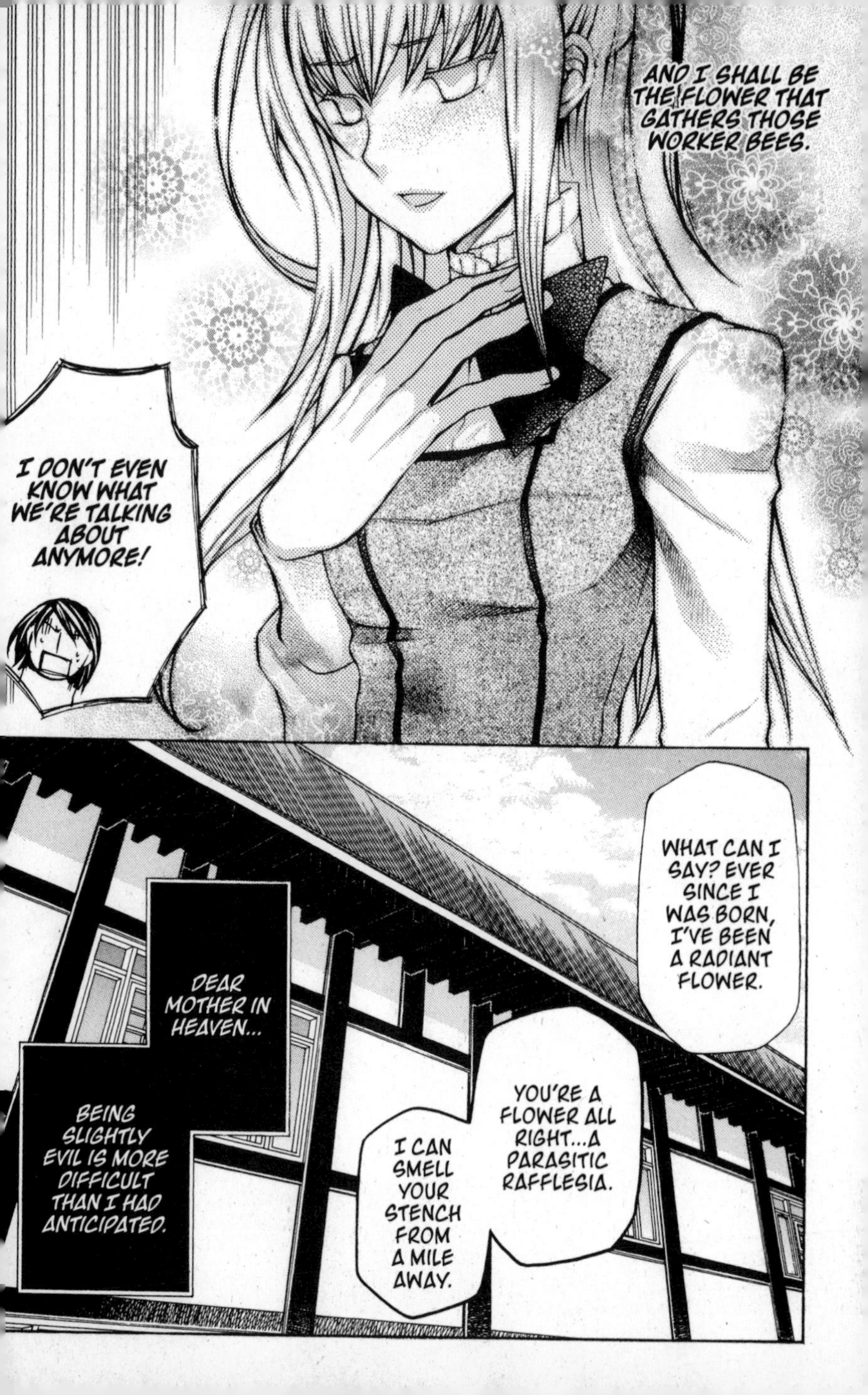
AND I SHALL BE THE FLOWER THAT GATHERS THOSE WORKER BEES.
I DON'T EVEN KNOW WHAT WE'RE TALKING ABOUT ANYMORE!
WHAT CAN I SAY? EVER SINCE I WAS BORN, I'VE BEEN A RADIANT FLOWER.
YOU'RE A FLOWER ALL RIGHT...A PARASITIC RAFFLESIA.
I CAN SMELL YOUR STENCH FROM A MILE AWAY.
DEAR MOTHER IN HEAVEN...
BEING SLIGHTLY EVIL IS MORE DIFFICULT THAN I HAD ANTICIPATED.

To be continued . . .

Maria✝Holic

There's more maidenly mischief
to be had in the next volume of...

**The sexual angst and comedic romance
continues! After receiving a letter from the
school president, Mariya just isn't himself
anymore. When Kanako spills tea, the usually
sadistic Mariya doesn't even get mad.
What's going on with our cross-dressing
brute?! The secret of the mysterious letter
and a hidden truth about the relationship
between the Mariya and Shizu will all be
revealed the next volume of Maria Holic!**

Maid Sama!™

The class president has a little secret she's keeping from the sexy bad boy in school...

"It's hard to deny this guilty pleasure when it looks like it's having so much fun." –About.com

Maid Sama!
Hiro Fujiwara
TOKYOPOP
4

The rogue hypnotist strikes again, this time planting the suggestion in Misaki that if she falls asleep, she'll wake up hating Usui! Well, hating him more than usual... So it's up to Usui to preserve their relationship (such as it is) by keeping Misaki awake as long as possible!

ROMANCE

T TEEN AGE 13+

BE SURE TO VISIT WWW.TOKYOPOP.COM/SHOP FOR EVERYTHING YOU COULD EVER WANT!

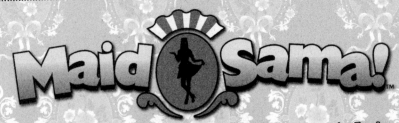

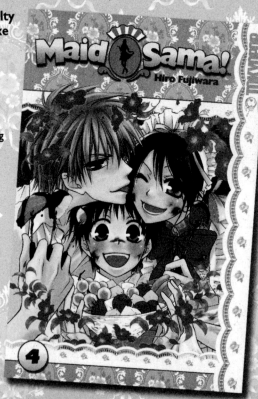

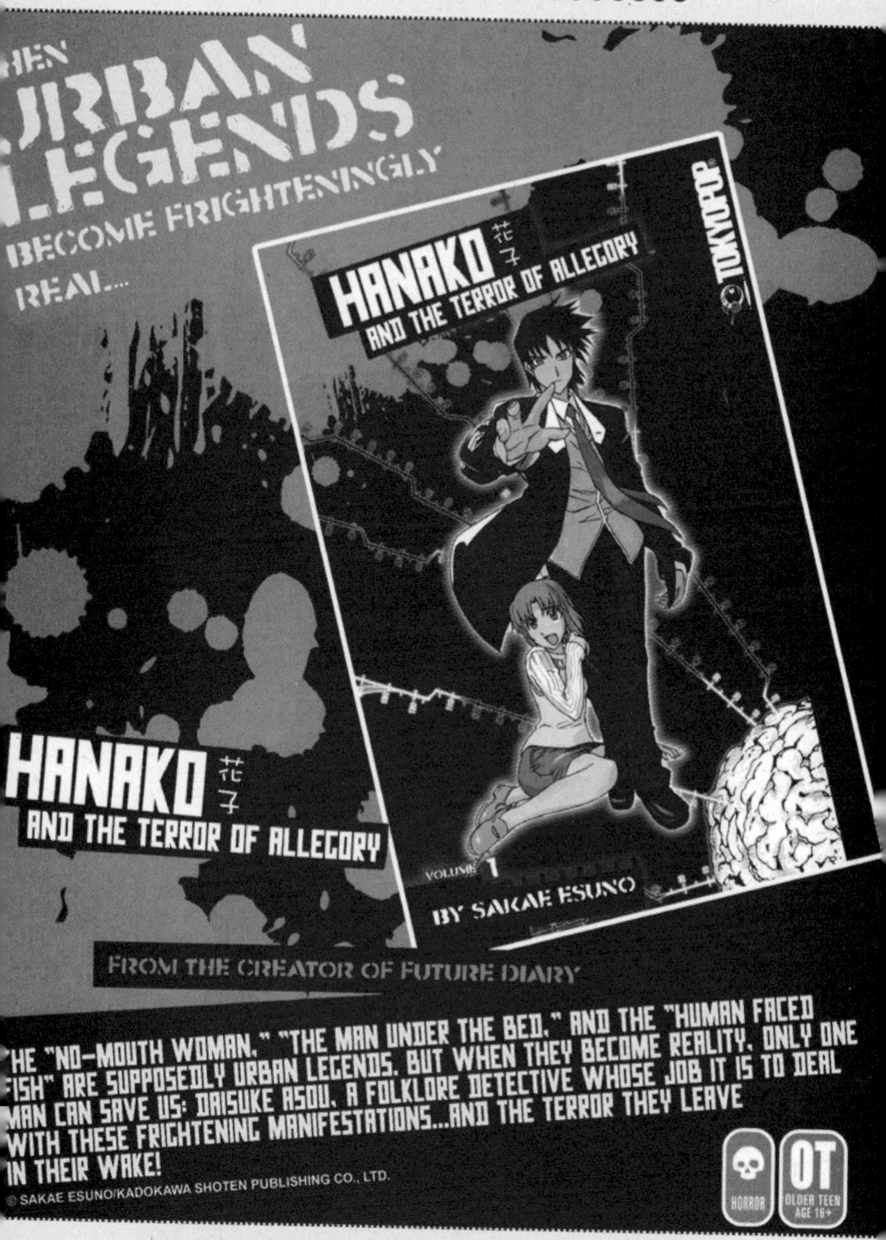
HEN URBAN LEGENDS BECOME FRIGHTENINGLY REAL....
HANAKO 花子 AND THE TERROR OF ALLEGORY
TOKYOPOP
VOLUME 1
BY SAKAE ESUNO
HANAKO 花子 AND THE TERROR OF ALLEGORY
FROM THE CREATOR OF FUTURE DIARY
HE "NO-MOUTH WOMAN," "THE MAN UNDER THE BED," AND THE "HUMAN FACED ISH" ARE SUPPOSEDLY URBAN LEGENDS. BUT WHEN THEY BECOME REALITY, ONLY ONE MAN CAN SAVE US: DAISUKE ASOU, A FOLKLORE DETECTIVE WHOSE JOB IT IS TO DEAL WITH THESE FRIGHTENING MANIFESTATIONS...AND THE TERROR THEY LEAVE IN THEIR WAKE!
© SAKAE ESUNO/KADOKAWA SHOTEN PUBLISHING CO., LTD.
HORROR
OT OLDER TEEN AGE 16+

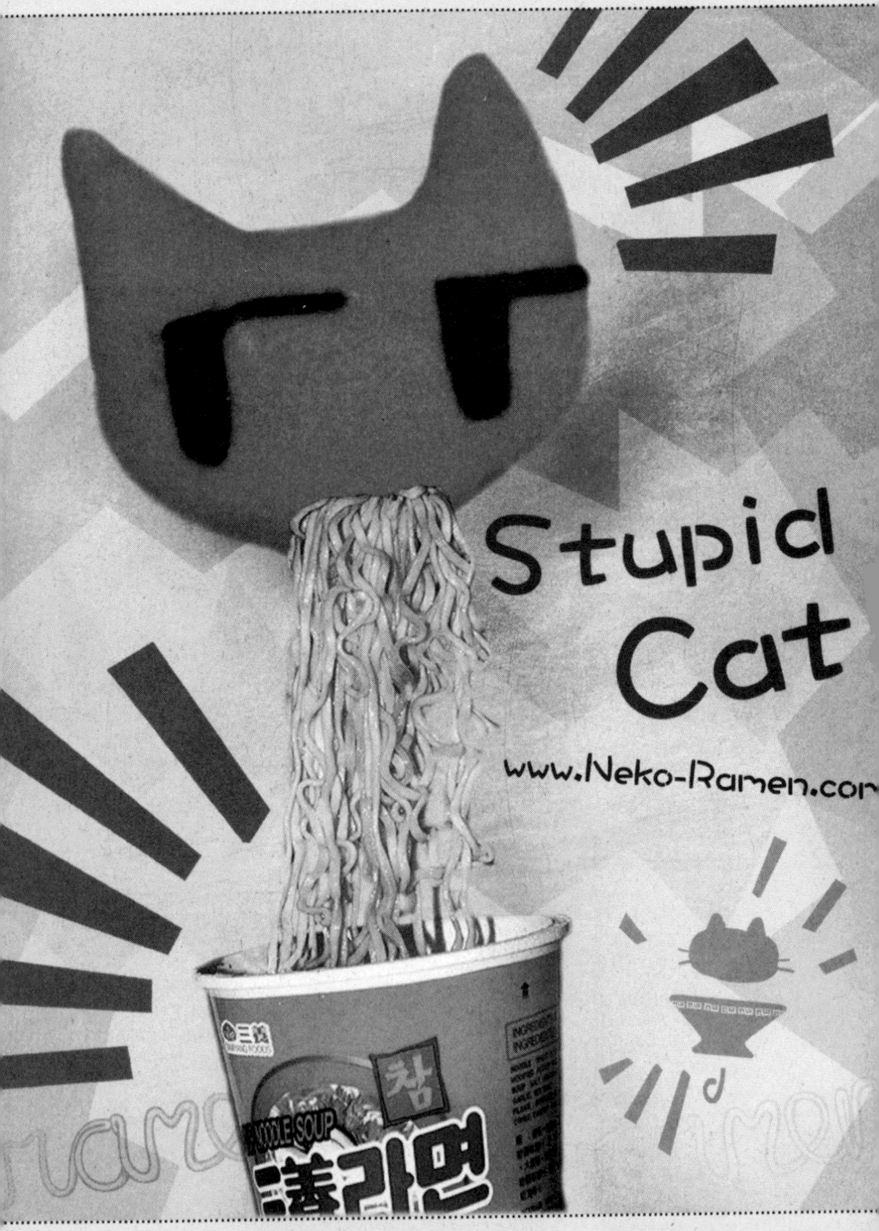
Stupid
Cat
www.Neko-Ramen.co
NOODLE SOUP
참

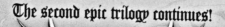

The second epic trilogy continues!

Ai fights to escape the clutches of her mysterious and malevolent captors, not knowing whether Kent, left behind on the Other Side, is even still alive. A frantic rescue mission commences, and in the end, even Ai's magical voice may not be enough to protect her from the trials of the Black Forest.

Dark secrets are revealed, and Ai must use all her strength and courage to face off against the new threat to Ai-Land. But will she ever see Kent again...?

"A very intriguing read that will satisfy old fans and create new fans, too."
– Bookloons

STOP!

This is the back of the book. You wouldn't want to spoil a great ending!

This book is printed "manga-style," in the authentic Japanese right-to-left format. Since none of the artwork has been flipped or altered, readers get to experience the story just as the creator intended. You've been asking for it, so TOKYOPOP® delivered: authentic, hot-off-the-press, and far more fun!

DIRECTIONS

If this is your first time reading manga-style, here's a quick guide to help you understand how it works.

It's easy... just start in the top right panel and follow the numbers. Have fun, and look for more 100% authentic manga from TOKYOPOP®!